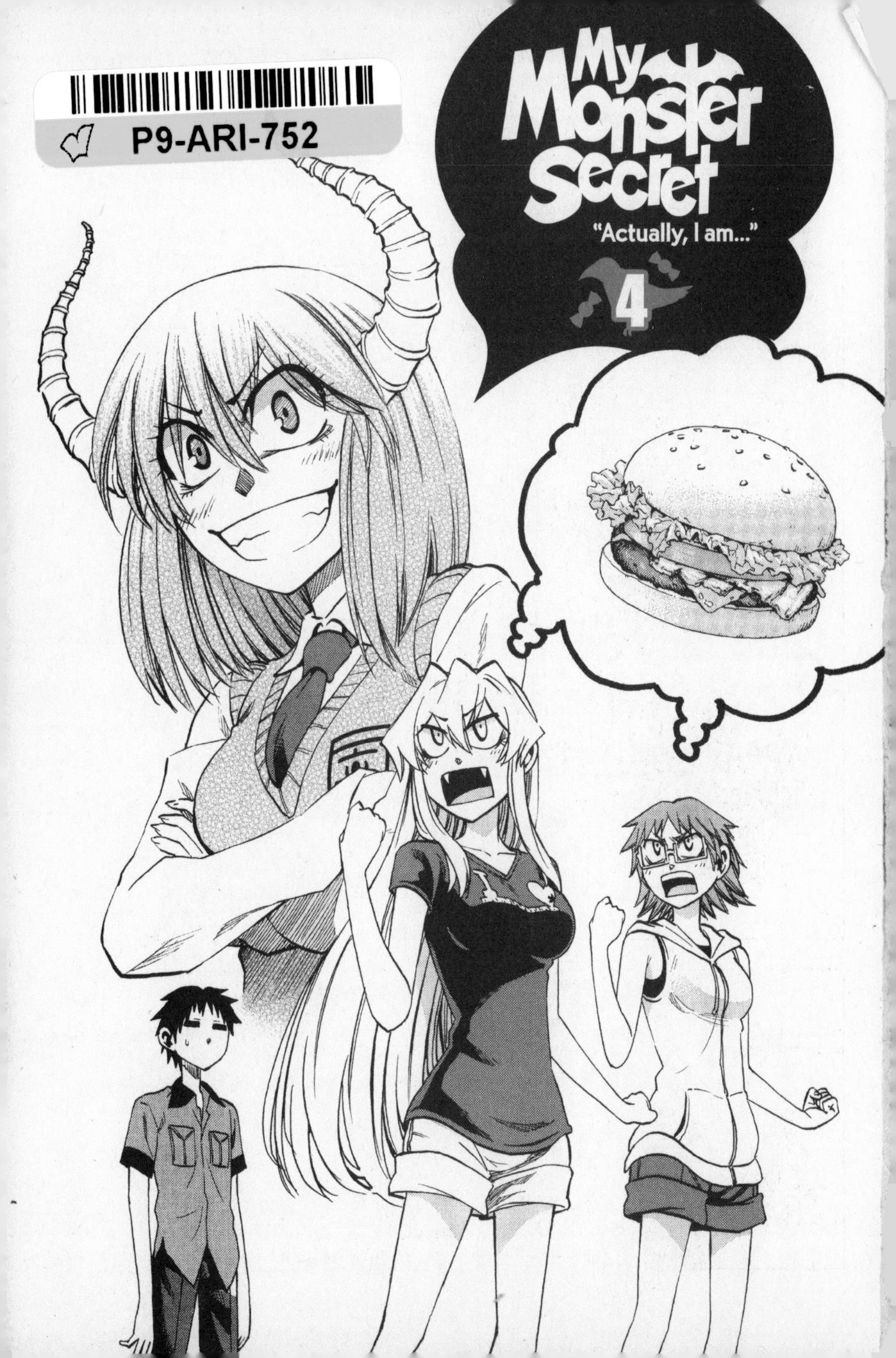
My Monster Secret
"Actually, I am..."
4

実(じつ)は私(わたし)は I am... Story & Character

After school one day, Kuromine Asahi opened the door to his classroom to confess his love to his crush Shiragami Youko...and discovered that she's actually a vampire! His goal was to tell Shiragami that he loved her, but he instead resolved to keep her secret--as a friend. It means they can continue to go to school together, but their problems are only beginning...

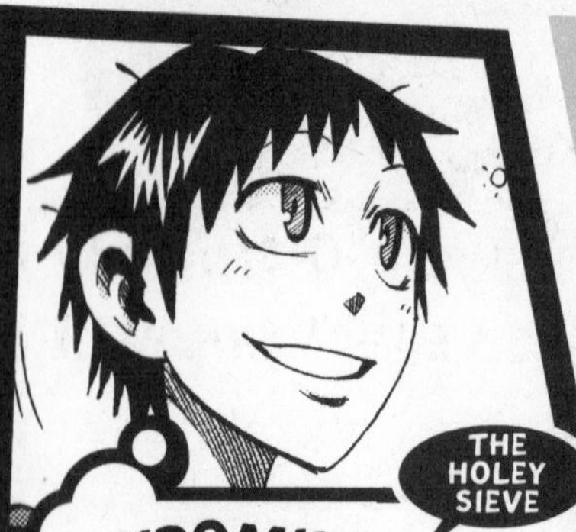

THE HOLEY SIEVE

KUROMINE ASAHI

The man with the worst poker face in the world, he's known as *The Sieve With A Hole In It*...because secrets slide right out of him. Now he has to hide the fact that Shiragami-san--the girl he's in love with--is a vampire.

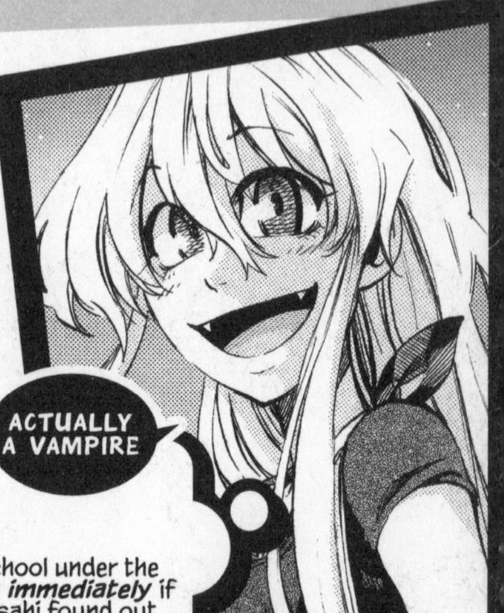

ACTUALLY A VAMPIRE

SHIRAGAMI YOUKO

She's attending a human high school under the condition that she'll ***stop going immediately*** if her true identity is discovered. Asahi found out (whoops), but she believes him when he says he'll keep her secret, and the two are now friends.

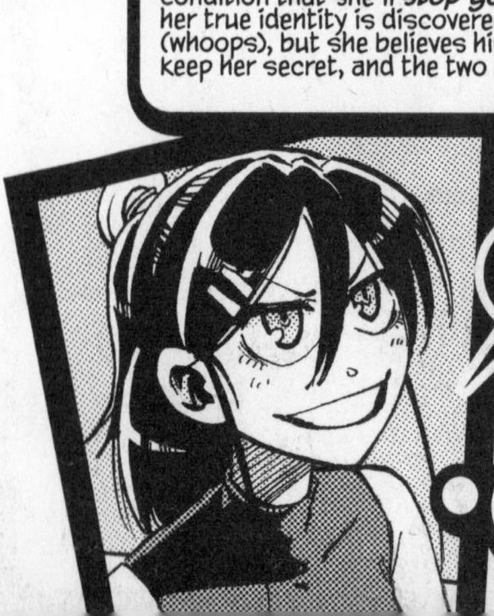

ACTUALLY AN ALIEN

AIZAWA NAGISA

This *Iron Lady*, a former crush of Asahi's, once mercilessly tore him to shreds before he could confess his love. She's currently posing as the representative of his class as she investigates Earth. Her true (tiny) form emerges from the screw-shaped cockpit on her head.

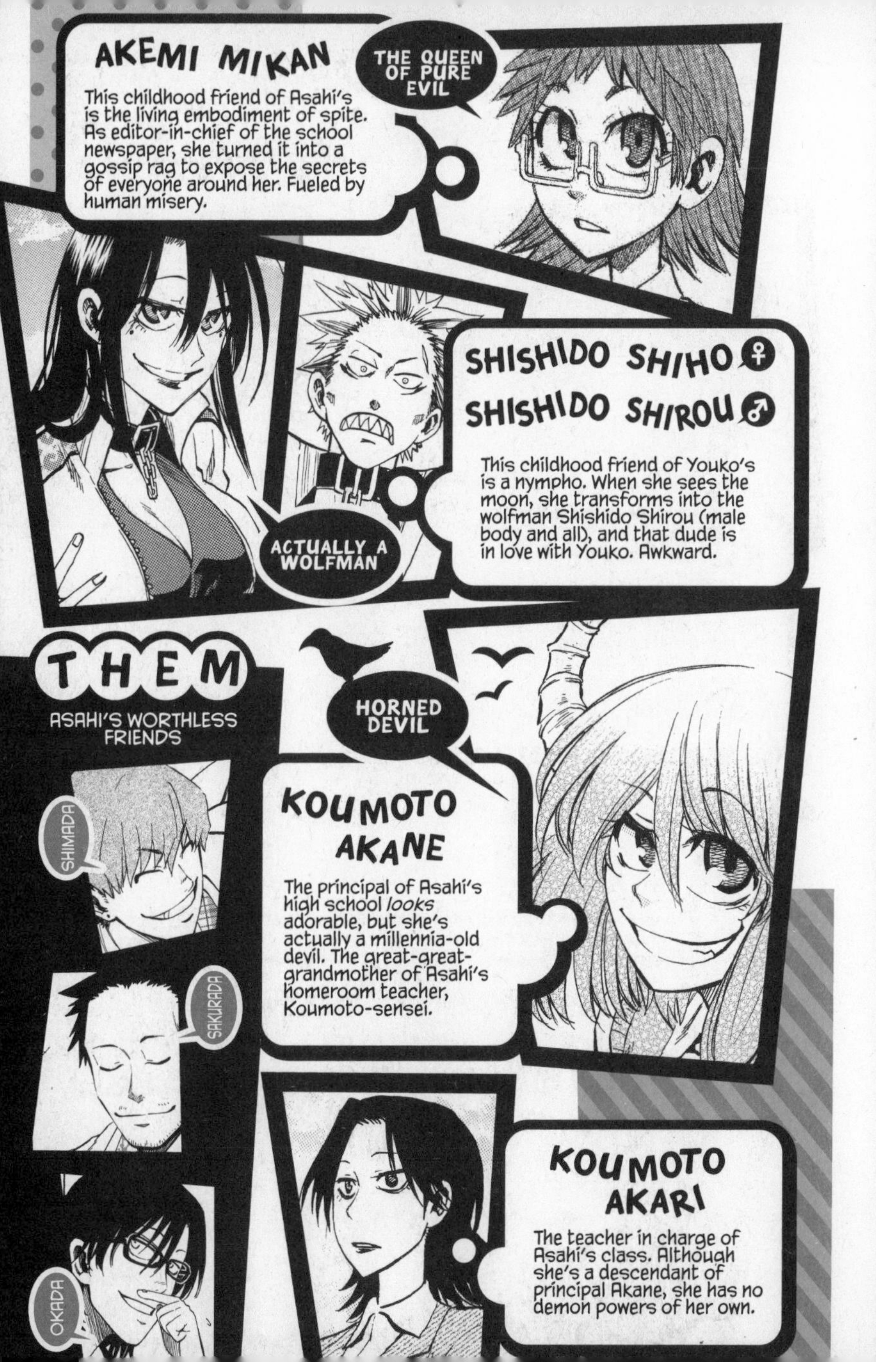
THE QUEEN OF PURE EVIL
AKEMI MIKAN
This childhood friend of Asahi's is the living embodiment of spite. As editor-in-chief of the school newspaper, she turned it into a gossip rag to expose the secrets of everyone around her. Fueled by human misery.
SHISHIDO SHIHO ♀
SHISHIDO SHIROU ♂
This childhood friend of Youko's is a nympho. When she sees the moon, she transforms into the wolfman Shishido Shirou (male body and all), and that dude is in love with Youko. Awkward.
ACTUALLY A WOLFMAN
HORNED DEVIL
KOUMOTO AKANE
The principal of Asahi's high school *looks* adorable, but she's actually a millennia-old devil. The great-great-grandmother of Asahi's homeroom teacher, Koumoto-sensei.
THEM
ASAHI'S WORTHLESS FRIENDS
SHIMADA
SAKURADA
OKADA
KOUMOTO AKARI
The teacher in charge of Asahi's class. Although she's a descendant of principal Akane, she has no demon powers of her own.

SEVEN SEAS ENTERTAINMENT PRESENTS

My Monster Secret

"Actually, I am...

story and art by Eiji Masuda

VOLUME 4

TRANSLATION
Alethea and Athena Nibley

ADAPTATION
Lianne Sentar

LETTERING AND LAYOUT
Annaliese Christman

LOGO DESIGN
Karis Page

COVER DESIGN
Nicky Lim

PROOFREADER
Shanti Whitesides

PRODUCTION MANAGER
Lissa Pattillo

EDITOR IN CHIEF
Adam Arnold

PUBLISHER
Jason DeAngelis

JITSUHA WATASHIHA Volume 4
© EIJI MASUDA 2013
Originally published in Japan in 2013 by Akita Publishing Co., Ltd.
English translation rights arranged with Akita Publishing Co., Ltd.
through TOHAN CORPORATION, Tokyo.

Seven Seas books may be purchased in bulk for promotional, educational, or business use. Please contact your local bookseller or the Macmillan Corporate and Premium Sales Department at 1-800-221-7945, extension 5442, or by e-mail at MacmillanSpecialMarkets@macmillan.com.

Seven Seas and the Seven Seas logo are trademarks of Seven Seas Entertainment, LLC. All rights reserved.

ISBN: 978-1-626923-45-4

Printed in Canada

First Printing: October 2016

10 9 8 7 6 5 4 3 2 1

FOLLOW US ONLINE: *www.gomanga.com*

READING DIRECTIONS

This book reads from *right to left*, Japanese style. If this is your first time reading manga, you start reading from the top right panel on each page and take it from there. If you get lost, just follow the numbered diagram here. It may seem backwards at first, but you'll get the hang of it! Have fun!!

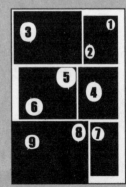

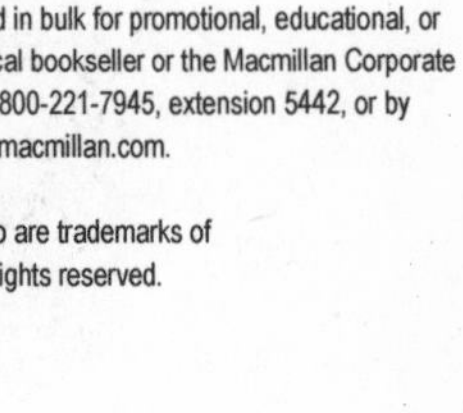

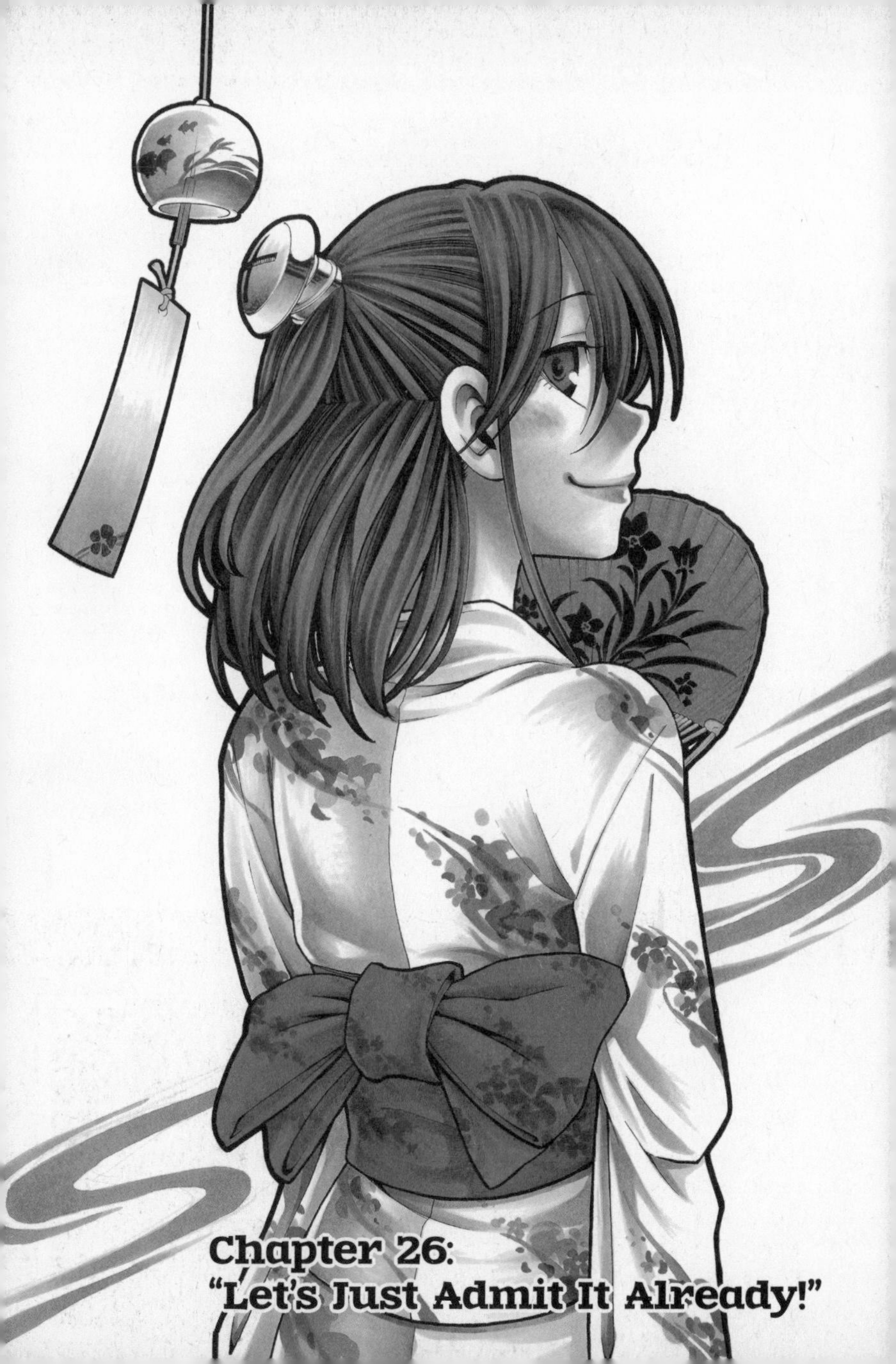

Chapter 26: “Let’s Just Admit It Already!”

TOP SECRET

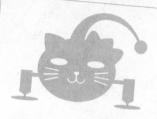

My Monster Secret 4

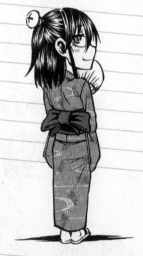

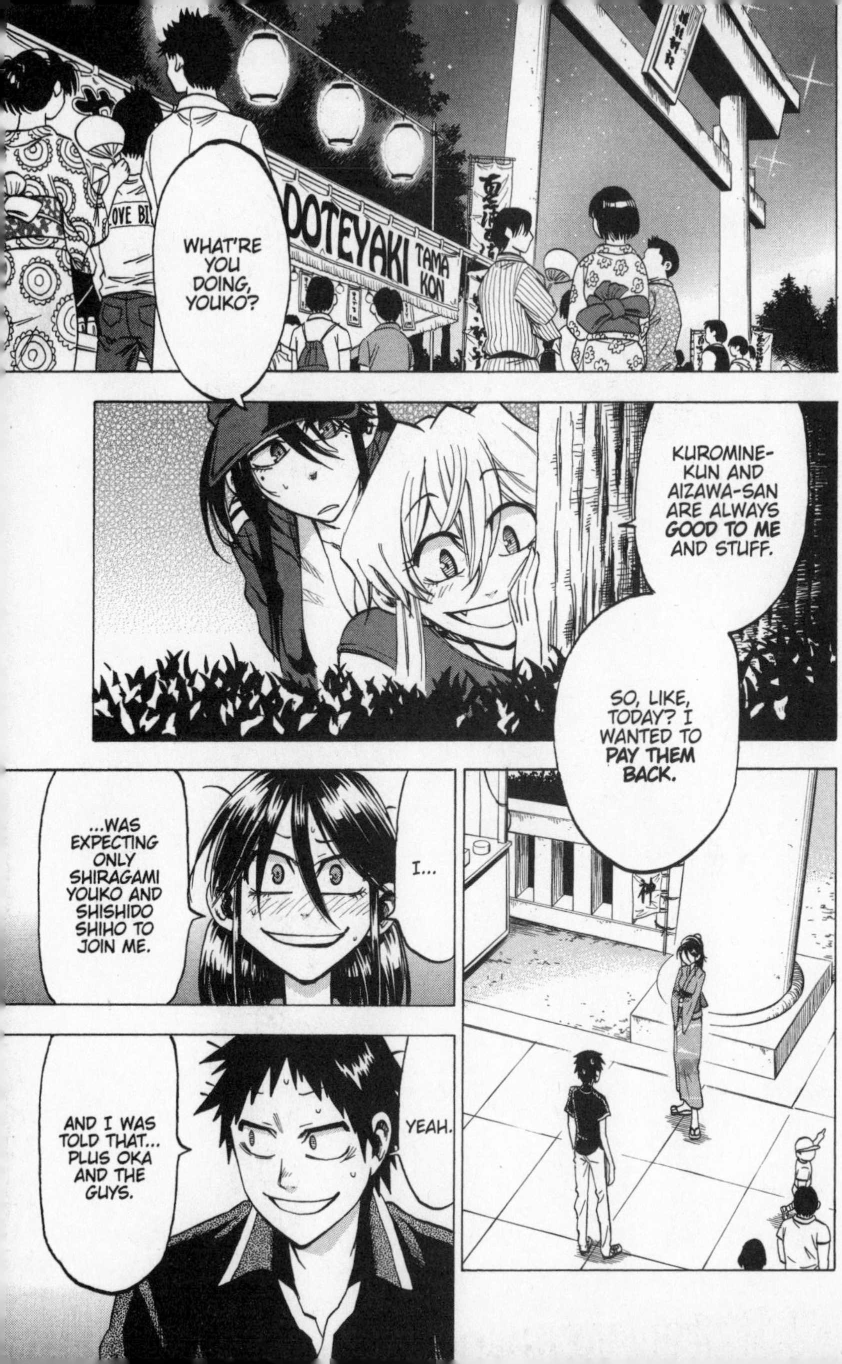
WHAT'RE YOU DOING, YOUKO?
DOTEYAKI
TAMA KON
KUROMINE-KUN AND AIZAWA-SAN ARE ALWAYS GOOD TO ME AND STUFF.
SO, LIKE, TODAY? I WANTED TO PAY THEM BACK.
I...
...WAS EXPECTING ONLY SHIRAGAMI YOUKO AND SHISHIDO SHIHO TO JOIN ME.
YEAH.
AND I WAS TOLD THAT... PLUS OKA AND THE GUYS.

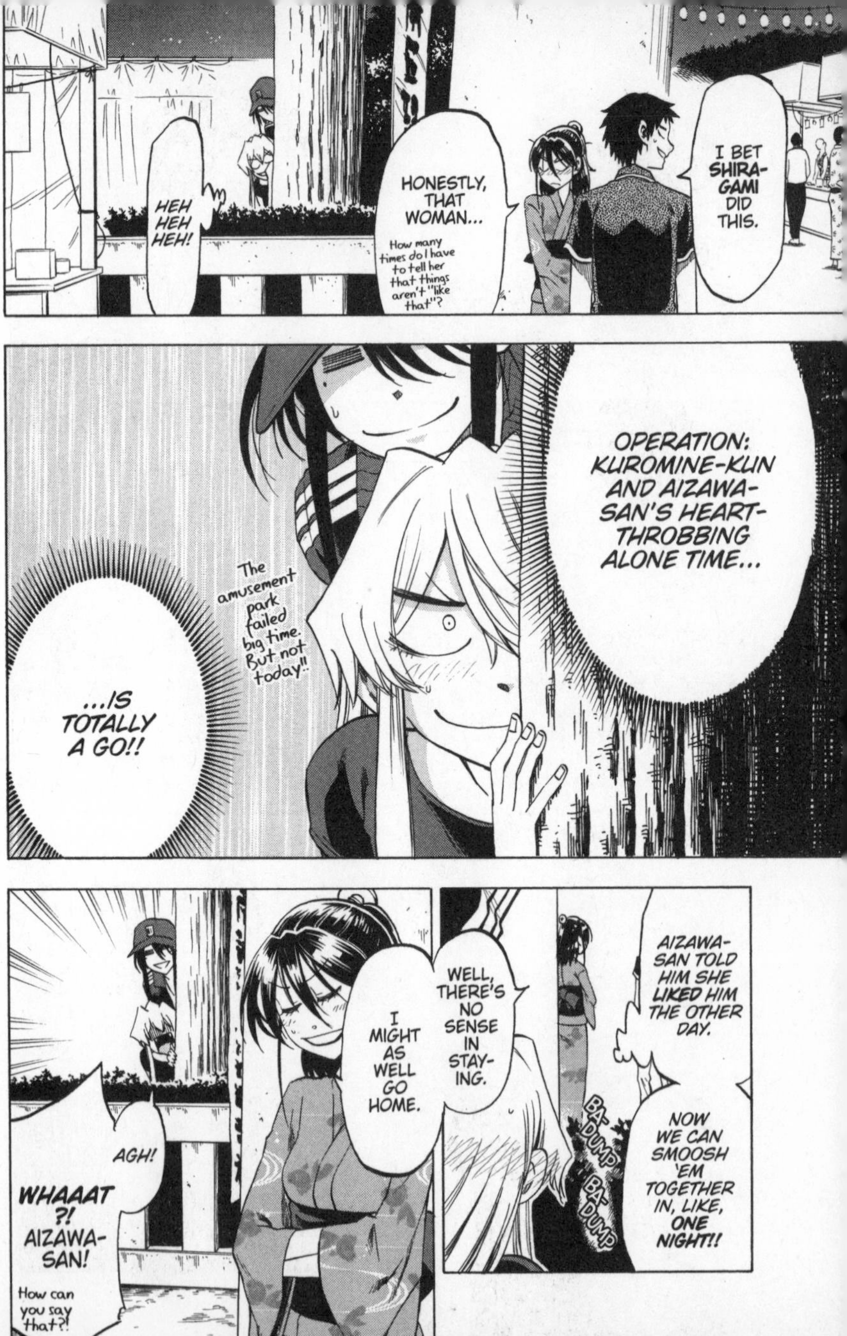
I BET SHIRAGAMI DID THIS.
HONESTLY, THAT WOMAN...
How many times do I have to tell her that things aren't "like that"?
HEH HEH HEH!
OPERATION: KUROMINE-KUN AND AIZAWA-SAN'S HEART-THROBBING ALONE TIME...
The amusement park failed big time. But not today!!
...IS TOTALLY A GO!!
AIZAWA-SAN TOLD HIM SHE LIKED HIM THE OTHER DAY.
NOW WE CAN SMOOSH 'EM TOGETHER IN, LIKE, ONE NIGHT!!
BA-DUMP BA-DUMP
WELL, THERE'S NO SENSE IN STAYING.
I MIGHT AS WELL GO HOME.
AGH!
WHAAAT?! AIZAWA-SAN!
How can you say that?!

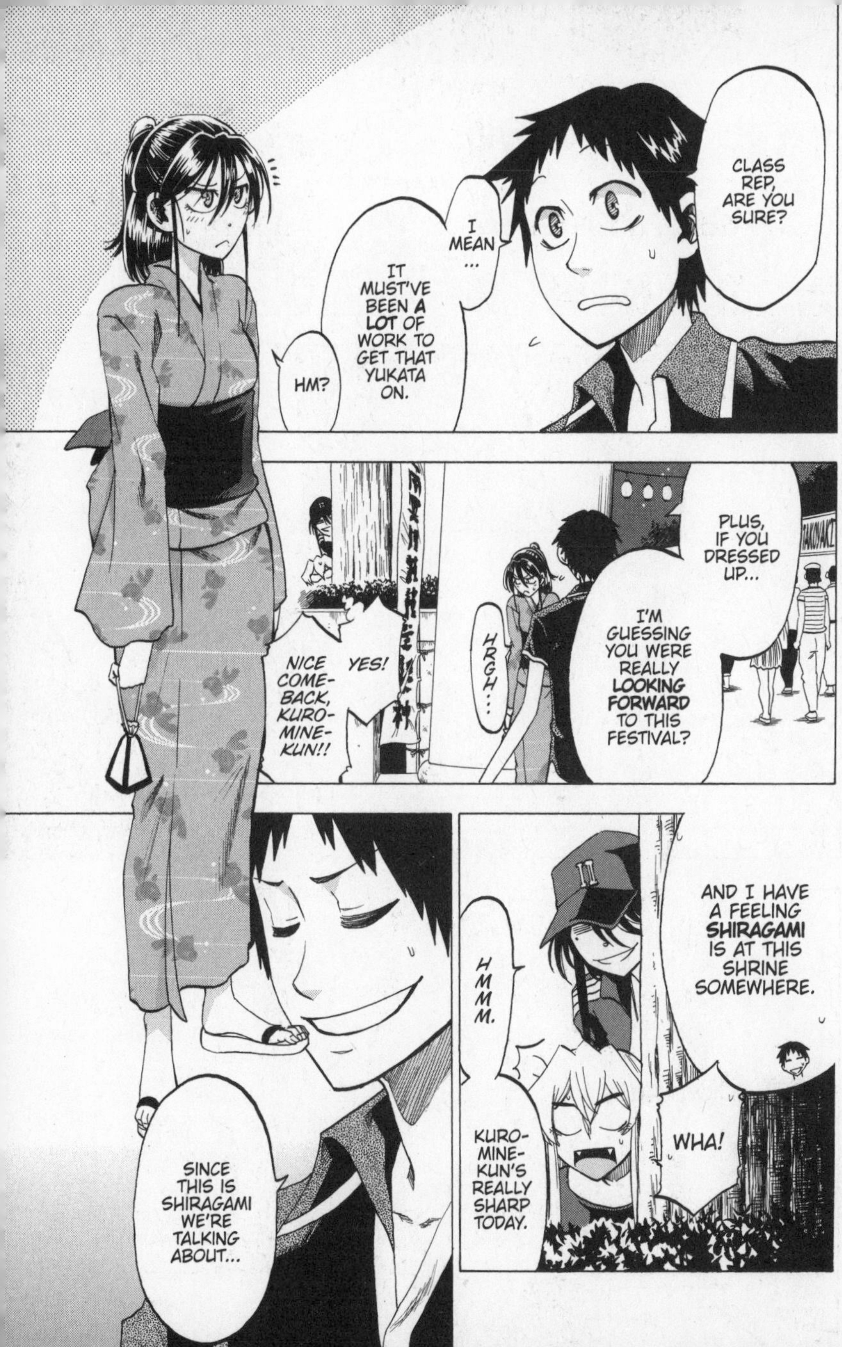

CLASS REP, ARE YOU SURE?
I MEAN ...
IT MUST'VE BEEN A LOT OF WORK TO GET THAT YUKATA ON.
HM?
PLUS, IF YOU DRESSED UP...
I'M GUESSING YOU WERE REALLY LOOKING FORWARD TO THIS FESTIVAL?
HRGH...
YES!
NICE COME-BACK, KURO-MINE-KUN!!
AND I HAVE A FEELING SHIRAGAMI IS AT THIS SHRINE SOMEWHERE.
HMMM.
WHA!
KURO-MINE-KUN'S REALLY SHARP TODAY.
SINCE THIS IS SHIRAGAMI WE'RE TALKING ABOUT...

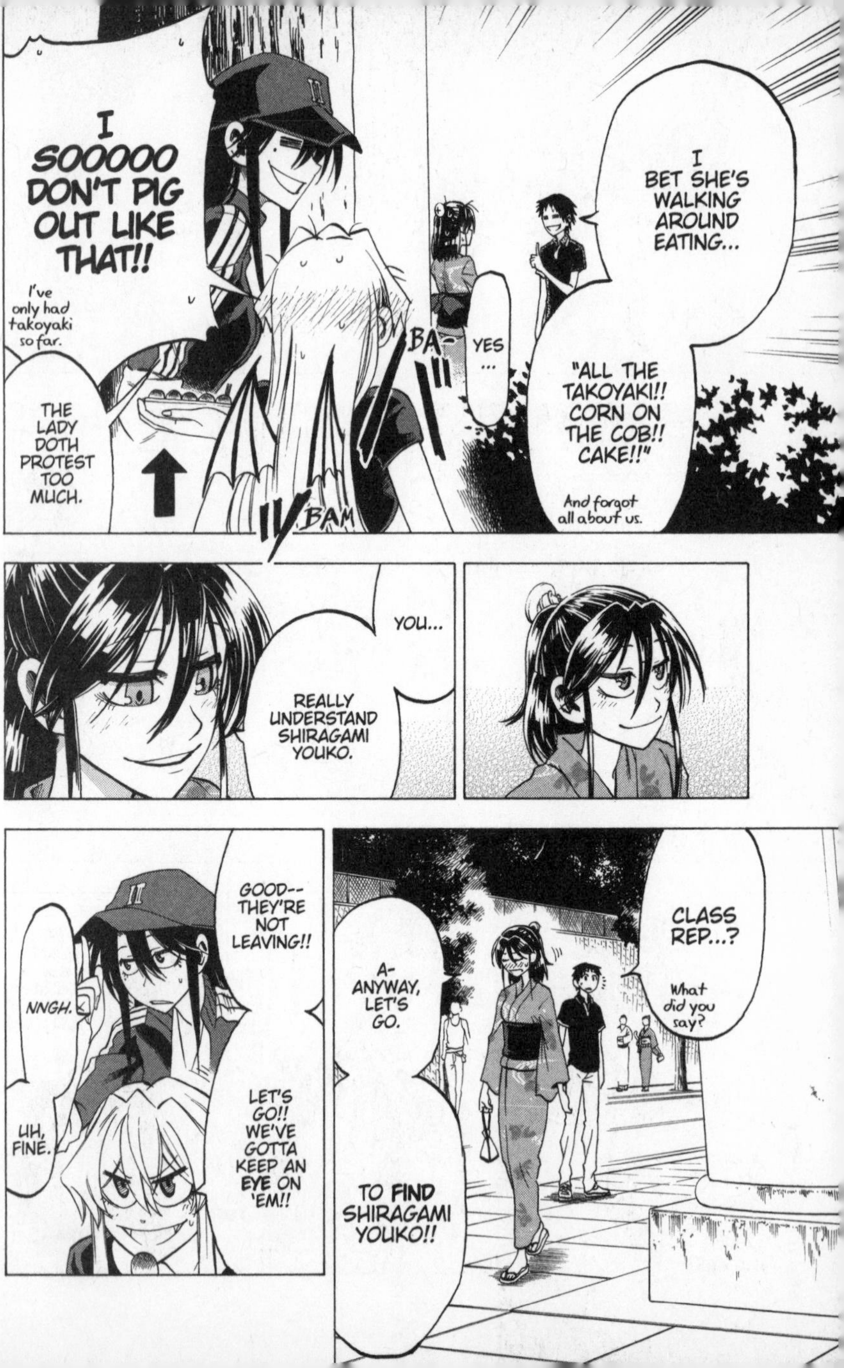
I BET SHE'S WALKING AROUND EATING...
"ALL THE TAKOYAKI!! CORN ON THE COB!! CAKE!!"
And forgot all about us.
YES ...
I SOOOOO DON'T PIG OUT LIKE THAT!!
I've only had takoyaki so far.
BA-
BAM
THE LADY DOTH PROTEST TOO MUCH.
YOU...
REALLY UNDERSTAND SHIRAGAMI YOUKO.
CLASS REP...?
What did you say?
A-ANYWAY, LET'S GO.
TO FIND SHIRAGAMI YOUKO!!
GOOD-- THEY'RE NOT LEAVING!!
NNGH.
LET'S GO!! WE'VE GOTTA KEEP AN EYE ON 'EM!!
UH, FINE.

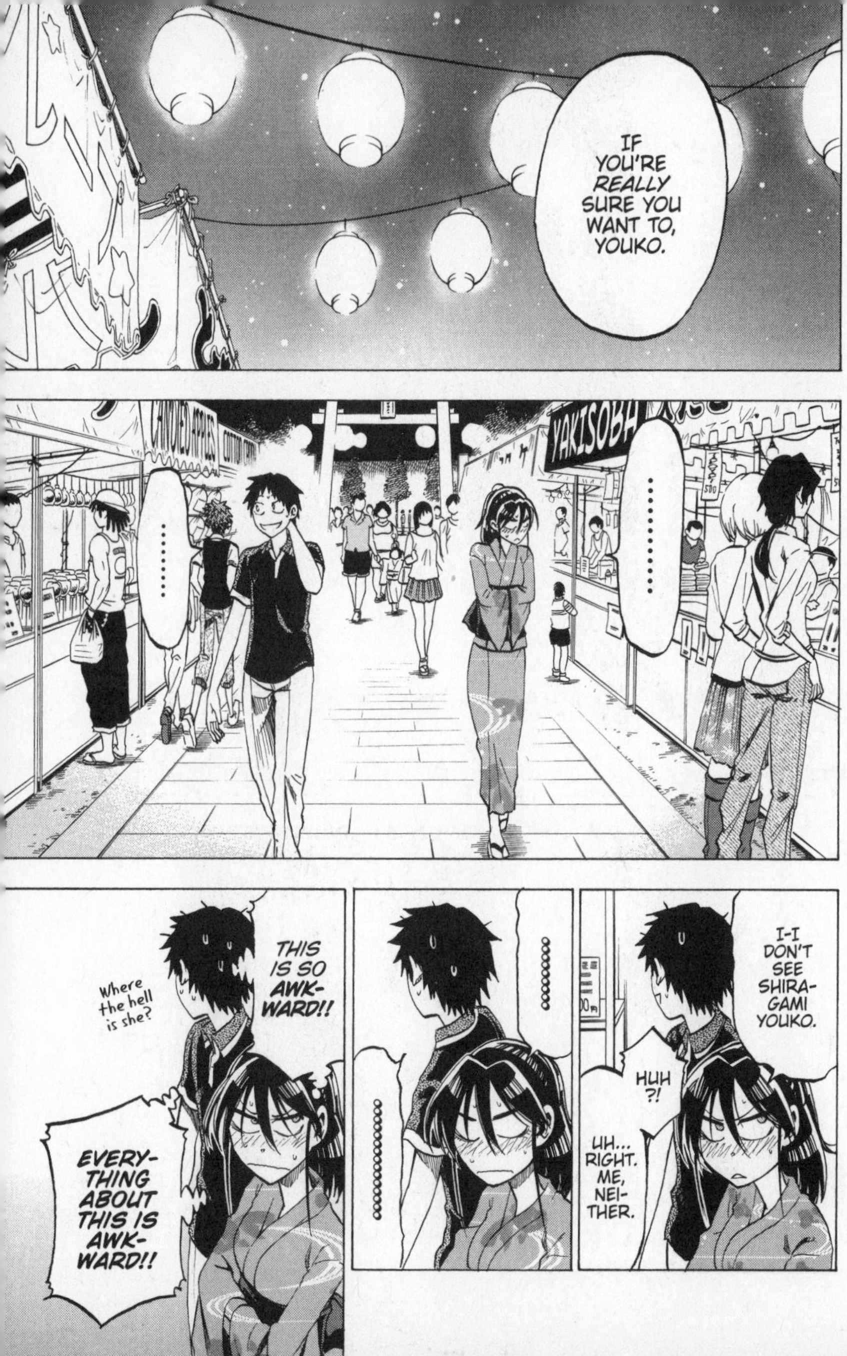
IF YOU'RE *REALLY* SURE YOU WANT TO, YOUKO.
YAKISOBA
......
CANDIED APPLES
......
I-I DON'T SEE SHIRAGAMI YOUKO.
HUH?!
UH... RIGHT. ME, NEITHER.
....
....
THIS IS SO AWKWARD!!
Where the hell is she?
EVERYTHING ABOUT THIS IS AWKWARD!!

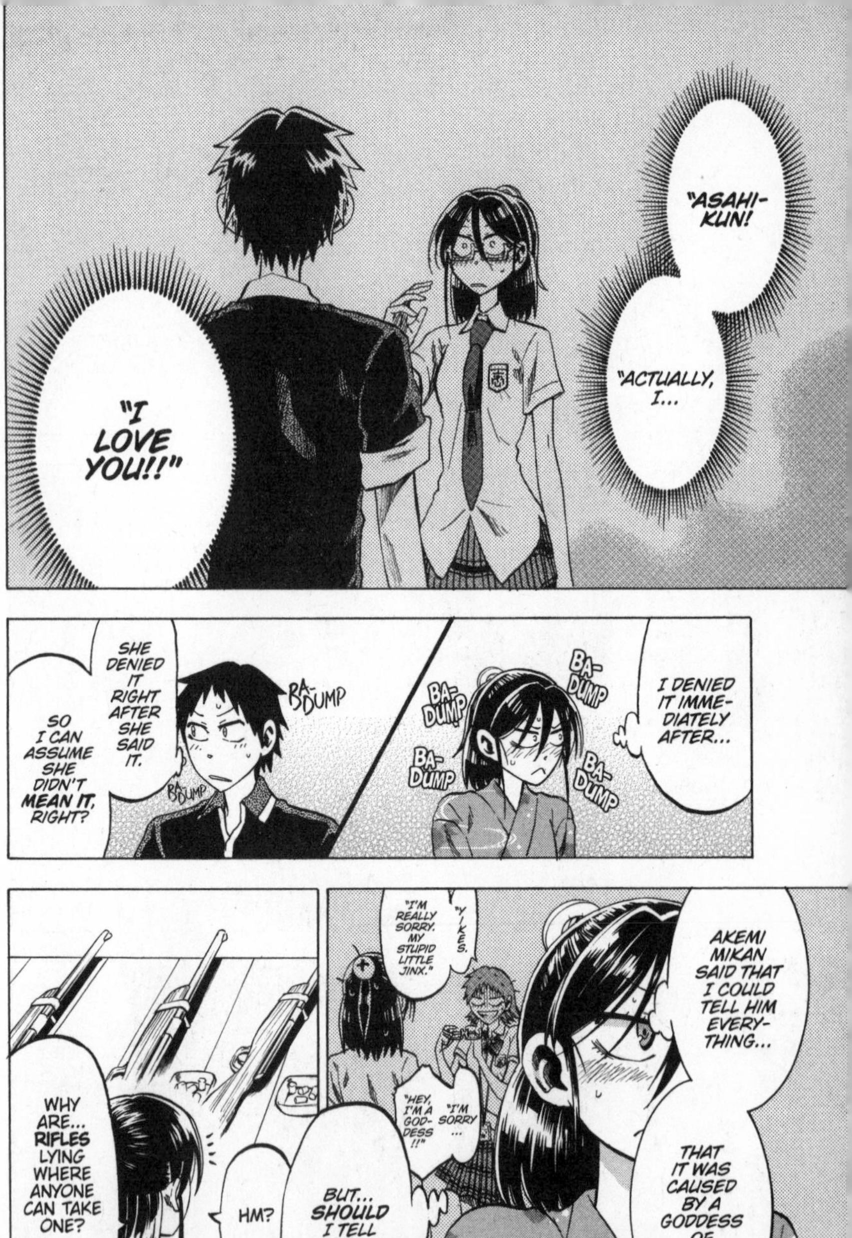
"ASAHI-KUN!
"ACTUALLY, I...
"I LOVE YOU!!"
BA-DUMP
BA-DUMP
BA-DUMP
BA-DUMP
I DENIED IT IMMEDIATELY AFTER...
SHE DENIED IT RIGHT AFTER SHE SAID IT.
BA-DUMP
SO I CAN ASSUME SHE DIDN'T MEAN IT, RIGHT?
BA-DUMP
AKEMI MIKAN SAID THAT I COULD TELL HIM EVERYTHING...
THAT IT WAS CAUSED BY A GODDESS OF FORTUNE.
"YIKES.
"I'M REALLY SORRY. MY STUPID LITTLE JINX."
"I'M SORRY ...
"HEY, I'M A GODDESS!!"
BUT... SHOULD I TELL HIM THAT?
HM?
WHY ARE... RIFLES LYING WHERE ANYONE CAN TAKE ONE?

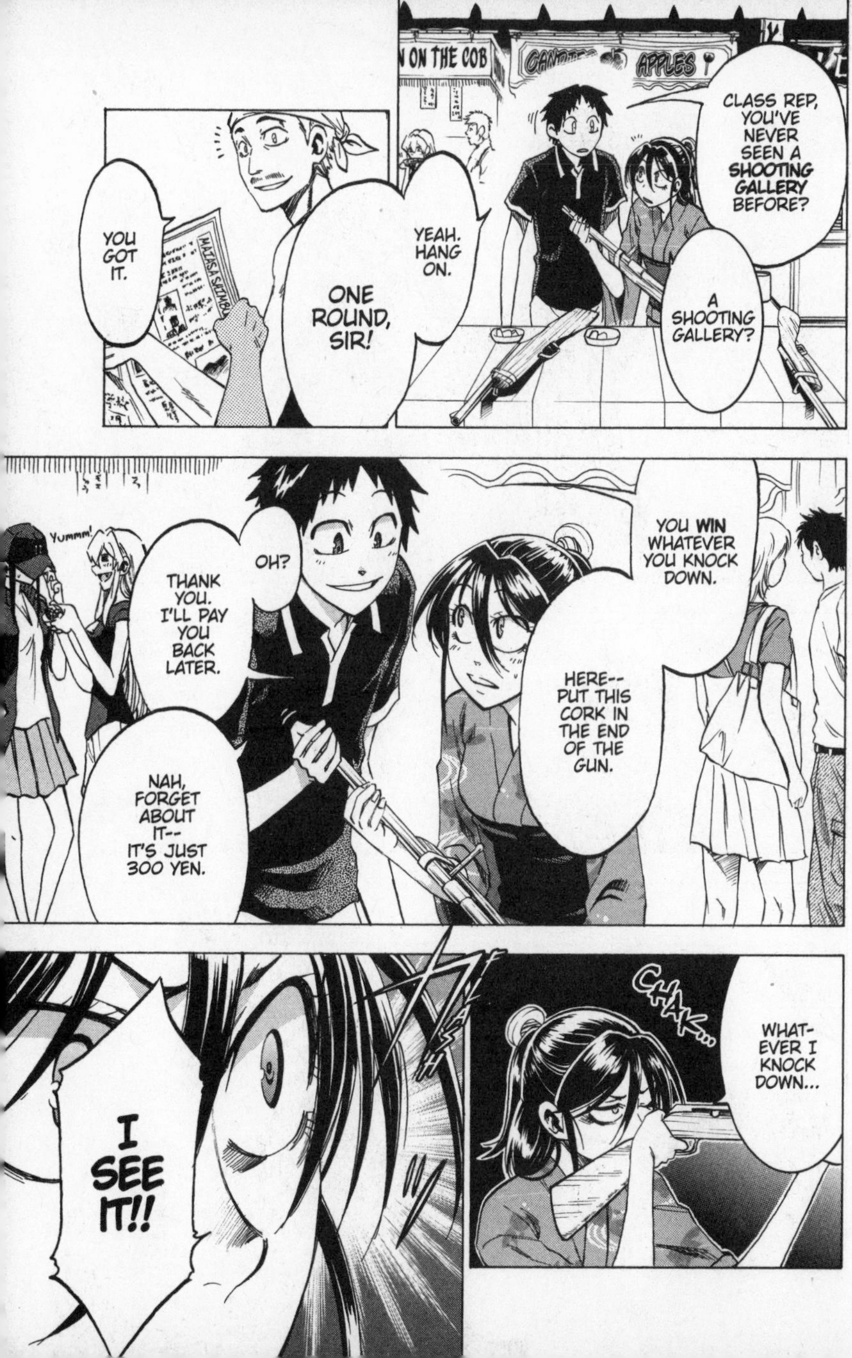
ON THE COB
APPLES
CLASS REP, YOU'VE NEVER SEEN A SHOOTING GALLERY BEFORE?
A SHOOTING GALLERY?
YEAH. HANG ON.
ONE ROUND, SIR!
YOU GOT IT.
YOU WIN WHATEVER YOU KNOCK DOWN.
HERE-- PUT THIS CORK IN THE END OF THE GUN.
OH?
THANK YOU. I'LL PAY YOU BACK LATER.
NAH, FORGET ABOUT IT-- IT'S JUST 300 YEN.
YUMMM!
CHAK...
WHAT-EVER I KNOCK DOWN...
I SEE IT!!

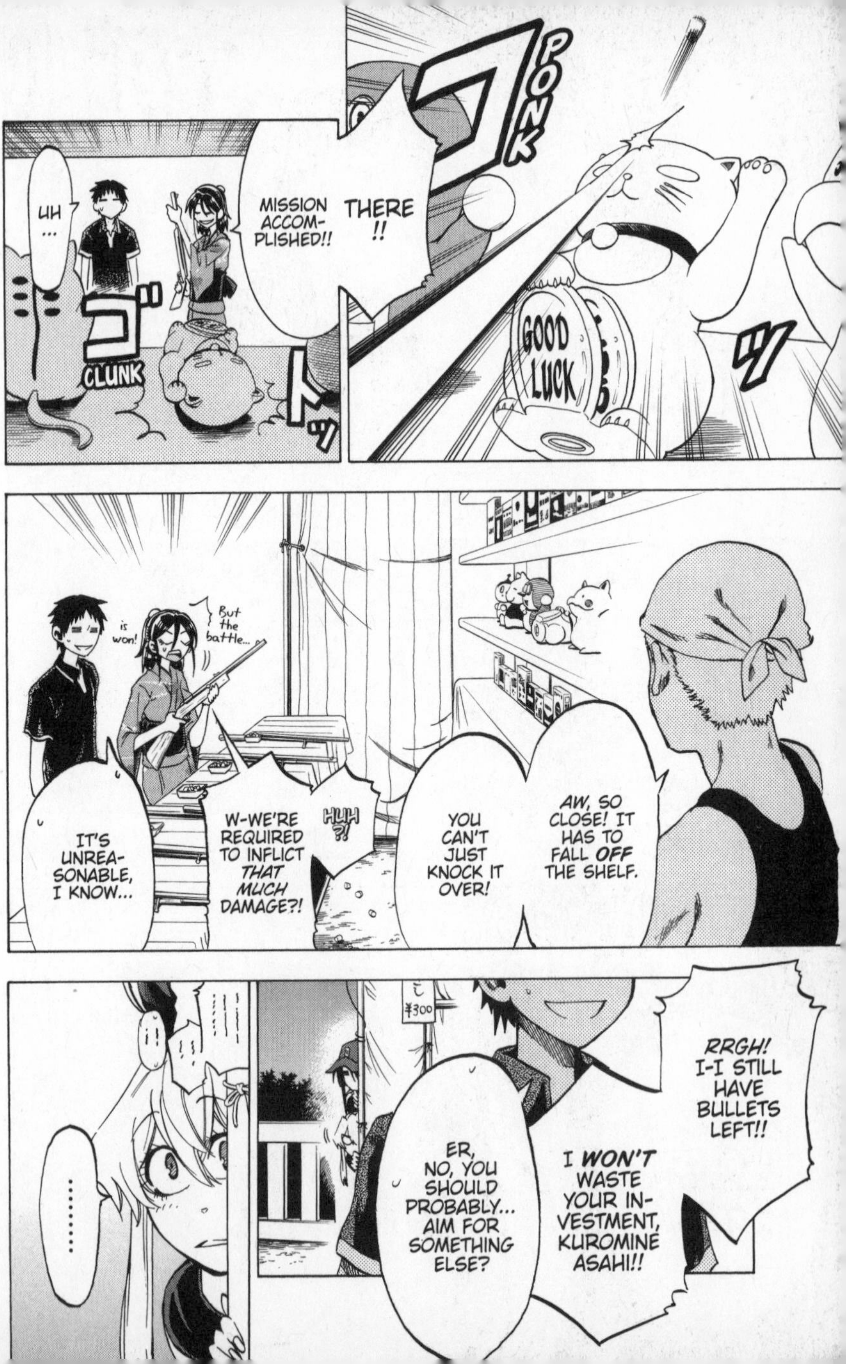
PONK
THERE!!
MISSION ACCOMPLISHED!!
GOOD LUCK
UH...
CLUNK
AW, SO CLOSE! IT HAS TO FALL OFF THE SHELF.
YOU CAN'T JUST KNOCK IT OVER!
HUH?!
W-WE'RE REQUIRED TO INFLICT THAT MUCH DAMAGE?!
But the battle... is won!
IT'S UNREASONABLE, I KNOW...
RRGH! I-I STILL HAVE BULLETS LEFT!!
I WON'T WASTE YOUR INVESTMENT, KUROMINE ASAHI!!
¥300
ER, NO, YOU SHOULD PROBABLY... AIM FOR SOMETHING ELSE?
!!
......

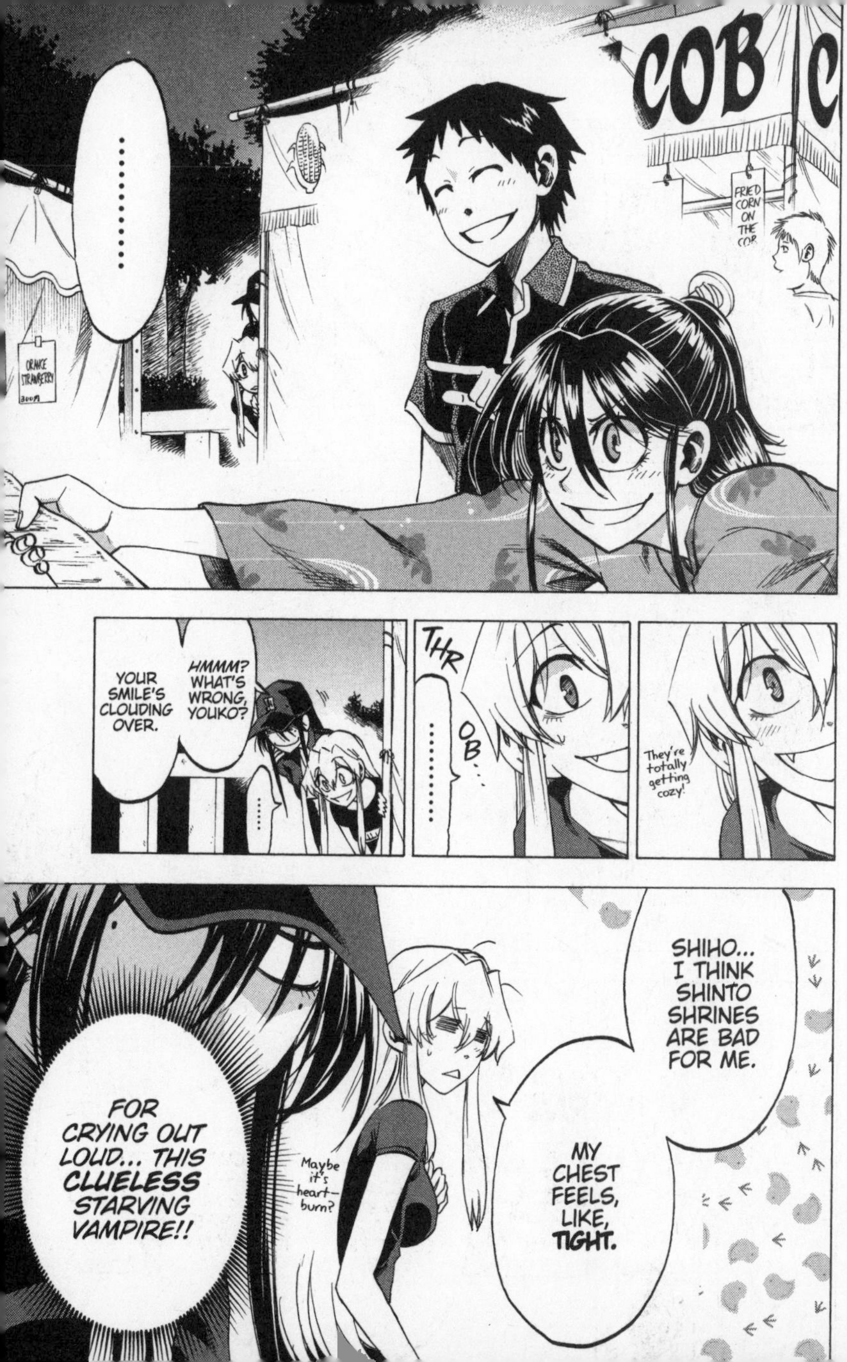
COB C
FRIED CORN ON THE COB
......
ORANGE STRAWBERRY
They're totally getting cozy!
THROB...
......
HMMM? WHAT'S WRONG, YOUKO?
YOUR SMILE'S CLOUDING OVER.
......
SHIHO... I THINK SHINTO SHRINES ARE BAD FOR ME.
MY CHEST FEELS, LIKE, TIGHT.
Maybe it's heart-burn?
FOR CRYING OUT LOUD... THIS CLUELESS STARVING VAMPIRE!!

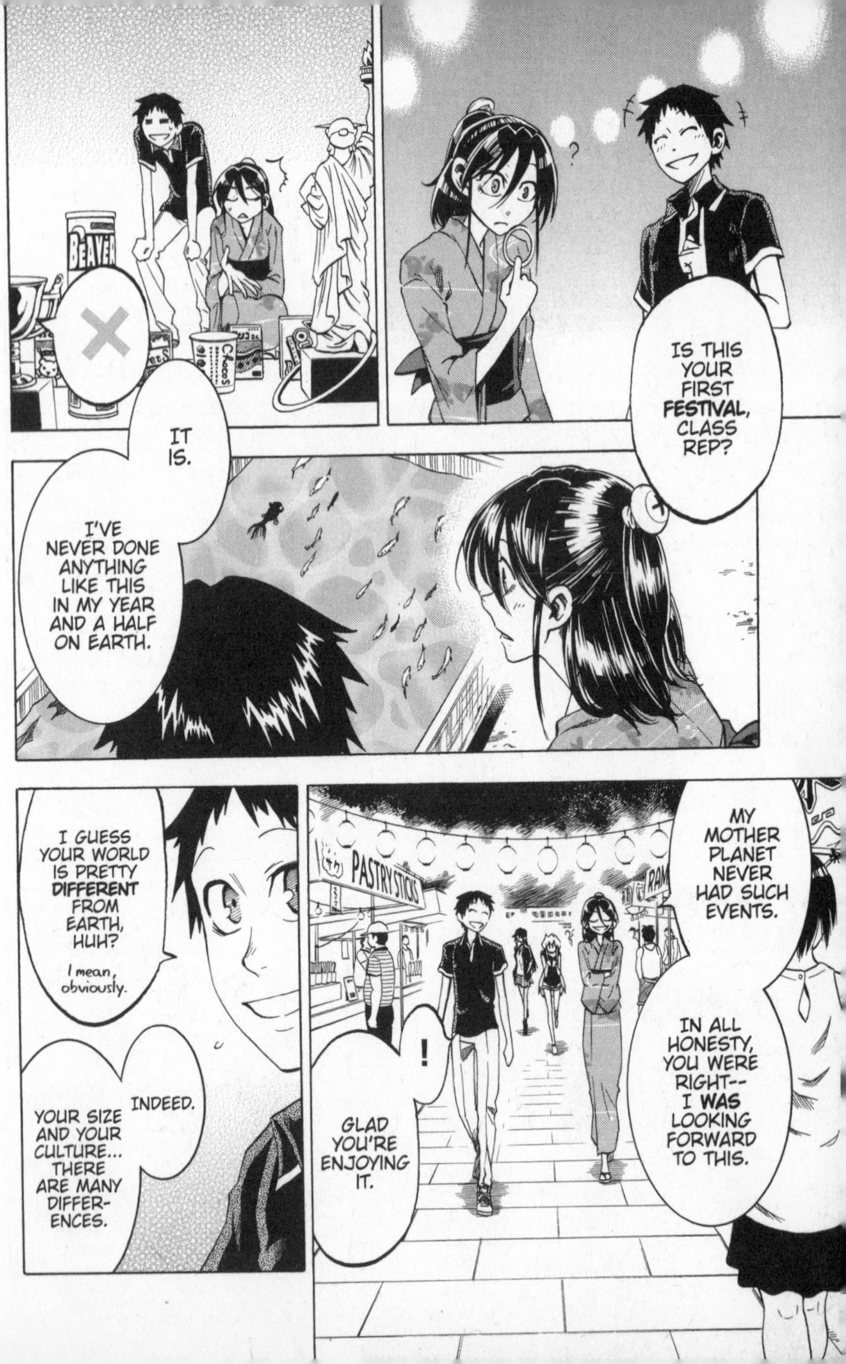
IS THIS YOUR FIRST **FESTIVAL**, CLASS REP?
BEAVER
×
IT IS.
I'VE NEVER DONE ANYTHING LIKE THIS IN MY YEAR AND A HALF ON EARTH.
MY MOTHER PLANET NEVER HAD SUCH EVENTS.
IN ALL HONESTY, YOU WERE RIGHT-- I **WAS** LOOKING FORWARD TO THIS.
PASTRY STICKS
!
GLAD YOU'RE ENJOYING IT.
I GUESS YOUR WORLD IS PRETTY **DIFFERENT** FROM EARTH, HUH?
I mean, obviously.
INDEED.
YOUR SIZE AND YOUR CULTURE... THERE ARE MANY DIFFER-ENCES.

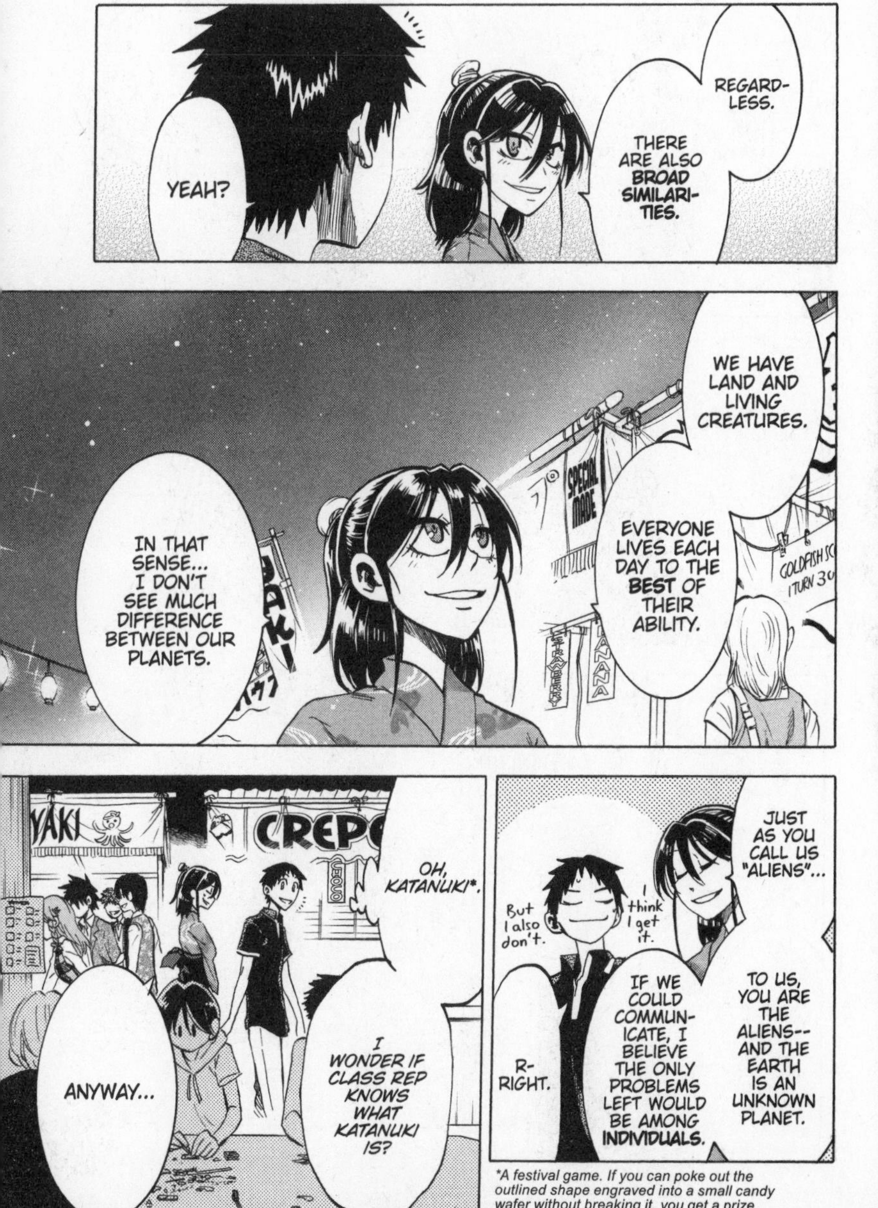
REGARD-
LESS.
THERE ARE ALSO BROAD SIMILARI-TIES.
YEAH?
WE HAVE LAND AND LIVING CREATURES.
EVERYONE LIVES EACH DAY TO THE BEST OF THEIR ABILITY.
IN THAT SENSE... I DON'T SEE MUCH DIFFERENCE BETWEEN OUR PLANETS.
SPECIAL MADE
JUST AS YOU CALL US "ALIENS"...
TO US, YOU ARE THE ALIENS-- AND THE EARTH IS AN UNKNOWN PLANET.
IF WE COULD COMMUN-ICATE, I BELIEVE THE ONLY PROBLEMS LEFT WOULD BE AMONG INDIVIDUALS.
I think I get it.
But I also don't.
R-RIGHT.
OH, KATANUKI*.
I WONDER IF CLASS REP KNOWS WHAT KATANUKI IS?
ANYWAY...
*A festival game. If you can poke out the outlined shape engraved into a small candy wafer without breaking it, you get a prize.

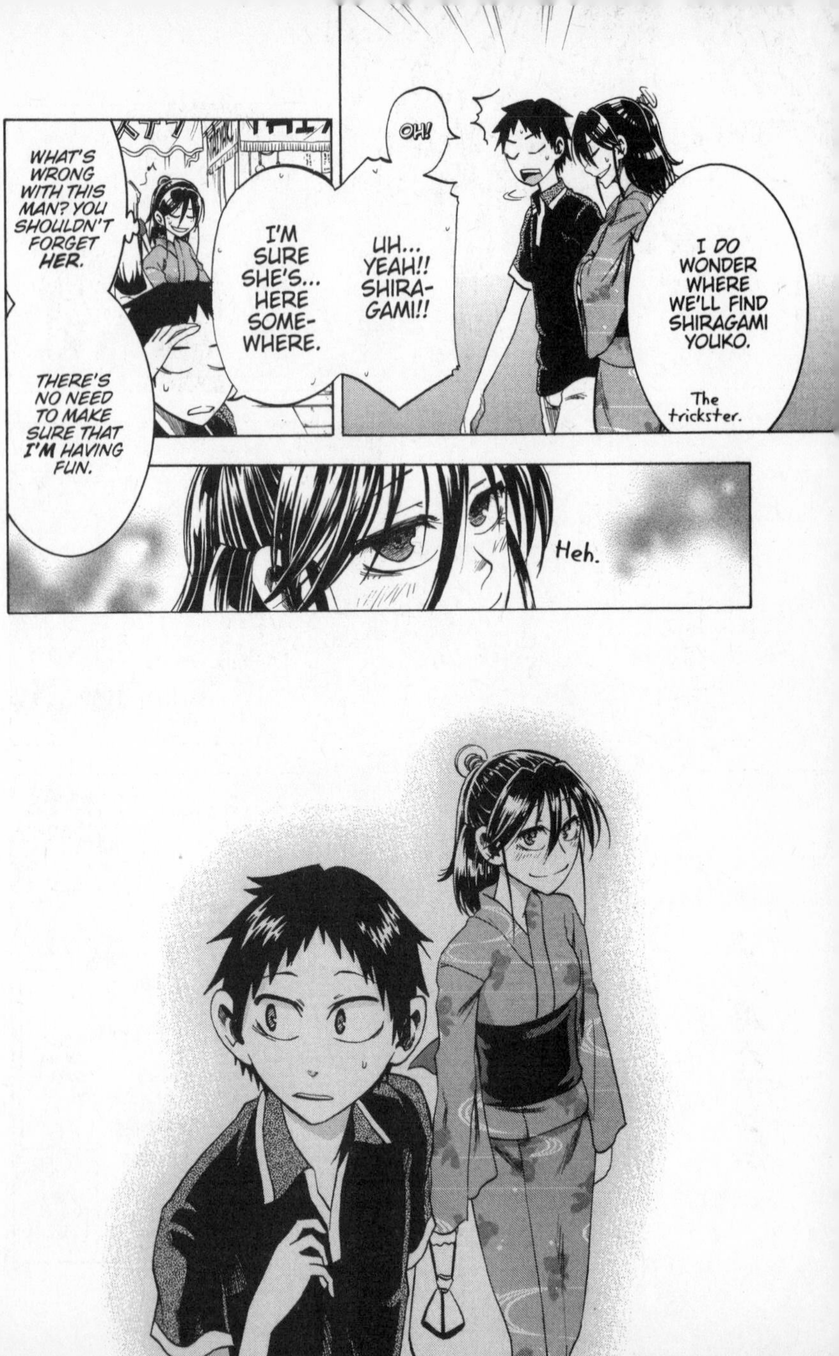
I DO WONDER WHERE WE'LL FIND SHIRAGAMI YOUKO.
The trickster.
OH!
UH... YEAH!! SHIRAGAMI!!
I'M SURE SHE'S... HERE SOMEWHERE.
WHAT'S WRONG WITH THIS MAN? YOU SHOULDN'T FORGET HER.
THERE'S NO NEED TO MAKE SURE THAT I'M HAVING FUN.
Heh.

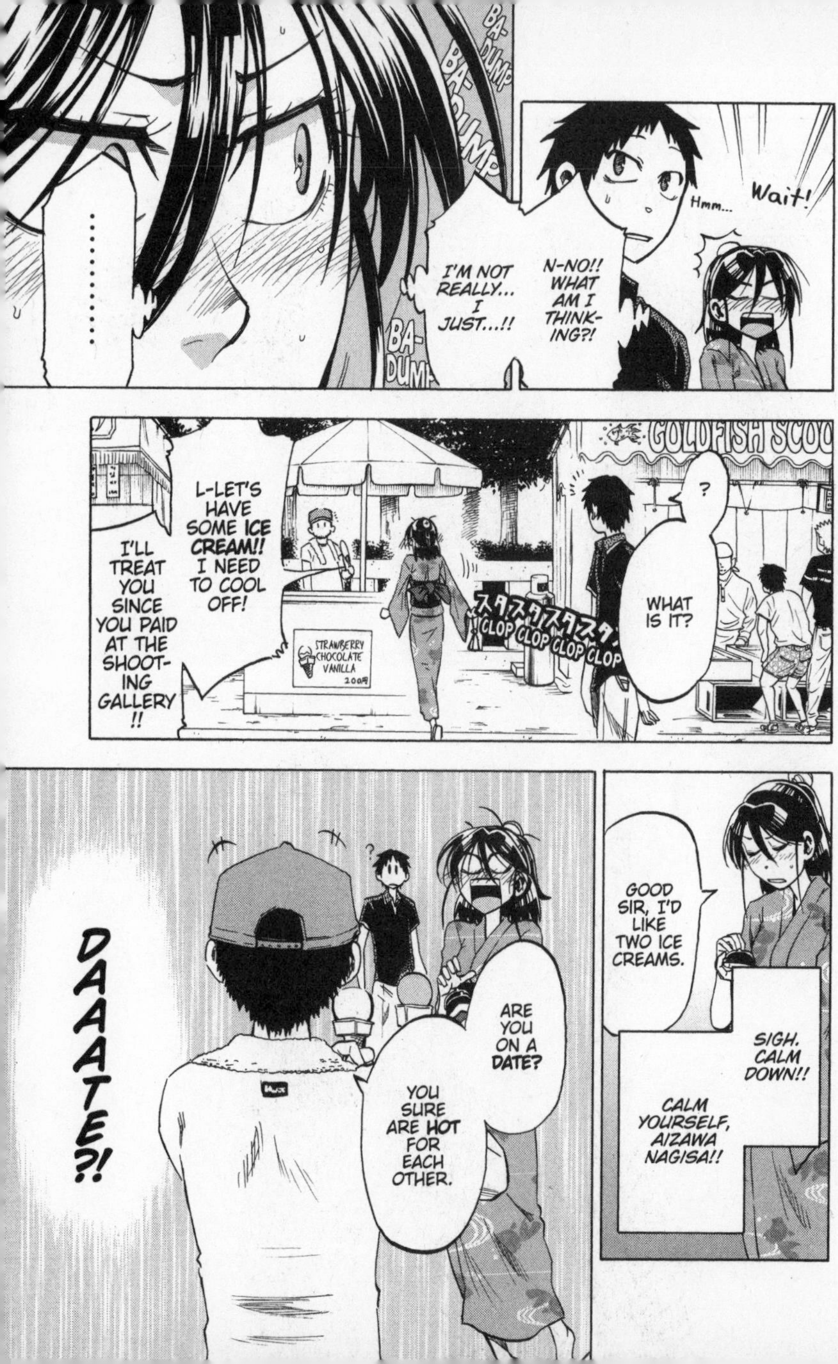
Wait!
Hmm...
N-NO!! WHAT AM I THINKING?!
I'M NOT REALLY... I JUST...!!
BA-DUMP
BA-DUMP
......
BA-DUMP
GOLDFISH SCOO
?
WHAT IS IT?
L-LET'S HAVE SOME ICE CREAM!! I NEED TO COOL OFF!
I'LL TREAT YOU SINCE YOU PAID AT THE SHOOTING GALLERY!!
STRAWBERRY CHOCOLATE VANILLA 200円
スタスタスタスタ
CLOP CLOP CLOP CLOP
GOOD SIR, I'D LIKE TWO ICE CREAMS.
SIGH. CALM DOWN!!
CALM YOURSELF, AIZAWA NAGISA!!
ARE YOU ON A DATE?
YOU SURE ARE HOT FOR EACH OTHER.
DAAATE?!

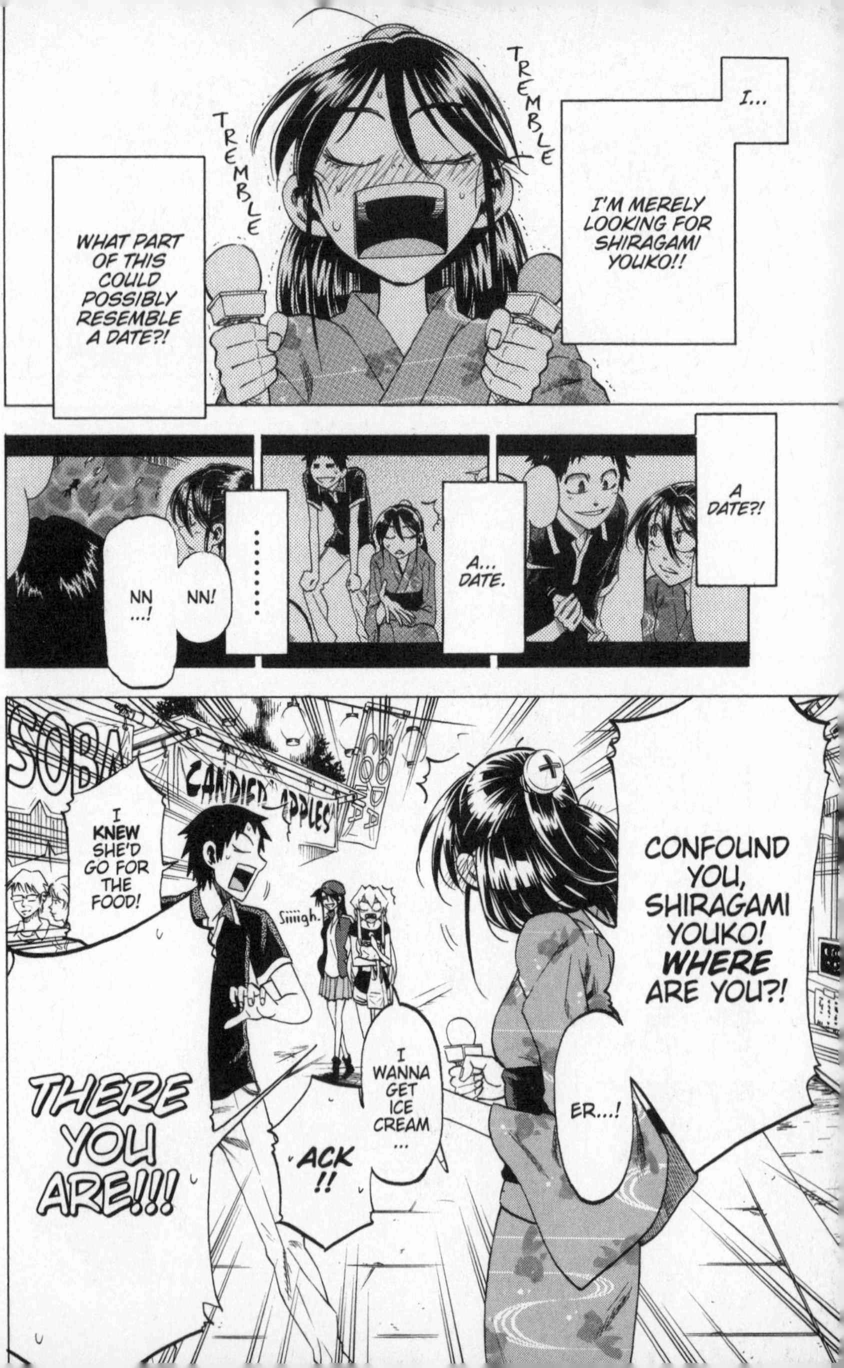
I...
I'M MERELY LOOKING FOR SHIRAGAMI YOUKO!!
TREMBLE
TREMBLE
WHAT PART OF THIS COULD POSSIBLY RESEMBLE A DATE?!
A DATE?!
A... DATE.
......
NN!
NN ...!
CONFOUND YOU, SHIRAGAMI YOUKO! WHERE ARE YOU?!
ER...!
I WANNA GET ICE CREAM ...
ACK !!
Siiiigh.
SOBA
CANDIED APPLES
I KNEW SHE'D GO FOR THE FOOD!
THERE YOU ARE!!!

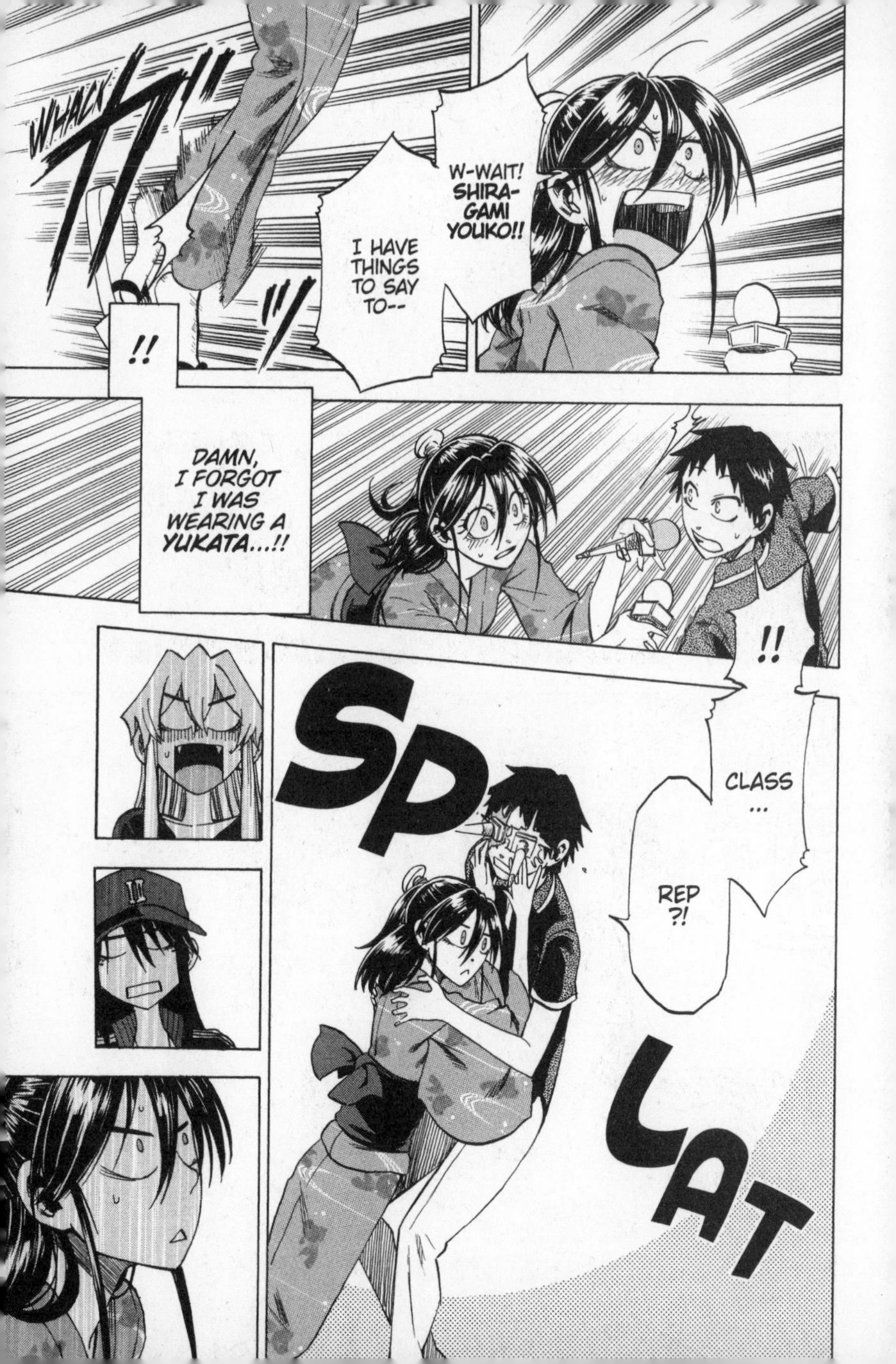

W-WAIT! SHIRAGAMI YOUKO!!
I HAVE THINGS TO SAY TO--
WHACK
!!
DAMN, I FORGOT I WAS WEARING A YUKATA...!!
!!
CLASS... REP?!
SPLAT

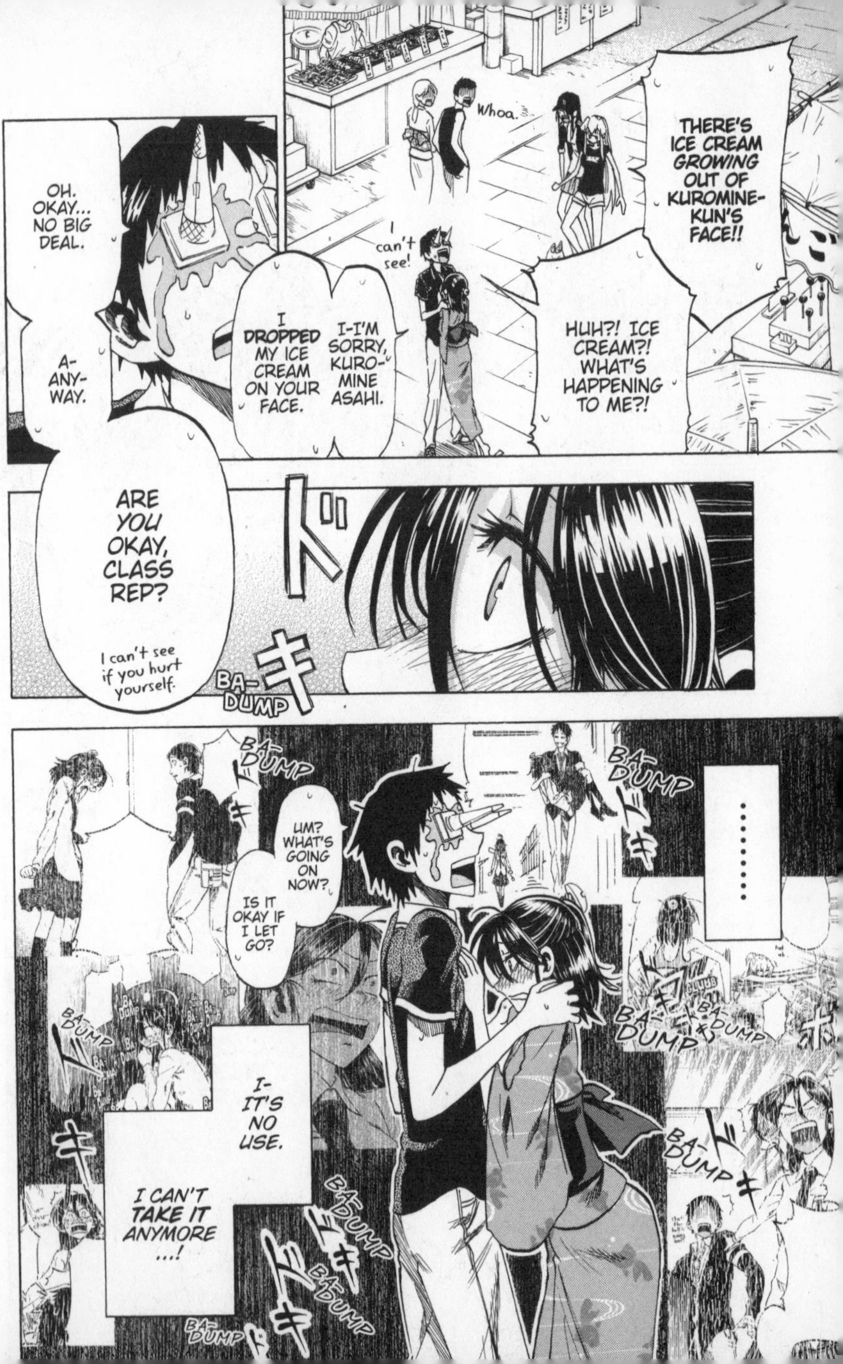
THERE'S ICE CREAM GROWING OUT OF KUROMINE-KUN'S FACE!!
Whoa.
I can't see!
HUH?! ICE CREAM?! WHAT'S HAPPENING TO ME?!
I-I'M SORRY, KUROMINE ASAHI.
I DROPPED MY ICE CREAM ON YOUR FACE.
OH. OKAY... NO BIG DEAL.
A-ANYWAY.
ARE YOU OKAY, CLASS REP?
I can't see if you hurt yourself.
BA-DUMP
BA-DUMP
BA-DUMP
....
UM? WHAT'S GOING ON NOW?
IS IT OKAY IF I LET GO?
BA-DUMP
BA-DUMP
BA-DUMP
I-IT'S NO USE.
I CAN'T TAKE IT ANYMORE...!
BA-DUMP
BA-DUMP
BA-DUMP

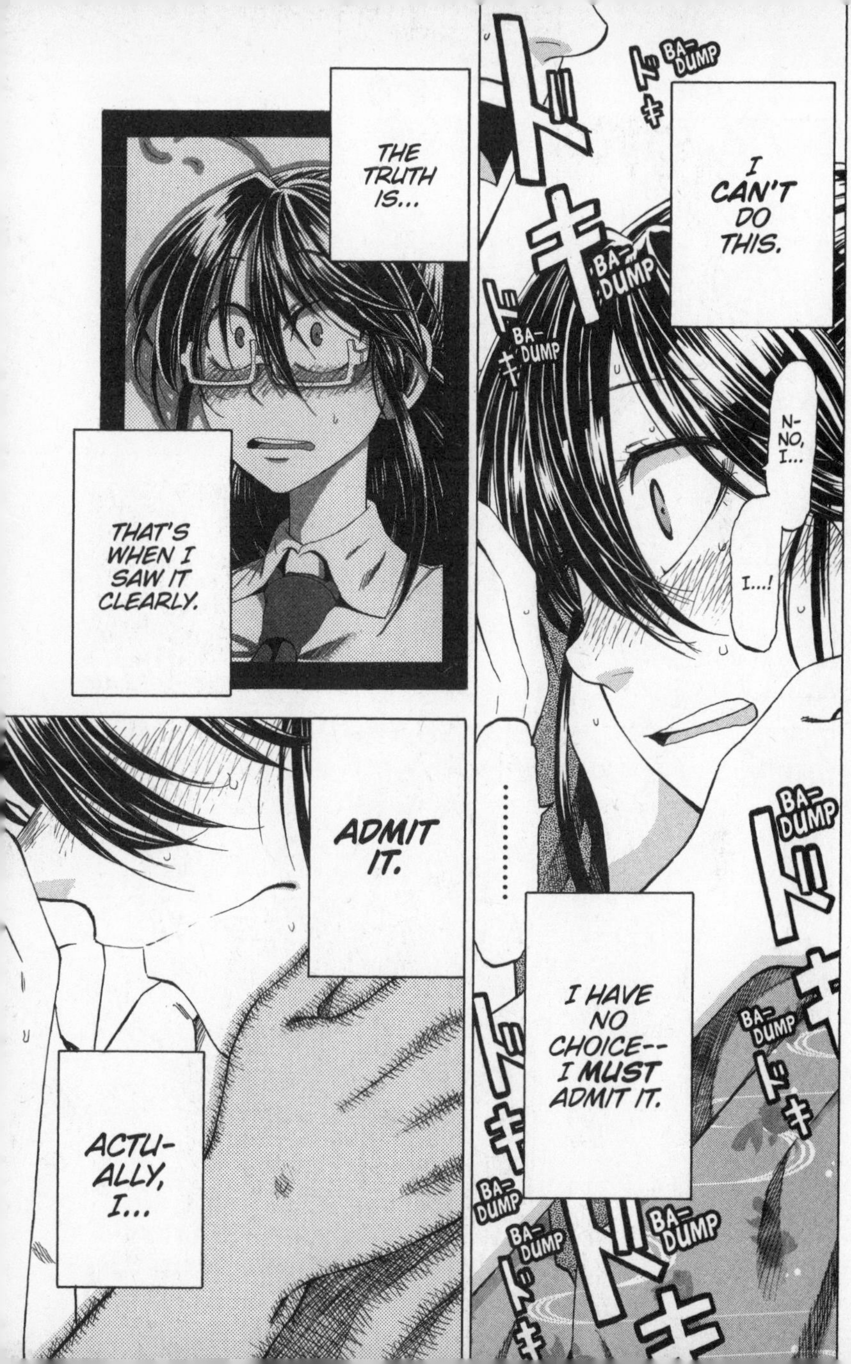
BA-DUMP
I CAN'T DO THIS.
BA-DUMP
BA-DUMP
N-NO, I...
I...!
......
BA-DUMP
I HAVE NO CHOICE-- I MUST ADMIT IT.
BA-DUMP
BA-DUMP
BA-DUMP
BA-DUMP
THE TRUTH IS...
THAT'S WHEN I SAW IT CLEARLY.
ADMIT IT.
ACTU-ALLY, I...

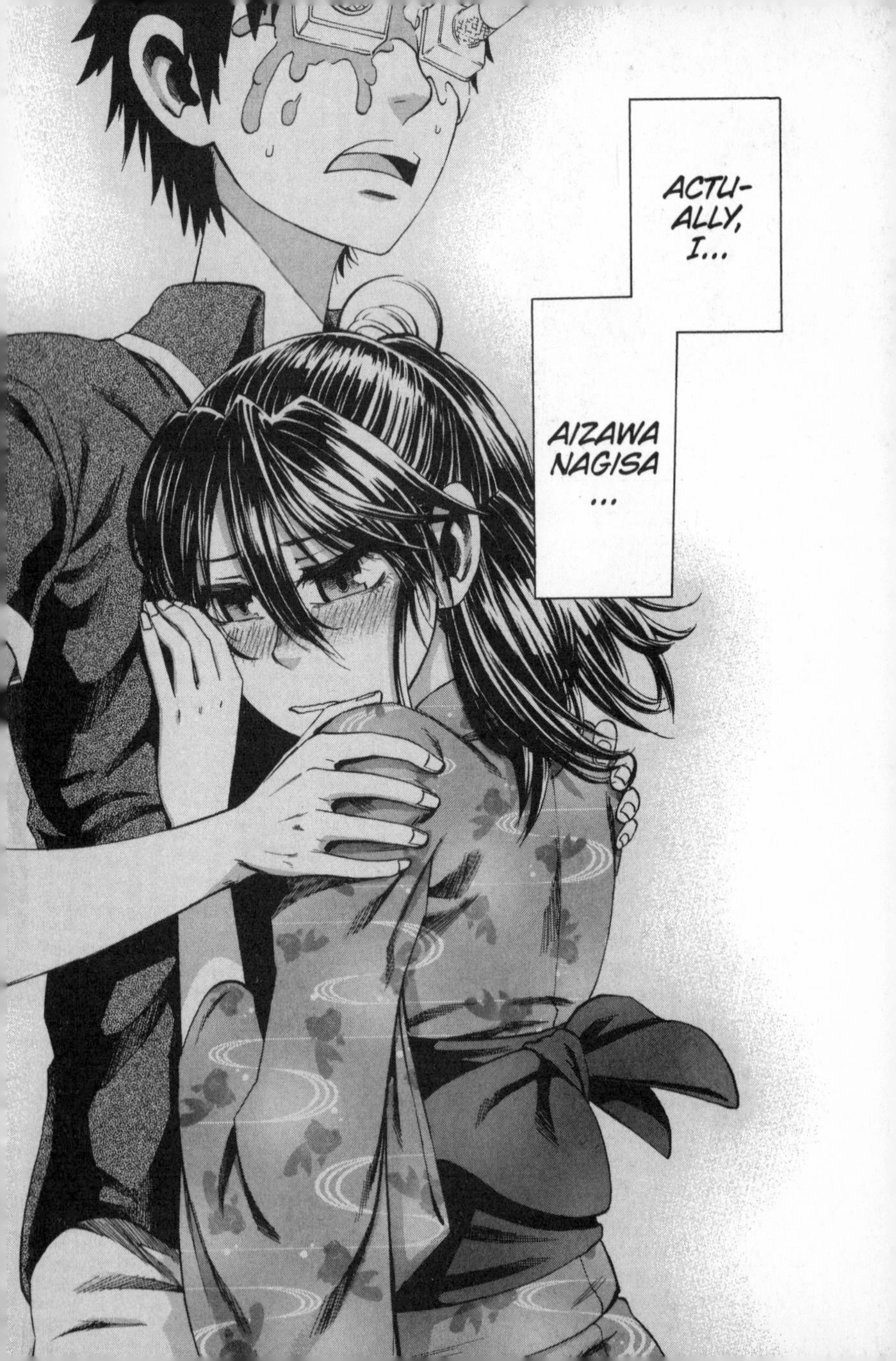
ACTU-
ALLY,
I...
AIZAWA
NAGISA
...

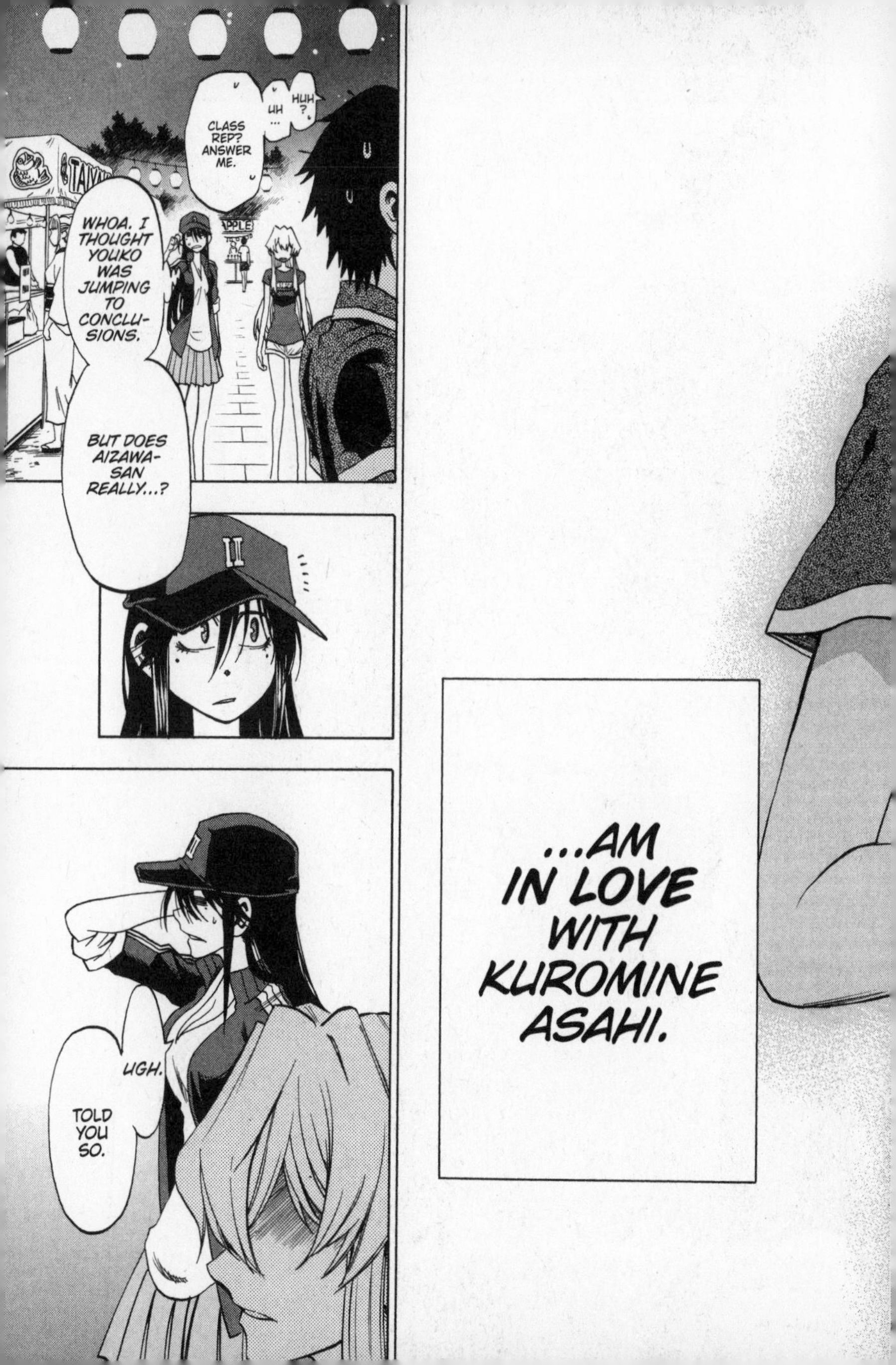
...AM IN LOVE WITH KUROMINE ASAHI.
HUH?
UH...
CLASS REP? ANSWER ME.
TAIYAKI
APPLE
WHOA. I THOUGHT YOUKO WAS JUMPING TO CONCLUSIONS.
BUT DOES AIZAWA-SAN REALLY...?
UGH.
TOLD YOU SO.

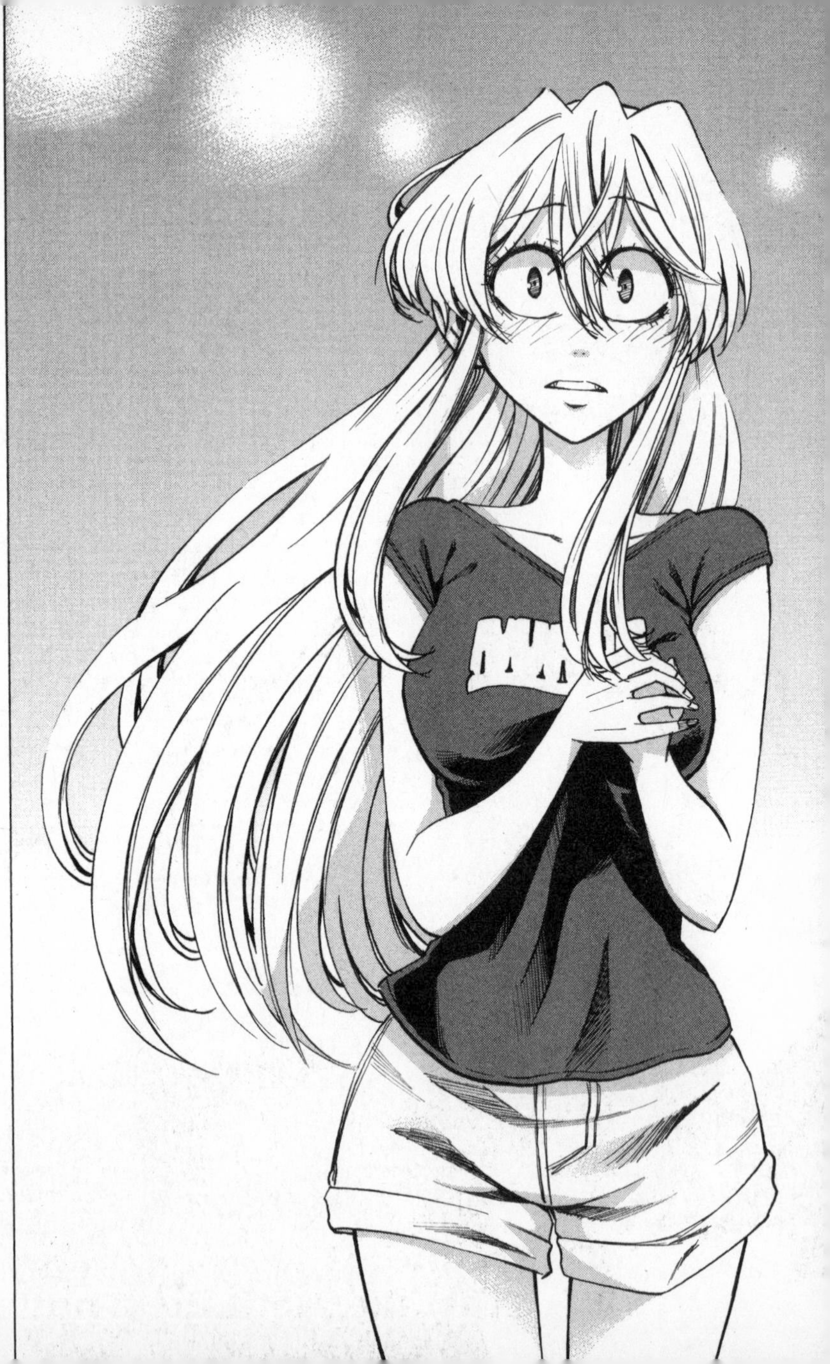

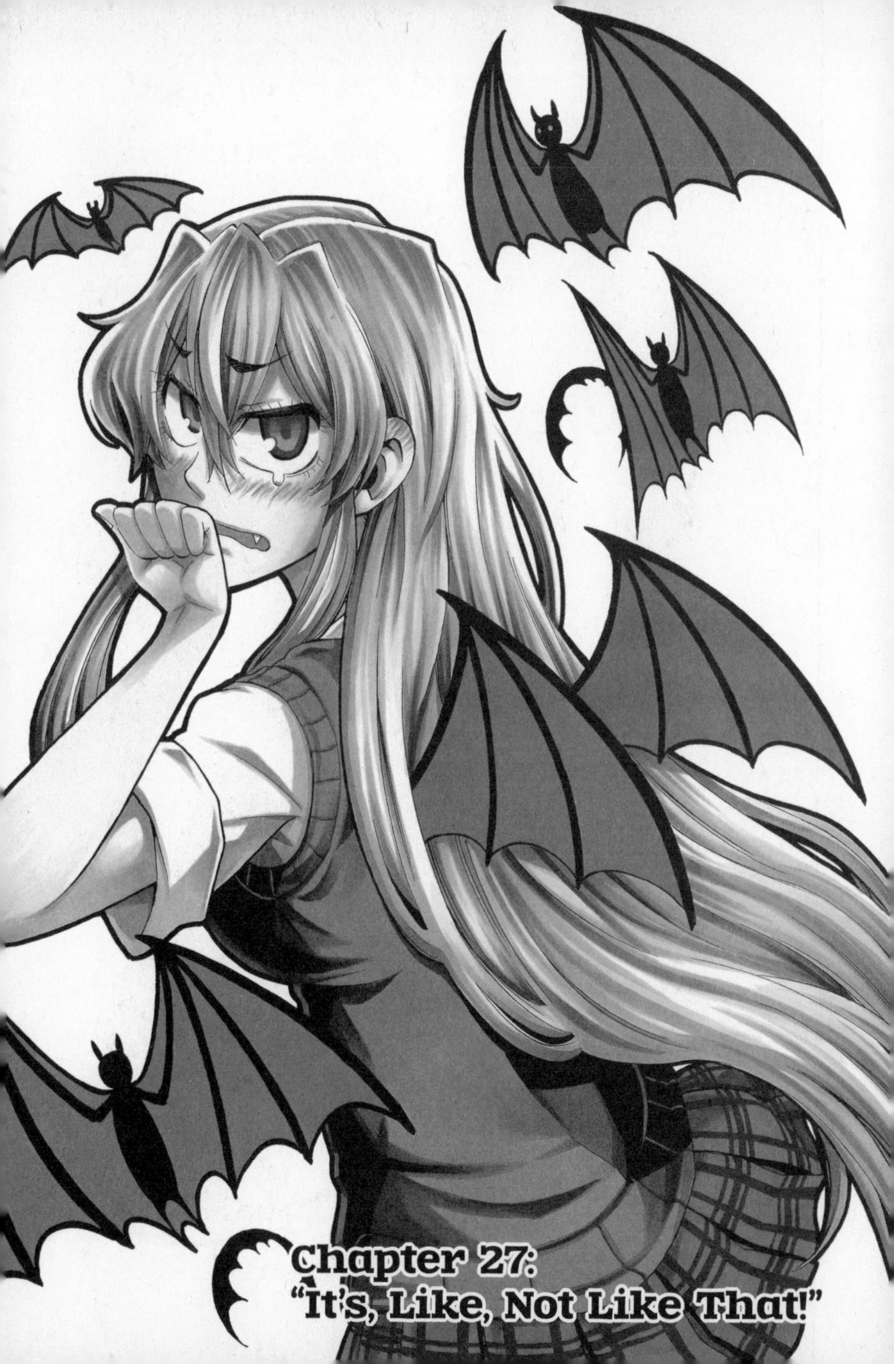
Chapter 27:
"It's, Like, Not Like That!"

TOP SECRET

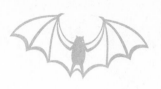

My Monster Secret 4

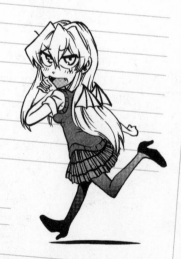

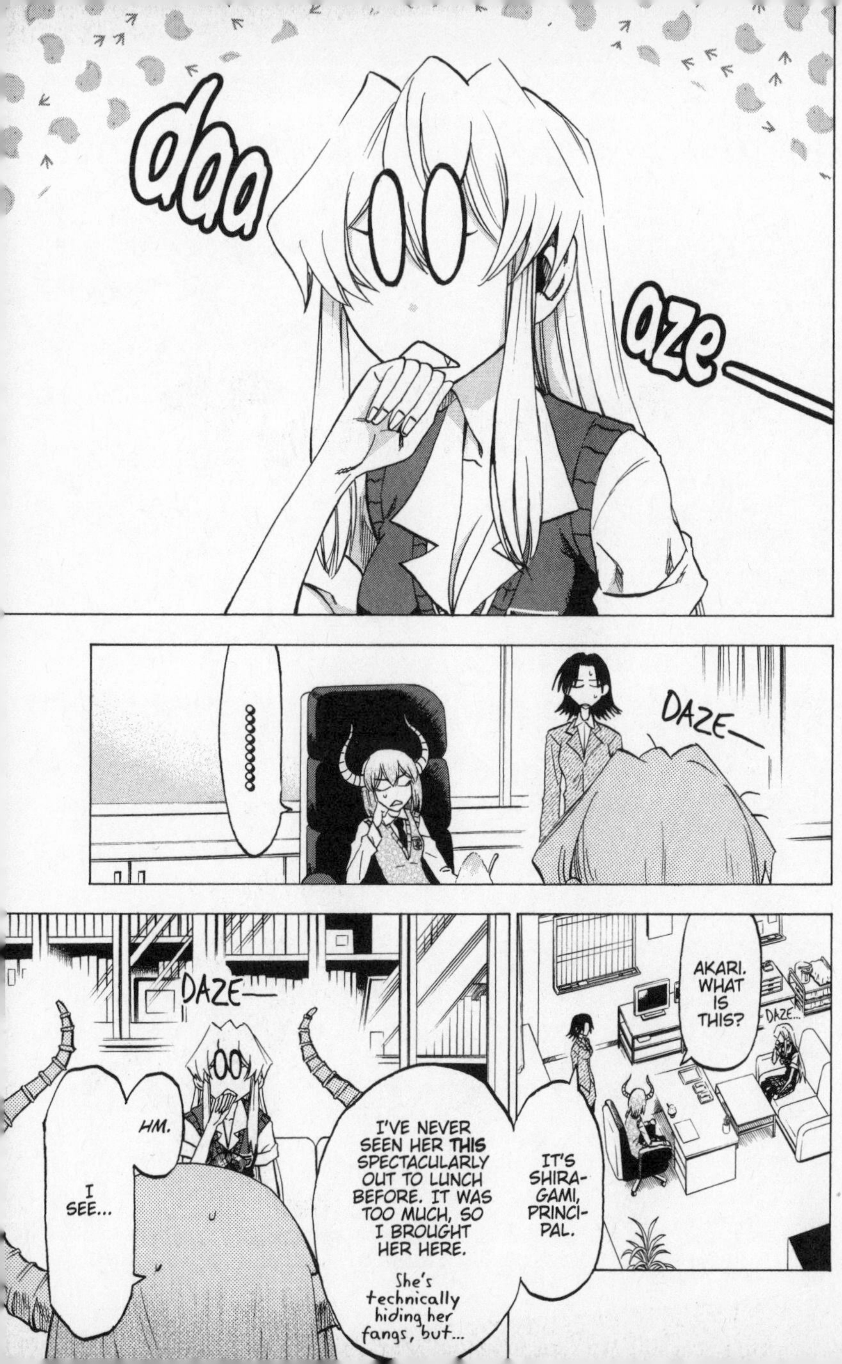
daa
aze—
……
DAZE—
AKARI. WHAT IS THIS?
DAZE...
IT'S SHIRA-GAMI, PRINCIPAL.
I'VE NEVER SEEN HER THIS SPECTACULARLY OUT TO LUNCH BEFORE. IT WAS TOO MUCH, SO I BROUGHT HER HERE.
She's technically hiding her fangs, but...
DAZE—
HM.
I SEE...

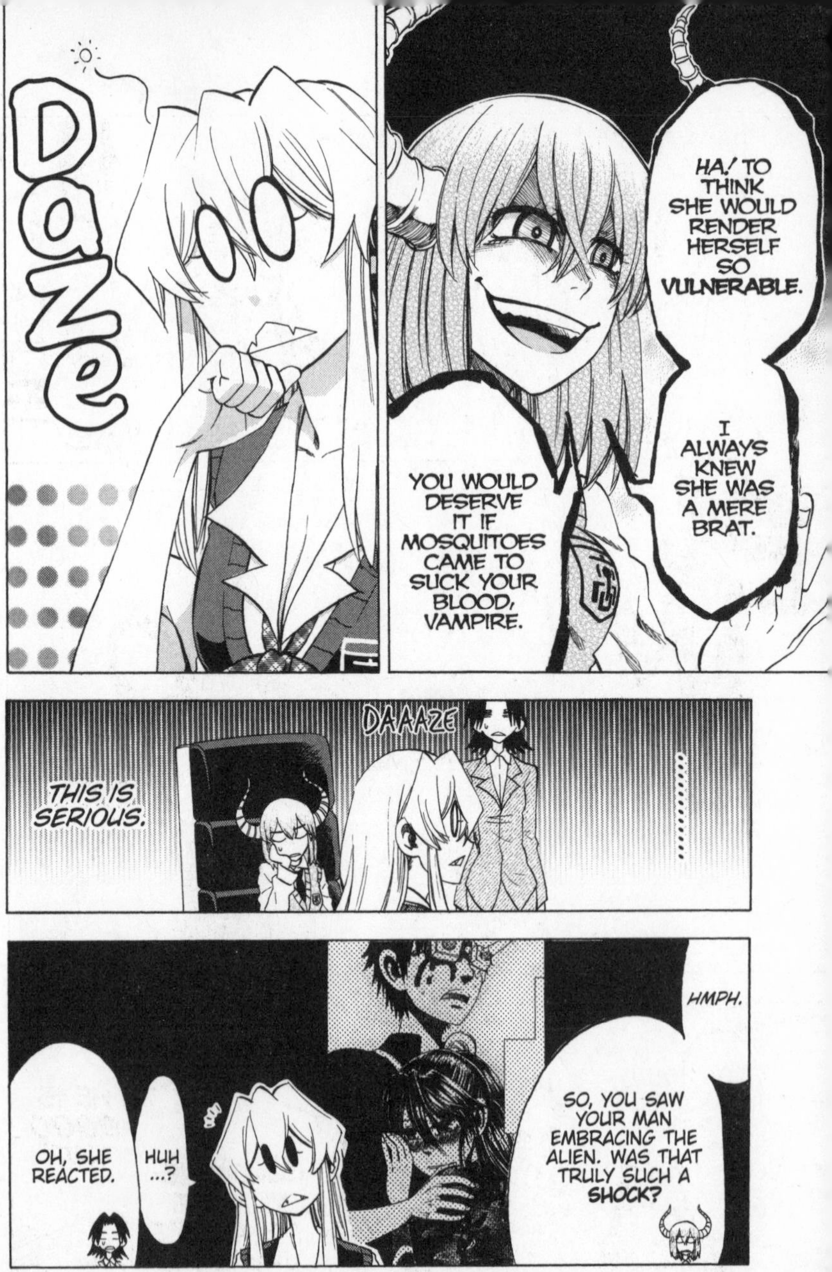
HA! TO THINK SHE WOULD RENDER HERSELF SO VULNERABLE.
I ALWAYS KNEW SHE WAS A MERE BRAT.
YOU WOULD DESERVE IT IF MOSQUITOES CAME TO SUCK YOUR BLOOD, VAMPIRE.
DAZE
DAAAZE
......
THIS IS SERIOUS.
HMPH.
SO, YOU SAW YOUR MAN EMBRACING THE ALIEN. WAS THAT TRULY SUCH A SHOCK?
HUH ...?
OH, SHE REACTED.

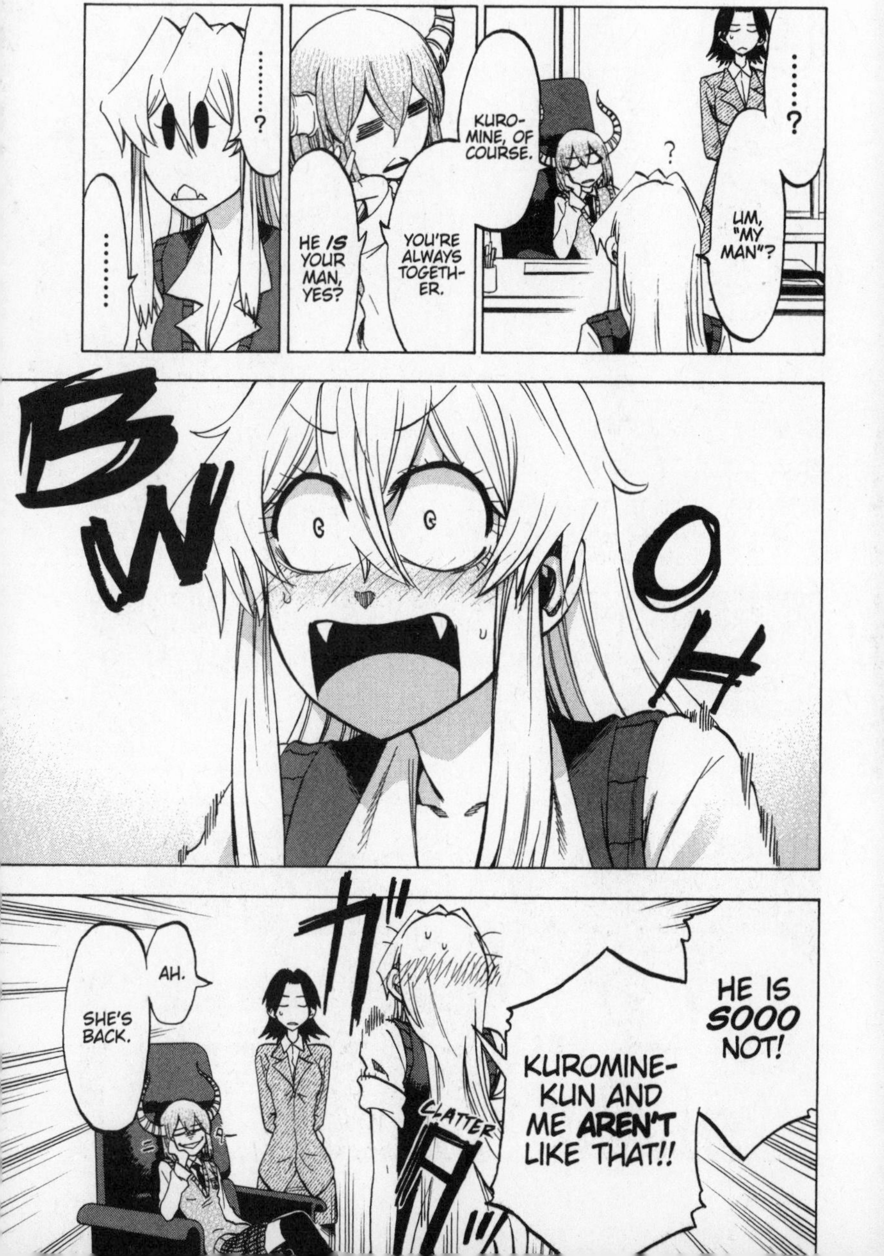
......?
?
UM, "MY MAN"?
KURO-MINE, OF COURSE.
YOU'RE ALWAYS TOGETH-ER.
HE IS YOUR MAN, YES?
......?
......
BWOH
HE IS SOOO NOT!
KUROMINE-KUN AND ME AREN'T LIKE THAT!!
CLATTER
AH.
SHE'S BACK.

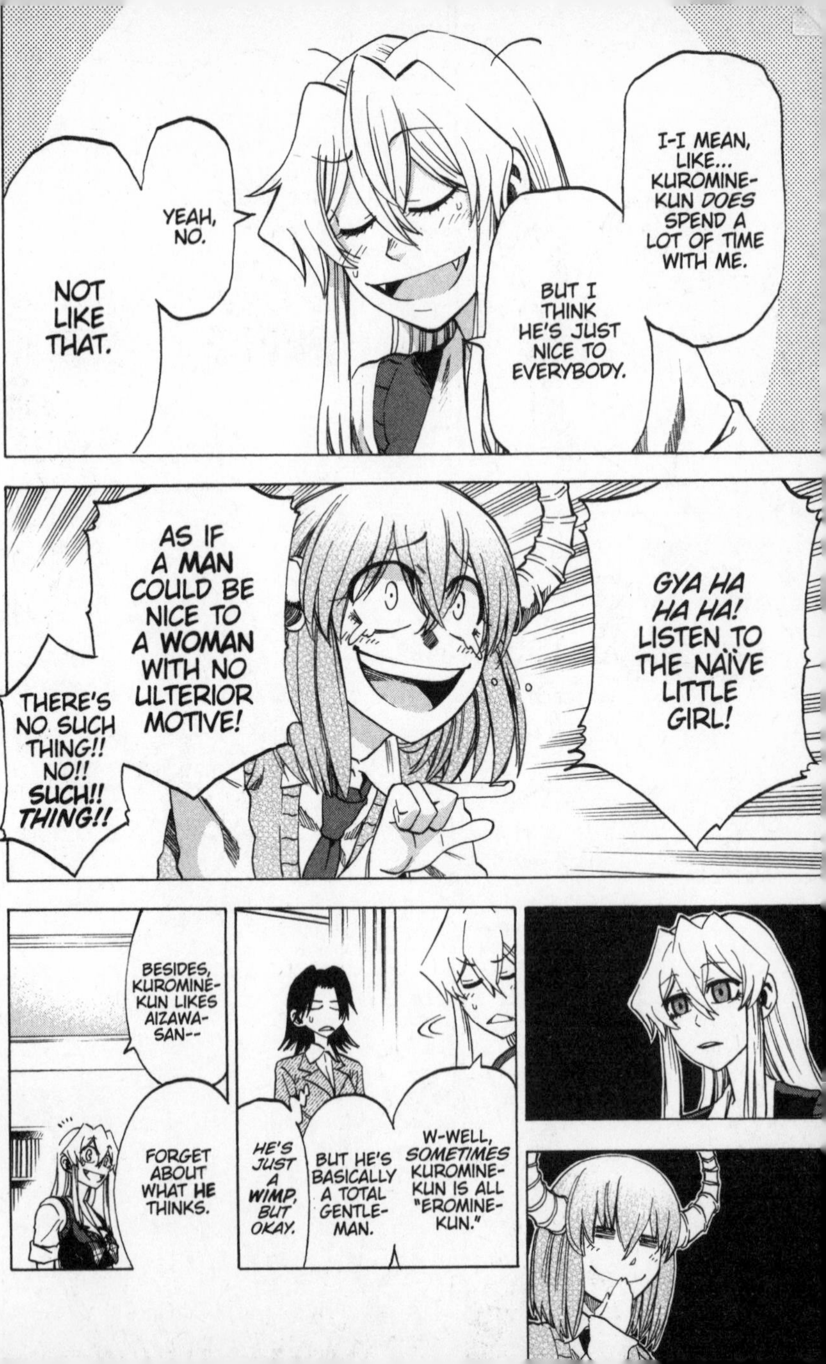
I-I MEAN, LIKE... KUROMINE-KUN DOES SPEND A LOT OF TIME WITH ME.
BUT I THINK HE'S JUST NICE TO EVERYBODY.
YEAH, NO.
NOT LIKE THAT.
GYA HA HA HA! LISTEN TO THE NAÏVE LITTLE GIRL!
AS IF A MAN COULD BE NICE TO A WOMAN WITH NO ULTERIOR MOTIVE!
THERE'S NO SUCH THING!! NO!! SUCH!! THING!!
W-WELL, SOMETIMES KUROMINE-KUN IS ALL "EROMINE-KUN."
BUT HE'S BASICALLY A TOTAL GENTLE-MAN.
HE'S JUST A WIMP, BUT OKAY.
BESIDES, KUROMINE-KUN LIKES AIZAWA-SAN--
FORGET ABOUT WHAT HE THINKS.

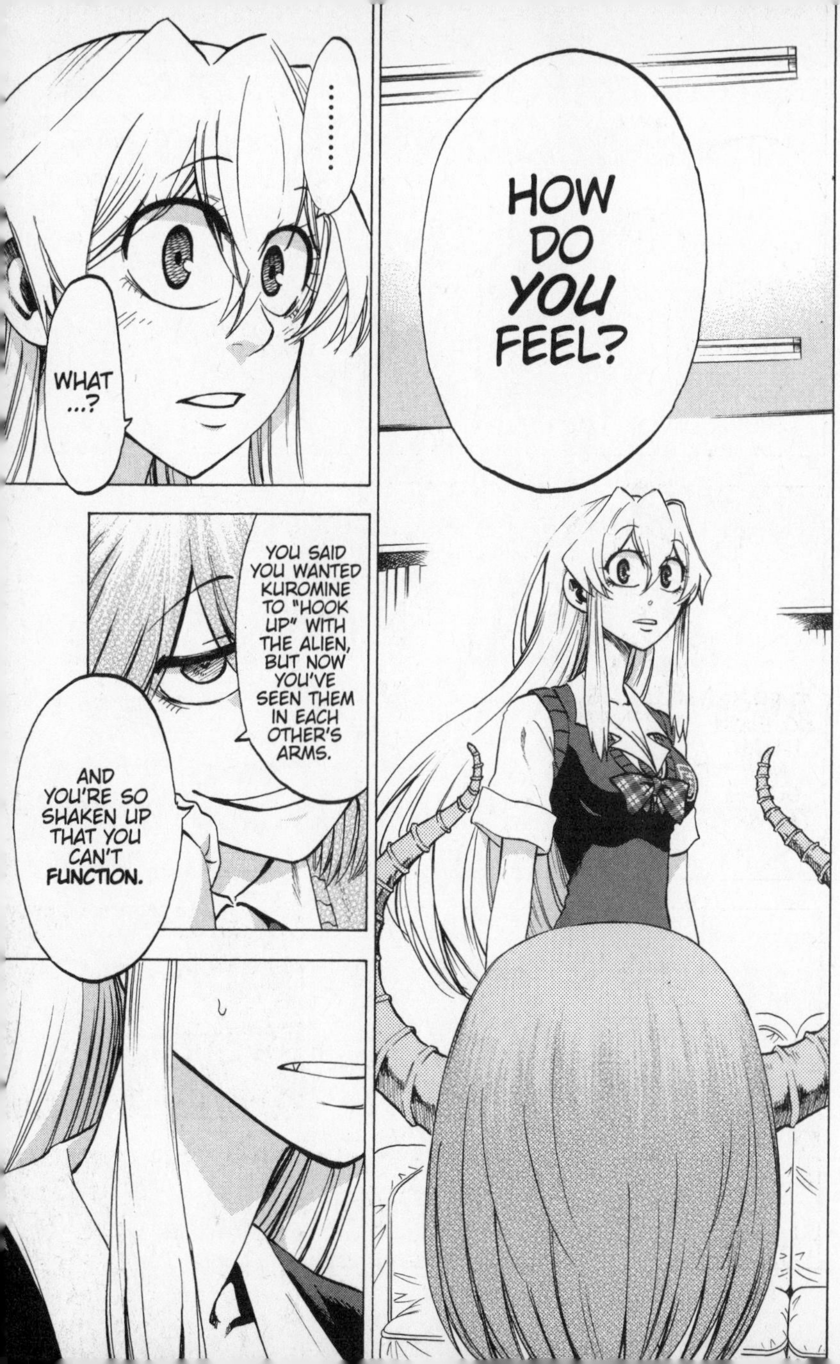
HOW DO YOU FEEL?
......
WHAT ...?
YOU SAID YOU WANTED KUROMINE TO "HOOK UP" WITH THE ALIEN, BUT NOW YOU'VE SEEN THEM IN EACH OTHER'S ARMS.
AND YOU'RE SO SHAKEN UP THAT YOU CAN'T FUNCTION.

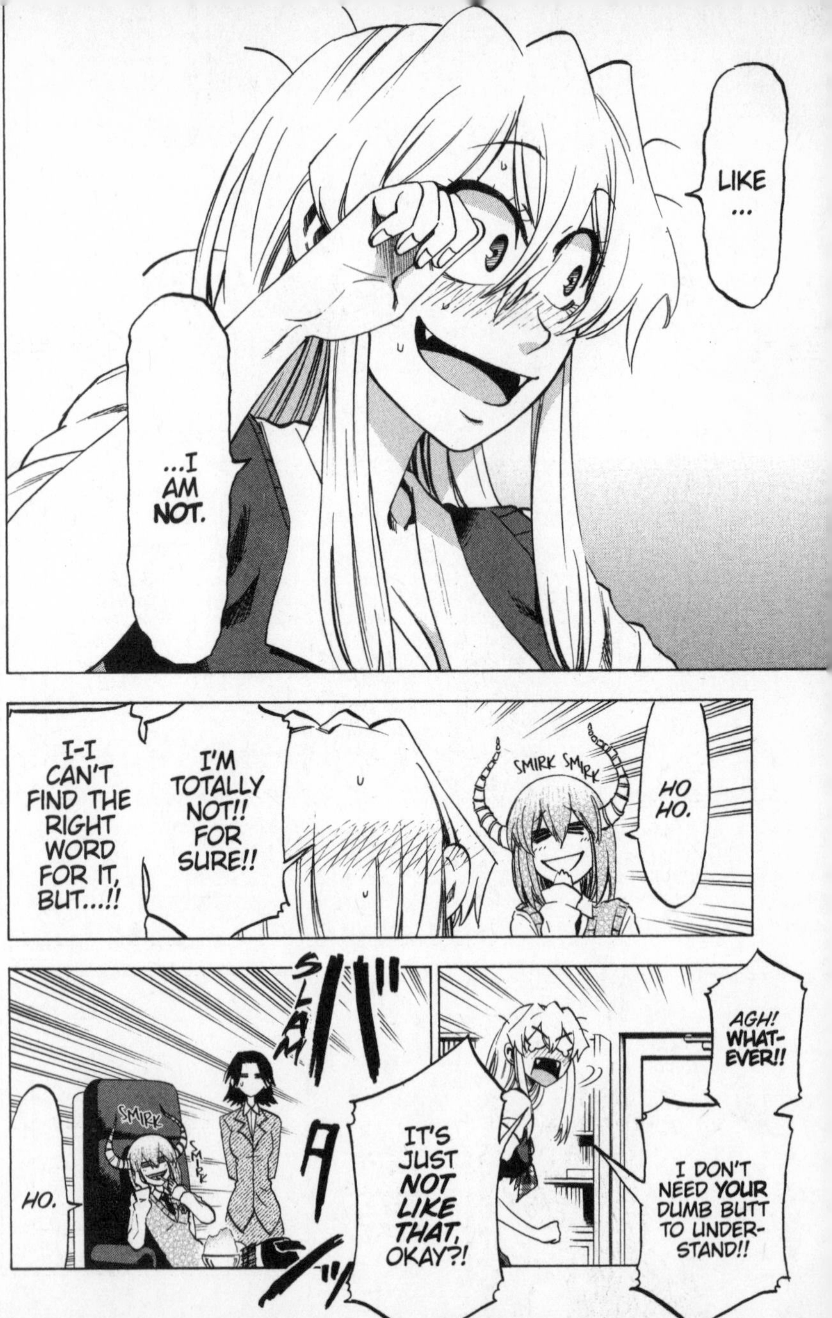
LIKE ...
...I AM NOT.
HO HO.
SMIRK SMIRK
I'M TOTALLY NOT!! FOR SURE!!
I-I CAN'T FIND THE RIGHT WORD FOR IT, BUT...!!
AGH! WHAT-EVER!!
I DON'T NEED YOUR DUMB BUTT TO UNDER-STAND!!
IT'S JUST NOT LIKE THAT, OKAY?!
SLAM
SMIRK
SMIRK
HO.

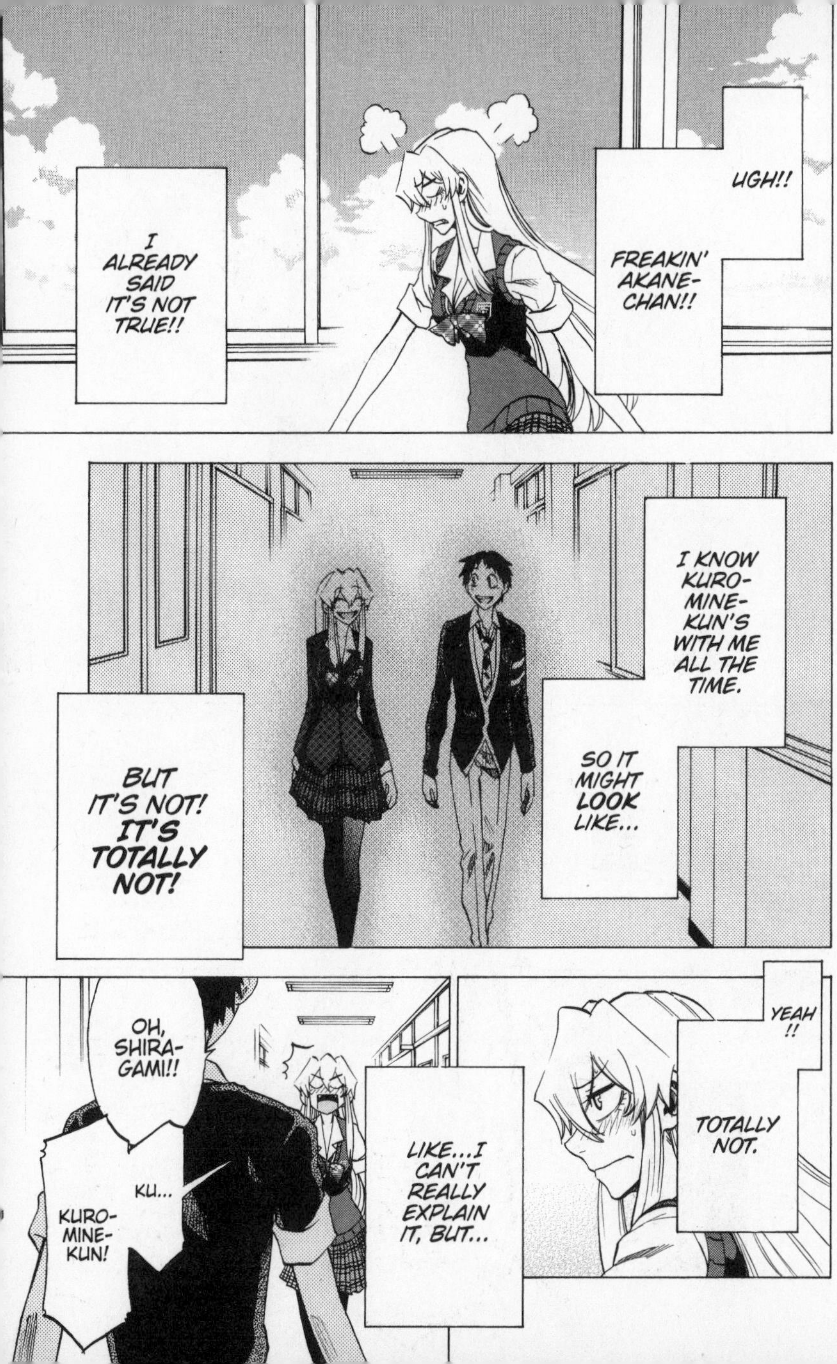
UGH!!
FREAKIN' AKANE-CHAN!!
I ALREADY SAID IT'S NOT TRUE!!
I KNOW KURO-MINE-KUN'S WITH ME ALL THE TIME.
SO IT MIGHT LOOK LIKE...
BUT IT'S NOT! IT'S TOTALLY NOT!
YEAH!!
TOTALLY NOT.
LIKE...I CAN'T REALLY EXPLAIN IT, BUT...
OH, SHIRA-GAMI!!
KU...
KURO-MINE-KUN!

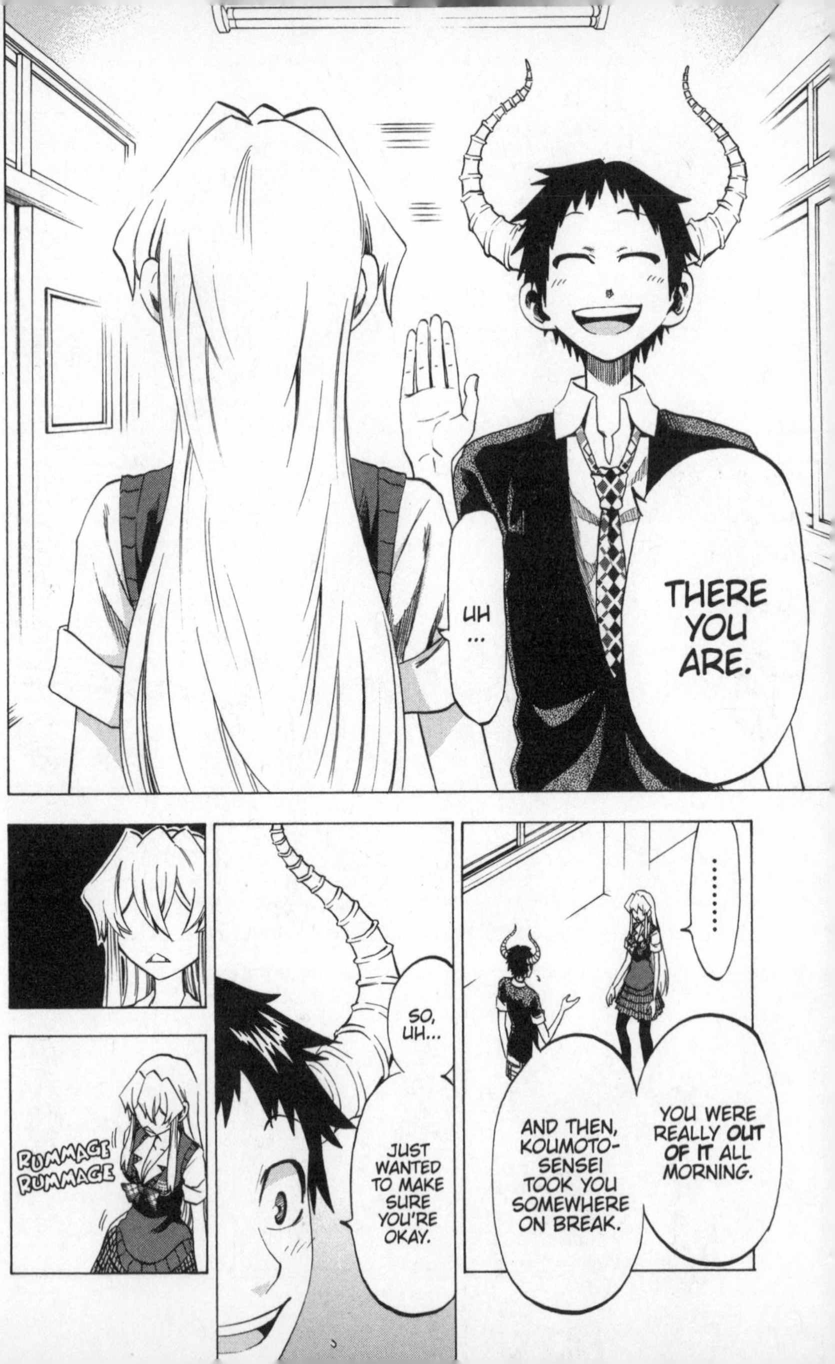
THERE YOU ARE.
UH...
......
YOU WERE REALLY OUT OF IT ALL MORNING.
AND THEN, KOUMOTO-SENSEI TOOK YOU SOMEWHERE ON BREAK.
SO, UH...
JUST WANTED TO MAKE SURE YOU'RE OKAY.
RUMMAGE RUMMAGE

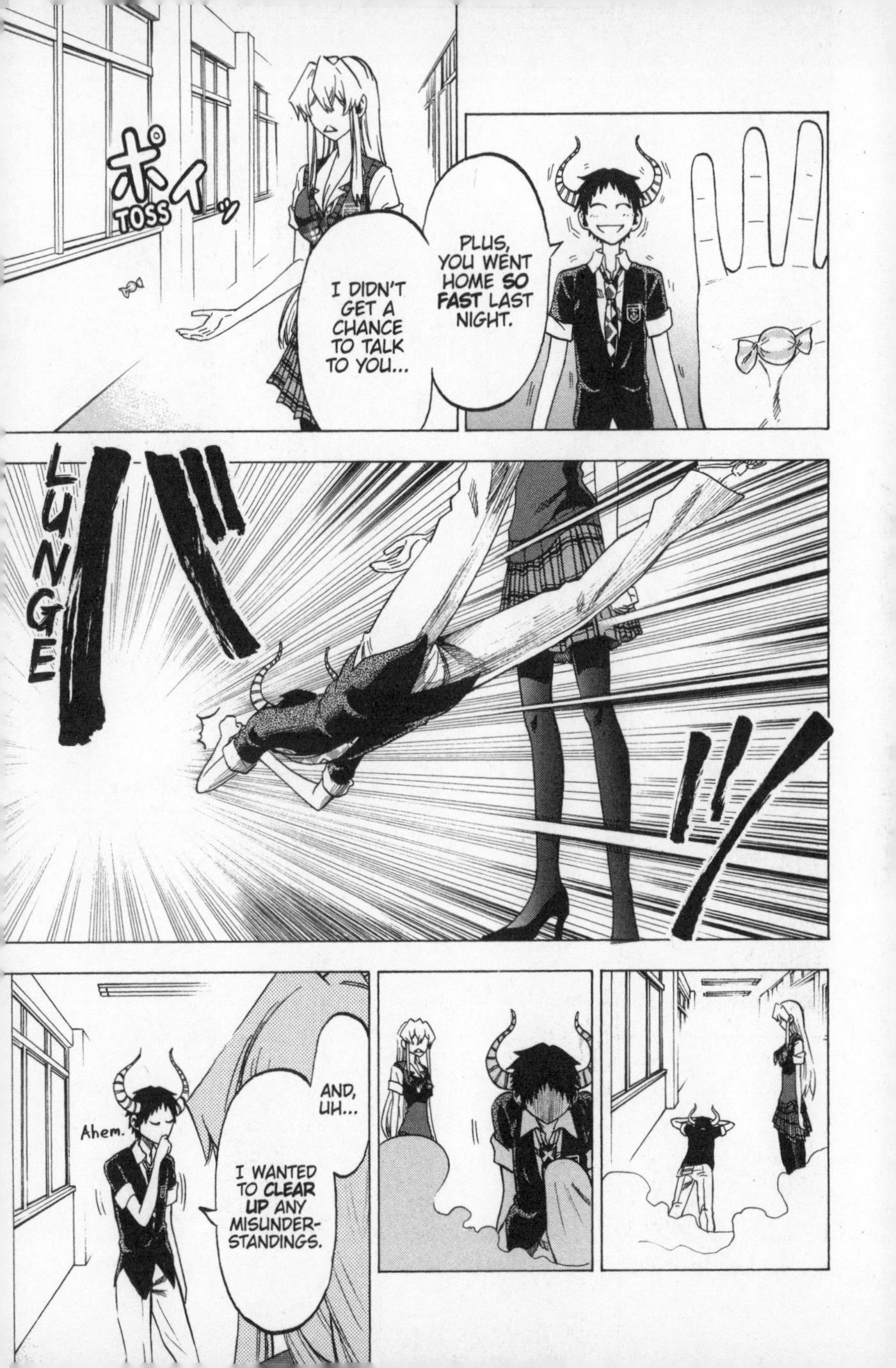

I DIDN'T GET A CHANCE TO TALK TO YOU...
PLUS, YOU WENT HOME SO FAST LAST NIGHT.
ポイッ
TOSS
LUNGE
AND, UH...
I WANTED TO CLEAR UP ANY MISUNDER-STANDINGS.
Ahem.

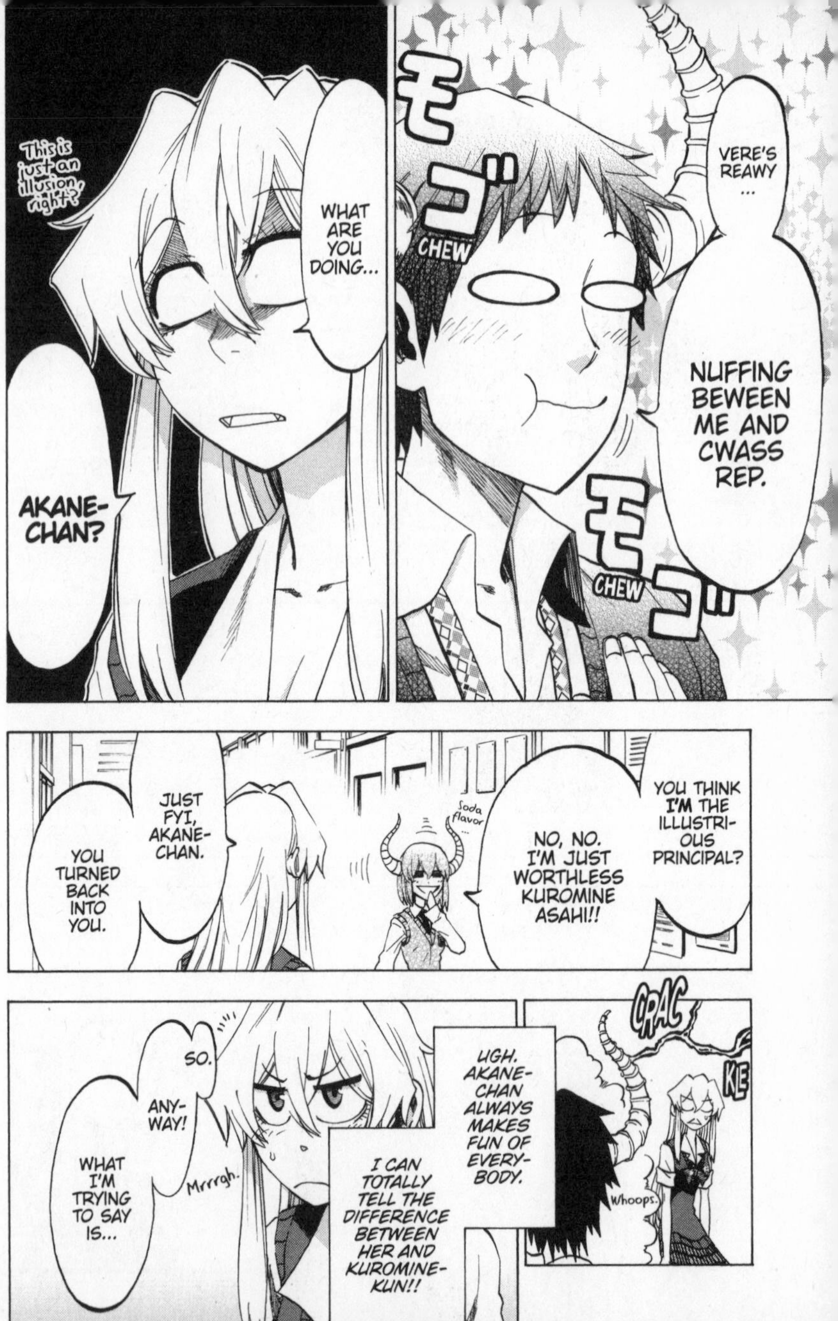

VERE'S REAWY ...
NUFFING BEWEEN ME AND CWASS REP.
CHEW
CHEW
WHAT ARE YOU DOING...
This is just an illusion, right?
AKANE-CHAN?
YOU THINK I'M THE ILLUSTRIOUS PRINCIPAL?
NO, NO. I'M JUST WORTHLESS KUROMINE ASAHI!!
Soda flavor ...
JUST FYI, AKANE-CHAN.
YOU TURNED BACK INTO YOU.
CRACKLE
UGH. AKANE-CHAN ALWAYS MAKES FUN OF EVERYBODY.
Whoops.
I CAN TOTALLY TELL THE DIFFERENCE BETWEEN HER AND KUROMINE-KUN!!
SO.
ANYWAY!
WHAT I'M TRYING TO SAY IS...
Mrrrgh.

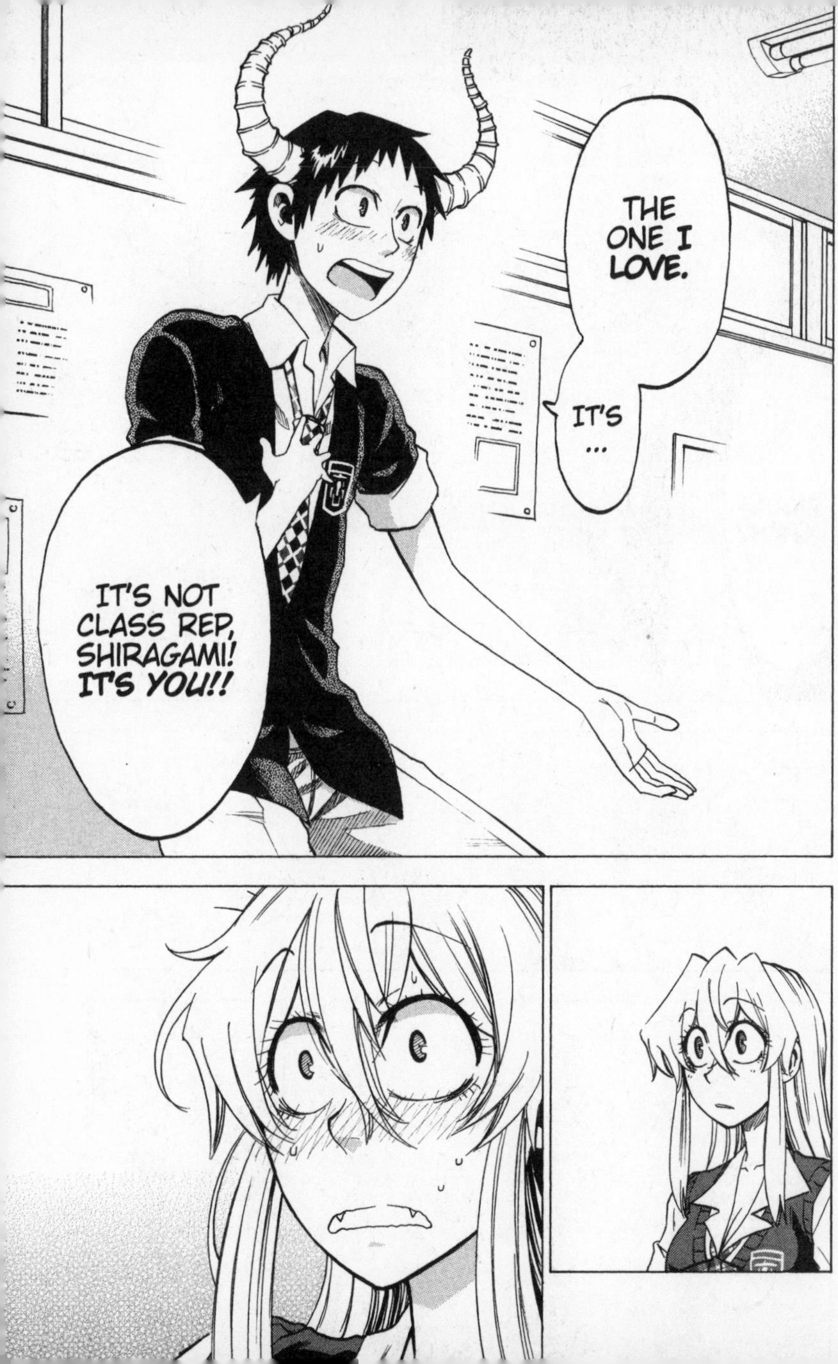
THE ONE I LOVE.
IT'S ...
IT'S NOT CLASS REP, SHIRAGAMI! IT'S *YOU*!!

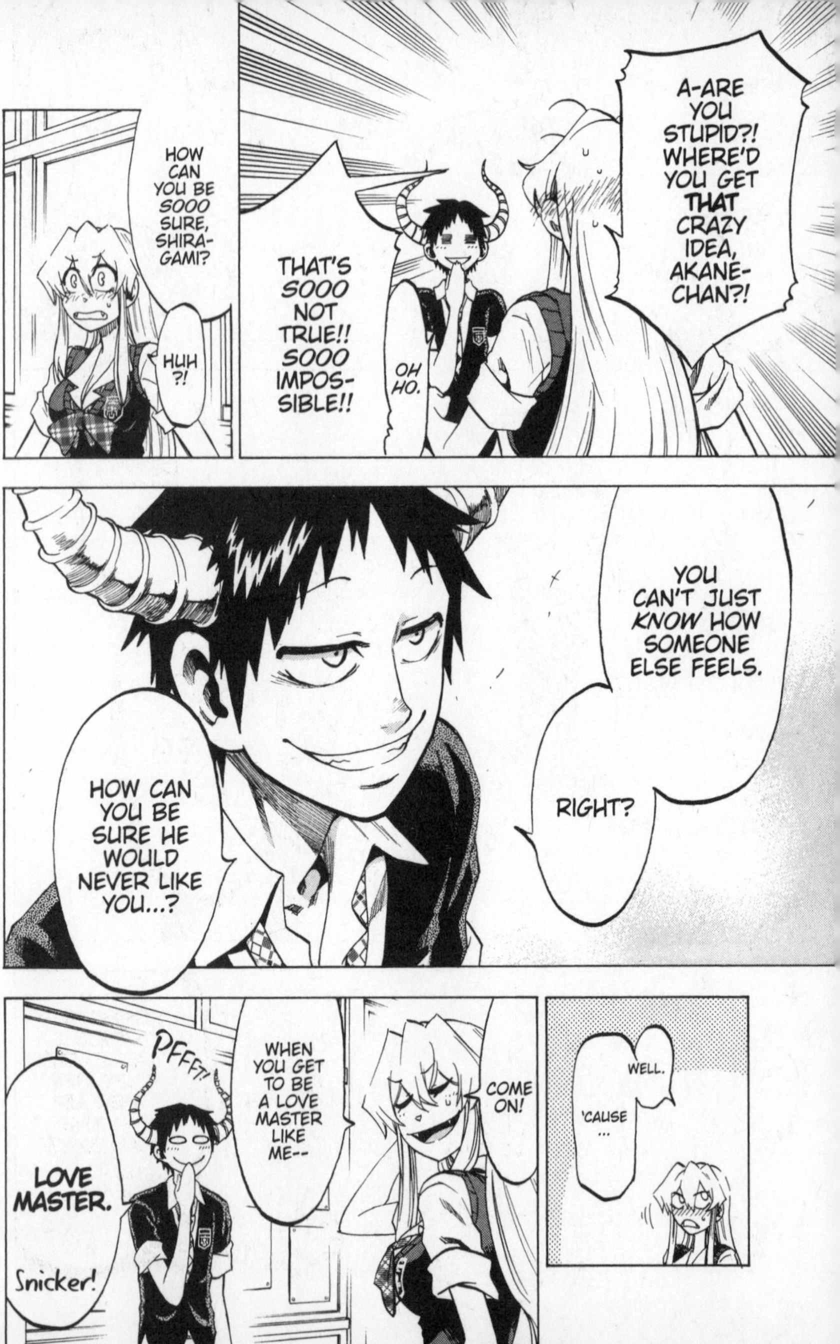
A-ARE YOU STUPID?! WHERE'D YOU GET THAT CRAZY IDEA, AKANE-CHAN?!
OH HO.
THAT'S SOOO NOT TRUE!! SOOO IMPOSSIBLE!!
HUH ?!
HOW CAN YOU BE SOOO SURE, SHIRA-GAMI?
YOU CAN'T JUST KNOW HOW SOMEONE ELSE FEELS.
RIGHT?
HOW CAN YOU BE SURE HE WOULD NEVER LIKE YOU...?
WELL.
'CAUSE ...
COME ON!
WHEN YOU GET TO BE A LOVE MASTER LIKE ME--
PFFFT!
LOVE MASTER.
Snicker!

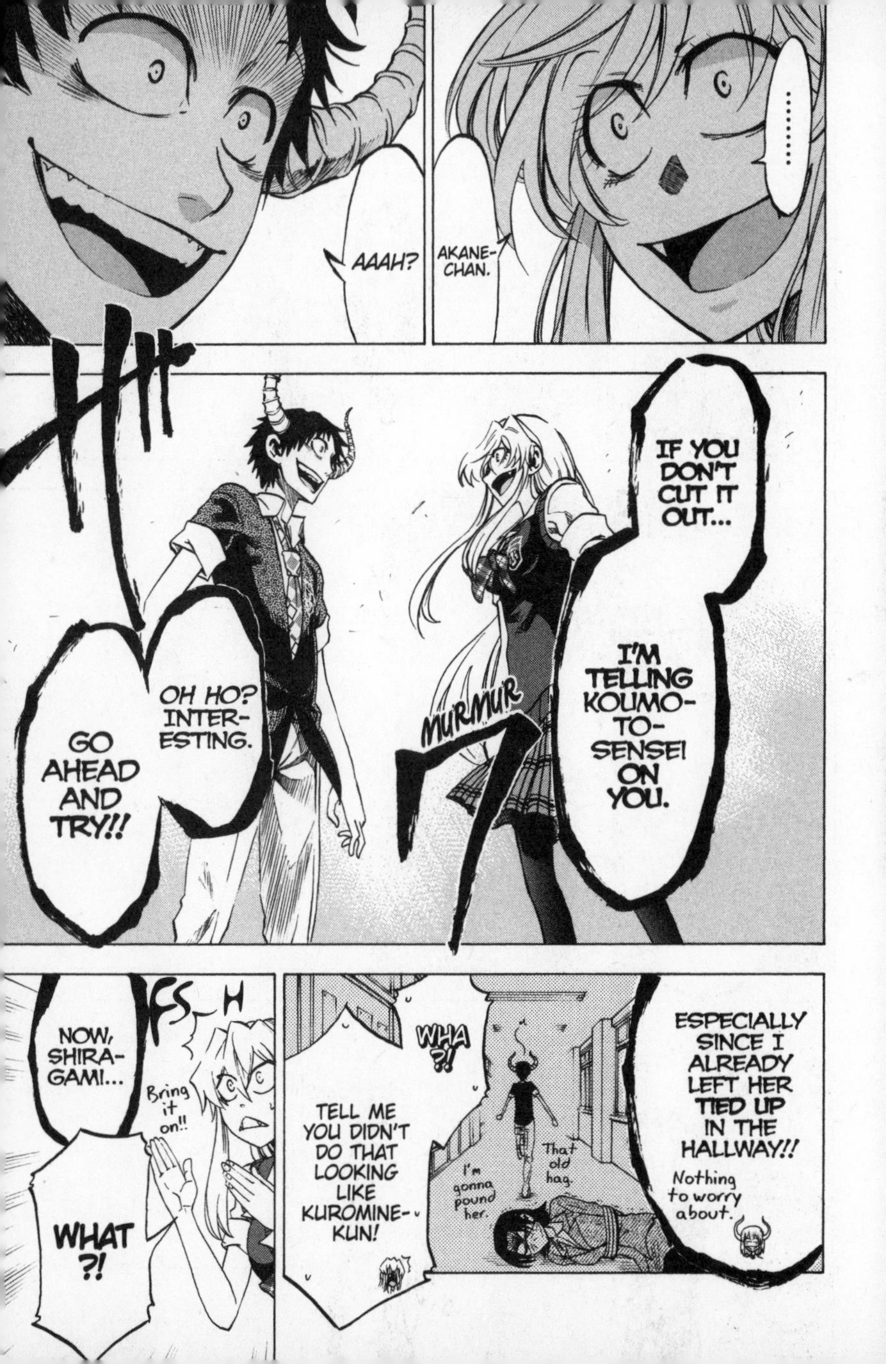
......
AKANE-CHAN.
AAAH?
IF YOU DON'T CUT IT OUT...
I'M TELLING KOUMOTO-SENSEI ON YOU.
MURMUR
OH HO? INTERESTING.
GO AHEAD AND TRY!!
ESPECIALLY SINCE I ALREADY LEFT HER TIED UP IN THE HALLWAY!!
Nothing to worry about.
That old hag.
I'm gonna pound her.
WHA ?!
TELL ME YOU DIDN'T DO THAT LOOKING LIKE KUROMINE-KUN!
FS-H
NOW, SHIRAGAMI...
Bring it on!!
WHAT ?!

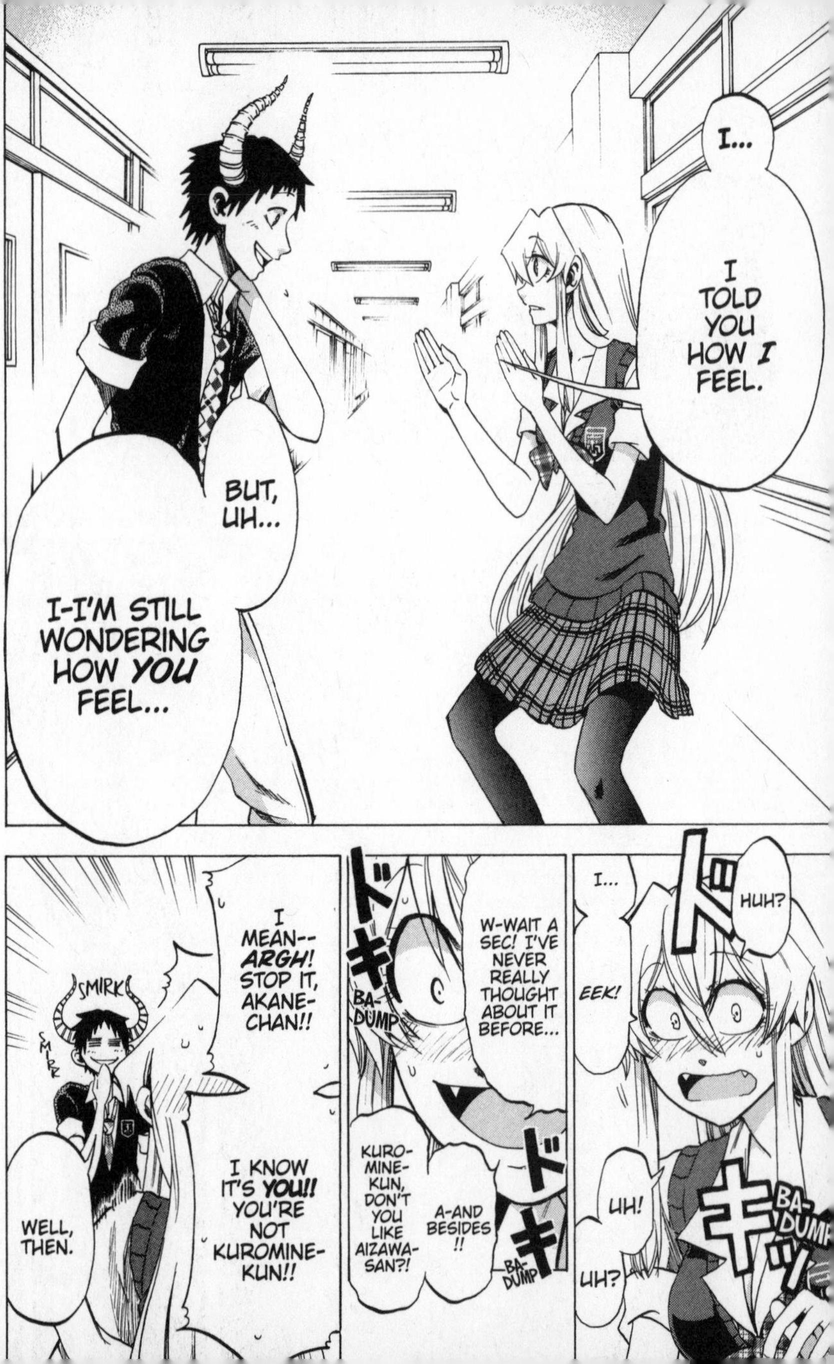
I...
I TOLD YOU HOW *I* FEEL.
BUT, UH...
I-I'M STILL WONDERING HOW *YOU* FEEL...
ドキッ
HUH?
I...
EEK!
UH!
BA-DUMP
UH?
W-WAIT A SEC! I'VE NEVER REALLY THOUGHT ABOUT IT BEFORE...
ドキ
BA-DUMP
A-AND BESIDES!!
KUROMINE-KUN, DON'T YOU LIKE AIZAWA-SAN?!
ドキ
BA-DUMP
I MEAN-- *ARGH*! STOP IT, AKANE-CHAN!!
I KNOW IT'S **YOU!!** YOU'RE NOT KUROMINE-KUN!!
SMIRK
SMIRK
WELL, THEN.

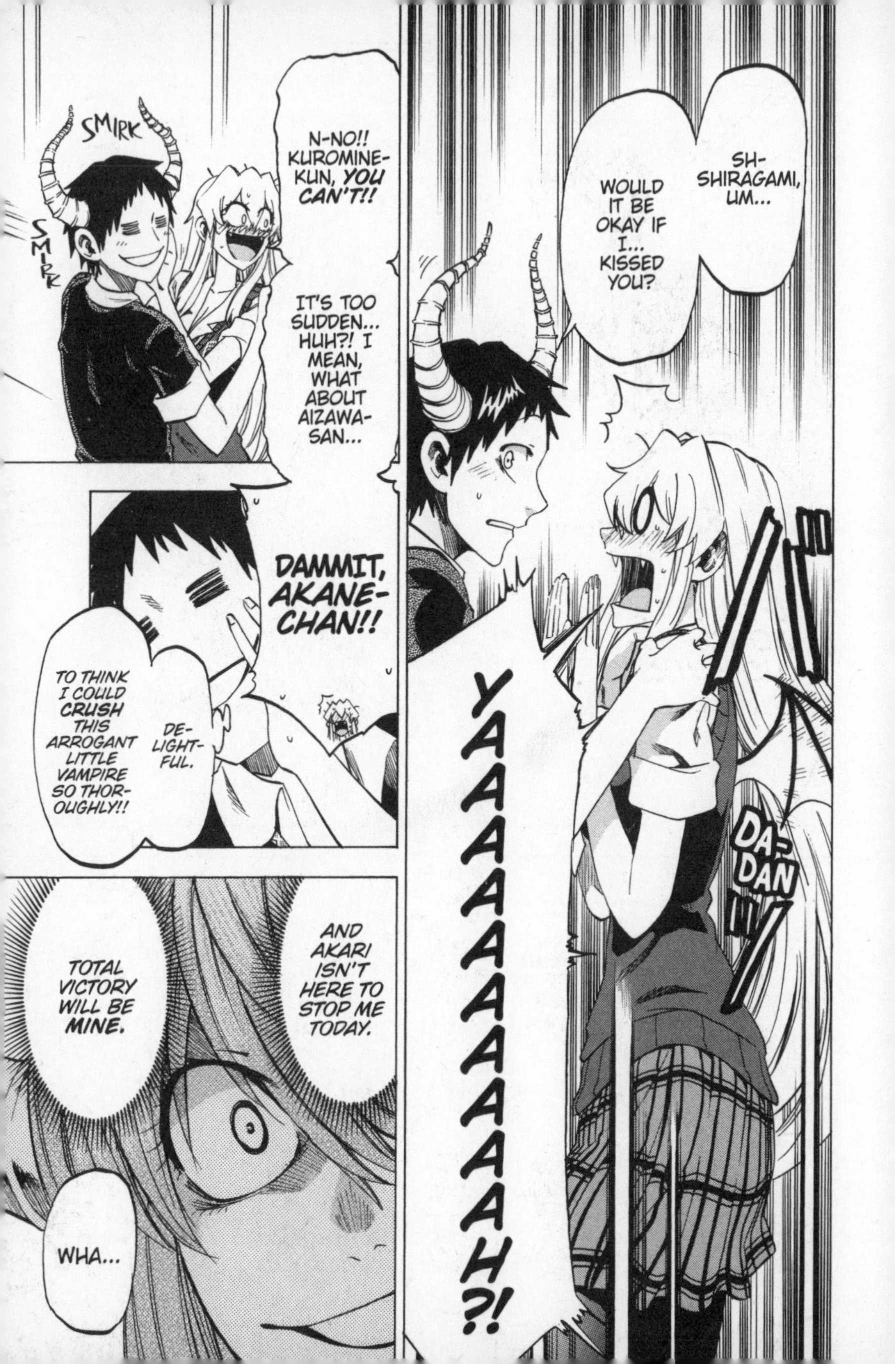
SH-SHIRAGAMI, UM...
WOULD IT BE OKAY IF I... KISSED YOU?
DA-DAN
YAAAAAAAAAAH?!
N-NO!! KUROMINE-KUN, YOU CAN'T!!
SMIRK
SMIRK
IT'S TOO SUDDEN... HUH?! I MEAN, WHAT ABOUT AIZAWA-SAN...
DAMMIT, AKANE-CHAN!!
DELIGHTFUL.
TO THINK I COULD CRUSH THIS ARROGANT LITTLE VAMPIRE SO THOROUGHLY!!
AND AKARI ISN'T HERE TO STOP ME TODAY.
TOTAL VICTORY WILL BE MINE.
WHA...

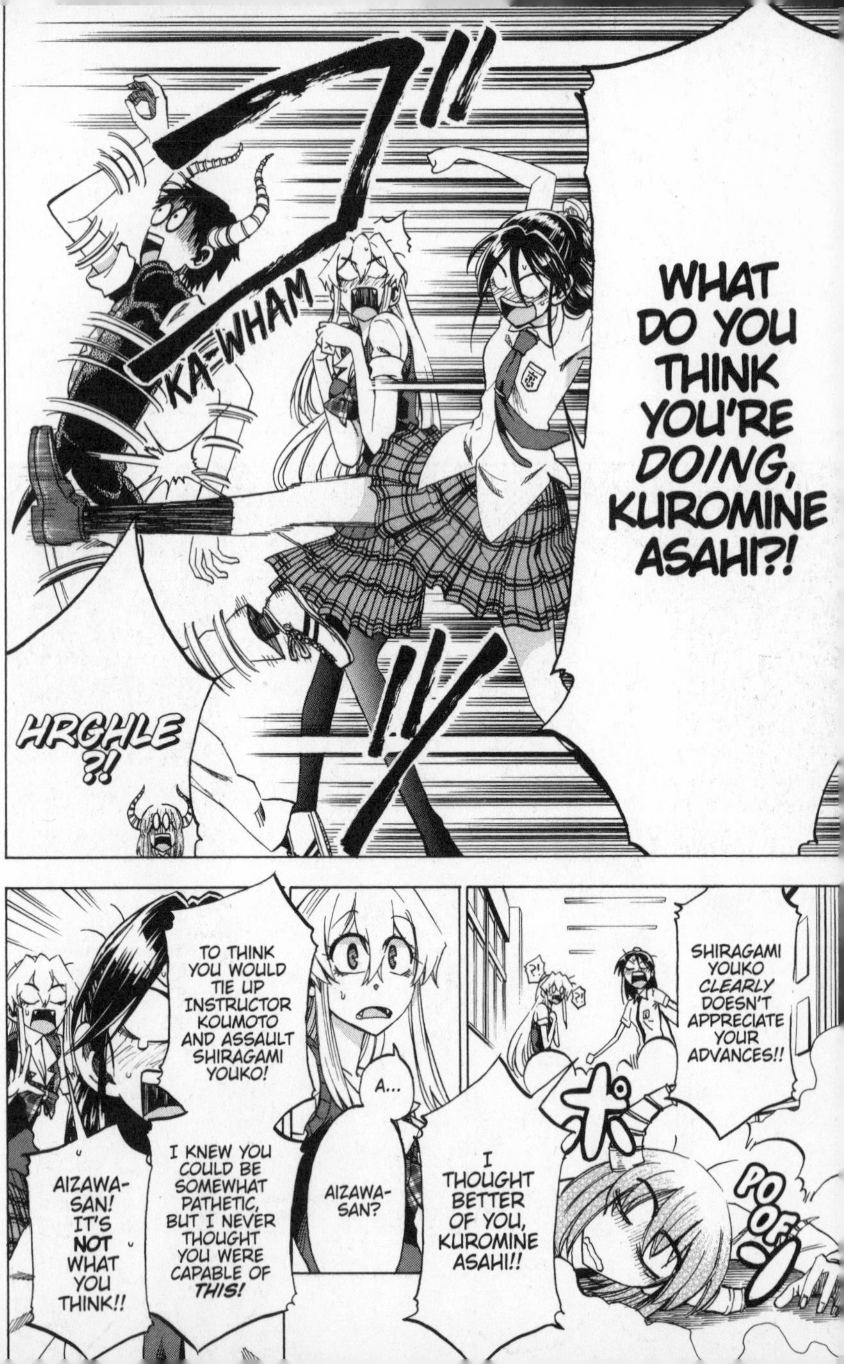
WHAT DO YOU THINK YOU'RE *DOING*, KUROMINE ASAHI?!
KA-WHAM
HRGHLE ?!
SHIRAGAMI YOUKO *CLEARLY* DOESN'T APPRECIATE YOUR ADVANCES!!
POOF
I THOUGHT BETTER OF YOU, KUROMINE ASAHI!!
TO THINK YOU WOULD TIE UP INSTRUCTOR KOUMOTO AND ASSAULT SHIRAGAMI YOUKO!
A...
AIZAWA-SAN?
I KNEW YOU COULD BE SOMEWHAT PATHETIC, BUT I NEVER THOUGHT YOU WERE CAPABLE OF ***THIS!***
AIZAWA-SAN! IT'S **NOT** WHAT YOU THINK!!

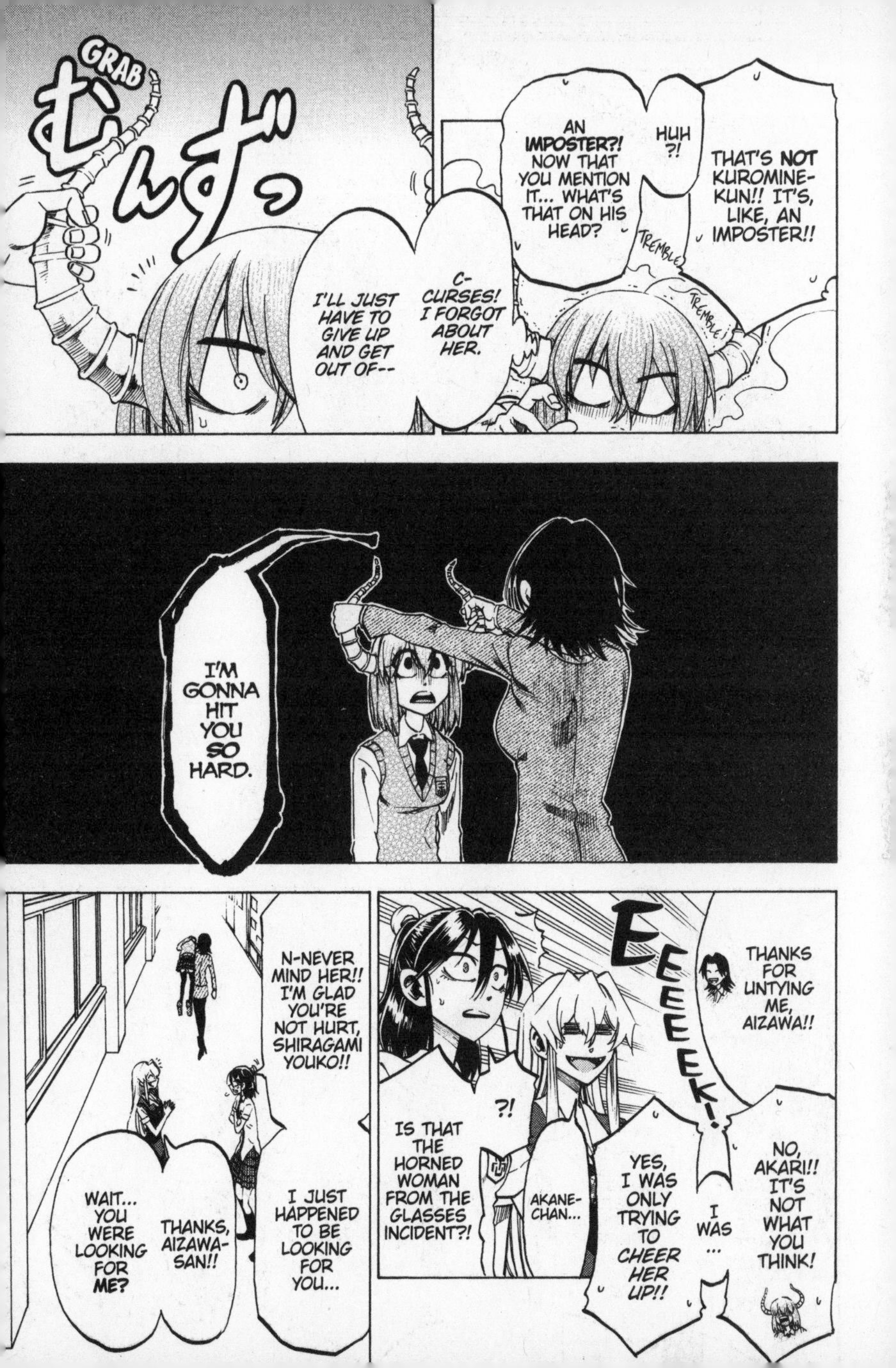
THAT'S NOT KUROMINE-KUN!! IT'S, LIKE, AN IMPOSTER!!
TREMBLE
TREMBLE
HUH ?!
AN IMPOSTER?! NOW THAT YOU MENTION IT... WHAT'S THAT ON HIS HEAD?
C-CURSES! I FORGOT ABOUT HER.
I'LL JUST HAVE TO GIVE UP AND GET OUT OF--
GRAB
むんずっ
I'M GONNA HIT YOU SO HARD.
THANKS FOR UNTYING ME, AIZAWA!!
EEEEEK!
NO, AKARI!! IT'S NOT WHAT YOU THINK!
I WAS ...
YES, I WAS ONLY TRYING TO CHEER HER UP!!
AKANE-CHAN...
?!
IS THAT THE HORNED WOMAN FROM THE GLASSES INCIDENT?!
N-NEVER MIND HER!! I'M GLAD YOU'RE NOT HURT, SHIRAGAMI YOUKO!!
I JUST HAPPENED TO BE LOOKING FOR YOU...
THANKS, AIZAWA-SAN!!
WAIT... YOU WERE LOOKING FOR ME?

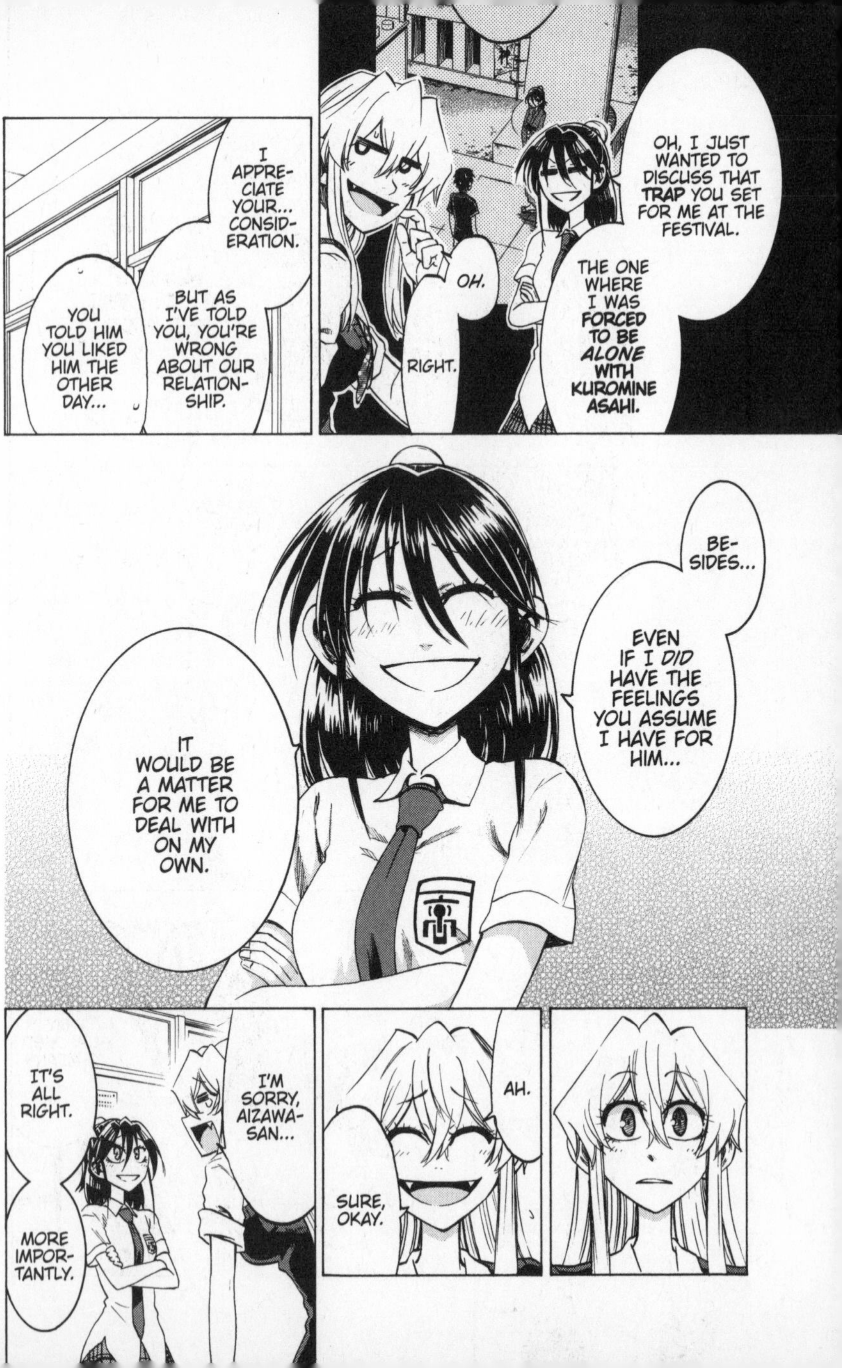
OH, I JUST WANTED TO DISCUSS THAT TRAP YOU SET FOR ME AT THE FESTIVAL.
THE ONE WHERE I WAS FORCED TO BE ALONE WITH KUROMINE ASAHI.
OH.
RIGHT.
I APPRECIATE YOUR... CONSIDERATION.
BUT AS I'VE TOLD YOU, YOU'RE WRONG ABOUT OUR RELATIONSHIP.
YOU TOLD HIM YOU LIKED HIM THE OTHER DAY...
BESIDES...
EVEN IF I DID HAVE THE FEELINGS YOU ASSUME I HAVE FOR HIM...
IT WOULD BE A MATTER FOR ME TO DEAL WITH ON MY OWN.
AH.
SURE, OKAY.
I'M SORRY, AIZAWA-SAN...
IT'S ALL RIGHT.
MORE IMPORTANTLY.

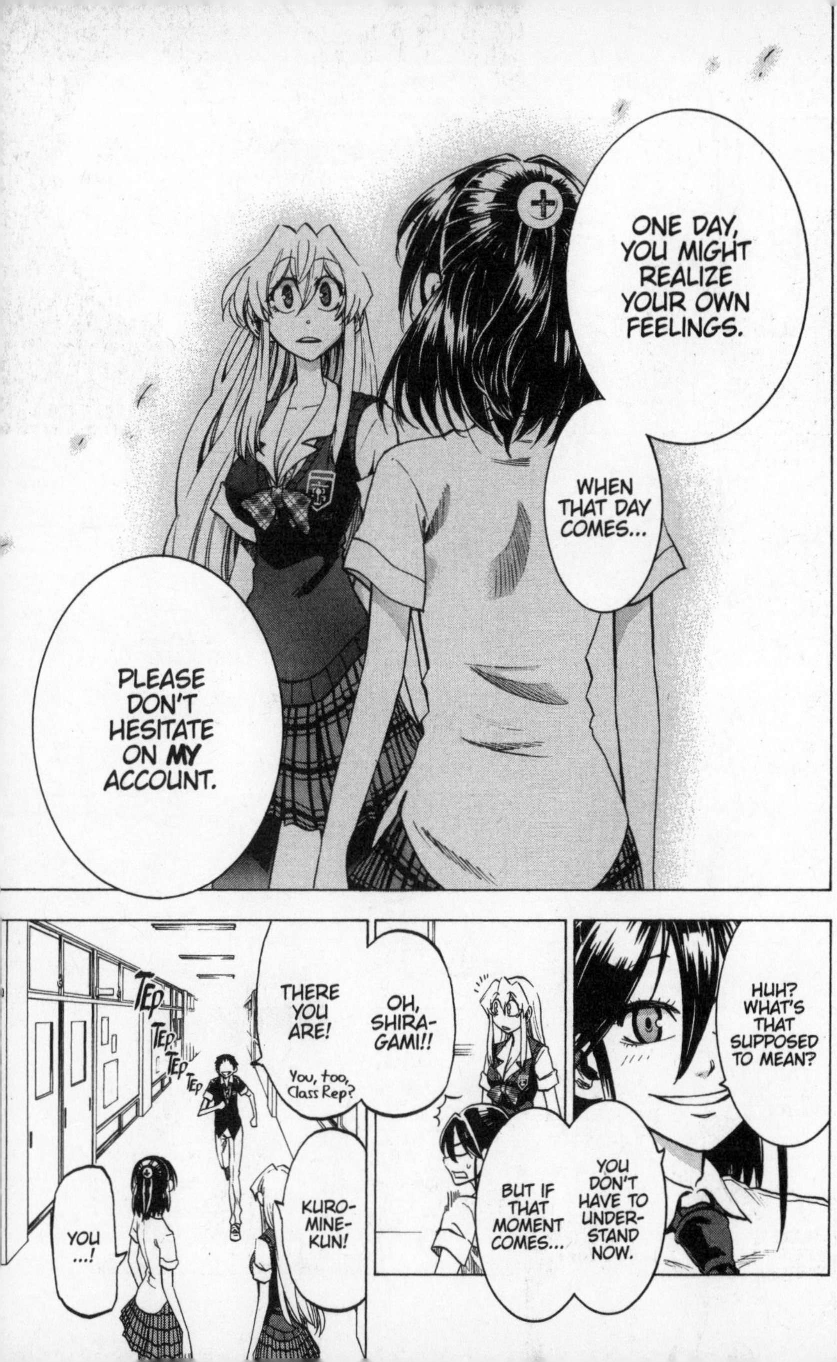
ONE DAY, YOU MIGHT REALIZE YOUR OWN FEELINGS.
WHEN THAT DAY COMES...
PLEASE DON'T HESITATE ON **MY** ACCOUNT.
HUH? WHAT'S THAT SUPPOSED TO MEAN?
YOU DON'T HAVE TO UNDER-STAND NOW.
BUT IF THAT MOMENT COMES...
OH, SHIRA-GAMI!!
THERE YOU ARE!
You, too, Class Rep?
TEP TEP TEP TEP
KURO-MINE-KUN!
YOU ...!

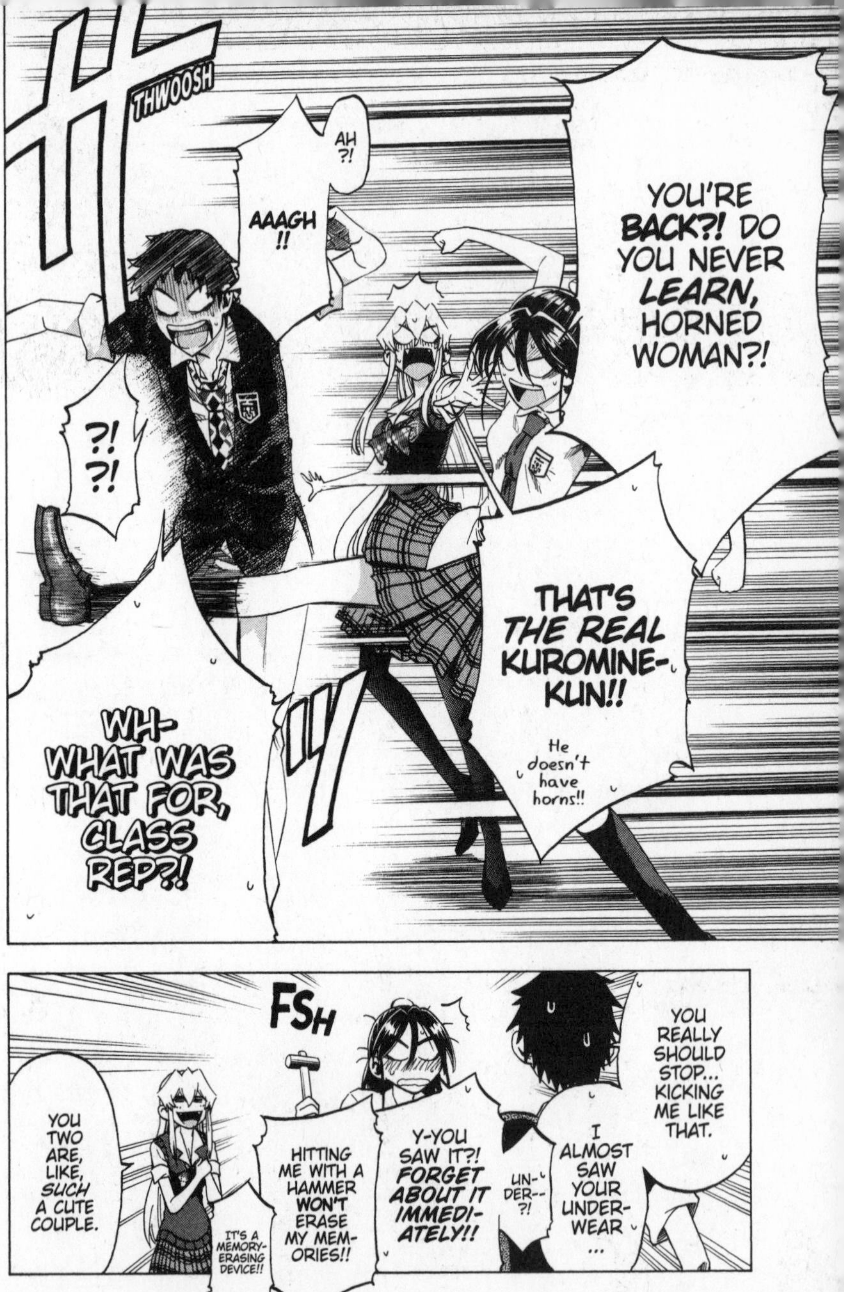
YOU'RE BACK?! DO YOU NEVER LEARN, HORNED WOMAN?!
AH?!
THWOOSH
AAAGH!!
THAT'S THE REAL KUROMINE-KUN!!
He doesn't have horns!!
?!?!
WH-WHAT WAS THAT FOR, CLASS REP?!
YOU REALLY SHOULD STOP... KICKING ME LIKE THAT.
I ALMOST SAW YOUR UNDERWEAR...
UN-DER--?!
FSH
Y-YOU SAW IT?! FORGET ABOUT IT IMMEDIATELY!!
HITTING ME WITH A HAMMER WON'T ERASE MY MEMORIES!!
IT'S A MEMORY-ERASING DEVICE!!
YOU TWO ARE, LIKE, SUCH A CUTE COUPLE.

Chapter 28: "Let's Get the Elusive Hamburger!"

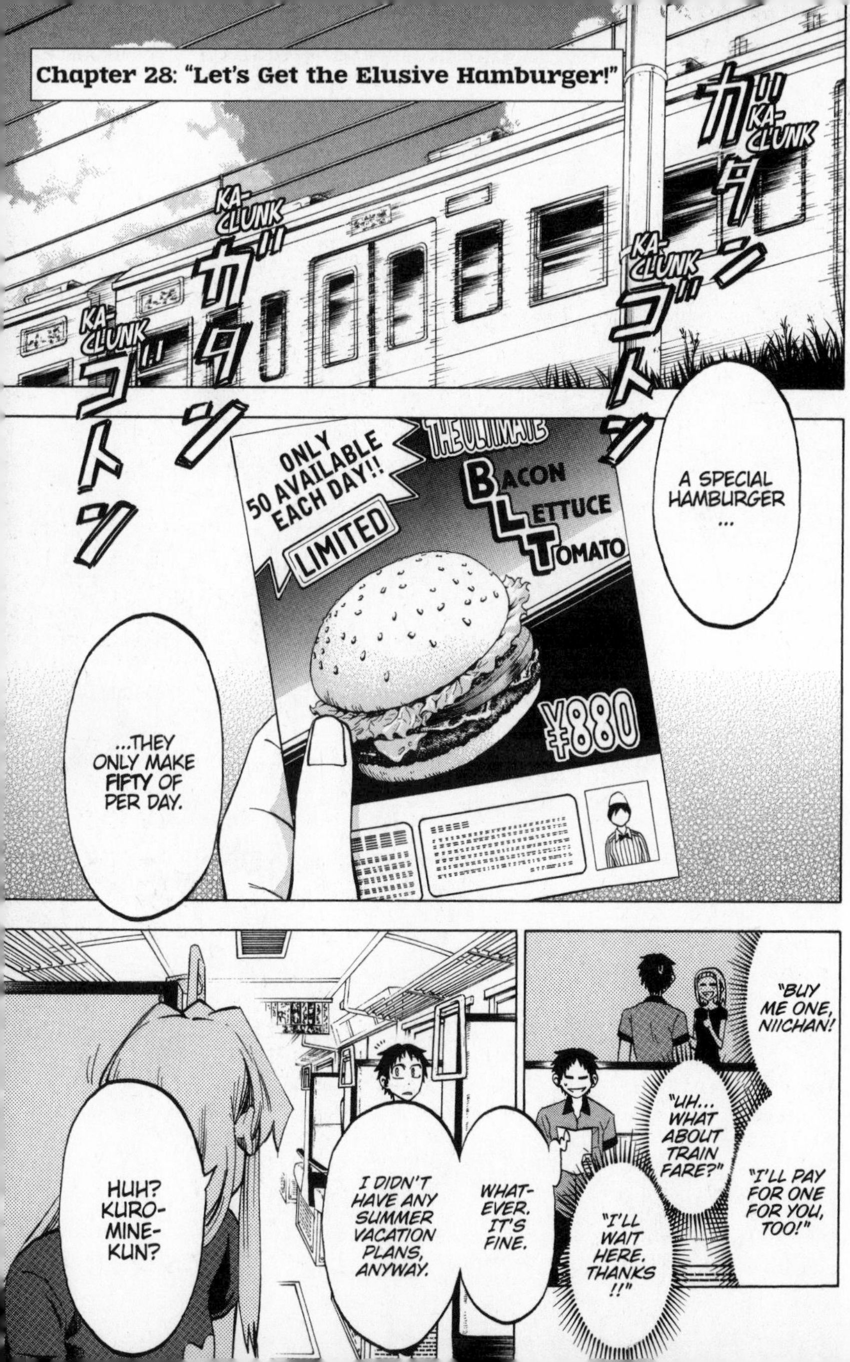
カタン
KA-CLUNK
コトッ
KA-CLUNK
カタッ
KA-CLUNK
コトッ
KA-CLUNK
A SPECIAL HAMBURGER ...
THE ULTIMATE BACON LETTUCE TOMATO
ONLY 50 AVAILABLE EACH DAY!!
LIMITED
¥880
...THEY ONLY MAKE FIFTY OF PER DAY.
"BUY ME ONE, NIICHAN!
"UH... WHAT ABOUT TRAIN FARE?"
"I'LL PAY FOR ONE FOR YOU, TOO!"
"I'LL WAIT HERE. THANKS!!"
WHAT-EVER. IT'S FINE.
I DIDN'T HAVE ANY SUMMER VACATION PLANS, ANYWAY.
HUH? KURO-MINE-KUN?

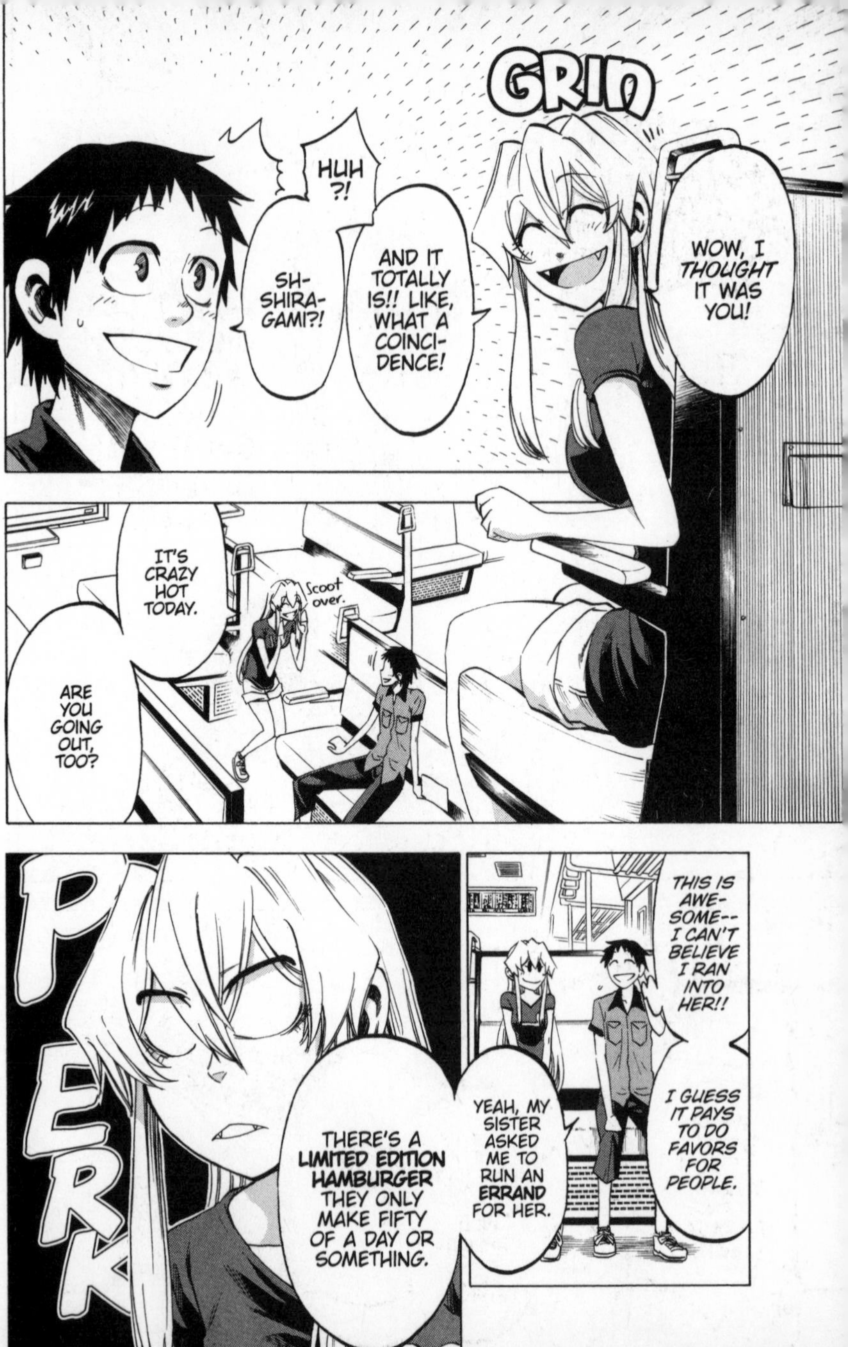
GRIN
WOW, I THOUGHT IT WAS YOU!
AND IT TOTALLY IS!! LIKE, WHAT A COINCIDENCE!
HUH ?!
SH- SHIRAGAMI?!
IT'S CRAZY HOT TODAY.
Scoot over.
ARE YOU GOING OUT, TOO?
THIS IS AWESOME-- I CAN'T BELIEVE I RAN INTO HER!!
I GUESS IT PAYS TO DO FAVORS FOR PEOPLE.
YEAH, MY SISTER ASKED ME TO RUN AN ERRAND FOR HER.
PERK
THERE'S A LIMITED EDITION HAMBURGER THEY ONLY MAKE FIFTY OF A DAY OR SOMETHING.

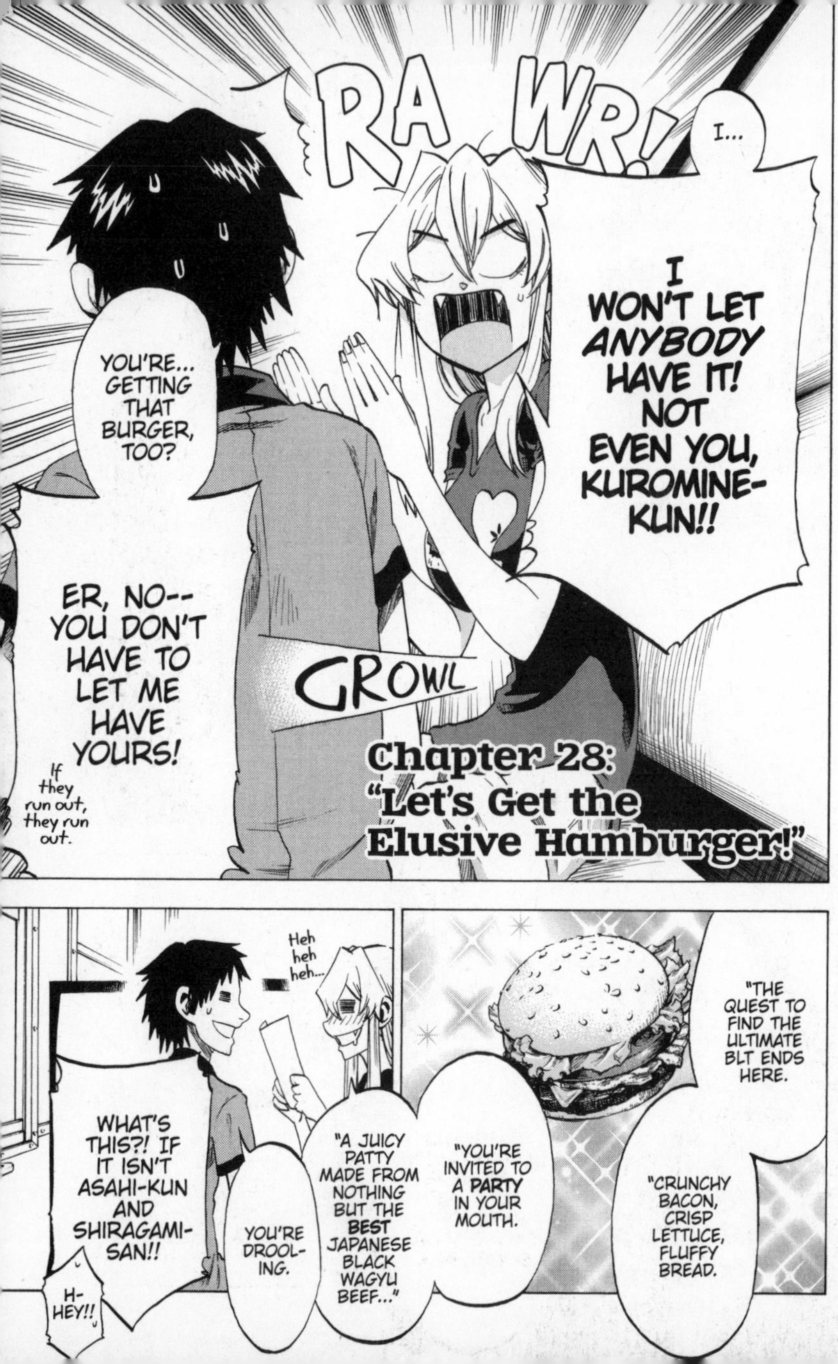
RAWR!
I...
I WON'T LET ANYBODY HAVE IT! NOT EVEN YOU, KUROMINE-KUN!!
YOU'RE... GETTING THAT BURGER, TOO?
GROWL
ER, NO-- YOU DON'T HAVE TO LET ME HAVE YOURS!
If they run out, they run out.
Chapter 28: "Let's Get the Elusive Hamburger!"
"THE QUEST TO FIND THE ULTIMATE BLT ENDS HERE.
"CRUNCHY BACON, CRISP LETTUCE, FLUFFY BREAD.
"YOU'RE INVITED TO A PARTY IN YOUR MOUTH.
"A JUICY PATTY MADE FROM NOTHING BUT THE BEST JAPANESE BLACK WAGYU BEEF..."
Heh heh heh...
YOU'RE DROOL-ING.
H-HEY!!
WHAT'S THIS?! IF IT ISN'T ASAHI-KUN AND SHIRAGAMI-SAN!!

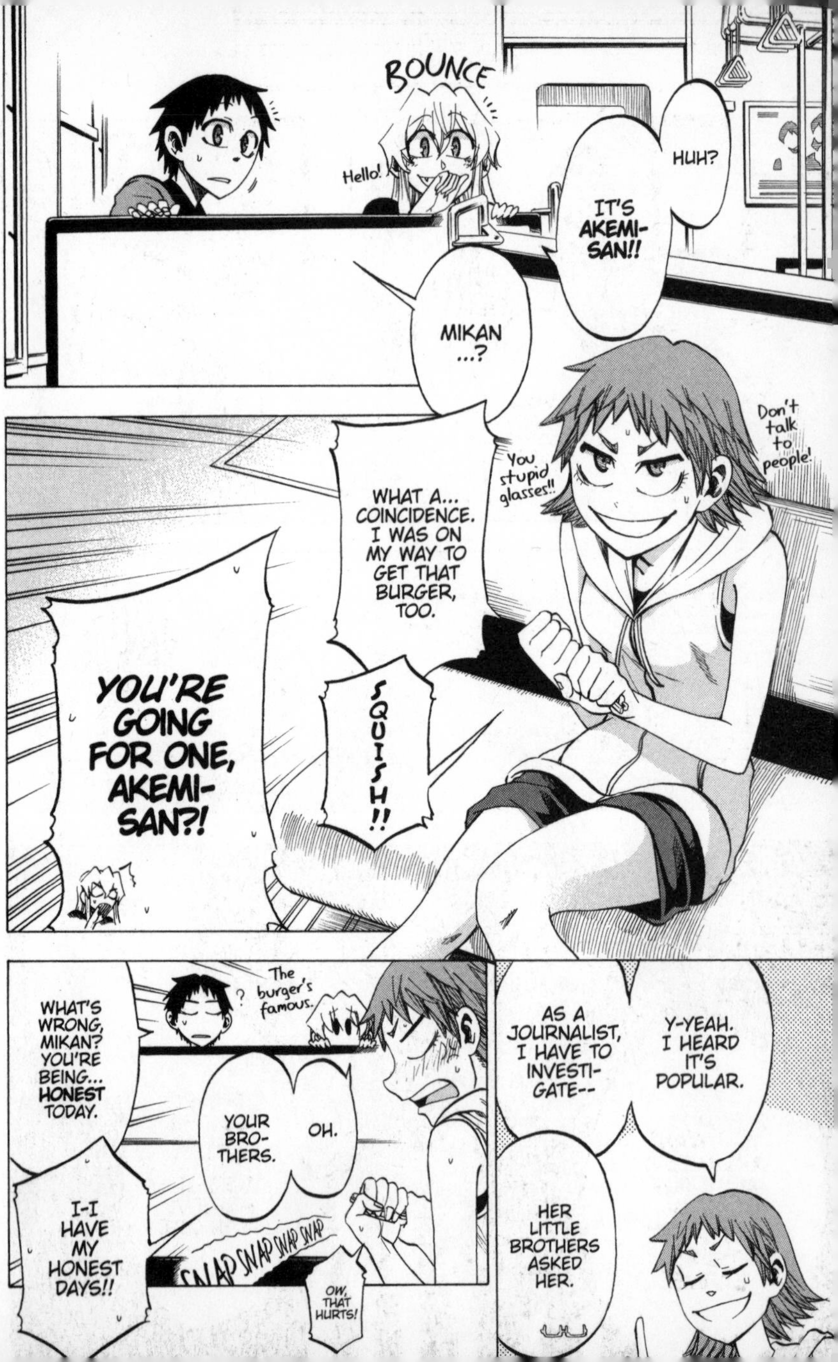
BOUNCE
HUH?
IT'S AKEMI-SAN!!
Hello!
MIKAN ...?
Don't talk to people!
You stupid glasses!!
WHAT A... COINCIDENCE. I WAS ON MY WAY TO GET THAT BURGER, TOO.
SQUISH!!
YOU'RE GOING FOR ONE, AKEMI-SAN?!
Y-YEAH. I HEARD IT'S POPULAR.
AS A JOURNALIST, I HAVE TO INVESTI-GATE--
HER LITTLE BROTHERS ASKED HER.
The burger's famous.
OH.
YOUR BRO-THERS.
WHAT'S WRONG, MIKAN? YOU'RE BEING... HONEST TODAY.
I-I HAVE MY HONEST DAYS!!
SNAP SNAP SNAP SNAP
OW, THAT HURTS!

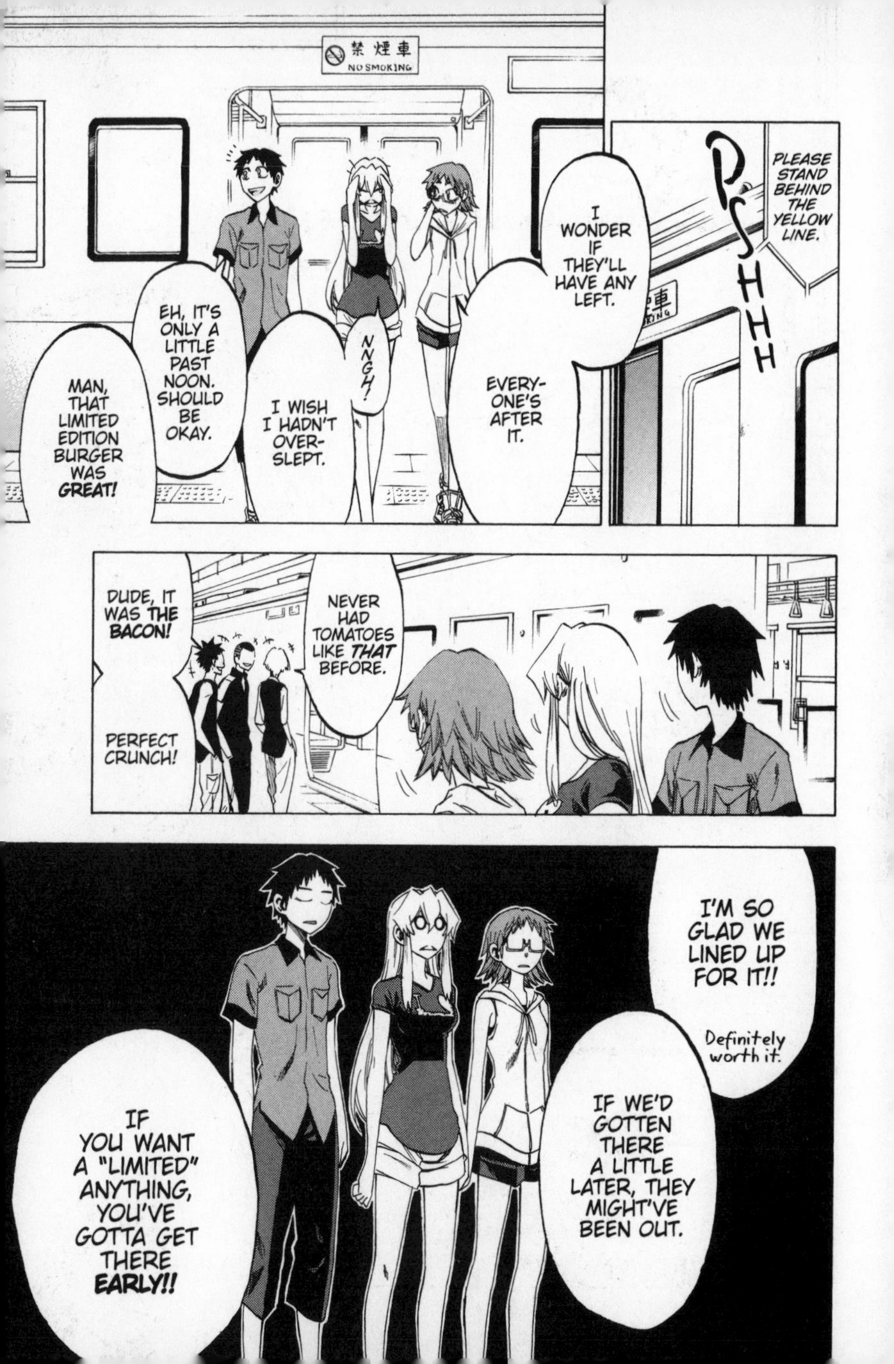
禁煙車
NO SMOKING
PSHHH
PLEASE STAND BEHIND THE YELLOW LINE.
I WONDER IF THEY'LL HAVE ANY LEFT.
EVERYONE'S AFTER IT.
NNGH!
I WISH I HADN'T OVERSLEPT.
EH, IT'S ONLY A LITTLE PAST NOON. SHOULD BE OKAY.
MAN, THAT LIMITED EDITION BURGER WAS GREAT!
NEVER HAD TOMATOES LIKE THAT BEFORE.
DUDE, IT WAS THE BACON!
PERFECT CRUNCH!
I'M SO GLAD WE LINED UP FOR IT!!
Definitely worth it.
IF WE'D GOTTEN THERE A LITTLE LATER, THEY MIGHT'VE BEEN OUT.
IF YOU WANT A "LIMITED" ANYTHING, YOU'VE GOTTA GET THERE EARLY!!

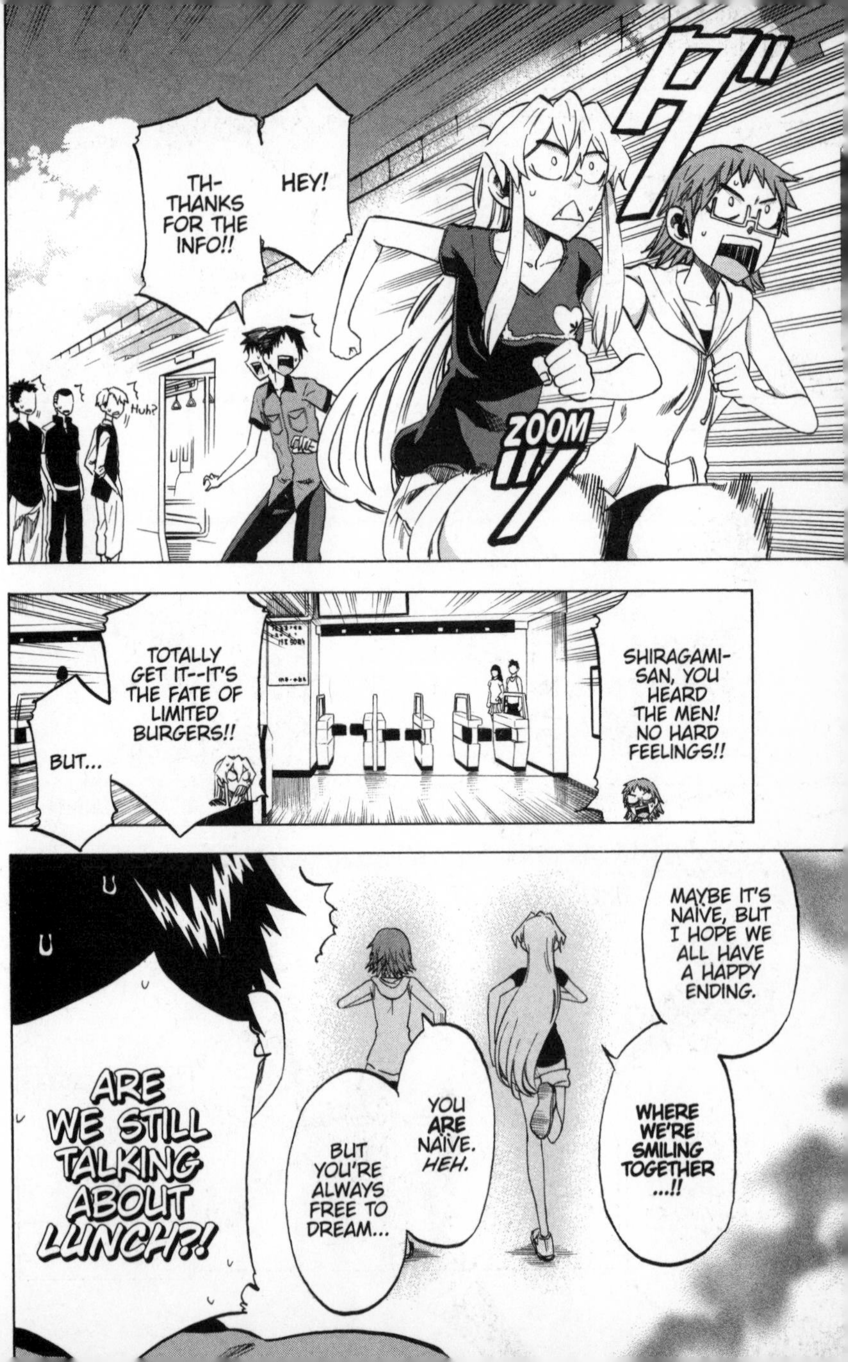
HEY!
TH- THANKS FOR THE INFO!!
Huh?
ZOOM
SHIRAGAMI-SAN, YOU HEARD THE MEN! NO HARD FEELINGS!!
TOTALLY GET IT--IT'S THE FATE OF LIMITED BURGERS!!
BUT...
MAYBE IT'S NAÏVE, BUT I HOPE WE ALL HAVE A HAPPY ENDING.
WHERE WE'RE SMILING TOGETHER ...!!
YOU ARE NAÏVE. HEH.
BUT YOU'RE ALWAYS FREE TO DREAM...
ARE WE STILL TALKING ABOUT LUNCH?!

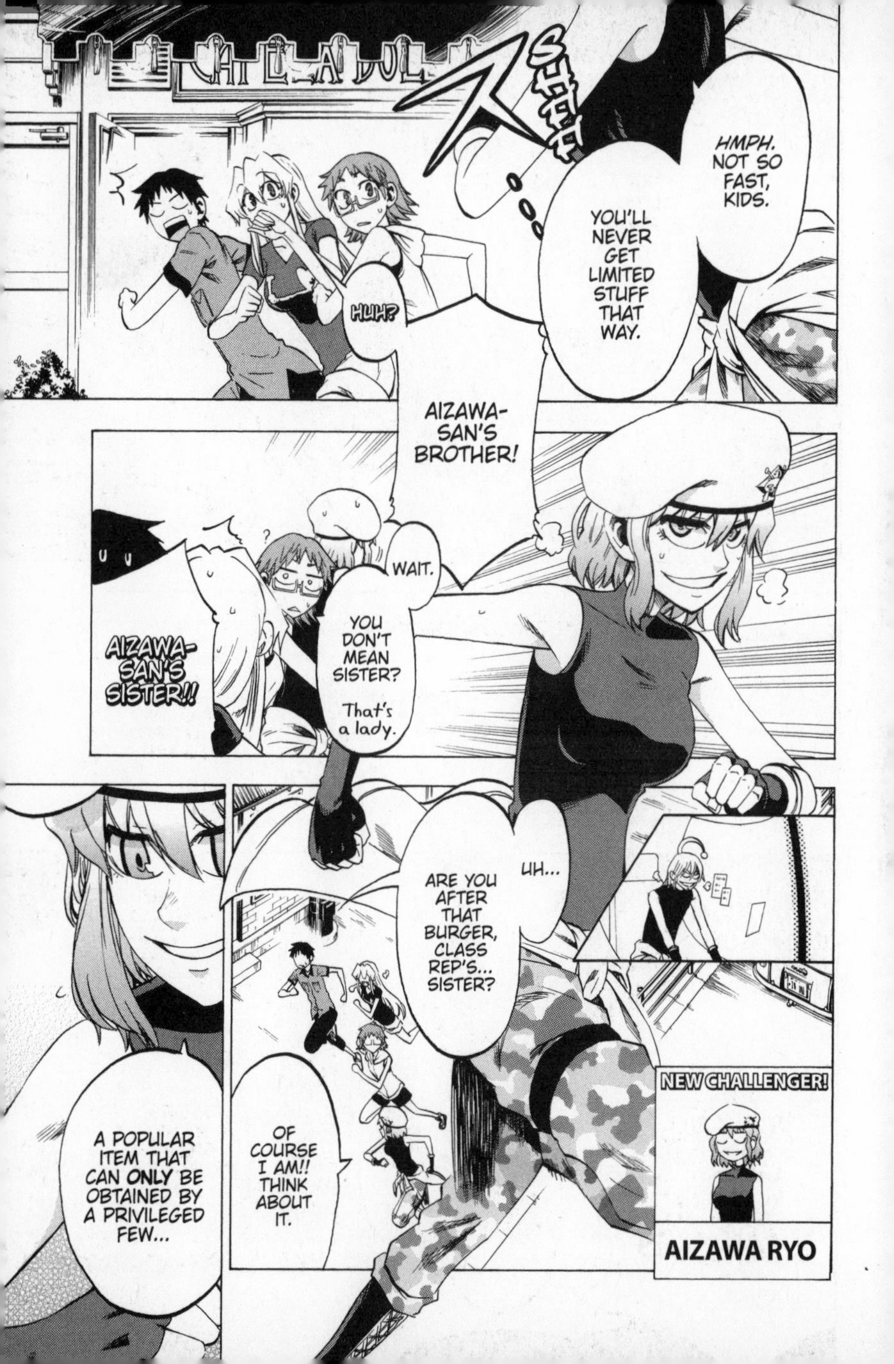
HMPH. NOT SO FAST, KIDS.
YOU'LL NEVER GET LIMITED STUFF THAT WAY.
HUH?
AIZAWA-SAN'S BROTHER!
WAIT.
YOU DON'T MEAN SISTER? That's a lady.
AIZAWA-SAN'S SISTER!!
UH...
ARE YOU AFTER THAT BURGER, CLASS REP'S... SISTER?
NEW CHALLENGER!
AIZAWA RYO
OF COURSE I AM!! THINK ABOUT IT.
A POPULAR ITEM THAT CAN **ONLY** BE OBTAINED BY A PRIVILEGED FEW...

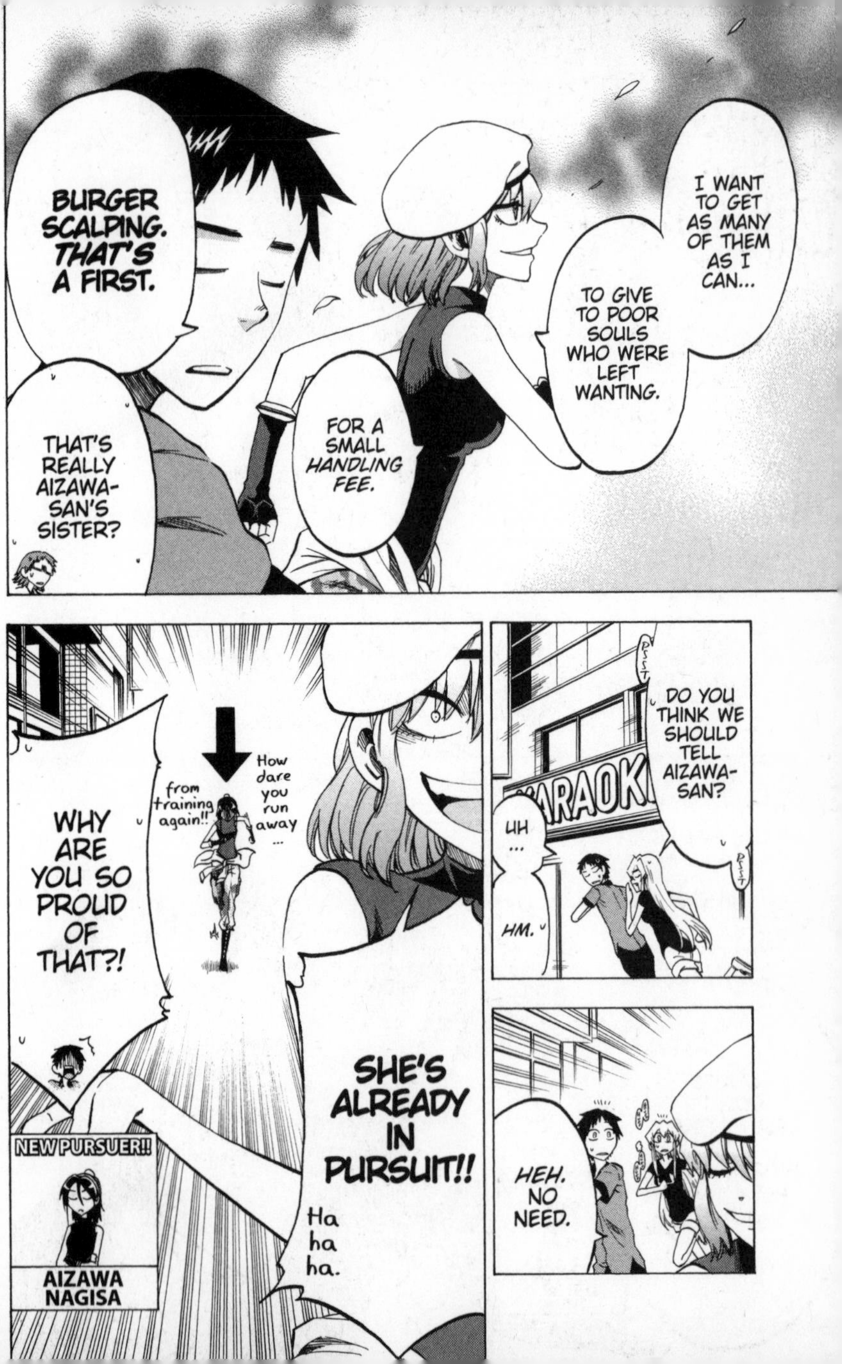
I WANT TO GET AS MANY OF THEM AS I CAN...
TO GIVE TO POOR SOULS WHO WERE LEFT WANTING.
FOR A SMALL HANDLING FEE.
BURGER SCALPING. THAT'S A FIRST.
THAT'S REALLY AIZAWA-SAN'S SISTER?
PSST
DO YOU THINK WE SHOULD TELL AIZAWA-SAN?
UH...
HM.
PSST
HEH. NO NEED.
SHE'S ALREADY IN PURSUIT!!
Ha ha ha.
How dare you run away from training again!!
WHY ARE YOU SO PROUD OF THAT?!
NEW PURSUER!!
AIZAWA NAGISA

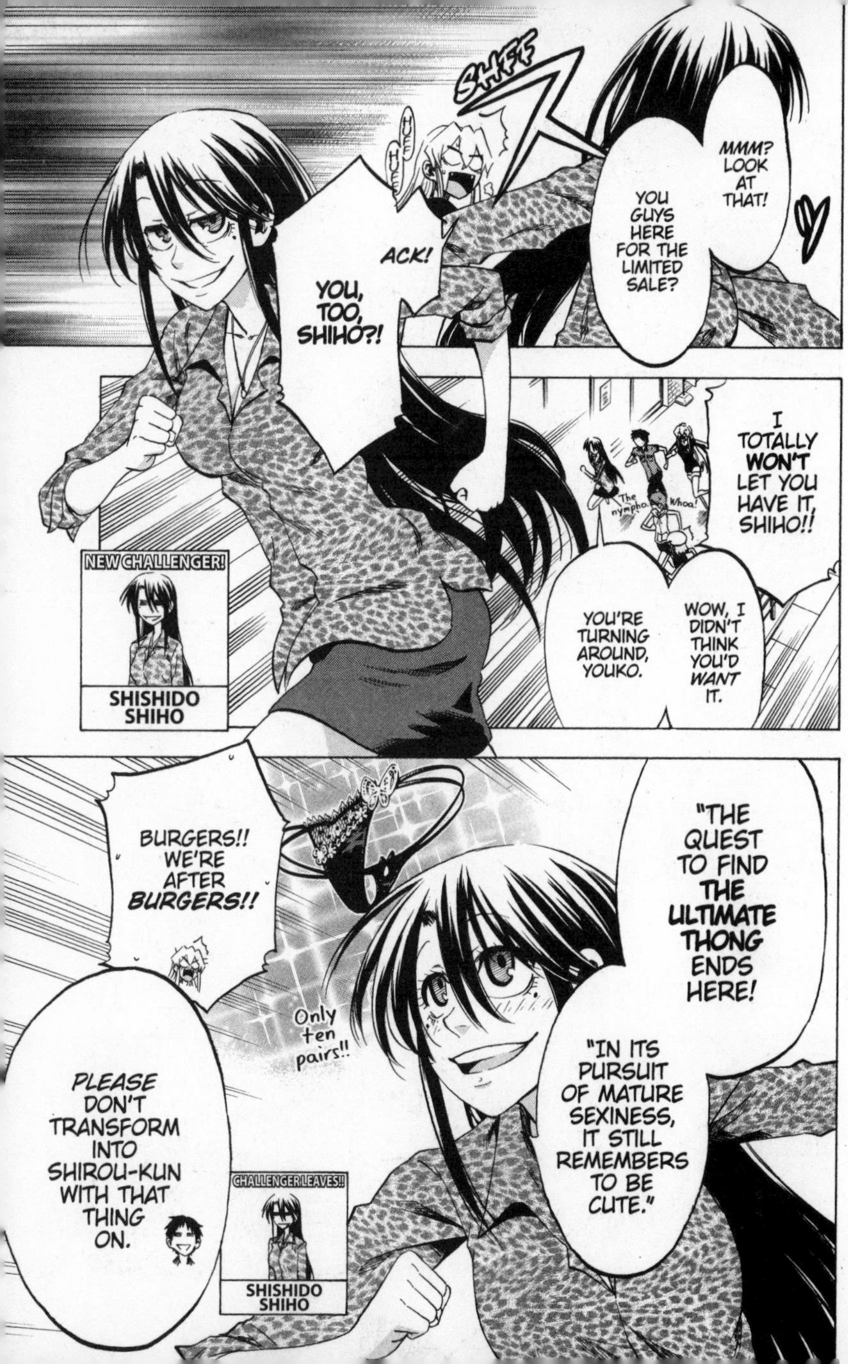
SHFF
MMM? LOOK AT THAT!
YOU GUYS HERE FOR THE LIMITED SALE?
HUFF HUFF
ACK!
YOU, TOO, SHIHO?!
I TOTALLY WON'T LET YOU HAVE IT, SHIHO!!
Whoa!
The nympho.
WOW, I DIDN'T THINK YOU'D WANT IT.
YOU'RE TURNING AROUND, YOUKO.
NEW CHALLENGER!
SHISHIDO SHIHO
"THE QUEST TO FIND THE ULTIMATE THONG ENDS HERE!
"IN ITS PURSUIT OF MATURE SEXINESS, IT STILL REMEMBERS TO BE CUTE."
Only ten pairs!!
BURGERS!! WE'RE AFTER BURGERS!!
PLEASE DON'T TRANSFORM INTO SHIROU-KUN WITH THAT THING ON.
CHALLENGER LEAVES!!
SHISHIDO SHIHO

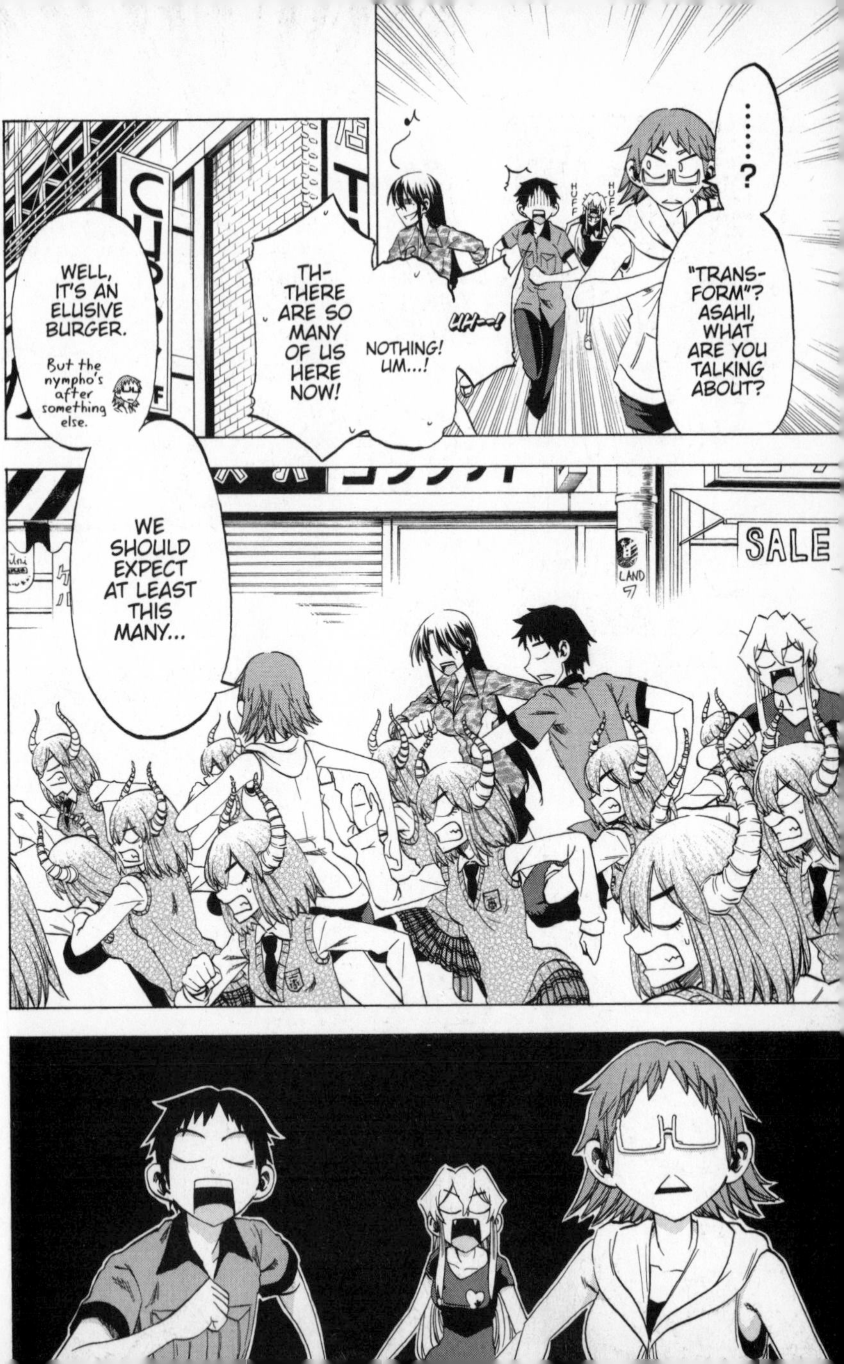
.....?
"TRANS-FORM"? ASAHI, WHAT ARE YOU TALKING ABOUT?
HUFF HUFF
UH--!
NOTHING! UM...!
TH- THERE ARE SO MANY OF US HERE NOW!
WELL, IT'S AN ELUSIVE BURGER.
But the nympho's after something else.
SALE
LAND
WE SHOULD EXPECT AT LEAST THIS MANY...

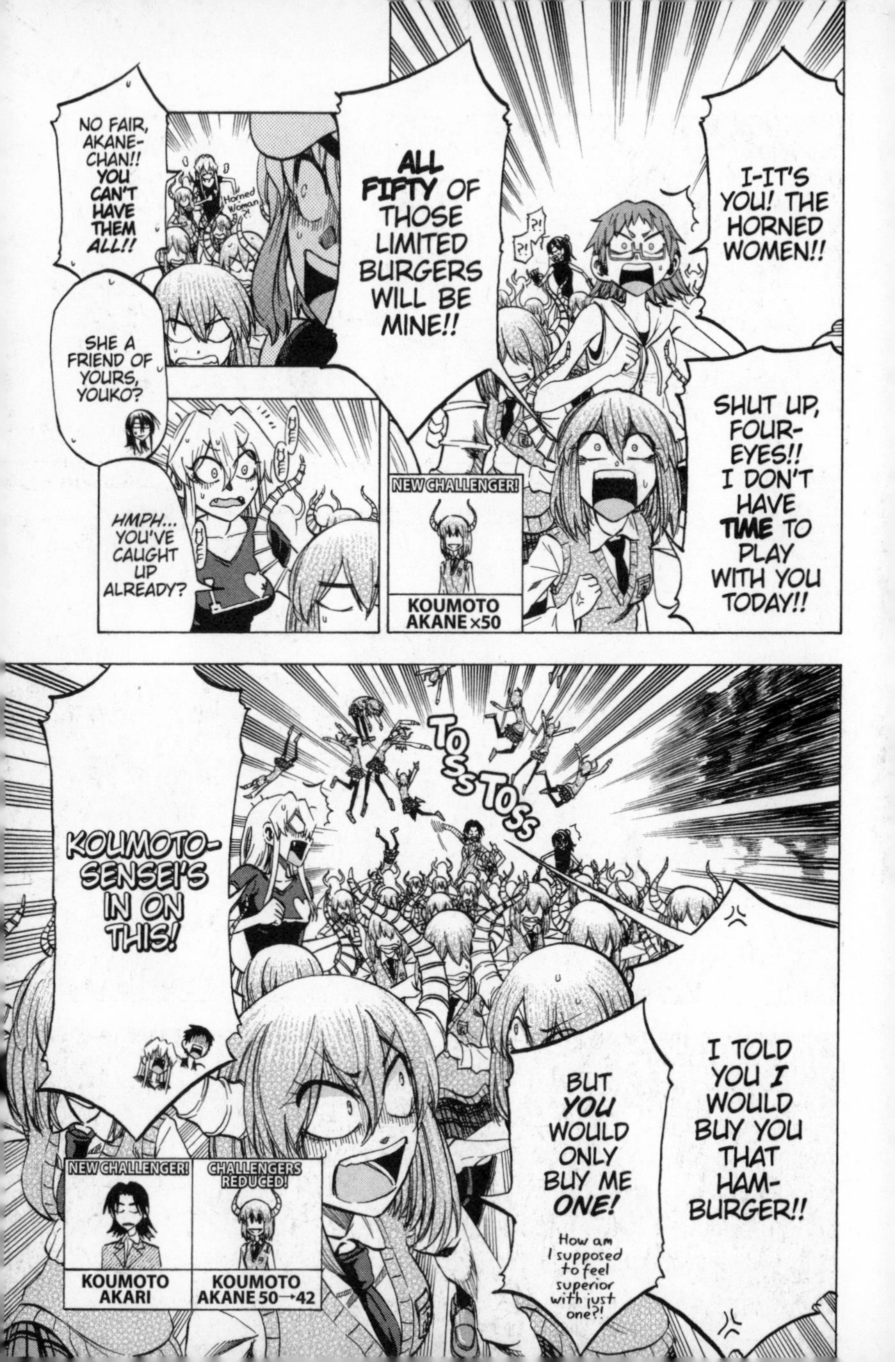
I-IT'S YOU! THE HORNED WOMEN!!
?!
?!
SHUT UP, FOUR-EYES!! I DON'T HAVE TIME TO PLAY WITH YOU TODAY!!
ALL FIFTY OF THOSE LIMITED BURGERS WILL BE MINE!!
NEW CHALLENGER!
KOUMOTO AKANE ×50
NO FAIR, AKANE-CHAN!! YOU CAN'T HAVE THEM ALL!!
Horned Woman?!
SHE A FRIEND OF YOURS, YOUKO?
HUFF HUFF HUFF
HMPH... YOU'VE CAUGHT UP ALREADY?
TOSS TOSS
I TOLD YOU I WOULD BUY YOU THAT HAMBURGER!!
BUT YOU WOULD ONLY BUY ME ONE!
How am I supposed to feel superior with just one?!
KOUMOTO-SENSEI'S IN ON THIS!
CHALLENGERS REDUCED!
KOUMOTO AKANE 50→42
NEW CHALLENGER!
KOUMOTO AKARI

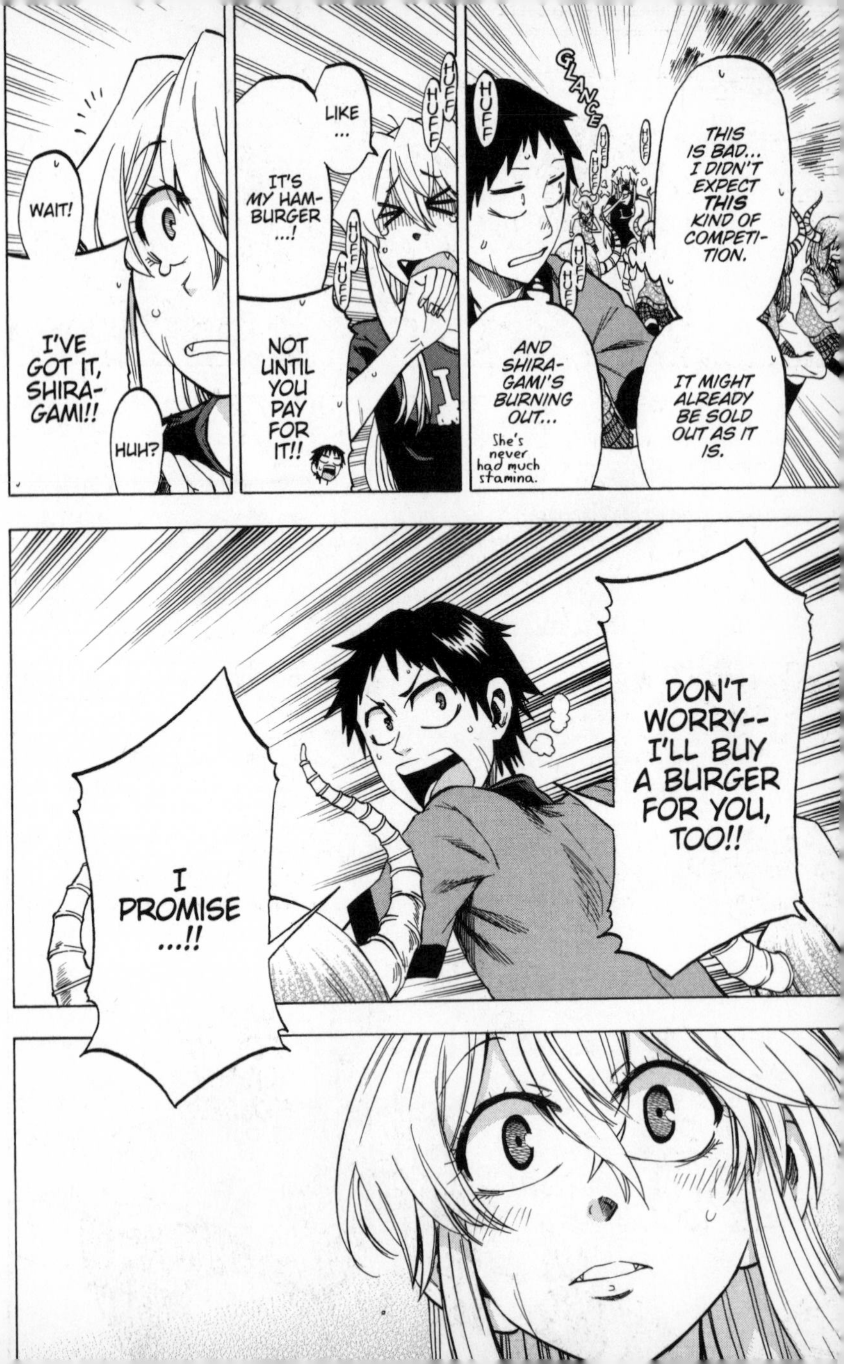
GLANCE
HUFF HUFF HUFF
THIS IS BAD... I DIDN'T EXPECT THIS KIND OF COMPETITION.
IT MIGHT ALREADY BE SOLD OUT AS IT IS.
HUFF HUFF HUFF
AND SHIRA-GAMI'S BURNING OUT...
She's never had much stamina.
HUFF HUFF
LIKE ...
IT'S MY HAM-BURGER ...!
HUFF HUFF
NOT UNTIL YOU PAY FOR IT!!
WAIT!
I'VE GOT IT, SHIRA-GAMI!!
HUH?
DON'T WORRY-- I'LL BUY A BURGER FOR YOU, TOO!!
I PROMISE ...!!

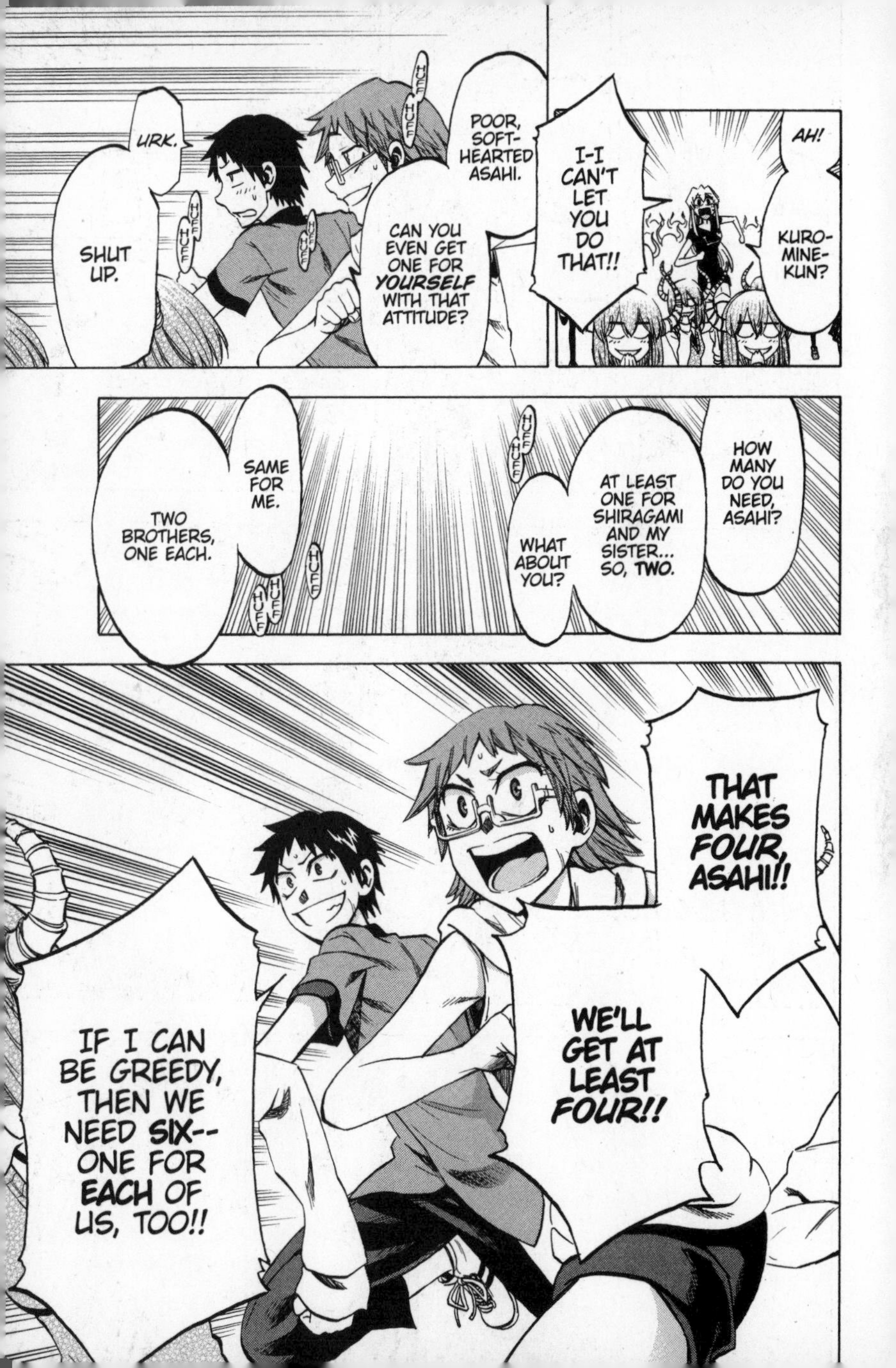
AH!
KURO-MINE-KUN?
I-I CAN'T LET YOU DO THAT!!
POOR, SOFT-HEARTED ASAHI.
CAN YOU EVEN GET ONE FOR YOURSELF WITH THAT ATTITUDE?
HUFF HUFF
HUFF HUFF
HUFF HUFF
URK.
SHUT UP.
HOW MANY DO YOU NEED, ASAHI?
AT LEAST ONE FOR SHIRAGAMI AND MY SISTER... SO, TWO.
HUFF HUFF
WHAT ABOUT YOU?
SAME FOR ME.
TWO BROTHERS, ONE EACH.
HUFF HUFF HUFF
THAT MAKES FOUR, ASAHI!!
WE'LL GET AT LEAST FOUR!!
IF I CAN BE GREEDY, THEN WE NEED SIX-- ONE FOR EACH OF US, TOO!!

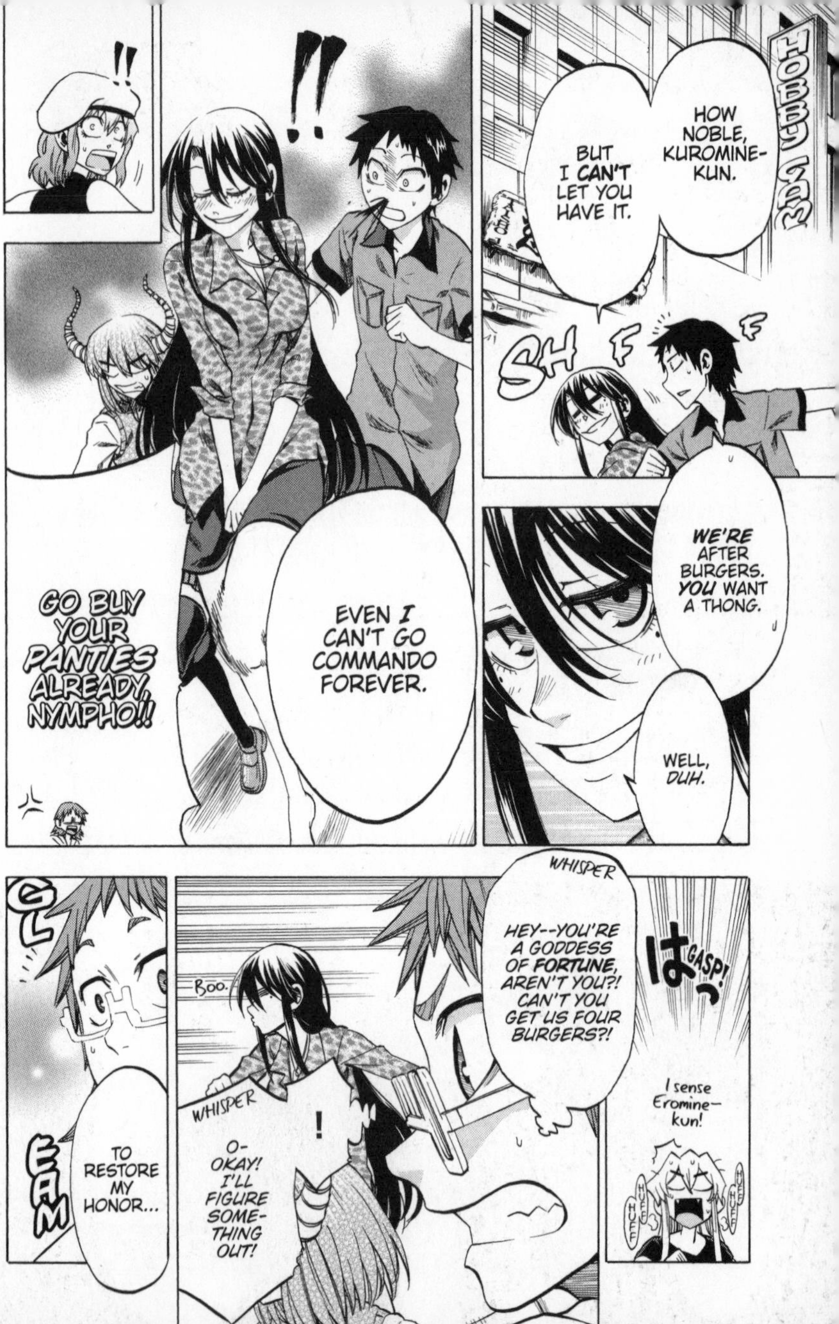
HOBBY GAM
HOW NOBLE, KUROMINE-KUN.
BUT I CAN'T LET YOU HAVE IT.
SH F F
WE'RE AFTER BURGERS. YOU WANT A THONG.
WELL, DUH.
!!
!!
EVEN I CAN'T GO COMMANDO FOREVER.
GO BUY YOUR PANTIES ALREADY, NYMPHO!!
I sense Eromine-kun!
HUFF HUFF HUFF HUFF
はっ GASP!
WHISPER
HEY--YOU'RE A GODDESS OF FORTUNE, AREN'T YOU?! CAN'T YOU GET US FOUR BURGERS?!
Boo.
WHISPER
O-OKAY! I'LL FIGURE SOMETHING OUT!
!
GLEAM
TO RESTORE MY HONOR...

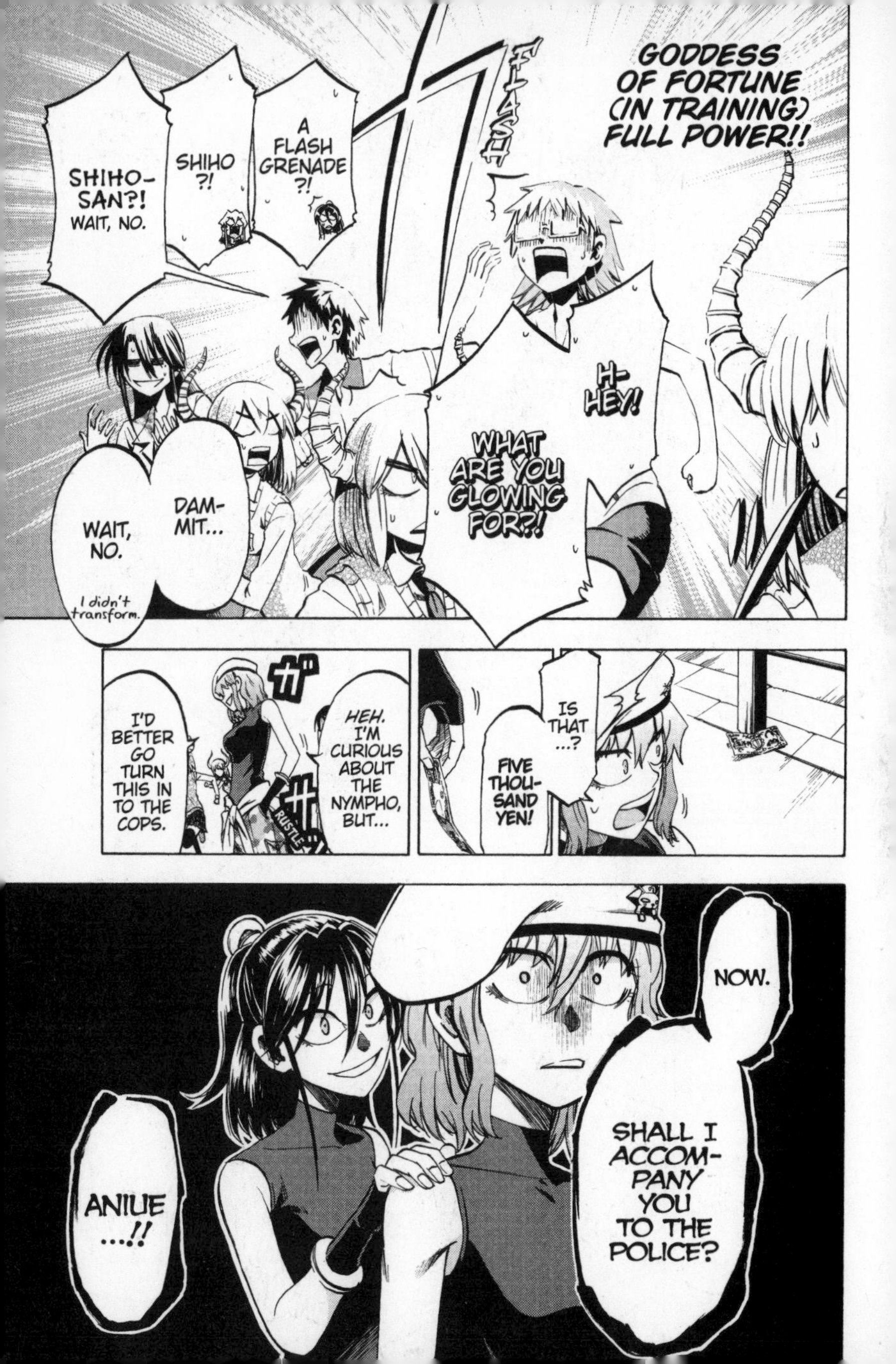
GODDESS OF FORTUNE (IN TRAINING) FULL POWER!!
FLASH
H-HEY!
WHAT ARE YOU GLOWING FOR?!
A FLASH GRENADE ?!
SHIHO ?!
SHIHO-SAN?! WAIT, NO.
DAM-MIT...
WAIT, NO.
I didn't transform.
IS THAT ...?
FIVE THOU-SAND YEN!
HEH. I'M CURIOUS ABOUT THE NYMPHO, BUT...
RUSTLE
I'D BETTER GO TURN THIS IN TO THE COPS.
NOW.
SHALL I ACCOM-PANY YOU TO THE POLICE?
ANIUE ...!!

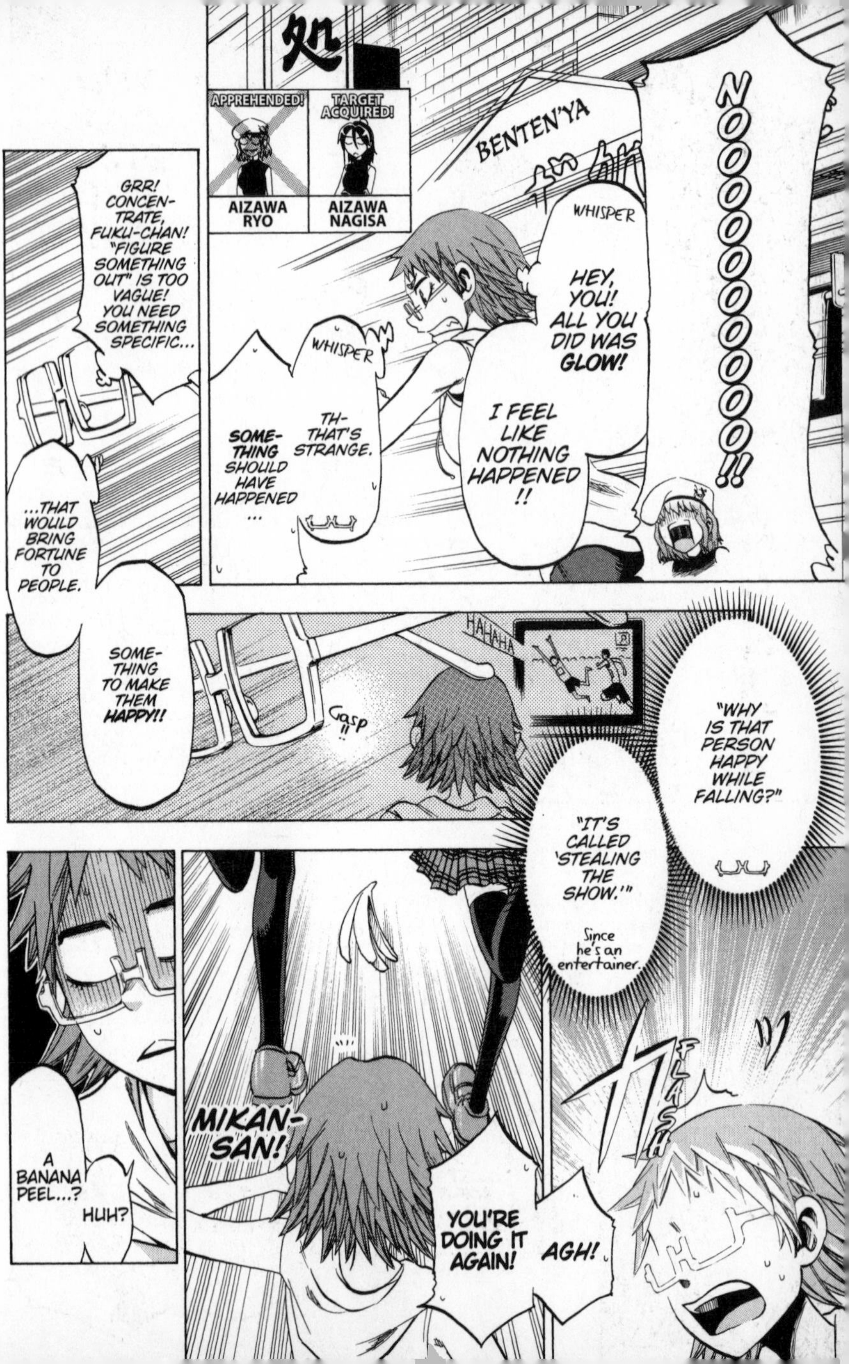
APPREHENDED!
AIZAWA RYO
TARGET ACQUIRED!
AIZAWA NAGISA
BENTEN'YA
NOOOOOOOOOOOOOO!!
WHISPER
HEY, YOU! ALL YOU DID WAS GLOW!
I FEEL LIKE NOTHING HAPPENED!!
WHISPER
TH- THAT'S STRANGE.
SOMETHING SHOULD HAVE HAPPENED...
GRR! CONCENTRATE, FUKU-CHAN! "FIGURE SOMETHING OUT" IS TOO VAGUE! YOU NEED SOMETHING SPECIFIC...
...THAT WOULD BRING FORTUNE TO PEOPLE.
SOMETHING TO MAKE THEM HAPPY!!
HAHAHA
Gasp!!
"WHY IS THAT PERSON HAPPY WHILE FALLING?"
"IT'S CALLED 'STEALING THE SHOW.'"
Since he's an entertainer.
FLASH
AGH!
YOU'RE DOING IT AGAIN!
MIKAN-SAN!
A BANANA PEEL...?
HUH?

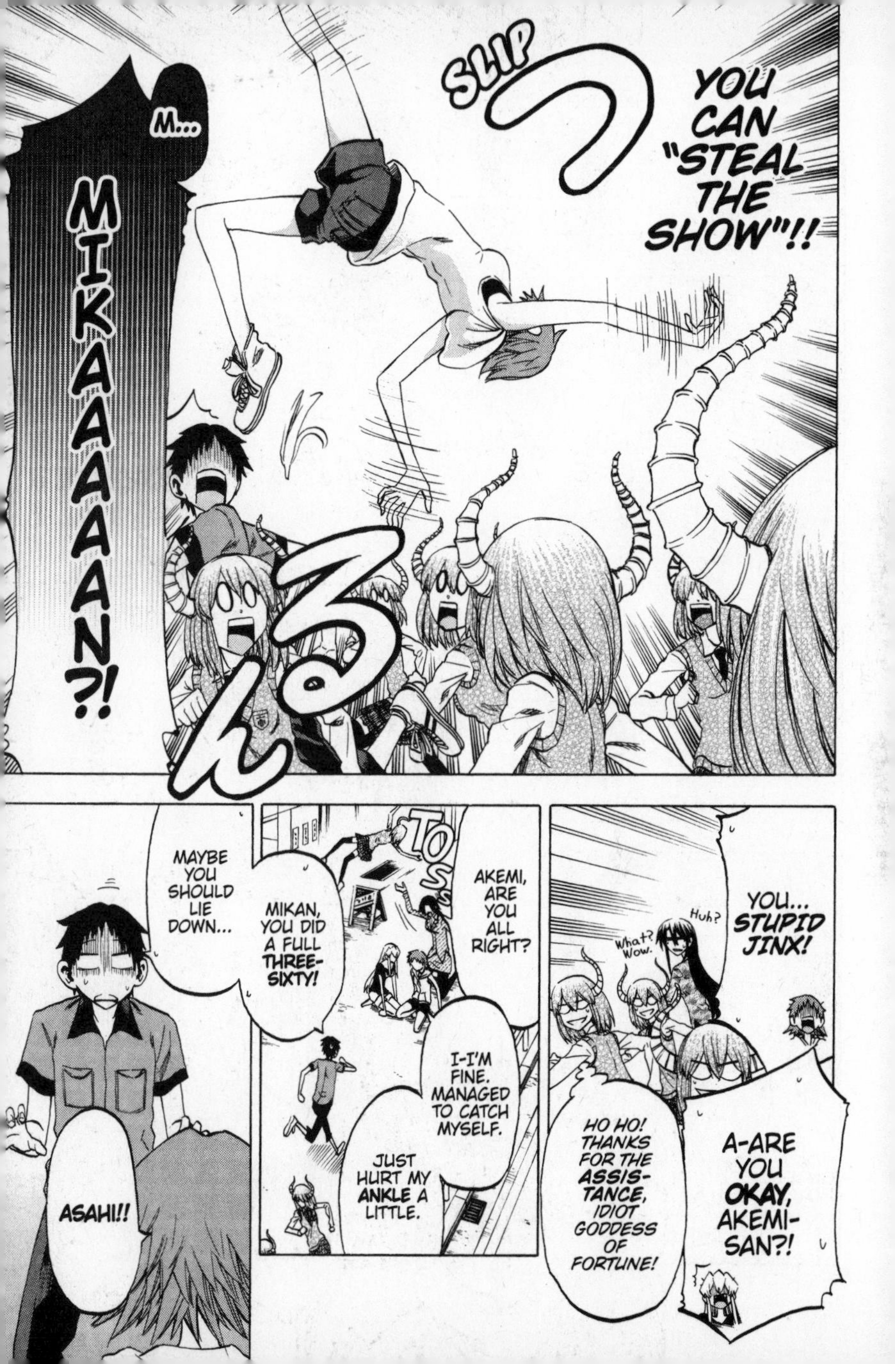
YOU CAN "STEAL THE SHOW"!!
SLIP
M...
MIKAAAAAAN?!
YOU... STUPID JINX!
Huh?
What? Wow.
A-ARE YOU OKAY, AKEMI-SAN?!
HO HO! THANKS FOR THE ASSIS-TANCE, IDIOT GODDESS OF FORTUNE!
TOSS
AKEMI, ARE YOU ALL RIGHT?
MIKAN, YOU DID A FULL THREE-SIXTY!
I-I'M FINE. MANAGED TO CATCH MYSELF.
JUST HURT MY ANKLE A LITTLE.
MAYBE YOU SHOULD LIE DOWN...
ASAHI!!

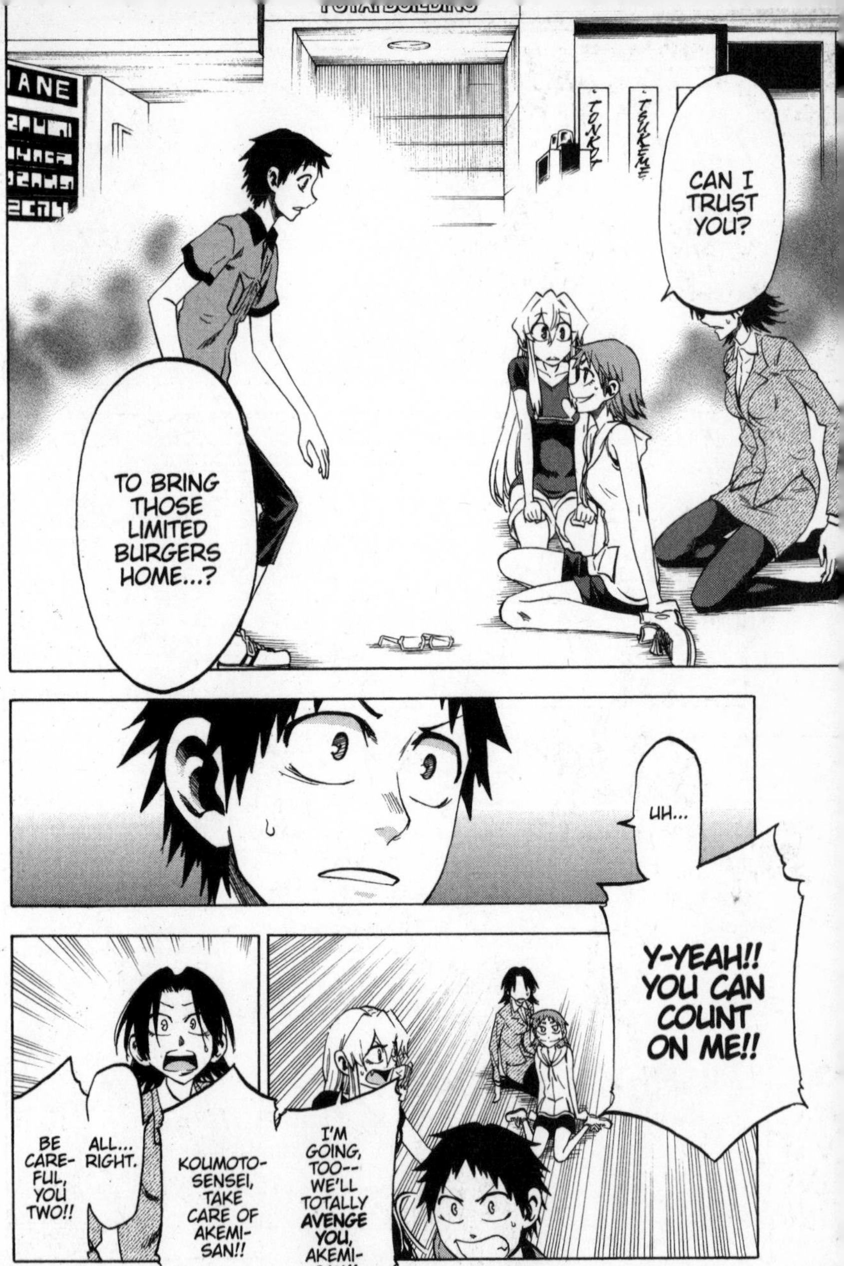
CAN I TRUST YOU?
TO BRING THOSE LIMITED BURGERS HOME...?
UH...
Y-YEAH!! YOU CAN COUNT ON ME!!
I'M GOING, TOO-- WE'LL TOTALLY AVENGE YOU, AKEMI-SAN!!
KOUMOTO-SENSEI, TAKE CARE OF AKEMI-SAN!!
ALL... RIGHT.
BE CAREFUL, YOU TWO!!

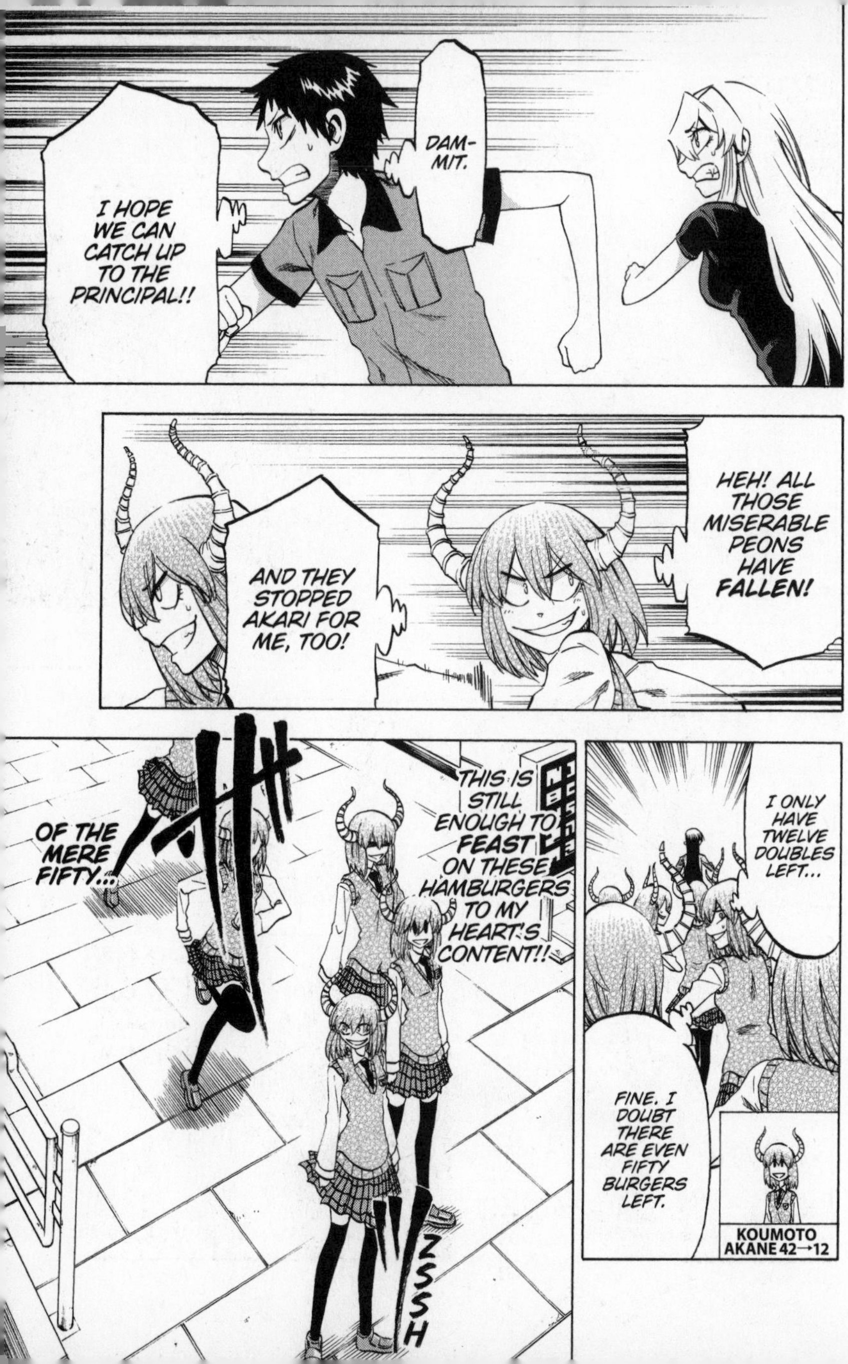
DAM-MIT.
I HOPE WE CAN CATCH UP TO THE PRINCIPAL!!
HEH! ALL THOSE MISERABLE PEONS HAVE FALLEN!
AND THEY STOPPED AKARI FOR ME, TOO!
I ONLY HAVE TWELVE DOUBLES LEFT...
FINE. I DOUBT THERE ARE EVEN FIFTY BURGERS LEFT.
KOUMOTO AKANE 42→12
THIS IS STILL ENOUGH TO FEAST ON THESE HAMBURGERS TO MY HEART'S CONTENT!!
OF THE MERE FIFTY...
ZSSH

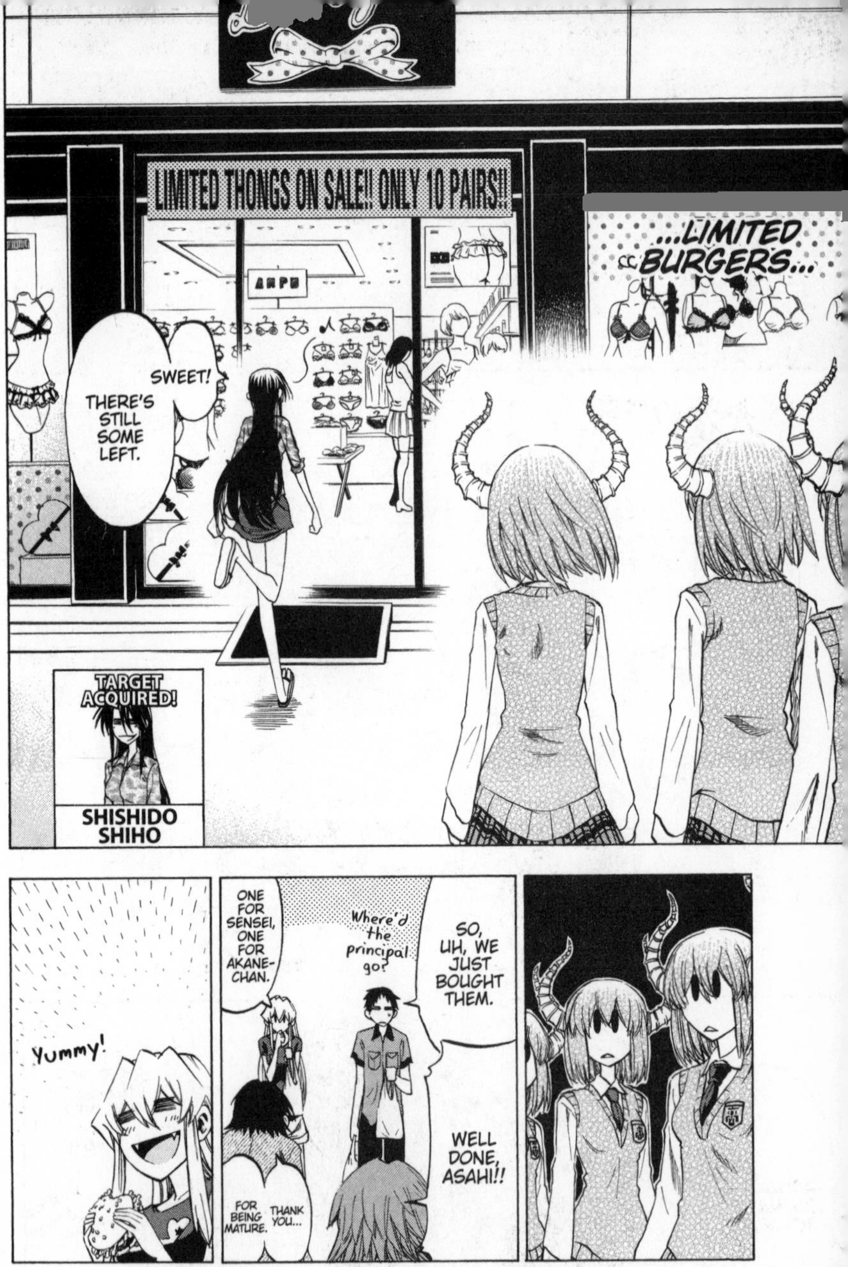
LIMITED THONGS ON SALE!! ONLY 10 PAIRS!!
...LIMITED BURGERS...
SWEET!
THERE'S STILL SOME LEFT.
TARGET ACQUIRED!
SHISHIDO SHIHO
SO, UH, WE JUST BOUGHT THEM.
Where'd the principal go?
ONE FOR SENSEI, ONE FOR AKANE-CHAN.
WELL DONE, ASAHI!!
THANK YOU...
FOR BEING MATURE.
Yummy!

Chapter 29: "Let's Ride in the New Car!"

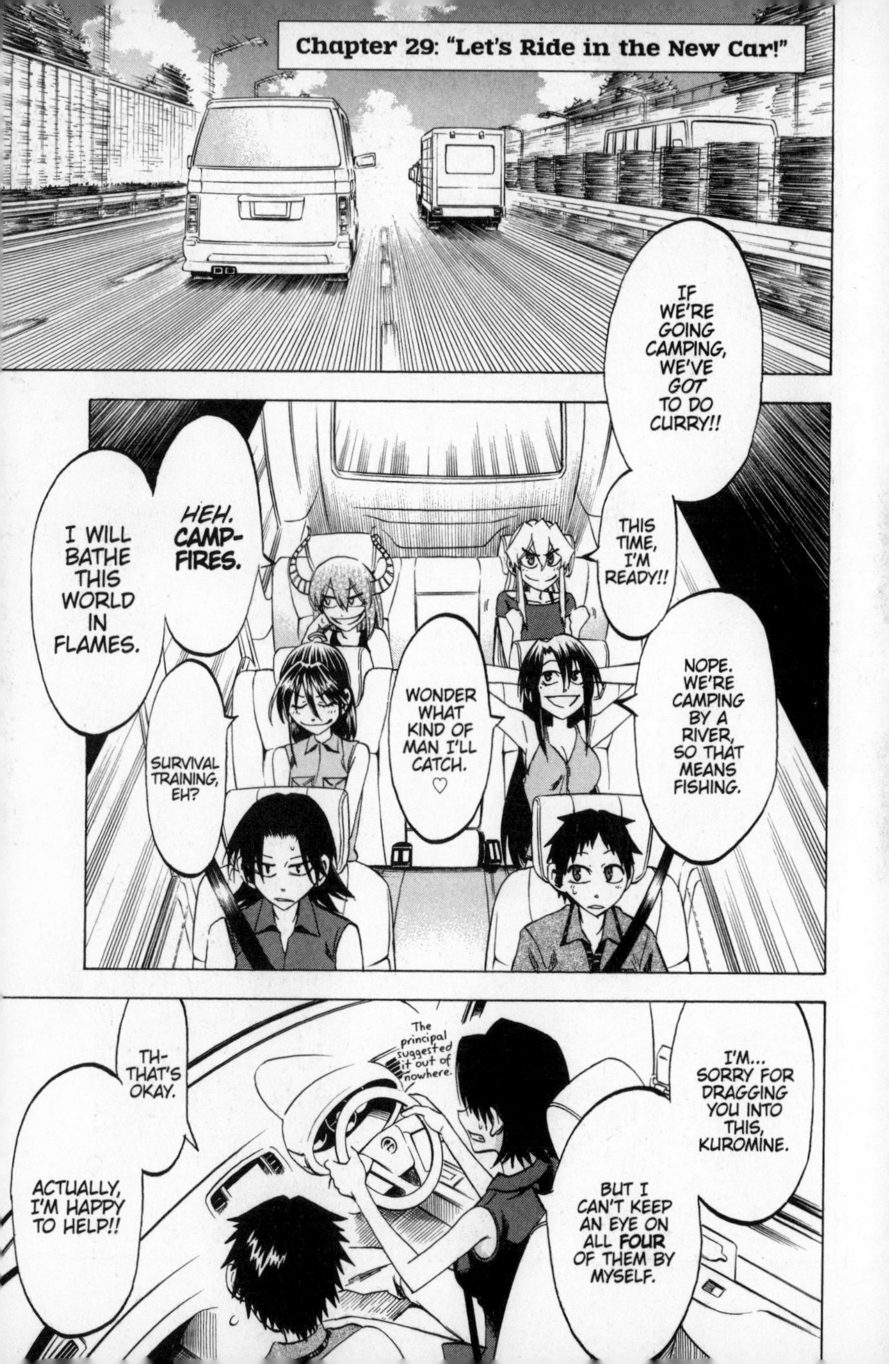
IF WE'RE GOING CAMPING, WE'VE GOT TO DO CURRY!!
THIS TIME, I'M READY!!
HEH. CAMPFIRES.
I WILL BATHE THIS WORLD IN FLAMES.
NOPE. WE'RE CAMPING BY A RIVER, SO THAT MEANS FISHING.
WONDER WHAT KIND OF MAN I'LL CATCH. ♡
SURVIVAL TRAINING, EH?
I'M... SORRY FOR DRAGGING YOU INTO THIS, KUROMINE.
The principal suggested it out of nowhere.
BUT I CAN'T KEEP AN EYE ON ALL FOUR OF THEM BY MYSELF.
TH-THAT'S OKAY.
ACTUALLY, I'M HAPPY TO HELP!!

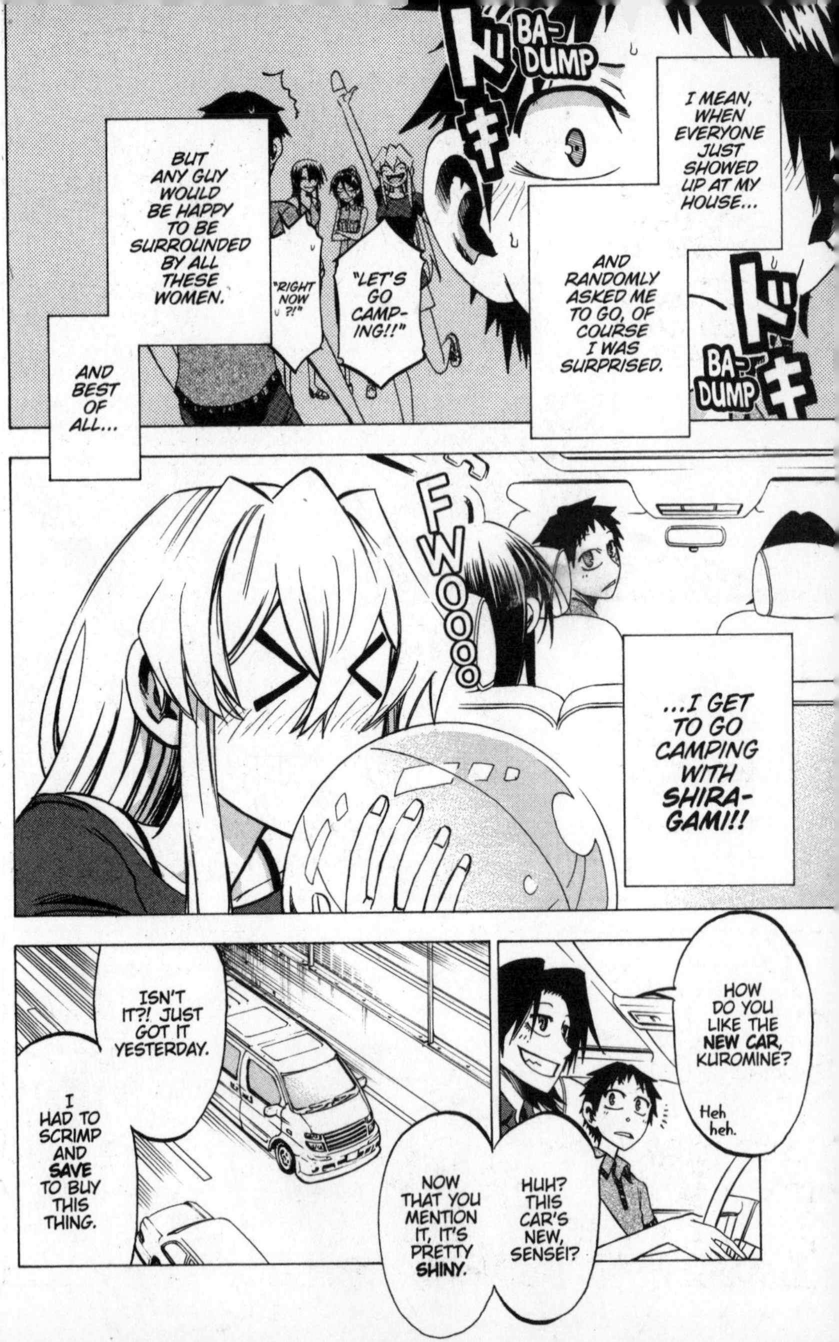
BA-DUMP
I MEAN, WHEN EVERYONE JUST SHOWED UP AT MY HOUSE...
AND RANDOMLY ASKED ME TO GO, OF COURSE I WAS SURPRISED.
BA-DUMP
"LET'S GO CAMPING!!"
"RIGHT NOW?!"
BUT ANY GUY WOULD BE HAPPY TO BE SURROUNDED BY ALL THESE WOMEN.
AND BEST OF ALL...
FWOOOO
...I GET TO GO CAMPING WITH SHIRAGAMI!!
HOW DO YOU LIKE THE NEW CAR, KUROMINE?
Heh heh.
HUH? THIS CAR'S NEW, SENSEI?
NOW THAT YOU MENTION IT, IT'S PRETTY SHINY.
ISN'T IT?! JUST GOT IT YESTERDAY.
I HAD TO SCRIMP AND SAVE TO BUY THIS THING.

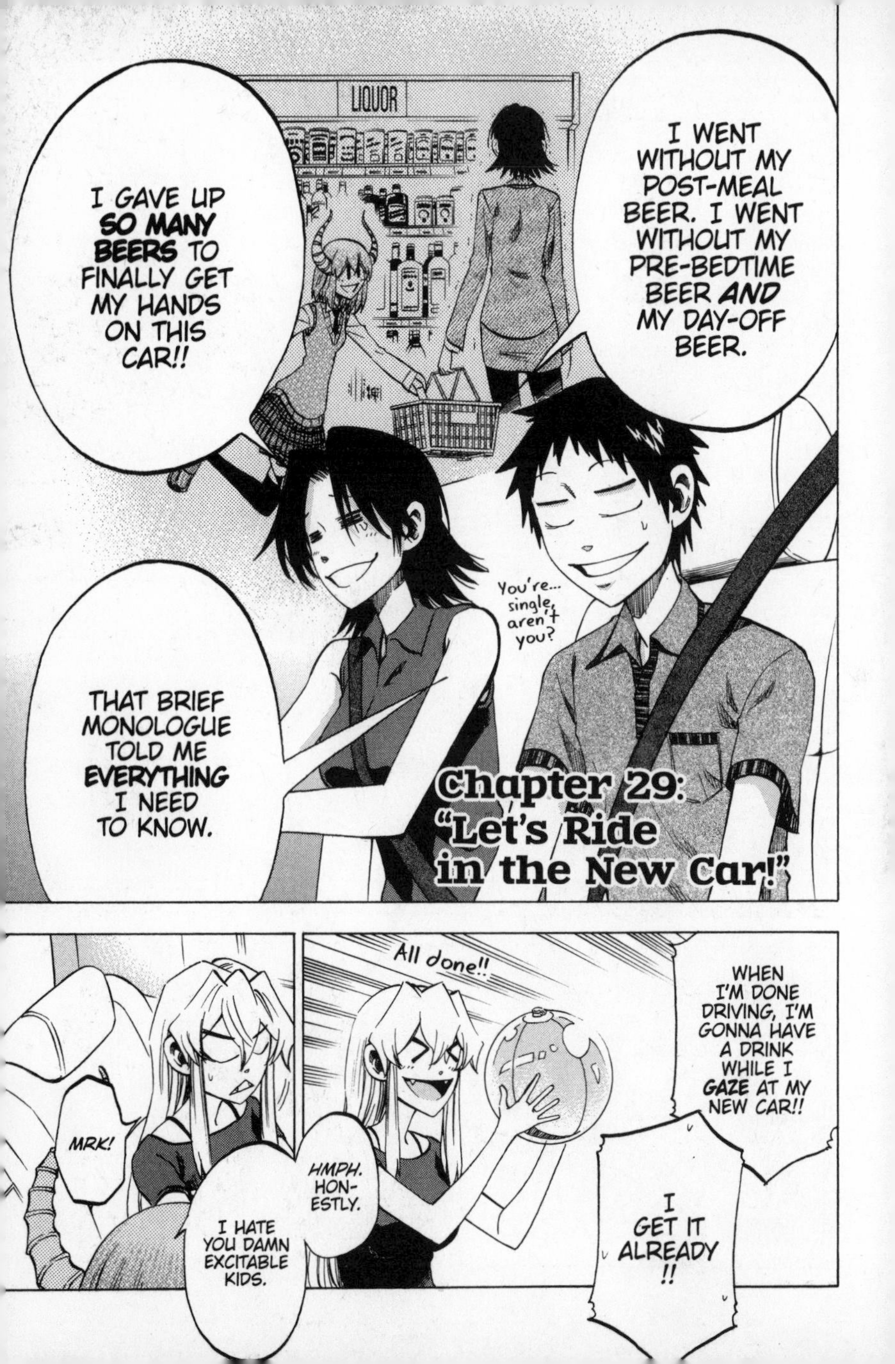
I WENT WITHOUT MY POST-MEAL BEER. I WENT WITHOUT MY PRE-BEDTIME BEER **AND** MY DAY-OFF BEER.
LIQUOR
I GAVE UP **SO MANY BEERS** TO FINALLY GET MY HANDS ON THIS CAR!!
You're... single, aren't you?
THAT BRIEF MONOLOGUE TOLD ME **EVERYTHING** I NEED TO KNOW.
Chapter 29: "Let's Ride in the New Car!"
All done!!
WHEN I'M DONE DRIVING, I'M GONNA HAVE A DRINK WHILE I **GAZE** AT MY NEW CAR!!
I GET IT ALREADY!!
HMPH. HON-ESTLY.
MRK!
I HATE YOU DAMN EXCITABLE KIDS.

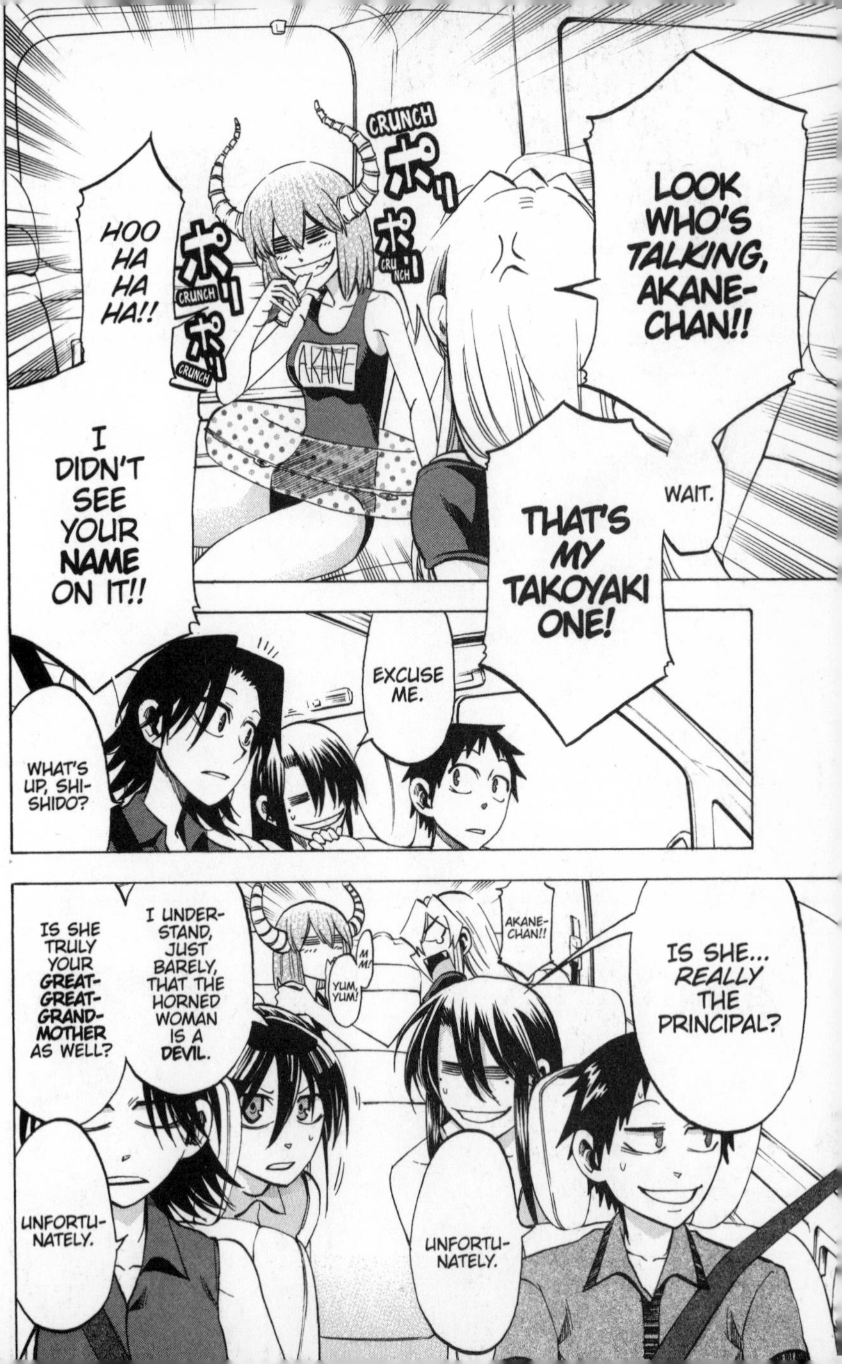
LOOK WHO'S TALKING, AKANE-CHAN!!
CRUNCH
CRUNCH
HOO HA HA HA!!
CRUNCH
CRUNCH
I DIDN'T SEE YOUR NAME ON IT!!
WAIT. THAT'S MY TAKOYAKI ONE!
EXCUSE ME.
WHAT'S UP, SHI-SHIDO?
IS SHE... REALLY THE PRINCIPAL?
AKANE-CHAN!!
MM!
YUM, YUM!
I UNDERSTAND, JUST BARELY, THAT THE HORNED WOMAN IS A DEVIL.
IS SHE TRULY YOUR GREAT-GREAT-GRANDMOTHER AS WELL?
UNFORTUNATELY.
UNFORTUNATELY.

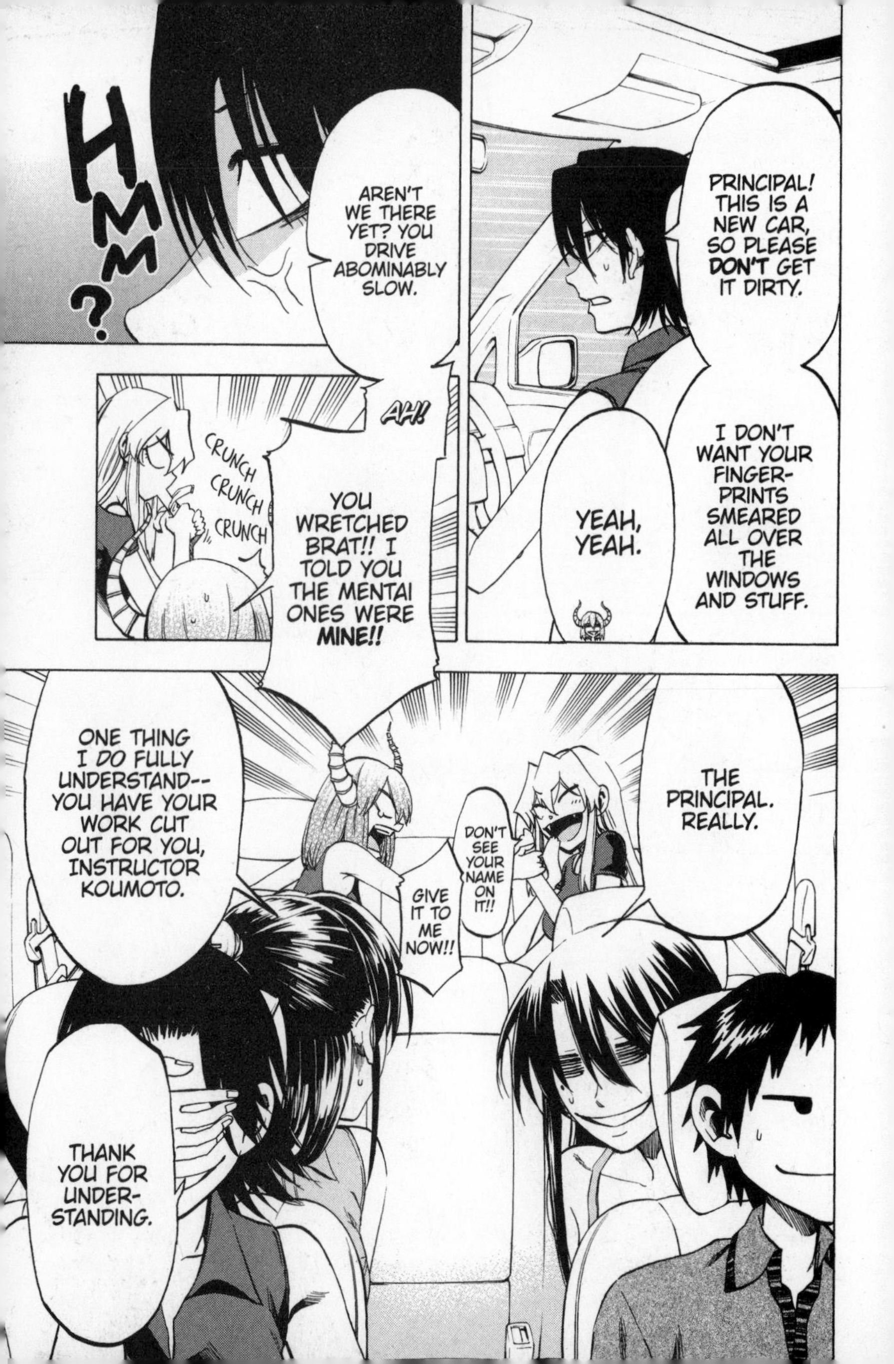
PRINCIPAL! THIS IS A NEW CAR, SO PLEASE DON'T GET IT DIRTY.
I DON'T WANT YOUR FINGER-PRINTS SMEARED ALL OVER THE WINDOWS AND STUFF.
YEAH, YEAH.
HMM?
AREN'T WE THERE YET? YOU DRIVE ABOMINABLY SLOW.
AH!
CRUNCH CRUNCH CRUNCH
YOU WRETCHED BRAT!! I TOLD YOU THE MENTAI ONES WERE MINE!!
THE PRINCIPAL. REALLY.
DON'T SEE YOUR NAME ON IT!!
GIVE IT TO ME NOW!!
ONE THING I DO FULLY UNDERSTAND-- YOU HAVE YOUR WORK CUT OUT FOR YOU, INSTRUCTOR KOUMOTO.
THANK YOU FOR UNDER-STANDING.

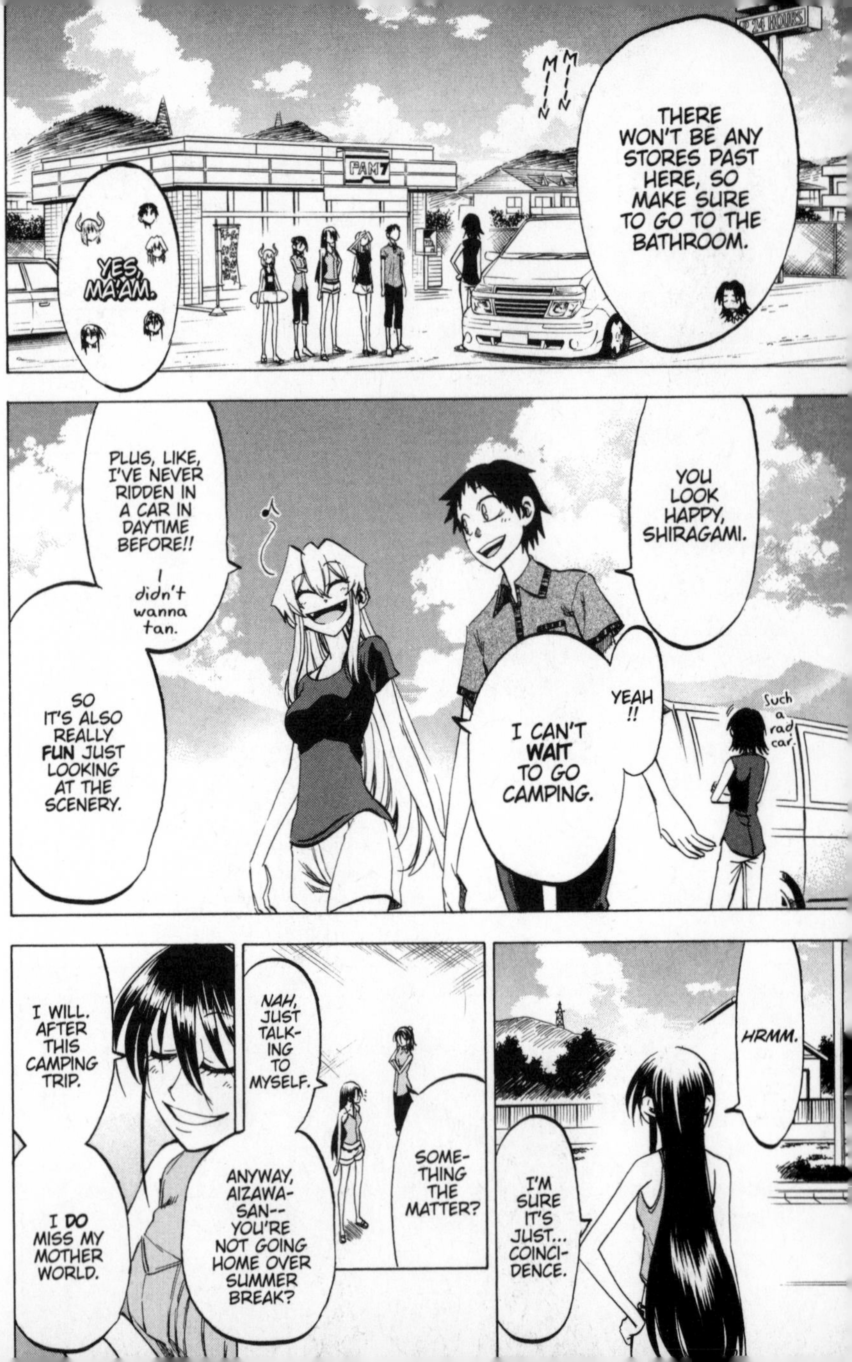
24 HOURS
THERE WON'T BE ANY STORES PAST HERE, SO MAKE SURE TO GO TO THE BATHROOM.
MIIN MIIN
FAM7
YES, MA'AM.
YOU LOOK HAPPY, SHIRAGAMI.
YEAH!!
I CAN'T WAIT TO GO CAMPING.
Such a rad car.
PLUS, LIKE, I'VE NEVER RIDDEN IN A CAR IN DAYTIME BEFORE!!
I didn't wanna tan.
SO IT'S ALSO REALLY FUN JUST LOOKING AT THE SCENERY.
HRMM.
I'M SURE IT'S JUST... COINCIDENCE.
SOMETHING THE MATTER?
NAH, JUST TALKING TO MYSELF.
ANYWAY, AIZAWA-SAN-- YOU'RE NOT GOING HOME OVER SUMMER BREAK?
I WILL. AFTER THIS CAMPING TRIP.
I DO MISS MY MOTHER WORLD.

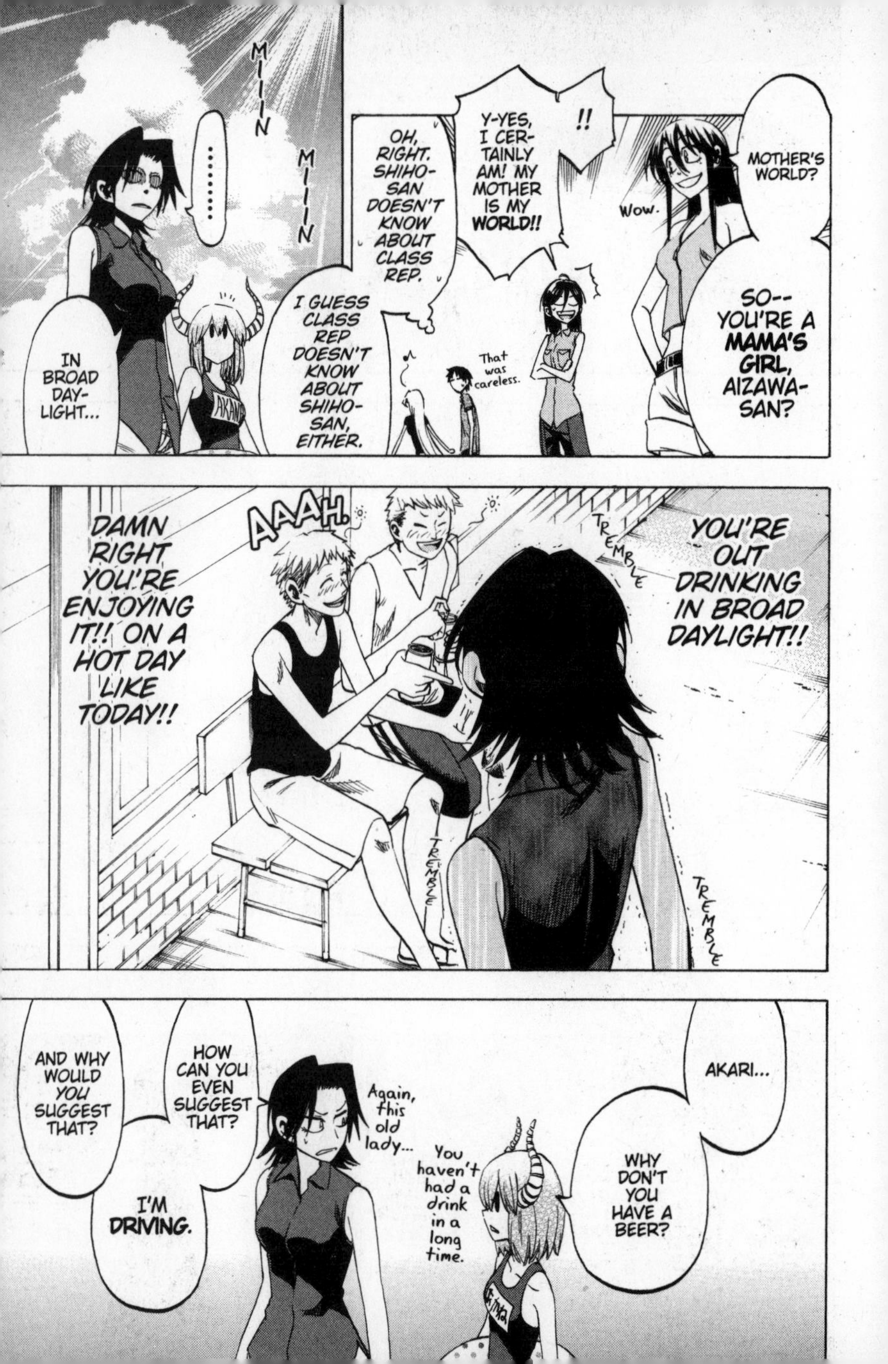
MOTHER'S WORLD?
Wow.
SO-- YOU'RE A MAMA'S GIRL, AIZAWA-SAN?
!!
Y-YES, I CER-TAINLY AM! MY MOTHER IS MY WORLD!!
That was careless.
OH, RIGHT. SHIHO-SAN DOESN'T KNOW ABOUT CLASS REP.
I GUESS CLASS REP DOESN'T KNOW ABOUT SHIHO-SAN, EITHER.
MIIIN
MIIIN
......
IN BROAD DAY-LIGHT...
YOU'RE OUT DRINKING IN BROAD DAYLIGHT!!
TREMBLE
AAAH.
DAMN RIGHT YOU'RE ENJOYING IT!! ON A HOT DAY LIKE TODAY!!
TREMBLE
TREMBLE
AKARI...
WHY DON'T YOU HAVE A BEER?
You haven't had a drink in a long time.
Again, this old lady...
HOW CAN YOU EVEN SUGGEST THAT?
AND WHY WOULD YOU SUGGEST THAT?
I'M DRIVING.

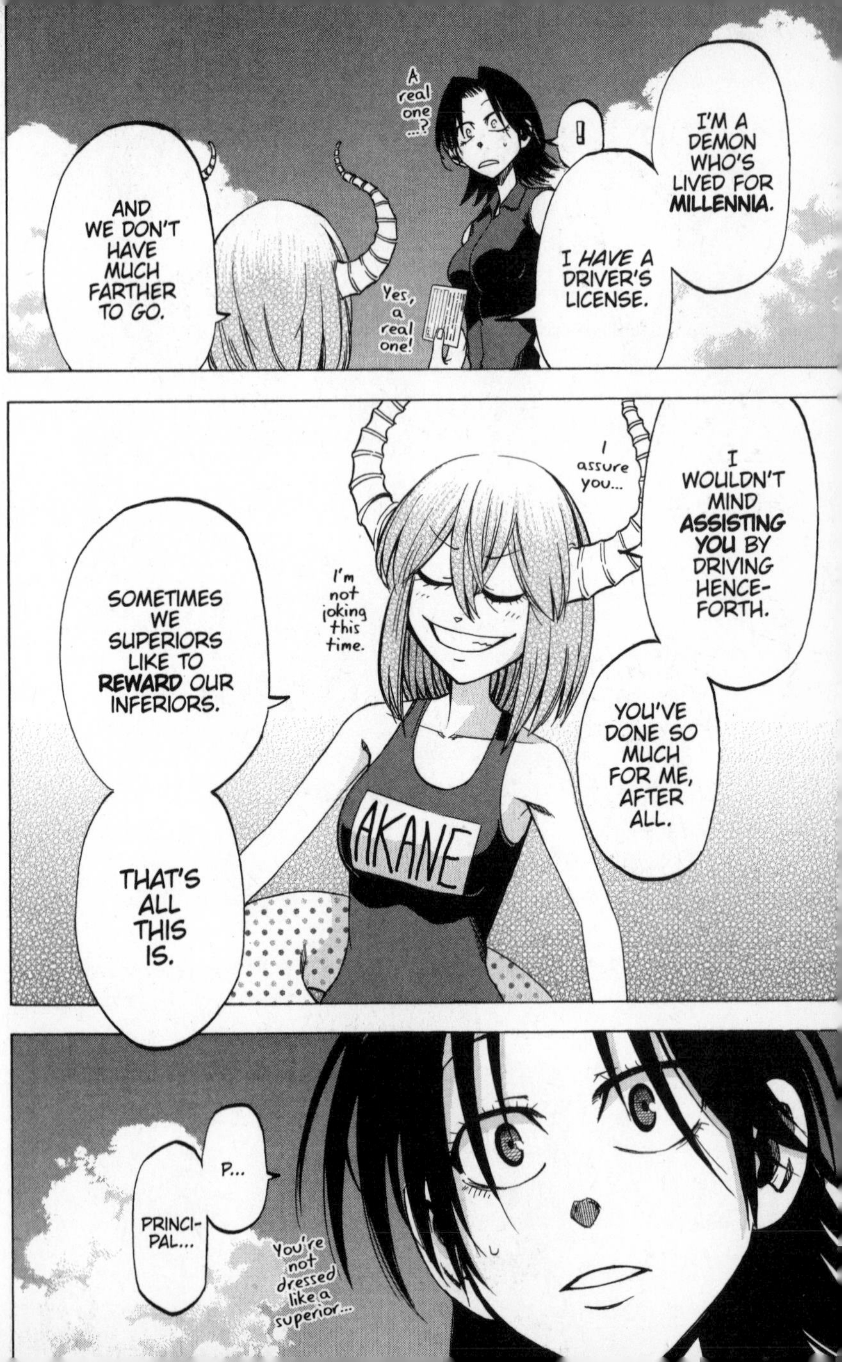
I'M A DEMON WHO'S LIVED FOR MILLENNIA.
I HAVE A DRIVER'S LICENSE.
!
A real one...?
Yes, a real one!
AND WE DON'T HAVE MUCH FARTHER TO GO.
I WOULDN'T MIND ASSISTING YOU BY DRIVING HENCE-FORTH.
I assure you...
YOU'VE DONE SO MUCH FOR ME, AFTER ALL.
I'm not joking this time.
SOMETIMES WE SUPERIORS LIKE TO REWARD OUR INFERIORS.
AKANE
THAT'S ALL THIS IS.
P...
PRINCI-PAL...
You're not dressed like a superior...

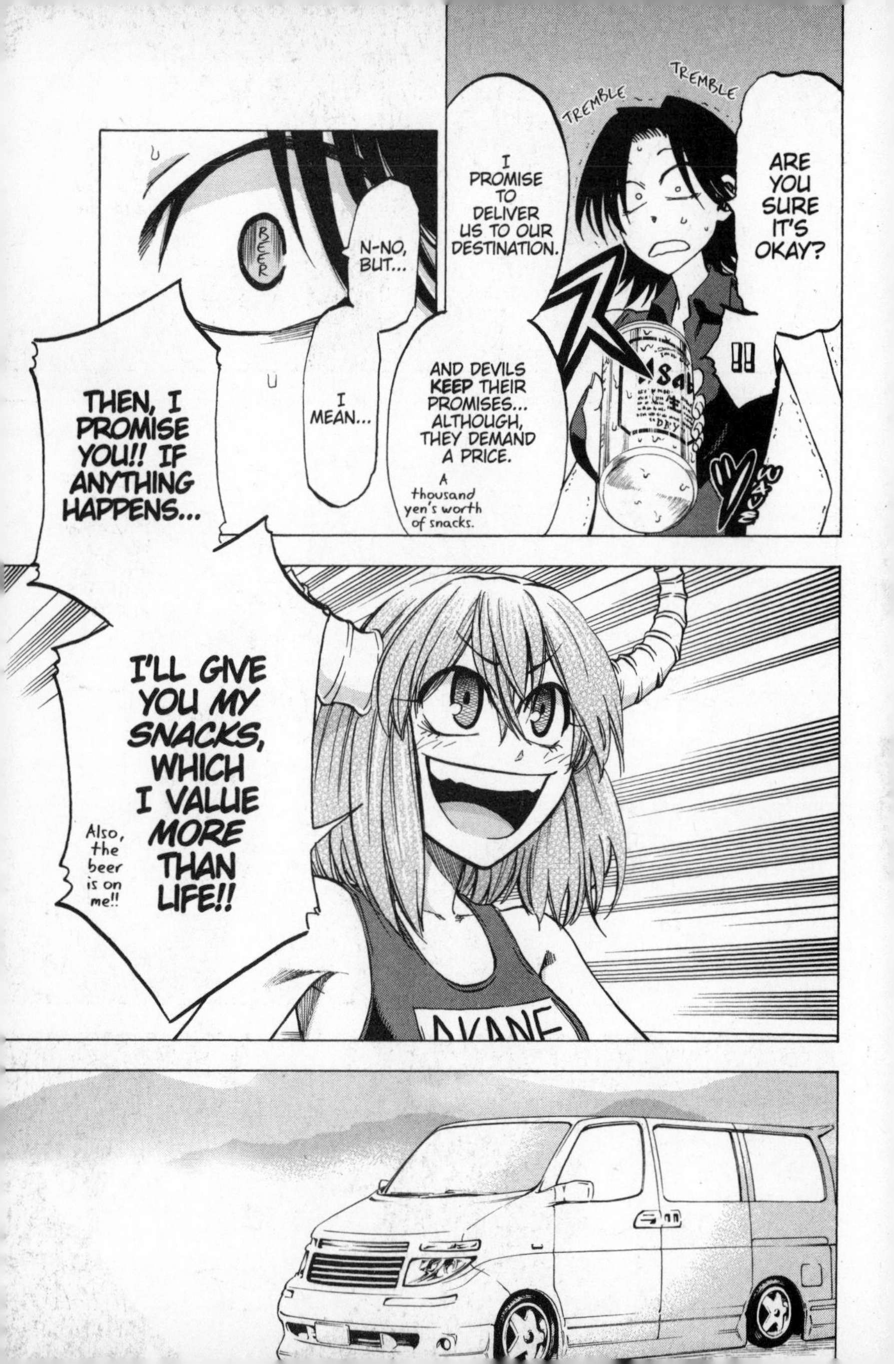
TREMBLE TREMBLE
ARE YOU SURE IT'S OKAY?
!!
WAVE
I PROMISE TO DELIVER US TO OUR DESTINATION.
AND DEVILS KEEP THEIR PROMISES... ALTHOUGH, THEY DEMAND A PRICE.
A thousand yen's worth of snacks.
BEER
N-NO, BUT...
I MEAN...
THEN, I PROMISE YOU!! IF ANYTHING HAPPENS...
I'LL GIVE YOU MY SNACKS, WHICH I VALUE MORE THAN LIFE!!
Also, the beer is on me!!
AKANE

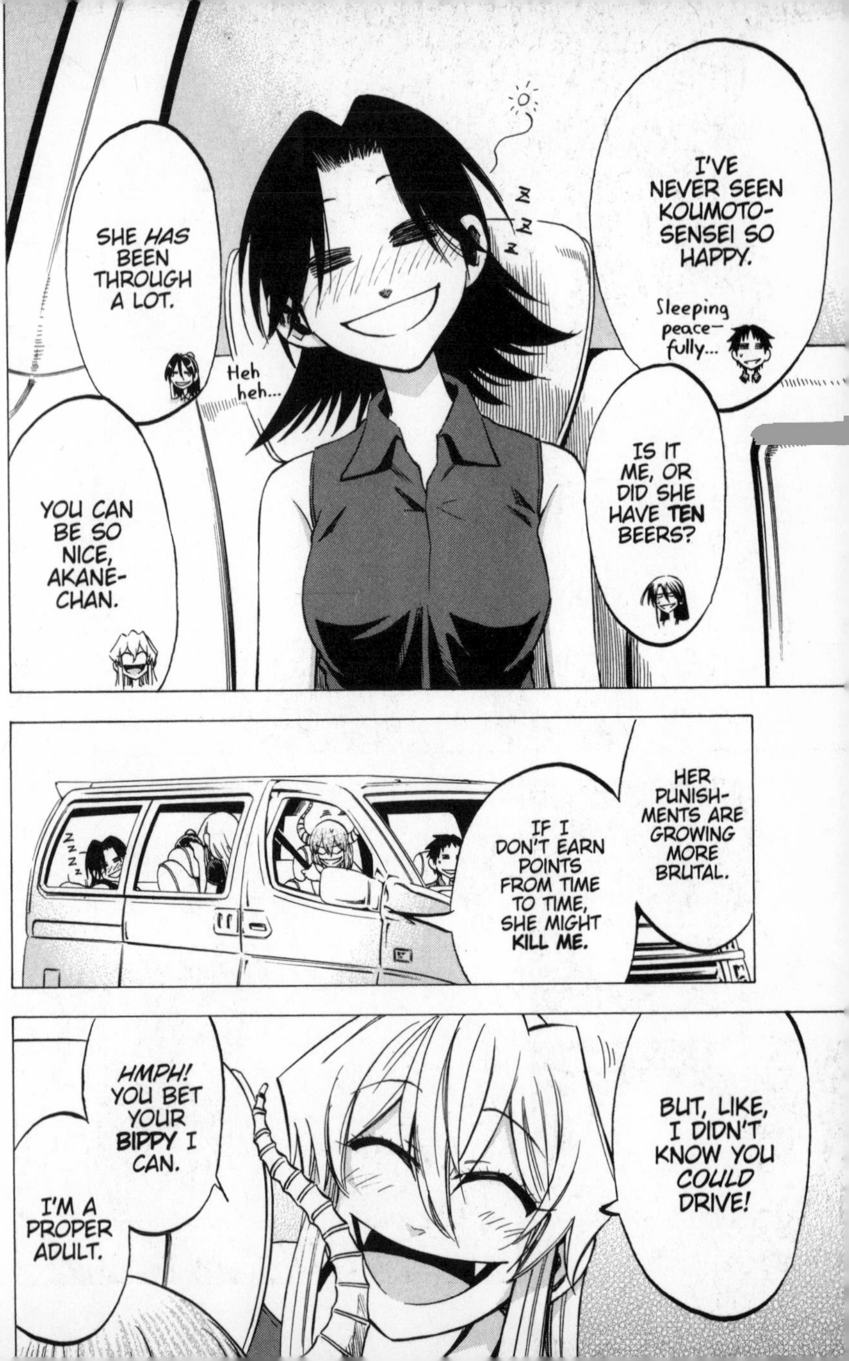
I'VE NEVER SEEN KOUMOTO-SENSEI SO HAPPY.
Sleeping peace-fully...
IS IT ME, OR DID SHE HAVE TEN BEERS?
Heh heh...
SHE HAS BEEN THROUGH A LOT.
YOU CAN BE SO NICE, AKANE-CHAN.
HER PUNISHMENTS ARE GROWING MORE BRUTAL.
IF I DON'T EARN POINTS FROM TIME TO TIME, SHE MIGHT KILL ME.
BUT, LIKE, I DIDN'T KNOW YOU COULD DRIVE!
HMPH! YOU BET YOUR BIPPY I CAN.
I'M A PROPER ADULT.

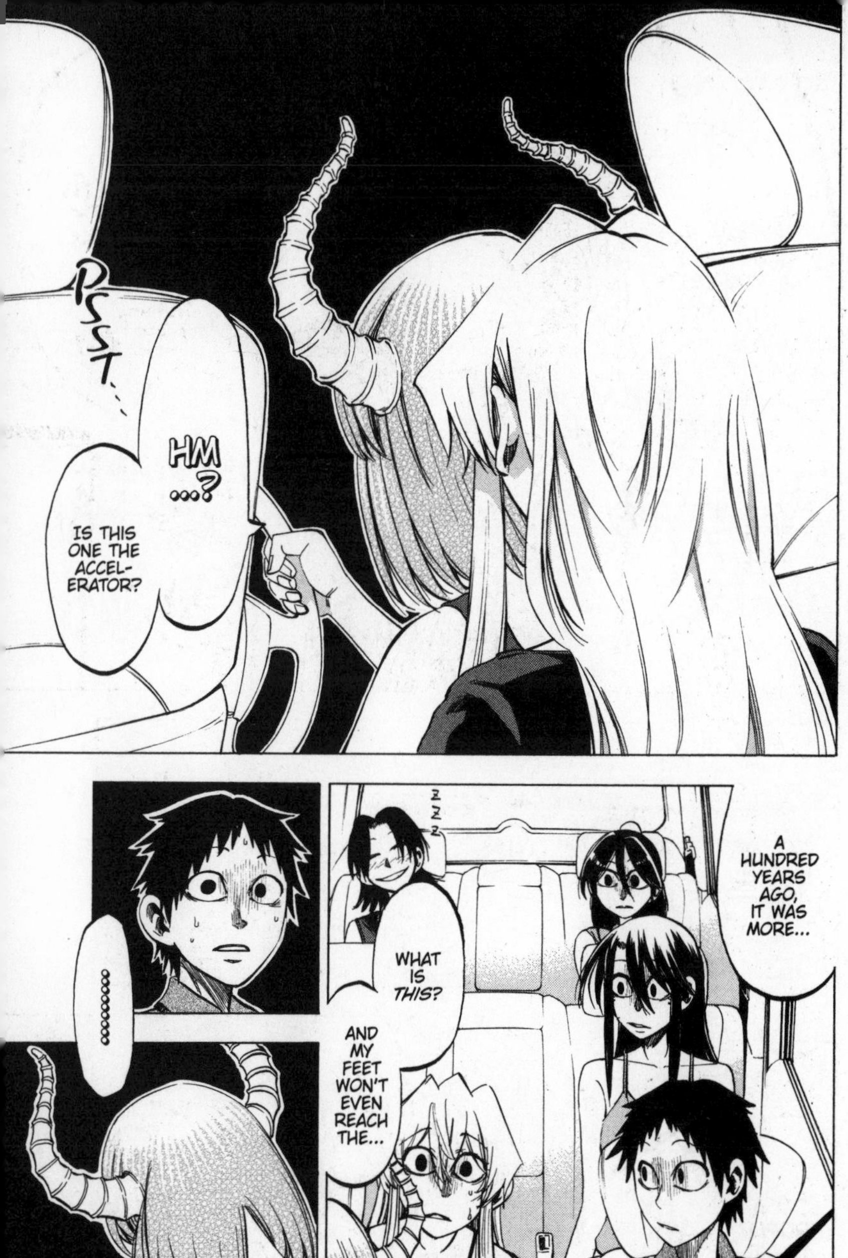
PSST...
HM ...?
IS THIS ONE THE ACCEL-ERATOR?
Z Z Z
A HUNDRED YEARS AGO, IT WAS MORE...
WHAT IS THIS?
AND MY FEET WON'T EVEN REACH THE...
....

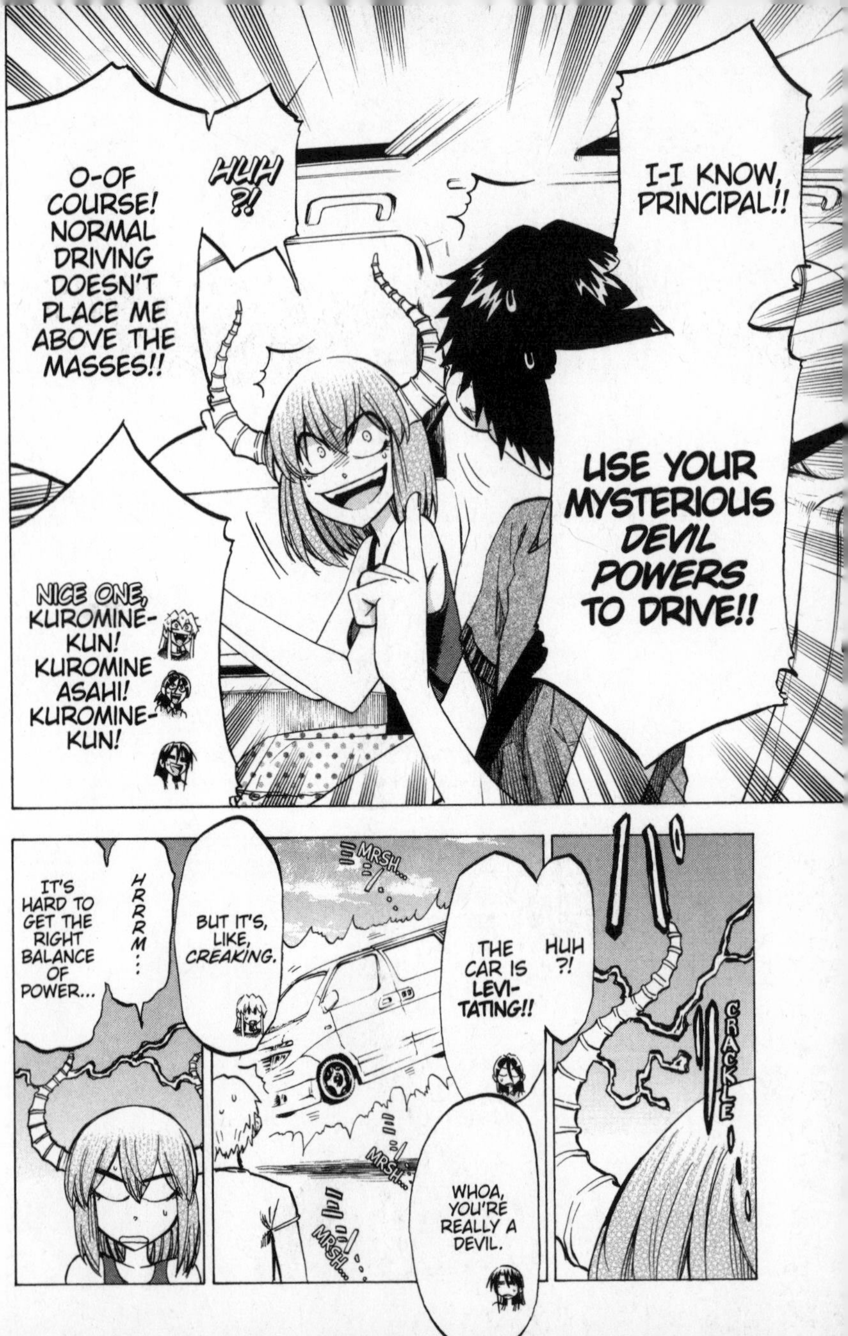
I-I KNOW, PRINCIPAL!!
HUH ?!
O-OF COURSE! NORMAL DRIVING DOESN'T PLACE ME ABOVE THE MASSES!!
USE YOUR MYSTERIOUS DEVIL POWERS TO DRIVE!!
NICE ONE, KUROMINE-KUN! KUROMINE ASAHI! KUROMINE-KUN!
HUH ?!
THE CAR IS LEVITATING!!
CRACKLE
WHOA, YOU'RE REALLY A DEVIL.
MRSH...
BUT IT'S, LIKE, CREAKING.
MRSH...
MRSH...
HRRRM...
IT'S HARD TO GET THE RIGHT BALANCE OF POWER...

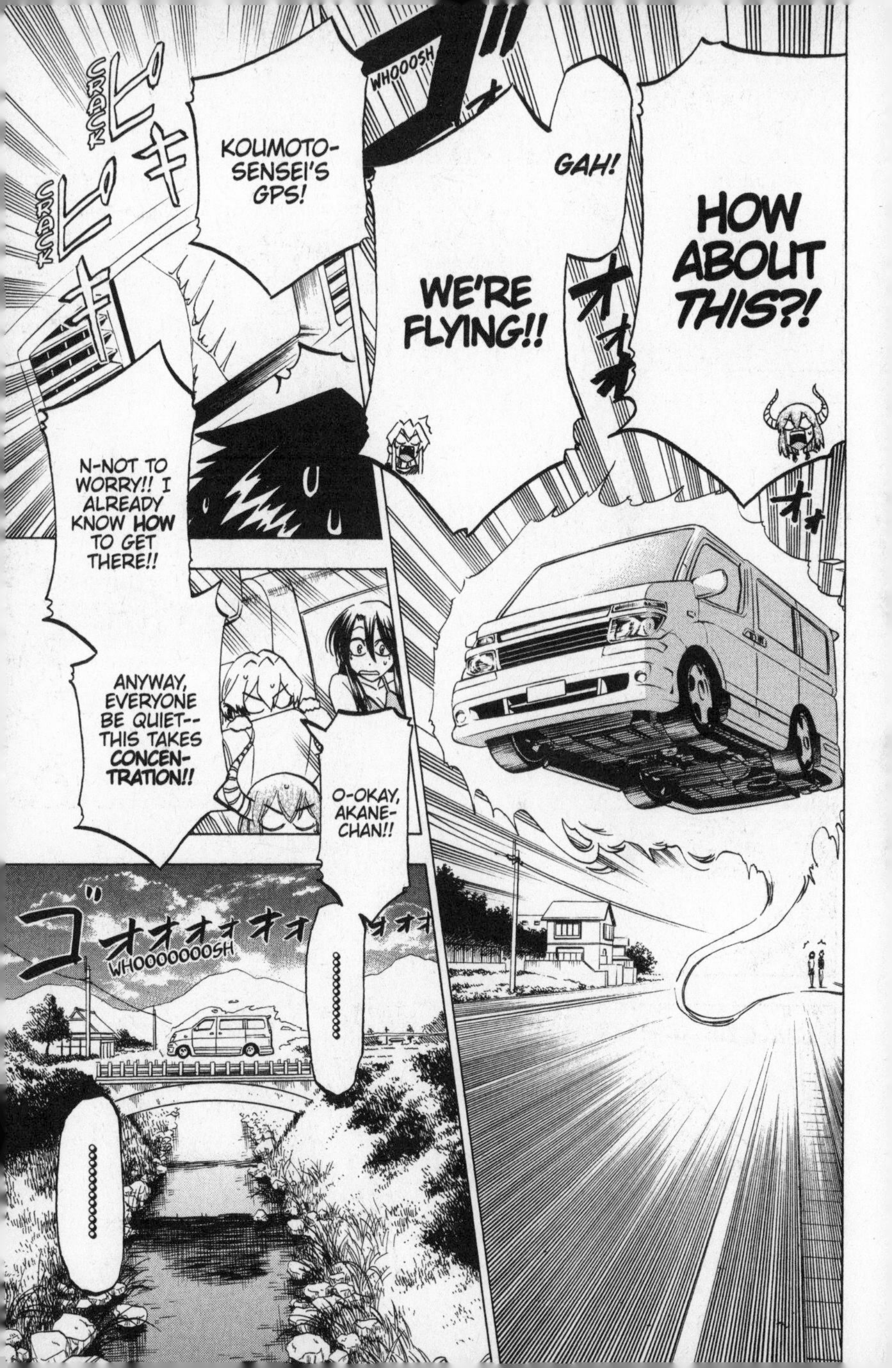
HOW ABOUT THIS?!
GAH!
WE'RE FLYING!!
WHOOOSH
KOUMOTO-SENSEI'S GPS!
CRACK
CRACK
N-NOT TO WORRY!! I ALREADY KNOW HOW TO GET THERE!!
ANYWAY, EVERYONE BE QUIET--THIS TAKES CONCENTRATION!!
O-OKAY, AKANE-CHAN!!
WHOOOOOOOOSH
....
....

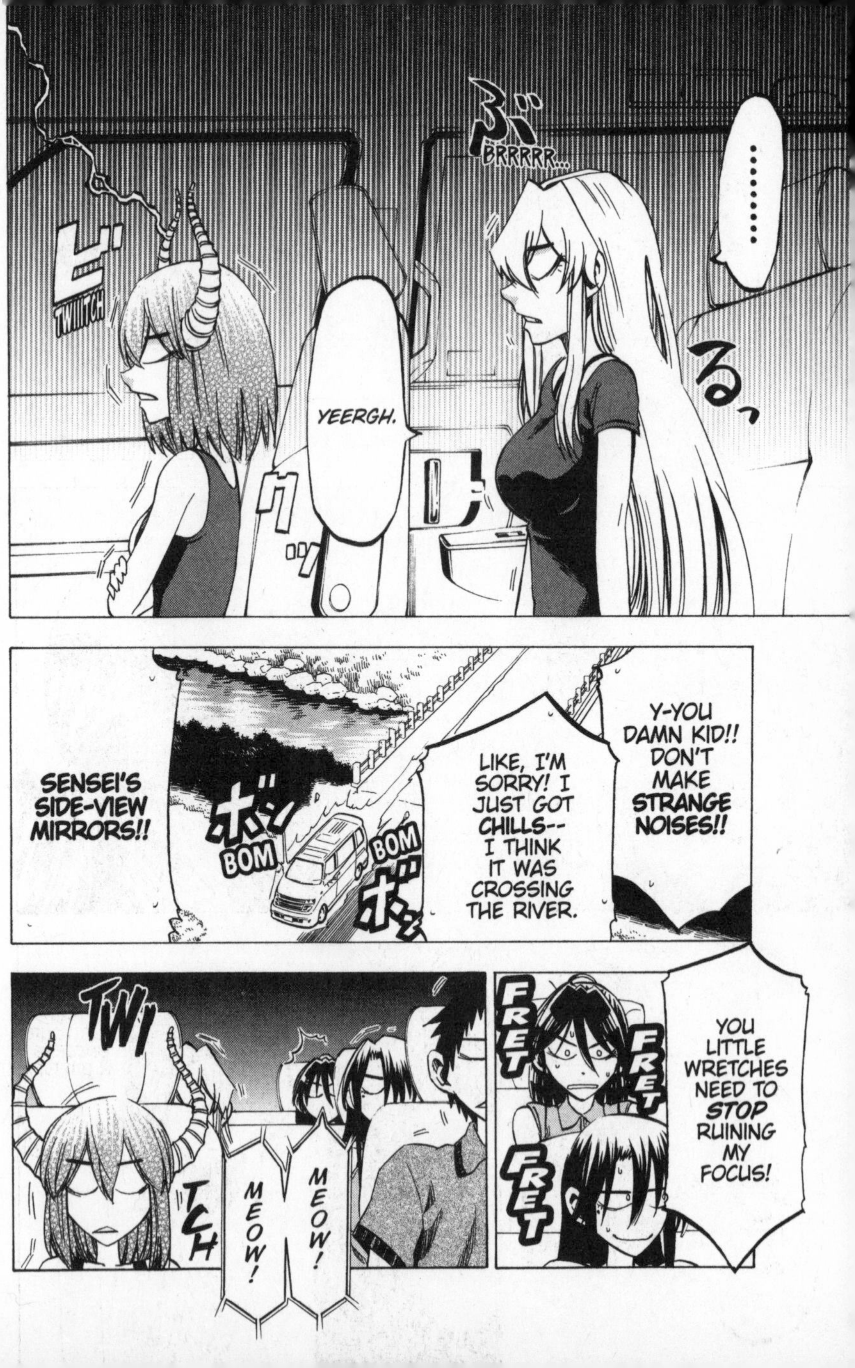

......
BRRRRR...
YEERGH.
TWIIITCH
Y-YOU DAMN KID!! DON'T MAKE STRANGE NOISES!!
LIKE, I'M SORRY! I JUST GOT CHILLS-- I THINK IT WAS CROSSING THE RIVER.
BOM
BOM
SENSEI'S SIDE-VIEW MIRRORS!!
YOU LITTLE WRETCHES NEED TO STOP RUINING MY FOCUS!
FRET
FRET
FRET
FRET
MEOW!
MEOW!
TWI
TCH

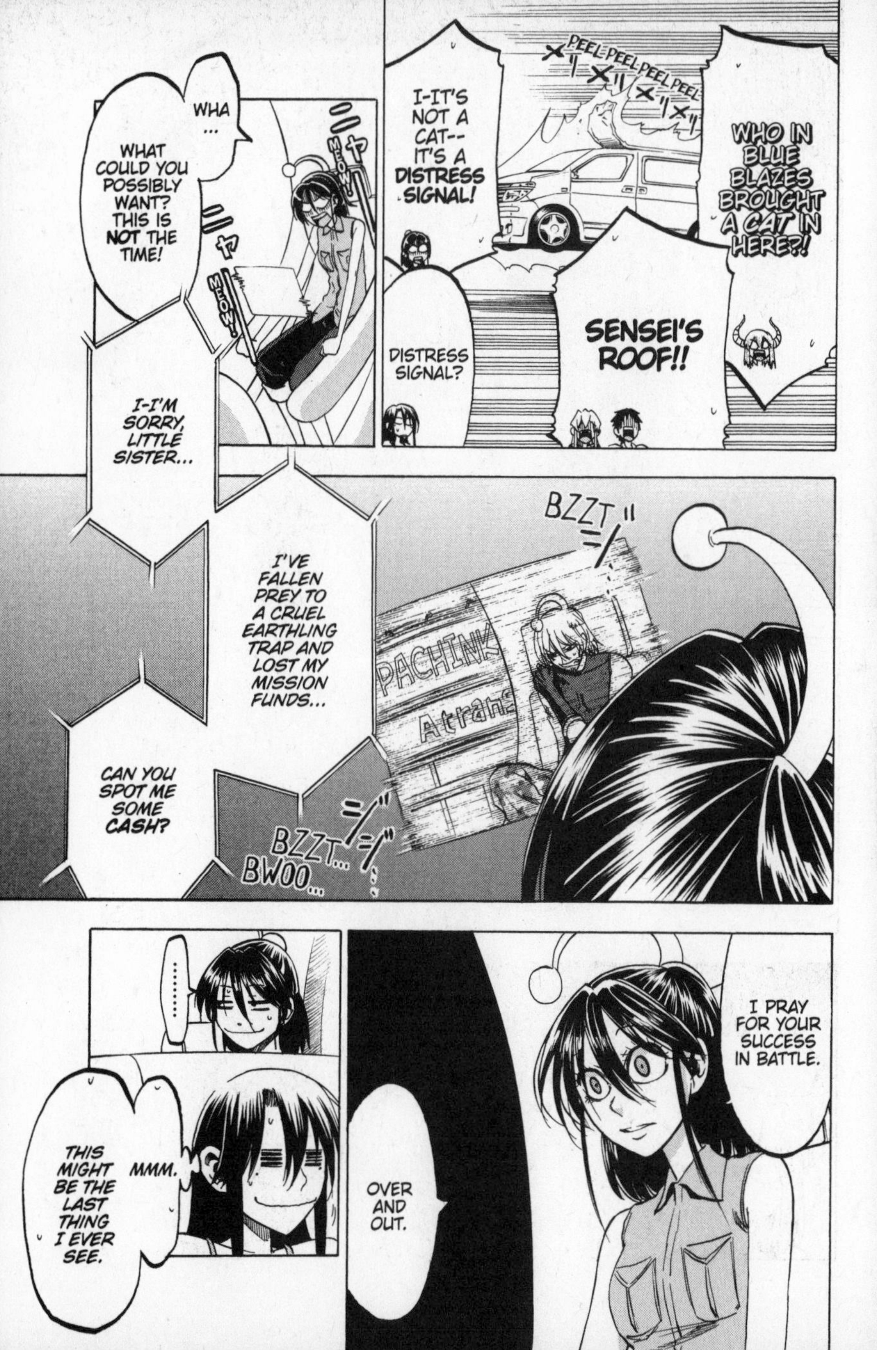
PEEL PEEL PEEL PEEL
WHO IN BLUE BLAZES BROUGHT A CAT IN HERE?!
SENSEI'S ROOF!!
I-IT'S NOT A CAT-- IT'S A DISTRESS SIGNAL!
DISTRESS SIGNAL?
MEOW!
MEOW!
WHA ...
WHAT COULD YOU POSSIBLY WANT? THIS IS NOT THE TIME!
I-I'M SORRY, LITTLE SISTER...
BZZT
I'VE FALLEN PREY TO A CRUEL EARTHLING TRAP AND LOST MY MISSION FUNDS...
CAN YOU SPOT ME SOME CASH?
BZZT... BWOO...
I PRAY FOR YOUR SUCCESS IN BATTLE.
OVER AND OUT.
......
MMM.
THIS MIGHT BE THE LAST THING I EVER SEE.

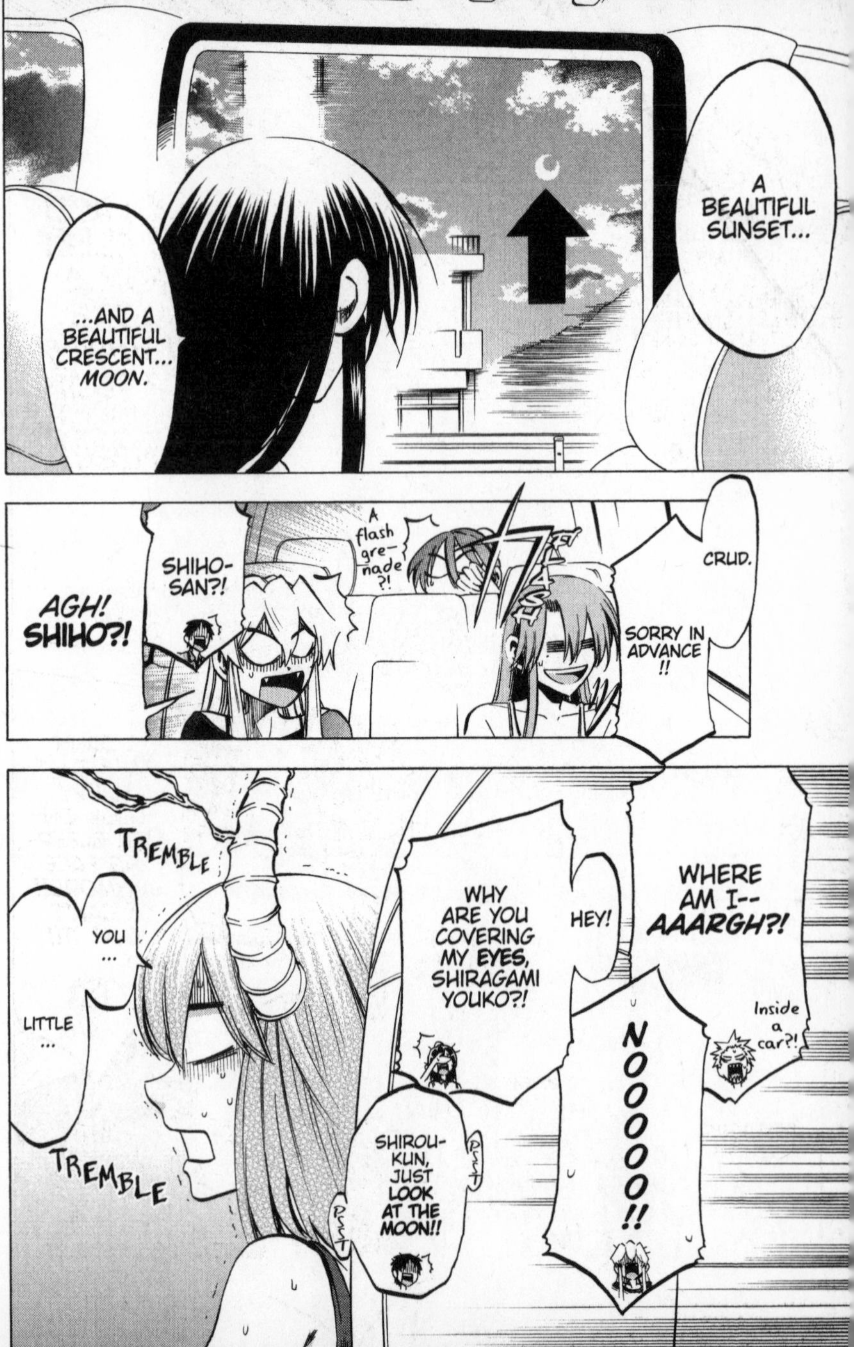
A BEAUTIFUL SUNSET...
...AND A BEAUTIFUL CRESCENT... MOON.
CRUD.
SORRY IN ADVANCE!!
FLASH
A flash gre-nade?!
SHIHO-SAN?!
AGH! SHIHO?!
WHERE AM I-- AAARGH?!
Inside a car?!
HEY!
WHY ARE YOU COVERING MY EYES, SHIRAGAMI YOUKO?!
NOOOOOO!!
SHIROU-KUN, JUST LOOK AT THE MOON!!
YOU...
LITTLE...
TREMBLE
TREMBLE

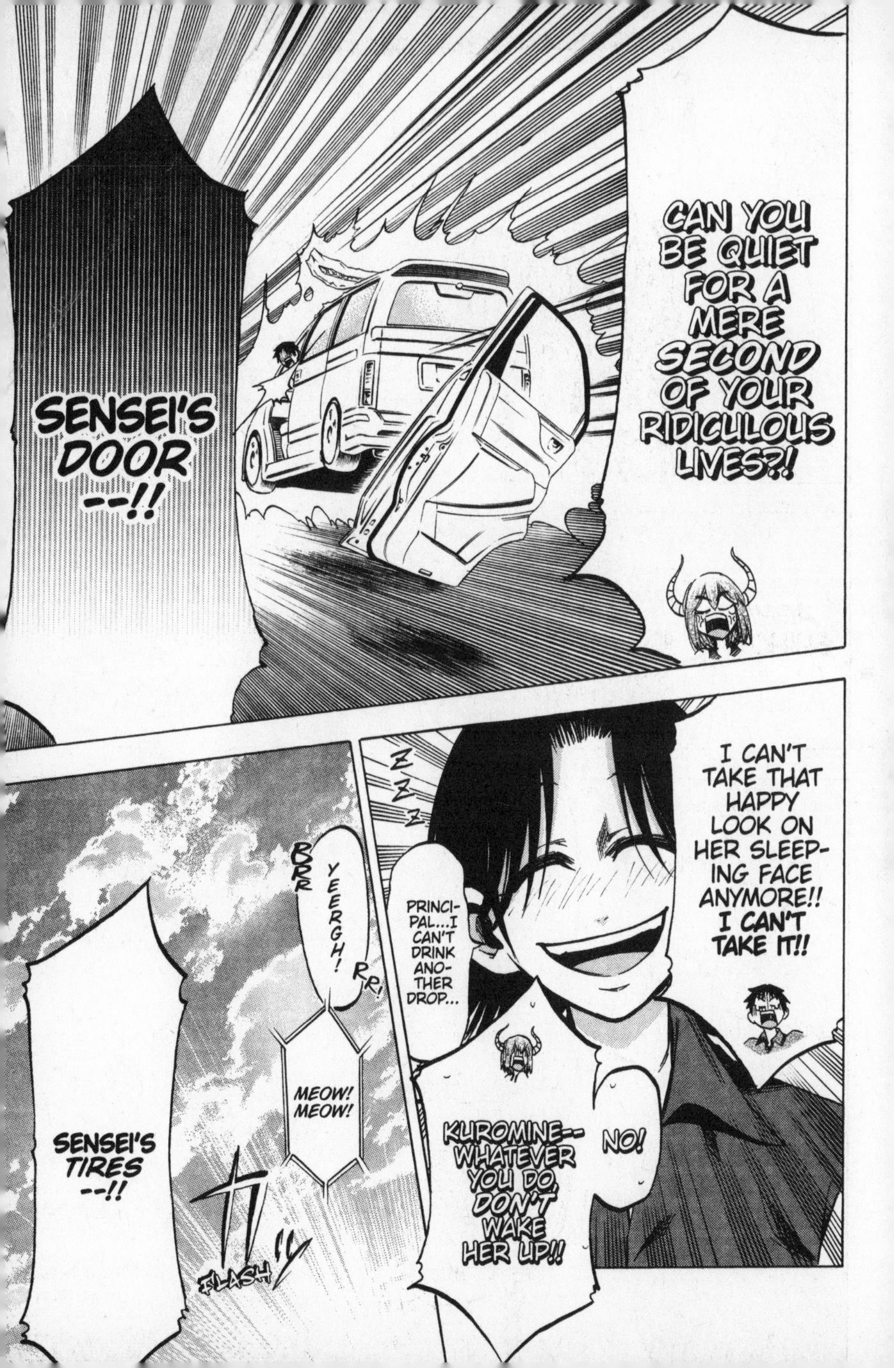
CAN YOU BE QUIET FOR A MERE SECOND OF YOUR RIDICULOUS LIVES?!
SENSEI'S DOOR --!!
I CAN'T TAKE THAT HAPPY LOOK ON HER SLEEPING FACE ANYMORE!! I CAN'T TAKE IT!!
ZZZ
PRINCI-PAL...I CAN'T DRINK ANO-THER DROP...
NO!
KUROMINE-- WHATEVER YOU DO, DON'T WAKE HER UP!!
YEERGH!
BRRR RR!
MEOW! MEOW!
SENSEI'S TIRES --!!
FLASH

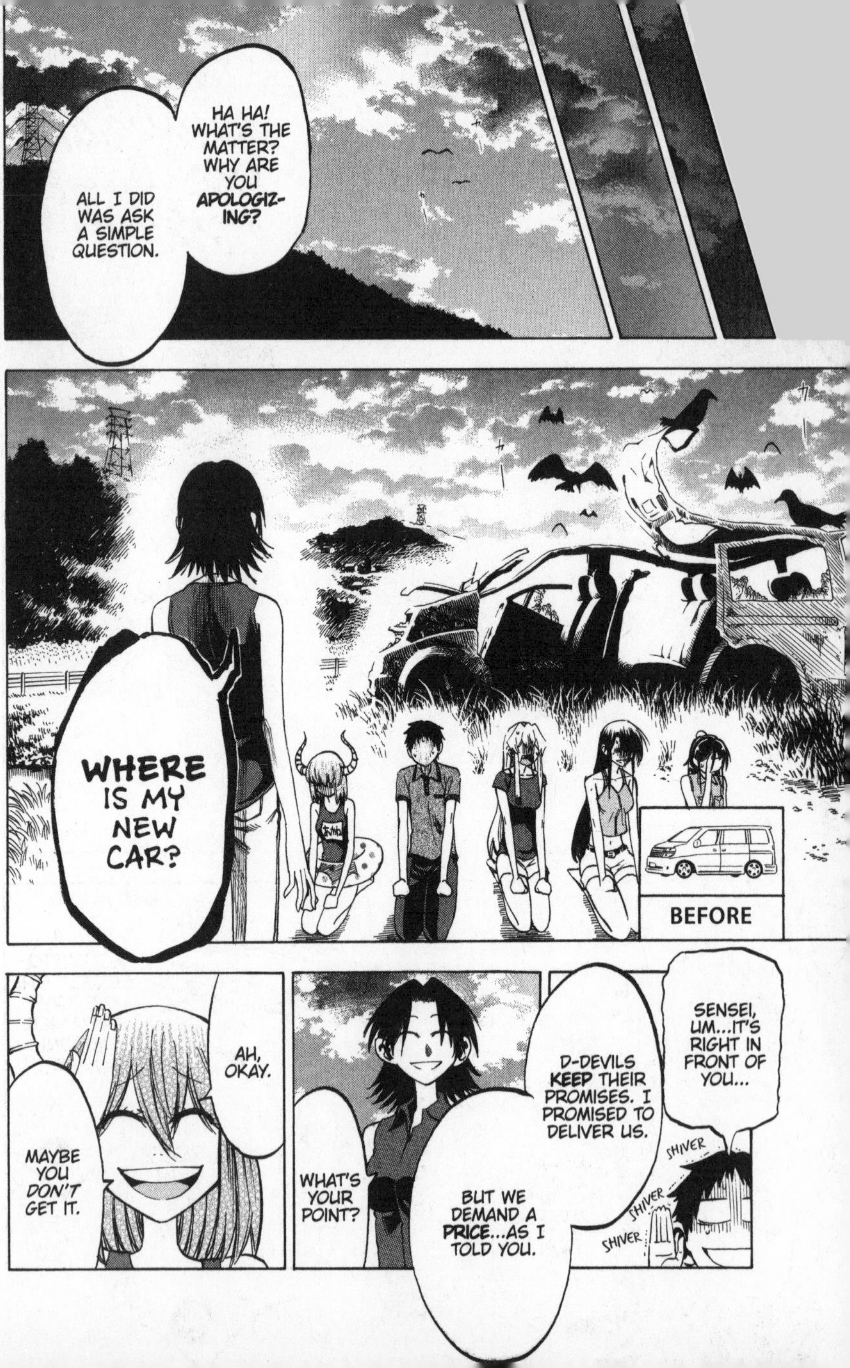
HA HA! WHAT'S THE MATTER? WHY ARE YOU APOLOGIZ-ING?
ALL I DID WAS ASK A SIMPLE QUESTION.
WHERE IS MY NEW CAR?
BEFORE
SENSEI, UM...IT'S RIGHT IN FRONT OF YOU...
SHIVER
SHIVER
SHIVER
D-DEVILS KEEP THEIR PROMISES. I PROMISED TO DELIVER US.
BUT WE DEMAND A PRICE...AS I TOLD YOU.
WHAT'S YOUR POINT?
AH, OKAY.
MAYBE YOU DON'T GET IT.

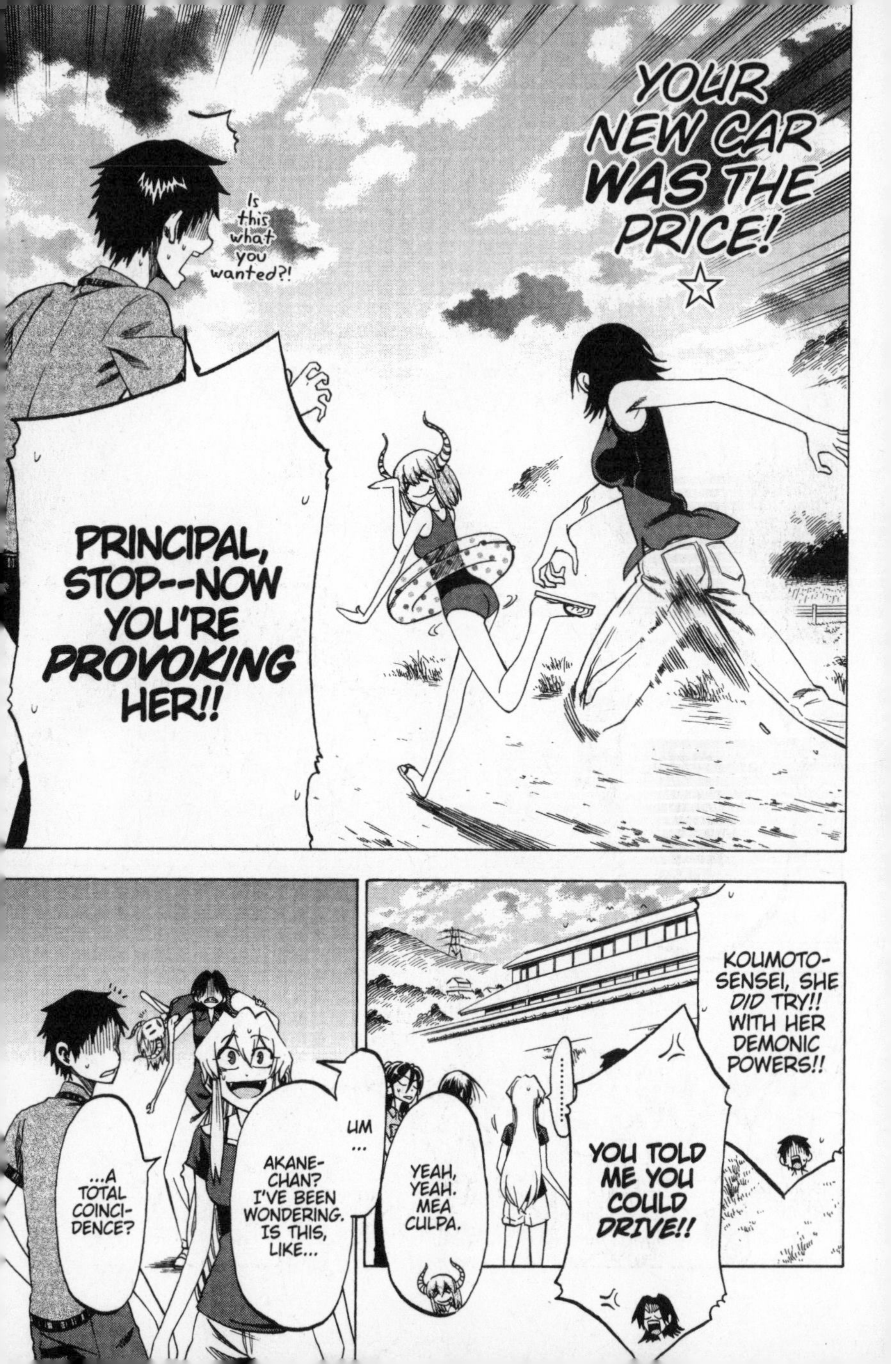
YOUR NEW CAR WAS THE PRICE! ☆
Is this what you wanted?!
PRINCIPAL, STOP--NOW YOU'RE *PROVOKING* HER!!
KOUMOTO-SENSEI, SHE *DID* TRY!! WITH HER DEMONIC POWERS!!
YOU TOLD ME YOU COULD *DRIVE*!!
......
YEAH, YEAH. MEA CULPA.
UM ...
AKANE-CHAN? I'VE BEEN WONDERING. IS THIS, LIKE...
...A TOTAL COINCI-DENCE?

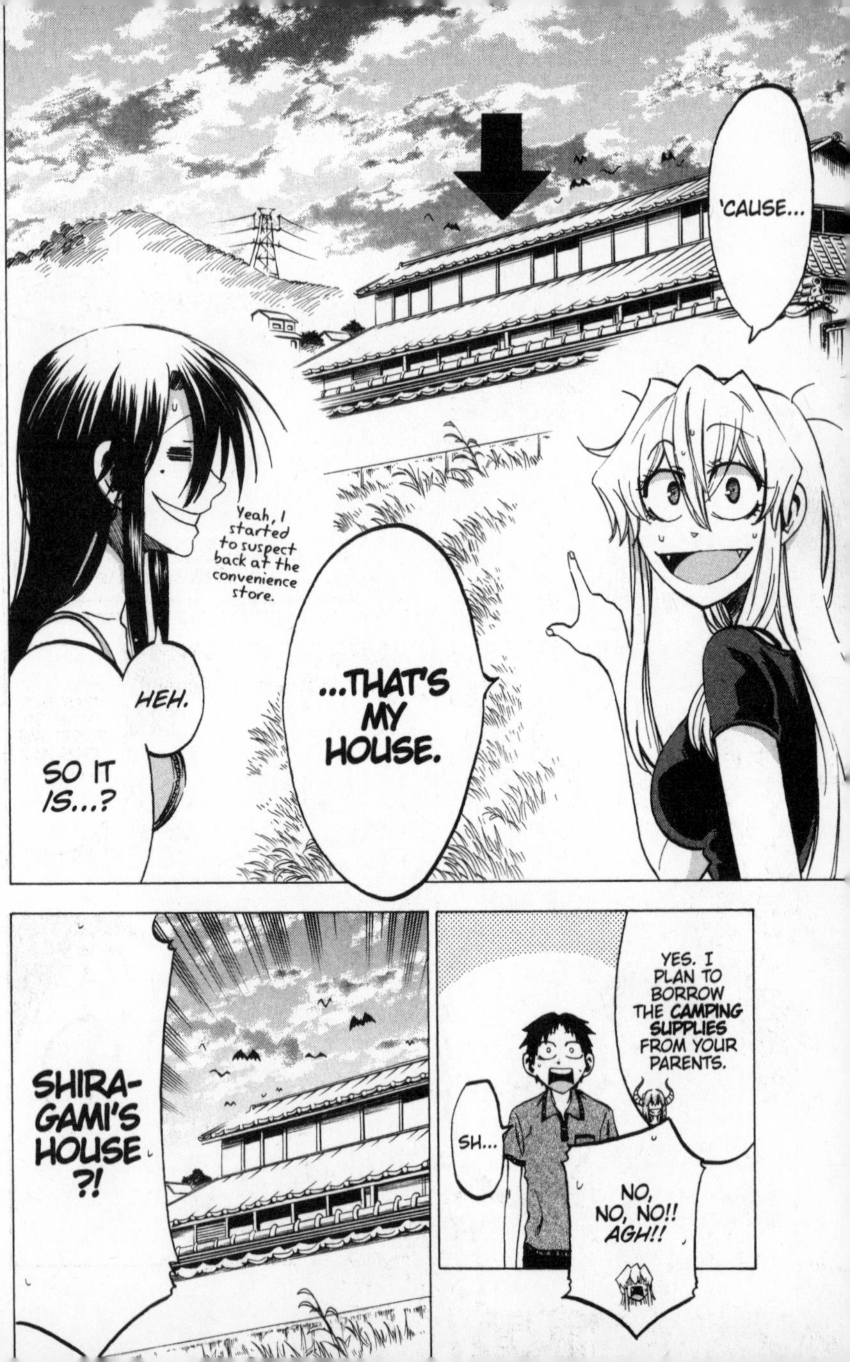
'CAUSE...
...THAT'S MY HOUSE.
Yeah, I started to suspect back at the convenience store.
HEH.
SO IT IS...?
YES. I PLAN TO BORROW THE CAMPING SUPPLIES FROM YOUR PARENTS.
SH...
NO, NO, NO!! AGH!!
SHIRA-GAMI'S HOUSE ?!

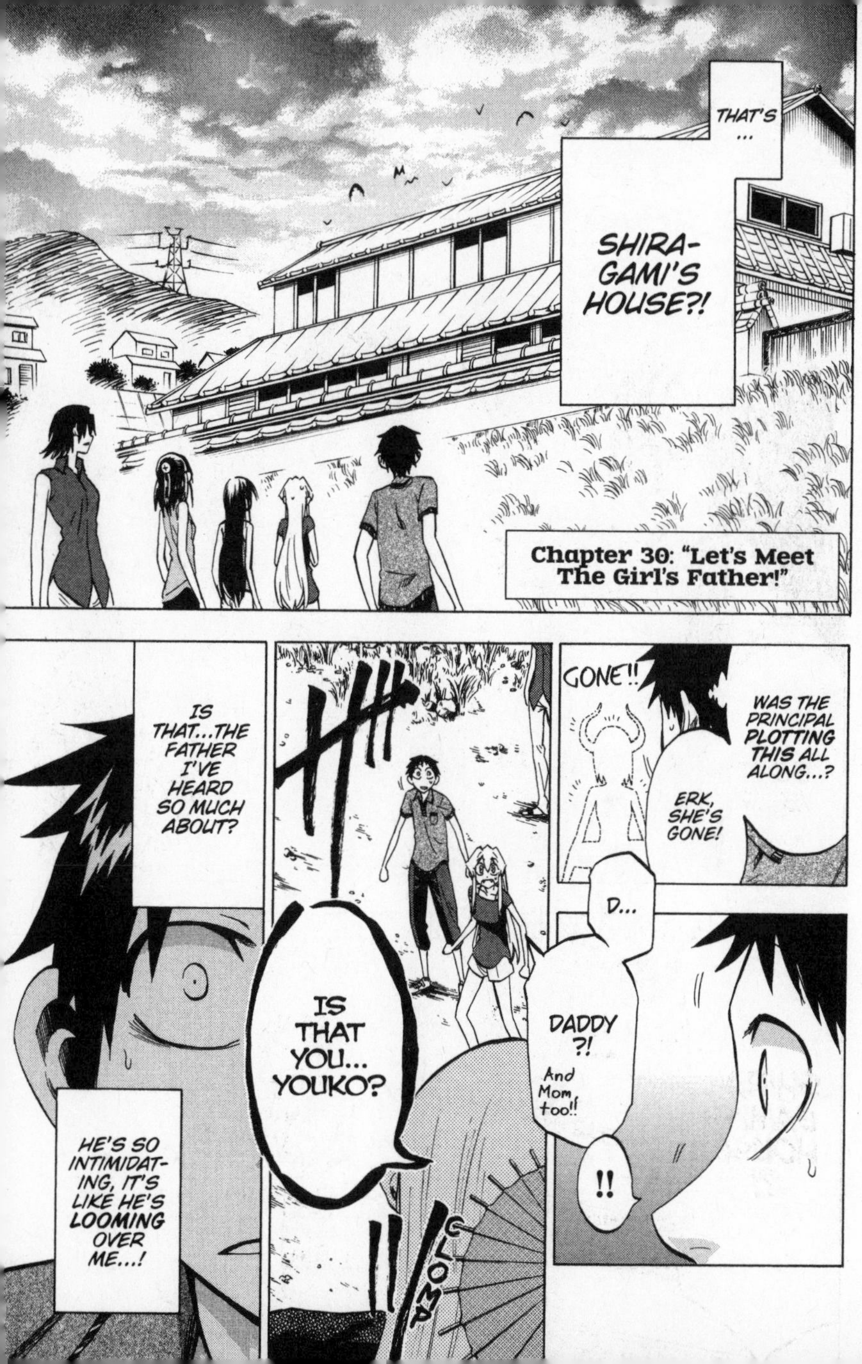
THAT'S ...
SHIRA-GAMI'S HOUSE?!
Chapter 30: "Let's Meet The Girl's Father!"
GONE!!
WAS THE PRINCIPAL PLOTTING THIS ALL ALONG...?
ERK, SHE'S GONE!
D...
DADDY ?!
And Mom too!!
!!
CLOMP
IS THAT YOU... YOUKO?
IS THAT...THE FATHER I'VE HEARD SO MUCH ABOUT?
HE'S SO INTIMIDAT-ING, IT'S LIKE HE'S LOOMING OVER ME...!

Chapter 30: "Let's Meet the Girl's Father!"

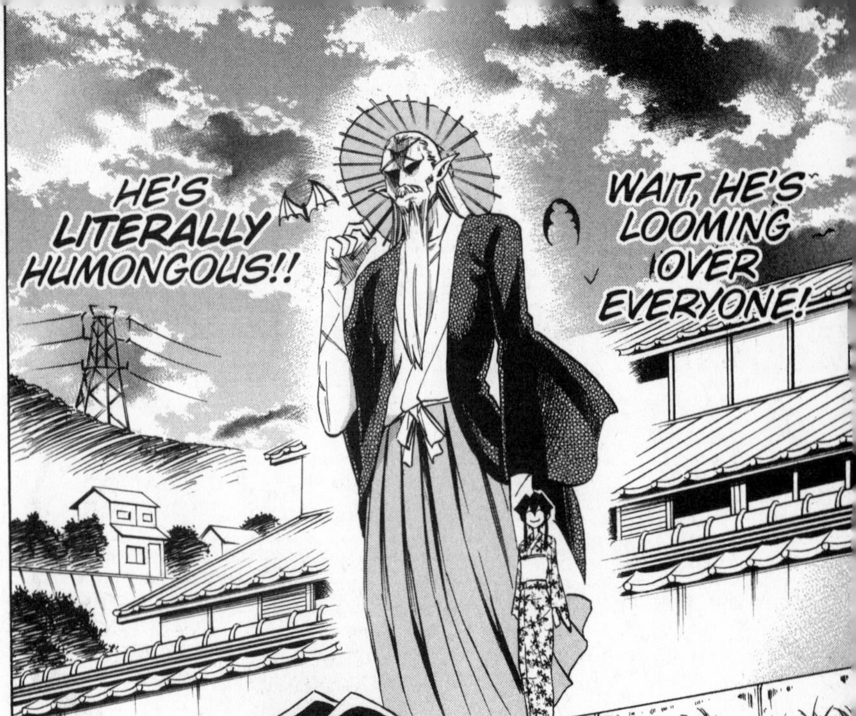
WAIT, HE'S LOOMING OVER EVERYONE!
HE'S LITERALLY HUMONGOUS!!

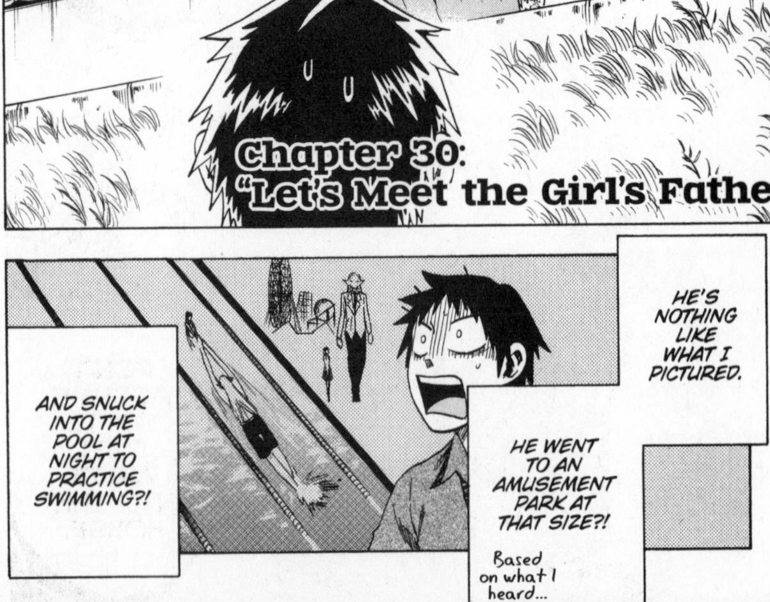
HE'S NOTHING LIKE WHAT I PICTURED.
HE WENT TO AN AMUSEMENT PARK AT THAT SIZE?!
Based on what I heard...
AND SNUCK INTO THE POOL AT NIGHT TO PRACTICE SWIMMING?!

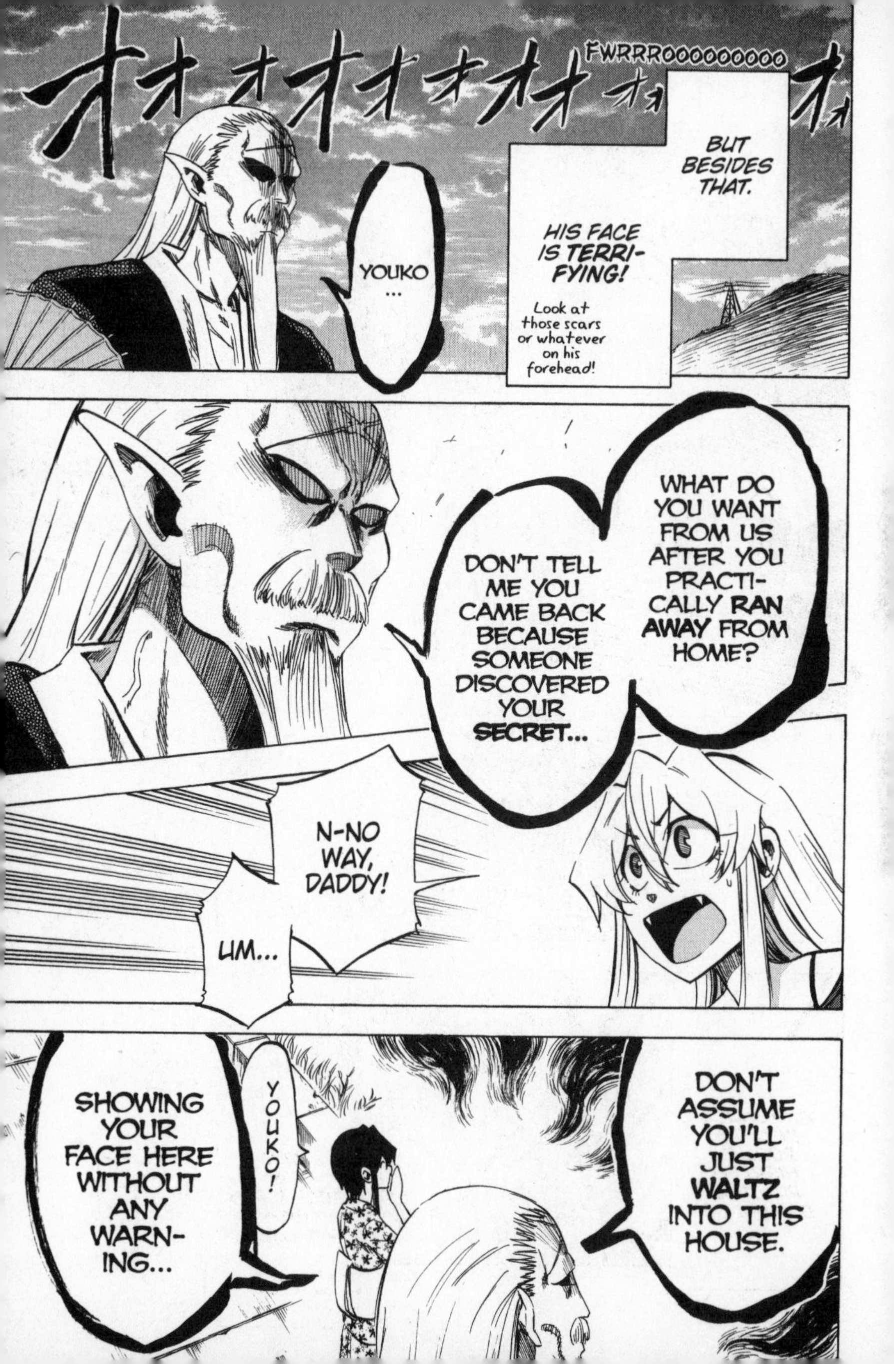
FWRRROOOOOOOOOO
BUT BESIDES THAT.
HIS FACE IS TERRI-FYING!
Look at those scars or whatever on his forehead!
YOUKO ...
WHAT DO YOU WANT FROM US AFTER YOU PRACTI-CALLY RAN AWAY FROM HOME?
DON'T TELL ME YOU CAME BACK BECAUSE SOMEONE DISCOVERED YOUR SECRET...
N-NO WAY, DADDY!
UM...
DON'T ASSUME YOU'LL JUST WALTZ INTO THIS HOUSE.
YOUKO!
SHOWING YOUR FACE HERE WITHOUT ANY WARN-ING...

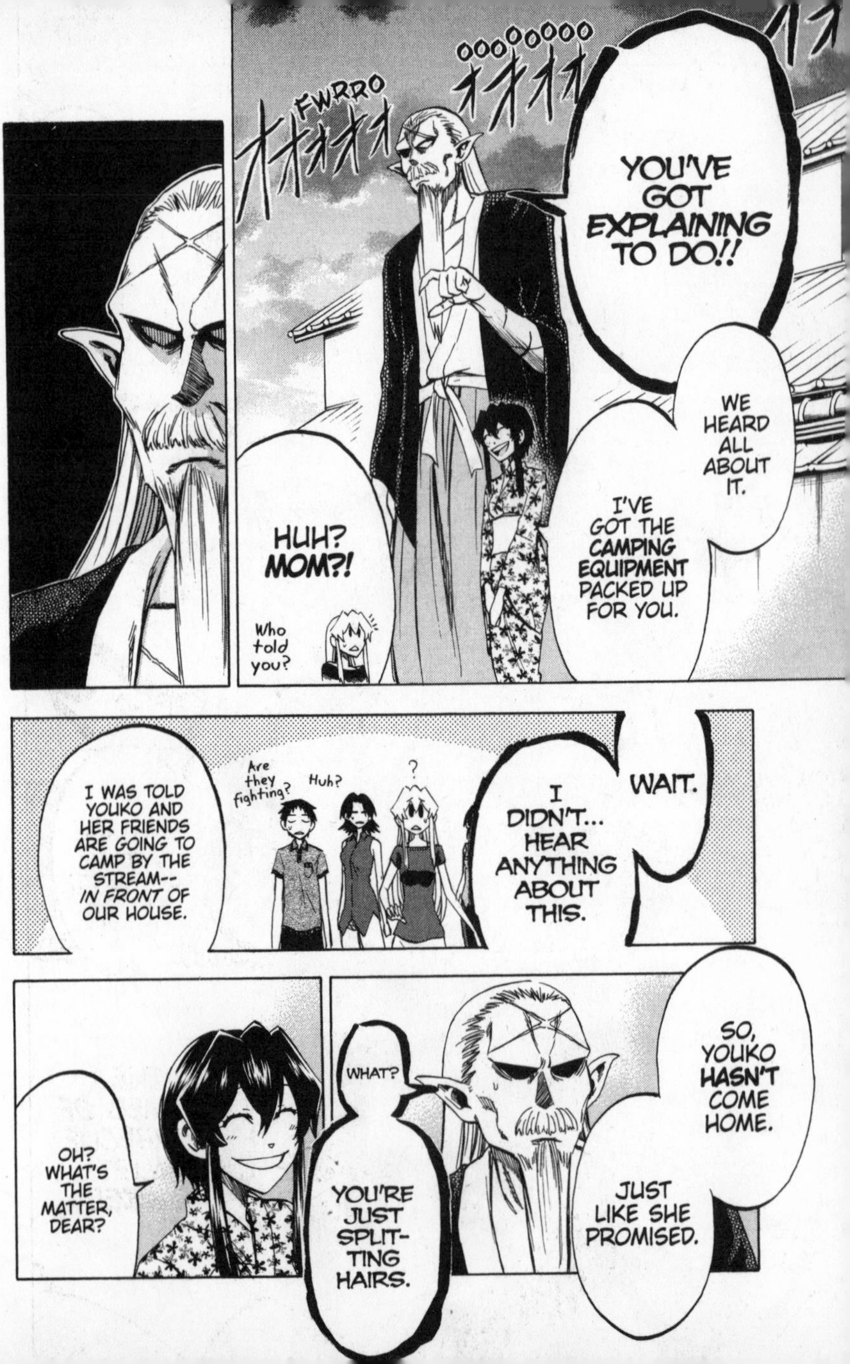
OOOOOOOO
FWRRO
YOU'VE GOT EXPLAINING TO DO!!
WE HEARD ALL ABOUT IT.
I'VE GOT THE CAMPING EQUIPMENT PACKED UP FOR YOU.
HUH? MOM?!
Who told you?
WAIT.
I DIDN'T... HEAR ANYTHING ABOUT THIS.
?
Huh?
Are they fighting?
I WAS TOLD YOUKO AND HER FRIENDS ARE GOING TO CAMP BY THE STREAM-- IN FRONT OF OUR HOUSE.
SO, YOUKO HASN'T COME HOME.
JUST LIKE SHE PROMISED.
WHAT?
YOU'RE JUST SPLIT-TING HAIRS.
OH? WHAT'S THE MATTER, DEAR?

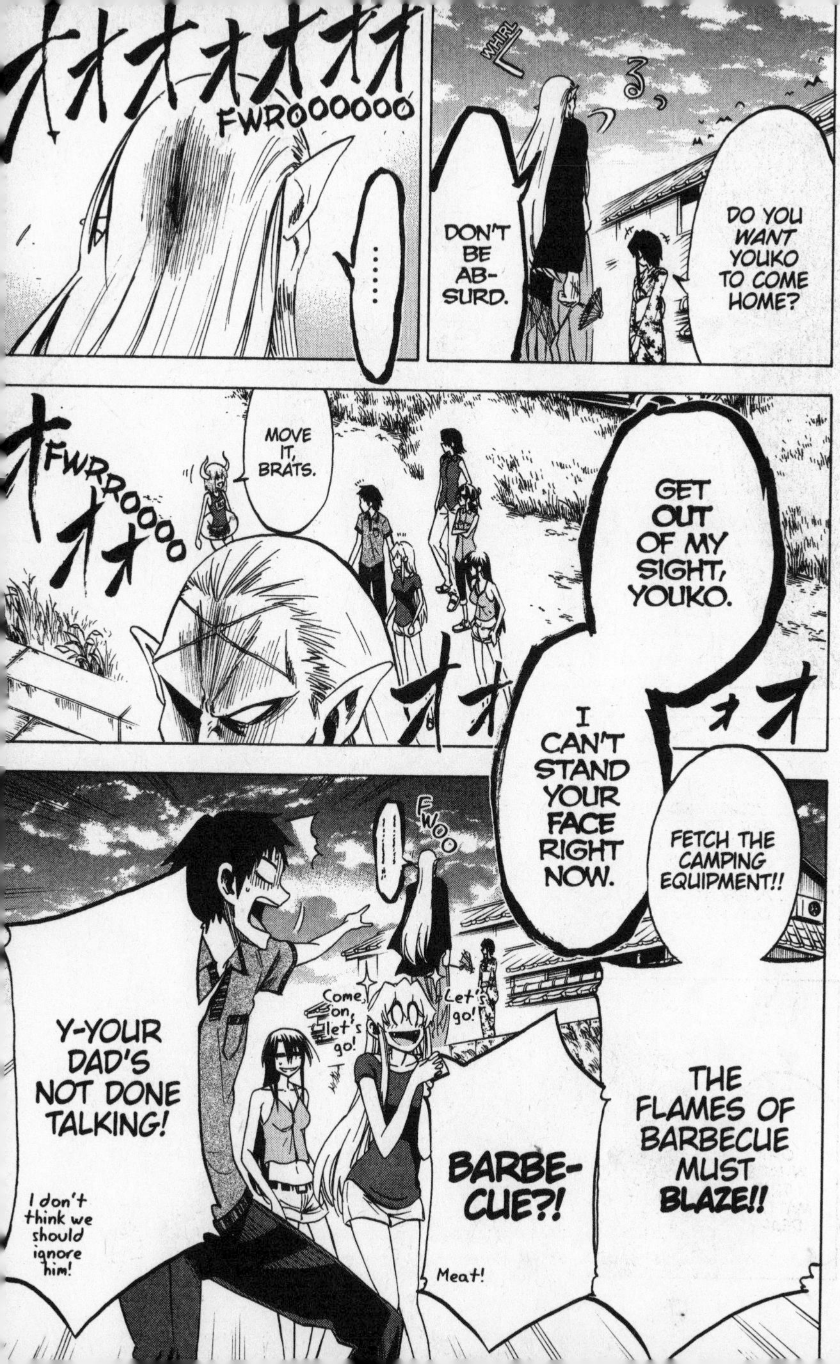
DO YOU WANT YOUKO TO COME HOME?
WHIRL
DON'T BE ABSURD.
FWROOOOOO
......
GET OUT OF MY SIGHT, YOUKO.
FWRRROOOOO
MOVE IT, BRATS.
I CAN'T STAND YOUR FACE RIGHT NOW.
FETCH THE CAMPING EQUIPMENT!!
FWOO
......
Let's go!
Come on, let's go!
THE FLAMES OF BARBECUE MUST BLAZE!!
BARBE-CUE?!
Meat!
Y-YOUR DAD'S NOT DONE TALKING!
I don't think we should ignore him!

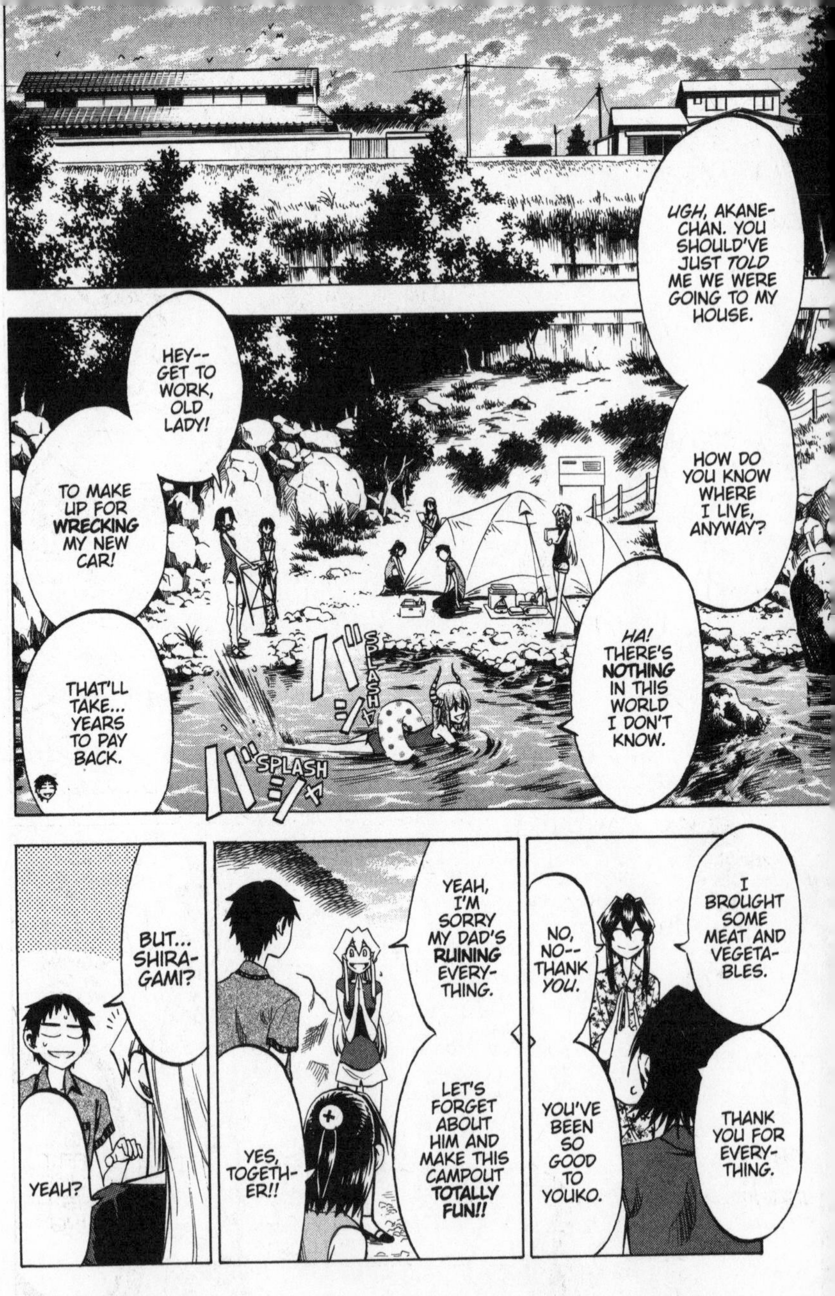
UGH, AKANE-CHAN. YOU SHOULD'VE JUST TOLD ME WE WERE GOING TO MY HOUSE.
HOW DO YOU KNOW WHERE I LIVE, ANYWAY?
HA! THERE'S NOTHING IN THIS WORLD I DON'T KNOW.
HEY-- GET TO WORK, OLD LADY!
TO MAKE UP FOR WRECKING MY NEW CAR!
THAT'LL TAKE... YEARS TO PAY BACK.
SPLASH
SPLASH
I BROUGHT SOME MEAT AND VEGETA-BLES.
NO, NO-- THANK YOU.
THANK YOU FOR EVERY-THING.
YOU'VE BEEN SO GOOD TO YOUKO.
YEAH, I'M SORRY MY DAD'S RUINING EVERY-THING.
LET'S FORGET ABOUT HIM AND MAKE THIS CAMPOUT TOTALLY FUN!!
YES, TOGETH-ER!!
BUT... SHIRA-GAMI?
YEAH?

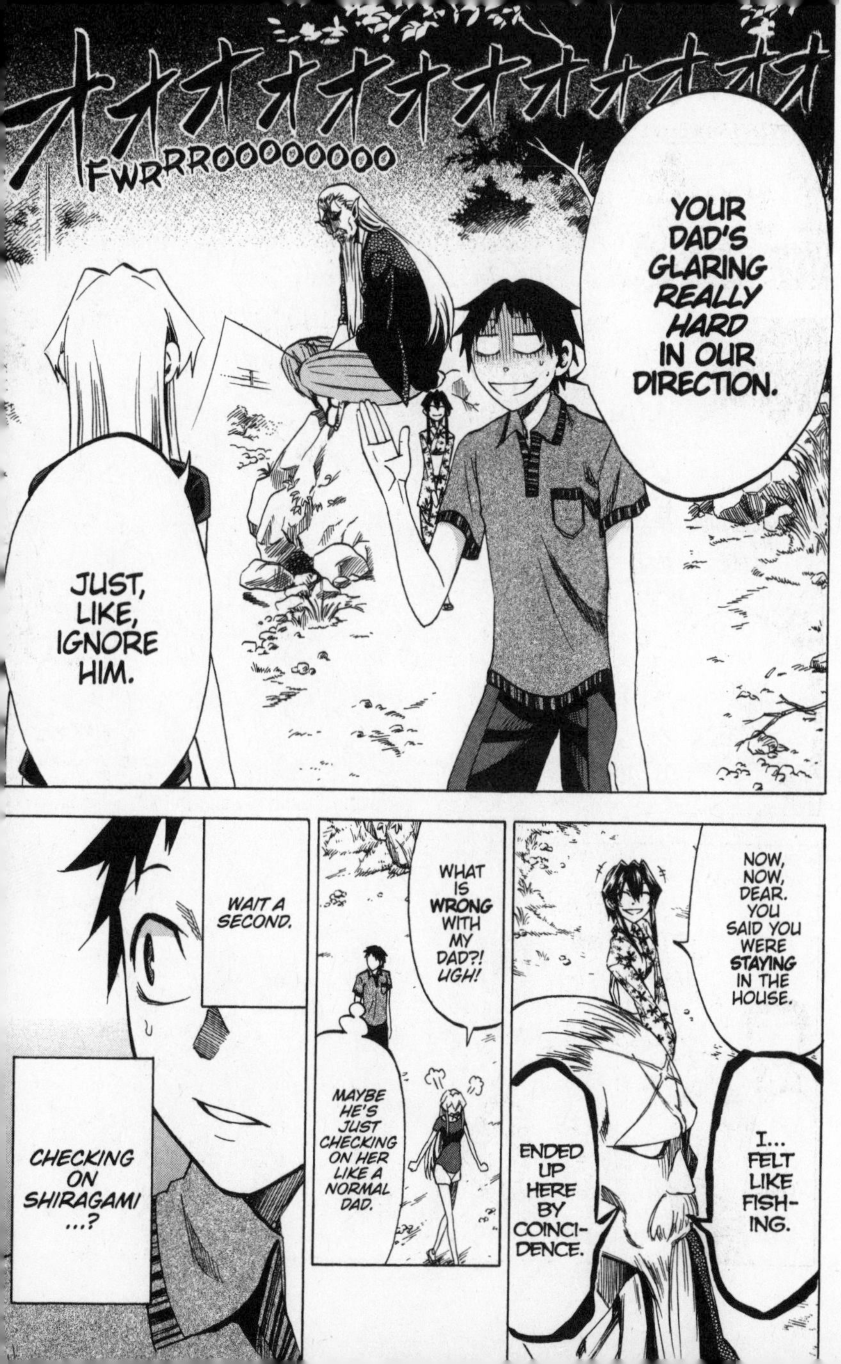
FWRRROOOOOOOO
YOUR DAD'S GLARING REALLY HARD IN OUR DIRECTION.
JUST, LIKE, IGNORE HIM.
NOW, NOW, DEAR. YOU SAID YOU WERE STAYING IN THE HOUSE.
I... FELT LIKE FISHING.
ENDED UP HERE BY COINCIDENCE.
WHAT IS WRONG WITH MY DAD?! UGH!
MAYBE HE'S JUST CHECKING ON HER LIKE A NORMAL DAD.
WAIT A SECOND.
CHECKING ON SHIRAGAMI ...?

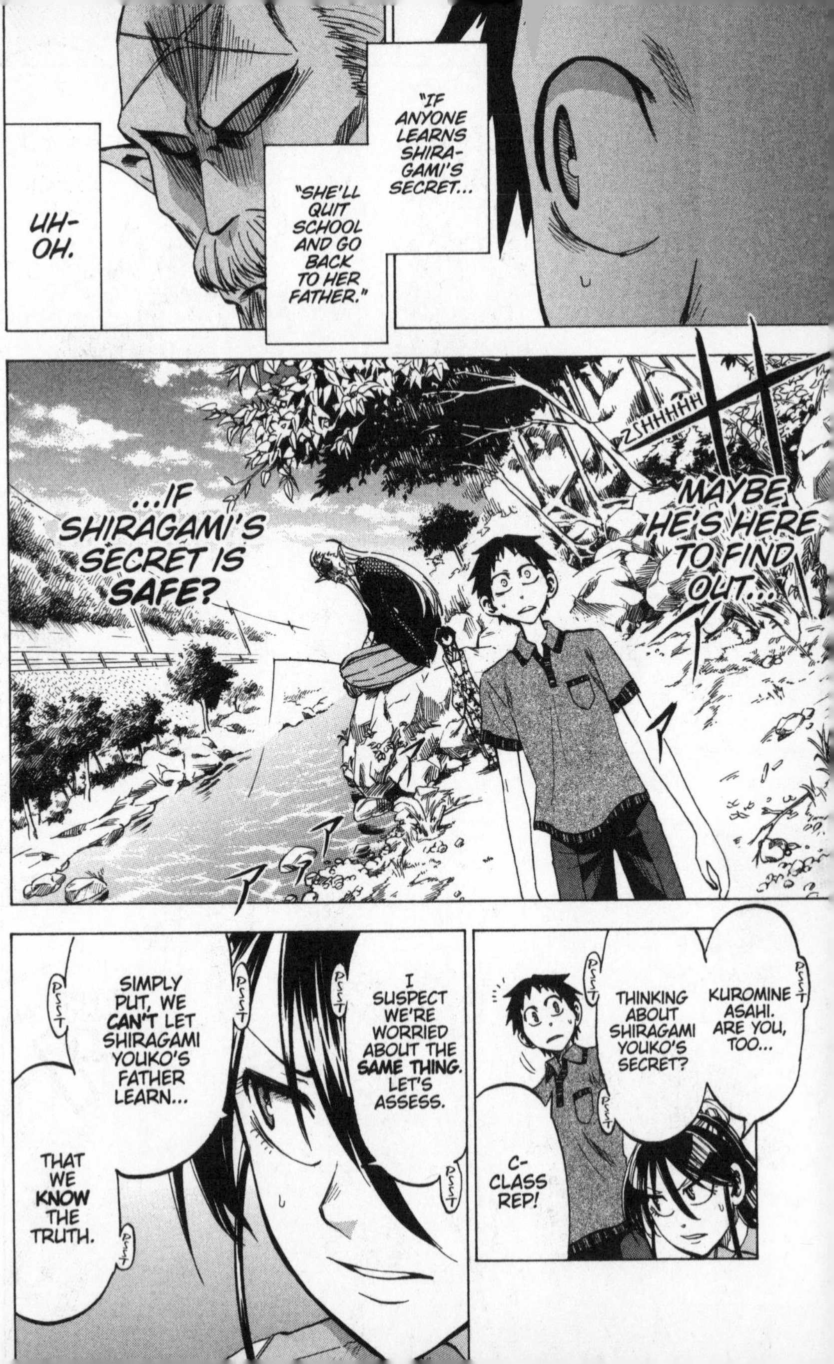
"IF ANYONE LEARNS SHIRA-GAMI'S SECRET...
"SHE'LL QUIT SCHOOL AND GO BACK TO HER FATHER."
UH-OH.
ZSHHHHH
MAYBE HE'S HERE TO FIND OUT...
...IF SHIRAGAMI'S SECRET IS SAFE?
PSST
KUROMINE ASAHI. ARE YOU, TOO...
THINKING ABOUT SHIRAGAMI YOUKO'S SECRET?
C-CLASS REP!
PSST
I SUSPECT WE'RE WORRIED ABOUT THE SAME THING. LET'S ASSESS.
SIMPLY PUT, WE CAN'T LET SHIRAGAMI YOUKO'S FATHER LEARN...
THAT WE KNOW THE TRUTH.

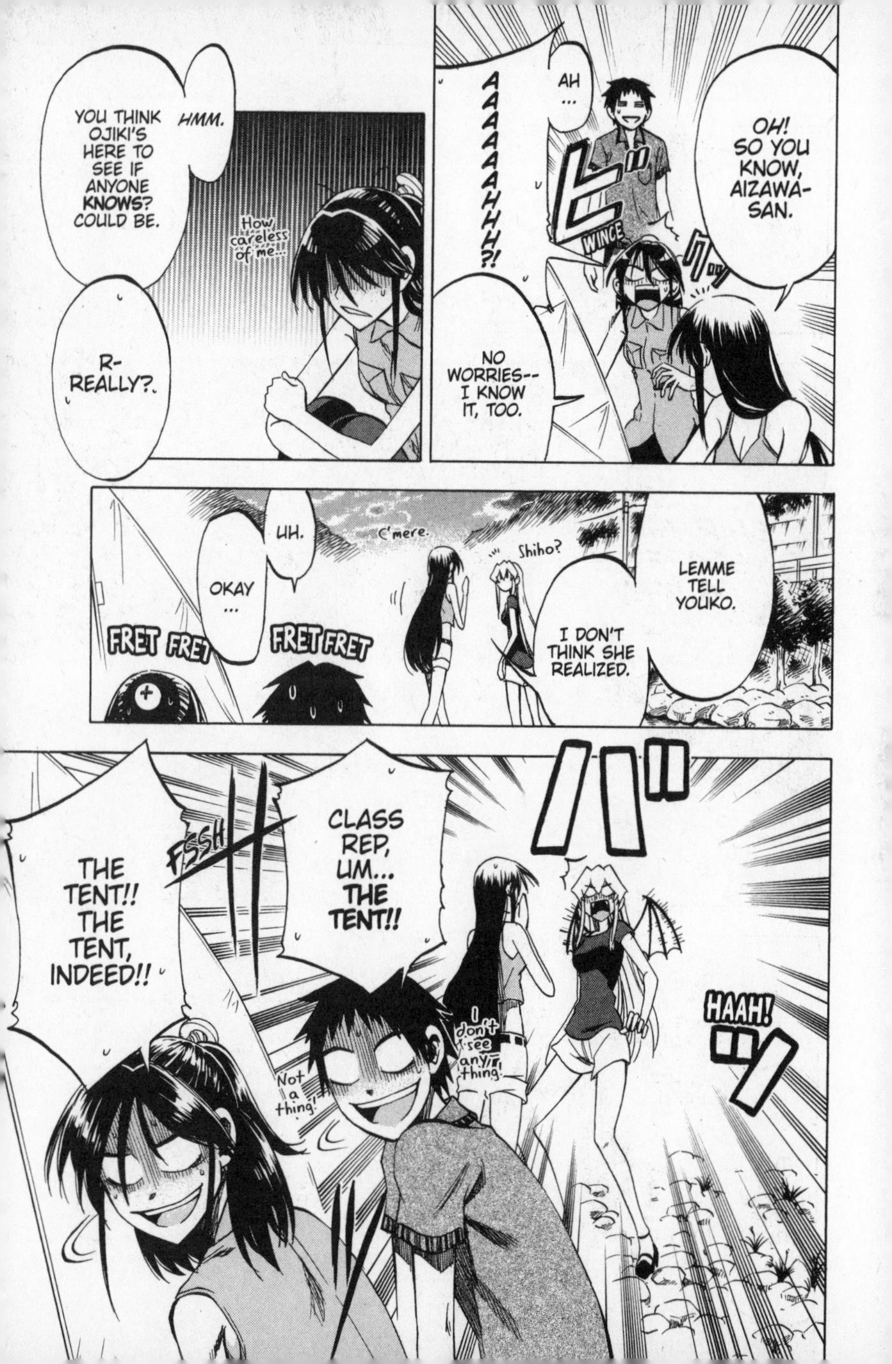
OH! SO YOU KNOW, AIZAWA-SAN.
AH ...
AAAAAAHHH?!
WINCE
NO WORRIES-- I KNOW IT, TOO.
HMM.
YOU THINK OJIKI'S HERE TO SEE IF ANYONE KNOWS? COULD BE.
How careless of me...
R-REALLY?.
LEMME TELL YOUKO.
I DON'T THINK SHE REALIZED.
Shiho?
C'mere.
UH.
OKAY ...
FRET FRET
FRET FRET
HAAH!
CLASS REP, UM... THE TENT!!
FSSH
THE TENT!! THE TENT, INDEED!!
I don't see any thing.
Not a thing!

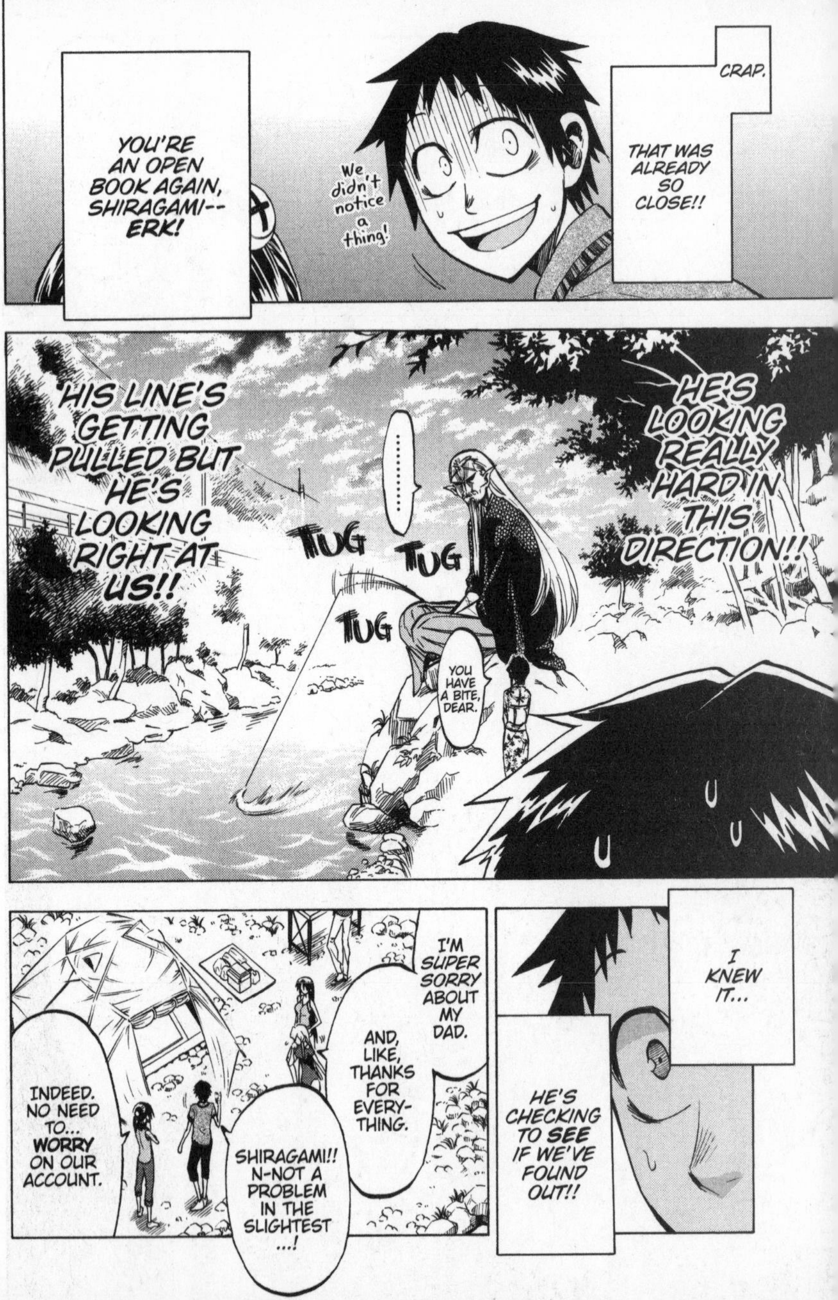
CRAP.
THAT WAS ALREADY SO CLOSE!!
We didn't notice a thing!
YOU'RE AN OPEN BOOK AGAIN, SHIRAGAMI-- ERK!
HE'S LOOKING REALLY HARD IN THIS DIRECTION!!
......
TUG
TUG
TUG
YOU HAVE A BITE, DEAR.
HIS LINE'S GETTING PULLED BUT HE'S LOOKING RIGHT AT US!!
I KNEW IT...
HE'S CHECKING TO SEE IF WE'VE FOUND OUT!!
I'M SUPER SORRY ABOUT MY DAD.
AND, LIKE, THANKS FOR EVERY-THING.
SHIRAGAMI!! N-NOT A PROBLEM IN THE SLIGHTEST ...!
INDEED. NO NEED TO... WORRY ON OUR ACCOUNT.

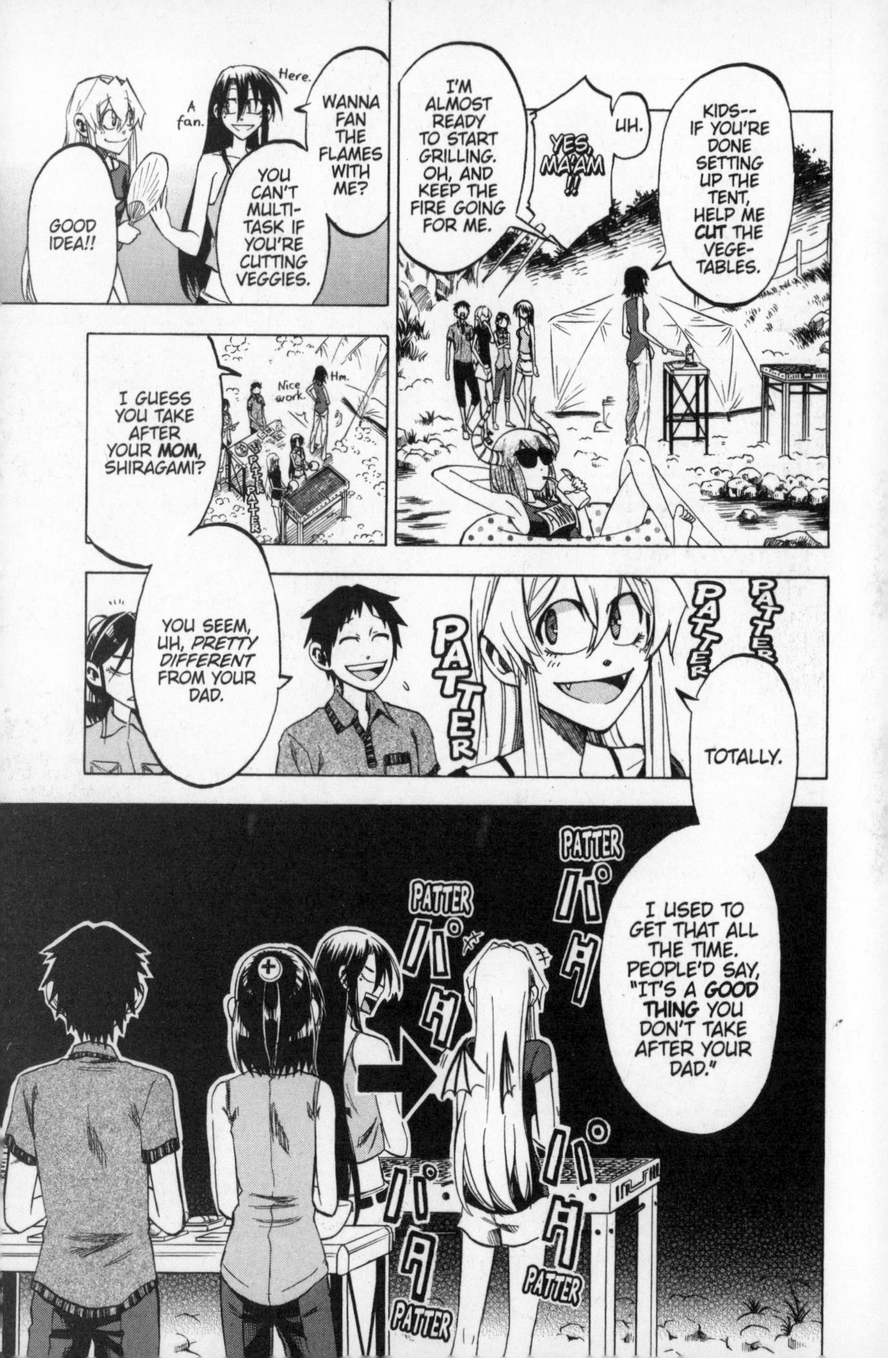
KIDS-- IF YOU'RE DONE SETTING UP THE TENT, HELP ME **CUT** THE VEGE-TABLES.
UH.
YES, MA'AM!!
I'M ALMOST READY TO START GRILLING. OH, AND KEEP THE FIRE GOING FOR ME.
WANNA FAN THE FLAMES WITH ME?
Here.
A fan.
YOU CAN'T MULTI-TASK IF YOU'RE CUTTING VEGGIES.
GOOD IDEA!!
Hm.
Nice work.
PATTER PATTER
I GUESS YOU TAKE AFTER YOUR **MOM**, SHIRAGAMI?
PATTER
PATTER
PATTER
YOU SEEM, UH, *PRETTY* *DIFFERENT* FROM YOUR DAD.
TOTALLY.
I USED TO GET THAT ALL THE TIME. PEOPLE'D SAY, "IT'S A **GOOD THING** YOU DON'T TAKE AFTER YOUR DAD."
PATTER
PATTER
PATTER
PATTER

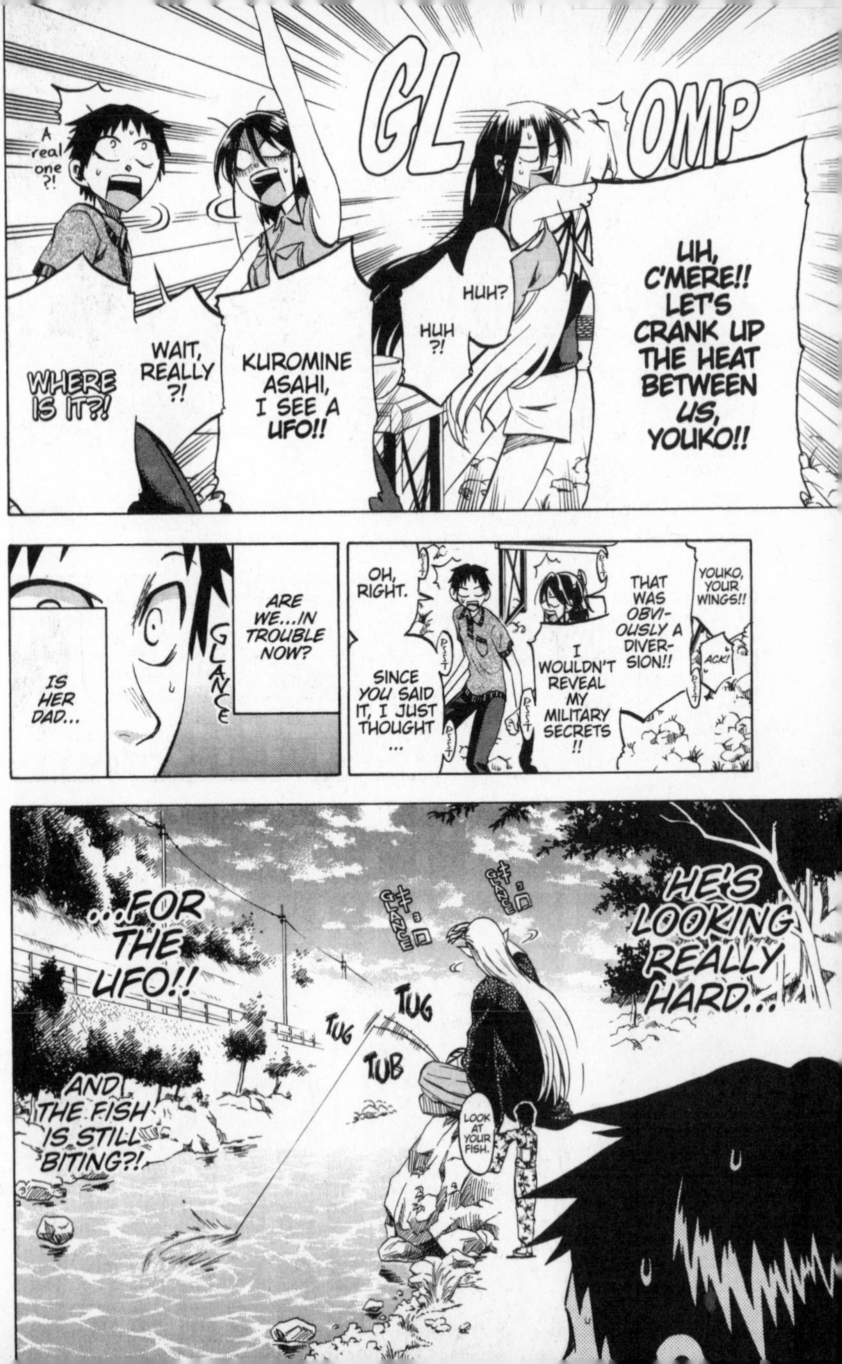
UH, C'MERE!! LET'S CRANK UP THE HEAT BETWEEN US, YOUKO!!
GLOMP
HUH?
HUH ?!
KUROMINE ASAHI, I SEE A UFO!!
WAIT, REALLY ?!
A real one ?!
WHERE IS IT?!
YOUKO, YOUR WINGS!!
ACK!
THAT WAS OBVIOUSLY A DIVERSION!!
I WOULDN'T REVEAL MY MILITARY SECRETS !!
OH, RIGHT.
SINCE YOU SAID IT, I JUST THOUGHT ...
ARE WE...IN TROUBLE NOW?
GLANCE
IS HER DAD...
HE'S LOOKING REALLY HARD...
GLANCE
GLANCE
TUG
TUG
TUB
LOOK AT YOUR FISH.
...FOR THE UFO!!
AND THE FISH IS STILL BITING?!

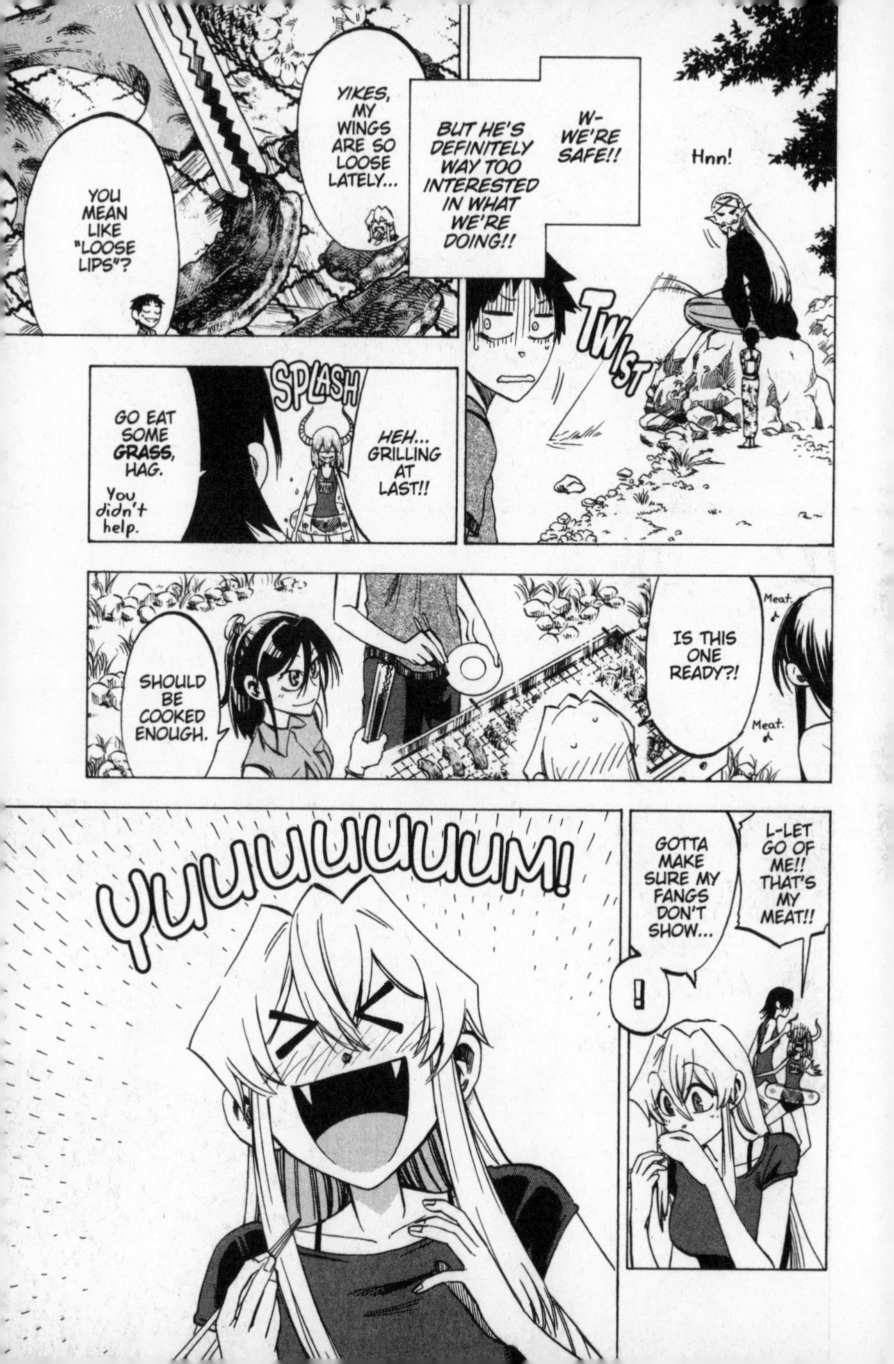
W-WE'RE SAFE!!
BUT HE'S DEFINITELY WAY TOO INTERESTED IN WHAT WE'RE DOING!!
Hnn!
TWIST
YIKES, MY WINGS ARE SO LOOSE LATELY...
YOU MEAN LIKE "LOOSE LIPS"?
HEH... GRILLING AT LAST!!
SPLASH
GO EAT SOME **GRASS**, HAG.
You didn't help.
Meat.
IS THIS ONE READY?!
Meat.
SHOULD BE COOKED ENOUGH.
L-LET GO OF ME!! THAT'S MY MEAT!!
GOTTA MAKE SURE MY FANGS DON'T SHOW...
!
YUUUUUUUM!

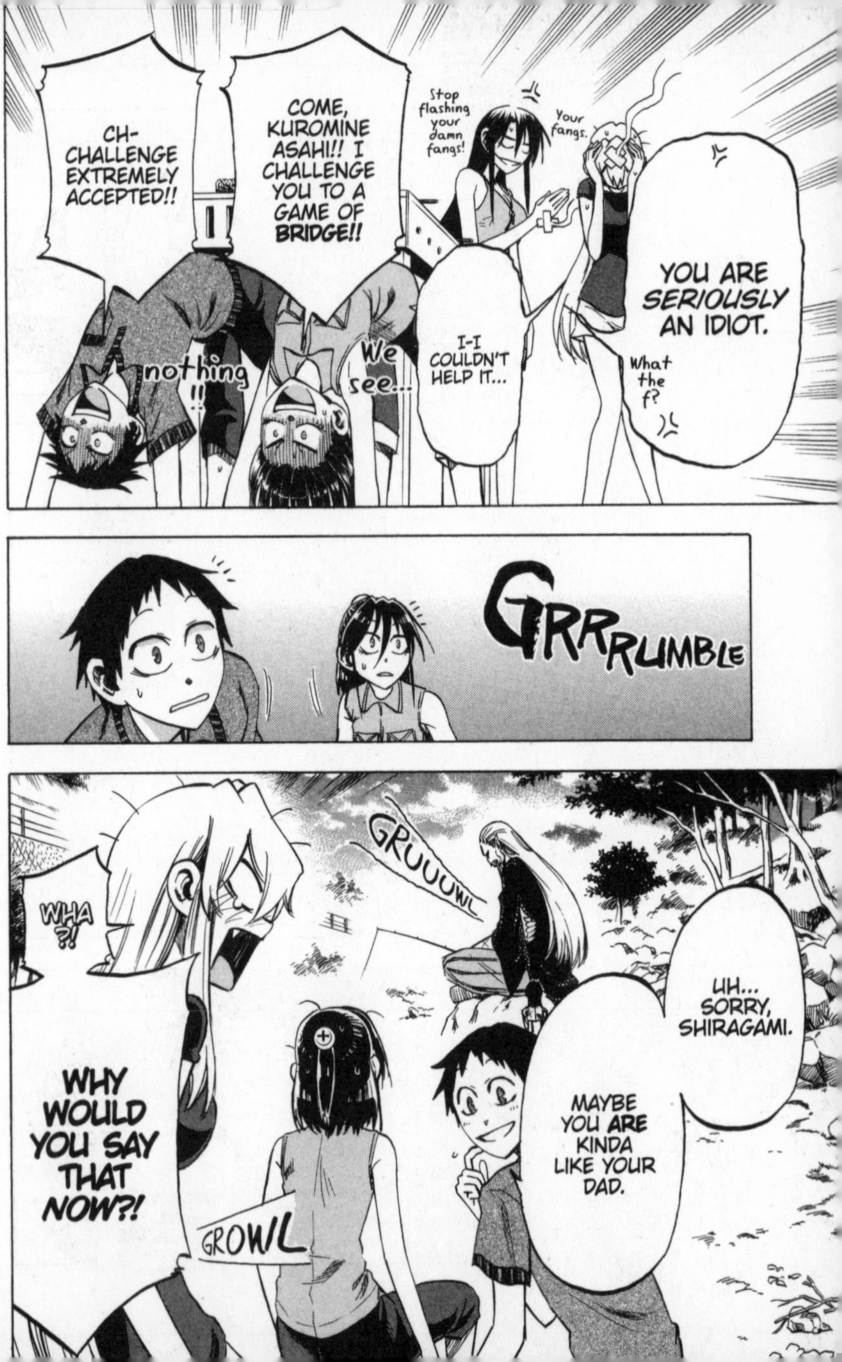
YOU ARE SERIOUSLY AN IDIOT.
Your fangs.
Stop flashing your damn fangs!
What the f?
I-I COULDN'T HELP IT...
COME, KUROMINE ASAHI!! I CHALLENGE YOU TO A GAME OF BRIDGE!!
CH-CHALLENGE EXTREMELY ACCEPTED!!
We see...
nothing!!
GRRRUMBLE
UH... SORRY, SHIRAGAMI.
MAYBE YOU ARE KINDA LIKE YOUR DAD.
GRUUUWL
WHA?!
WHY WOULD YOU SAY THAT NOW?!
GROWL

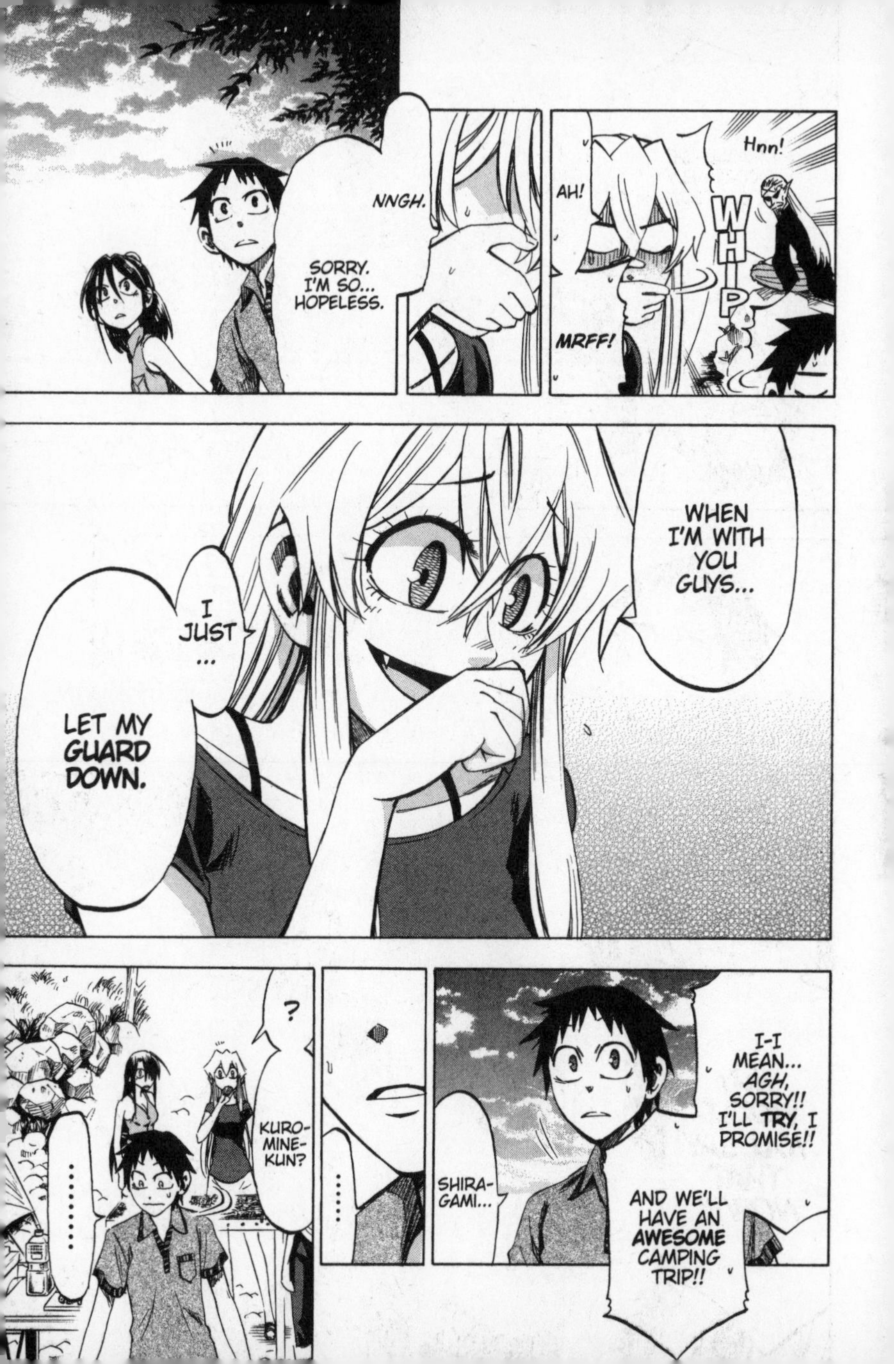
Hnn!
WHIP
AH!
MRFF!
NNGH.
SORRY. I'M SO... HOPELESS.
WHEN I'M WITH YOU GUYS...
I JUST ...
LET MY GUARD DOWN.
I-I MEAN... AGH, SORRY!! I'LL TRY, I PROMISE!!
SHIRA-GAMI...
AND WE'LL HAVE AN AWESOME CAMPING TRIP!!
......
?
KURO-MINE-KUN?
......

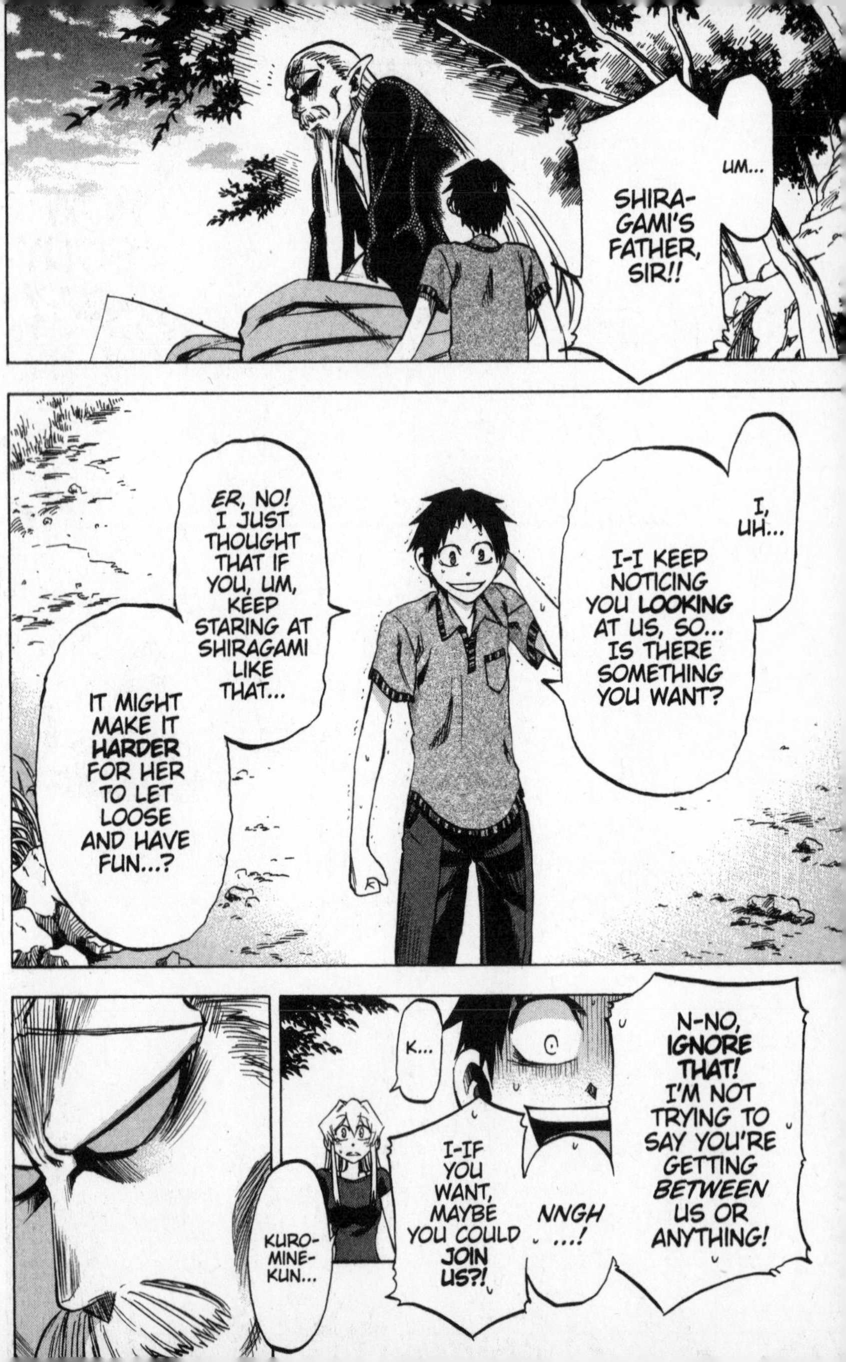
UM...
SHIRA-GAMI'S FATHER, SIR!!
I, UH...
I-I KEEP NOTICING YOU **LOOKING** AT US, SO... IS THERE SOMETHING YOU WANT?
ER, NO! I JUST THOUGHT THAT IF YOU, UM, KEEP STARING AT SHIRAGAMI LIKE THAT...
IT MIGHT MAKE IT **HARDER** FOR HER TO LET LOOSE AND HAVE FUN...?
N-NO, **IGNORE THAT!** I'M NOT TRYING TO SAY YOU'RE GETTING *BETWEEN* US OR ANYTHING!
NNGH ...!
I-IF YOU WANT, MAYBE YOU COULD **JOIN US?!**
K...
KURO-MINE-KUN...

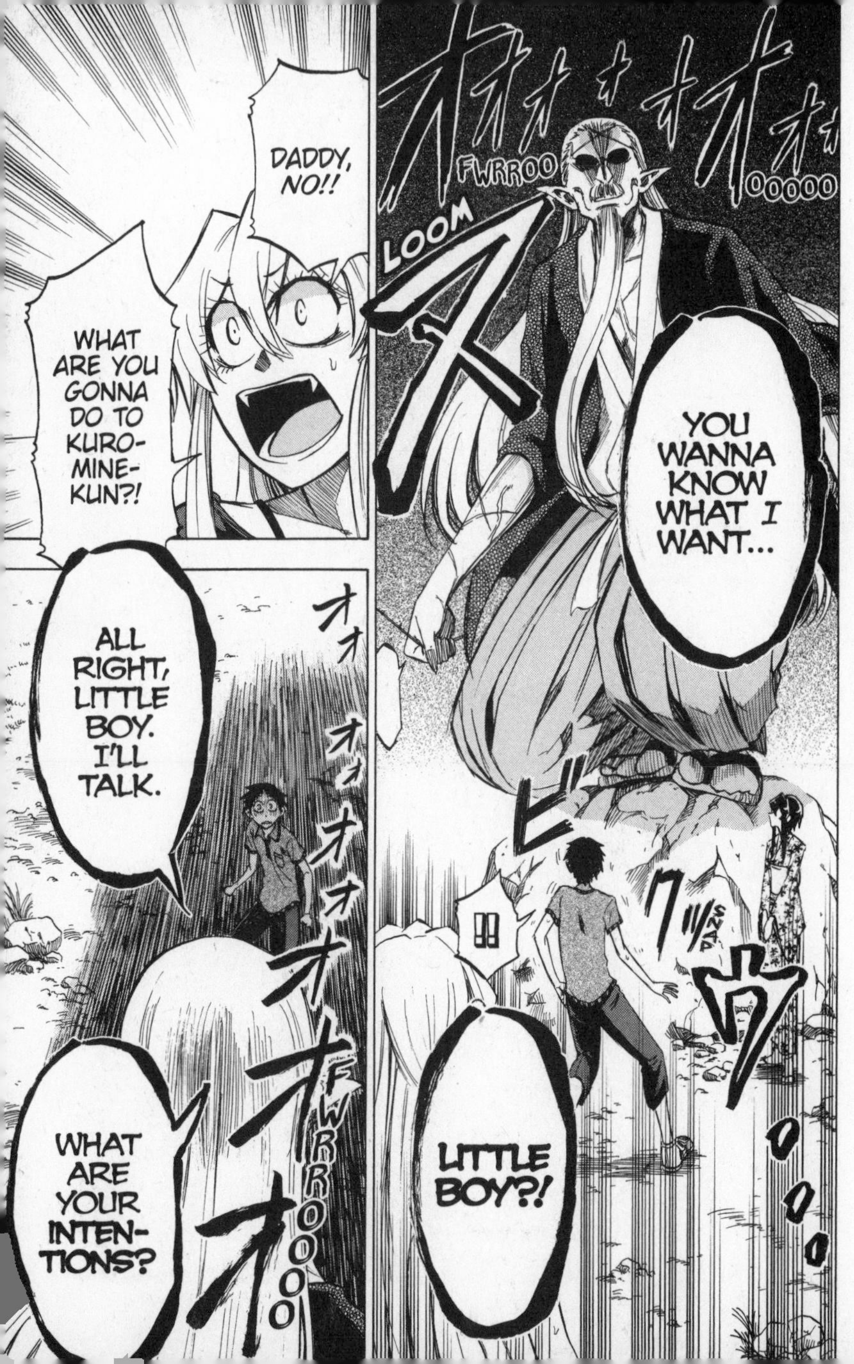
FWRROO
OOOOOO
LOOM
YOU WANNA KNOW WHAT I WANT...
DADDY, NO!!
WHAT ARE YOU GONNA DO TO KURO-MINE-KUN?!
!!
SNAP
LITTLE BOY?!
ALL RIGHT, LITTLE BOY. I'LL TALK.
FWRROOOOO
WHAT ARE YOUR INTEN-TIONS?

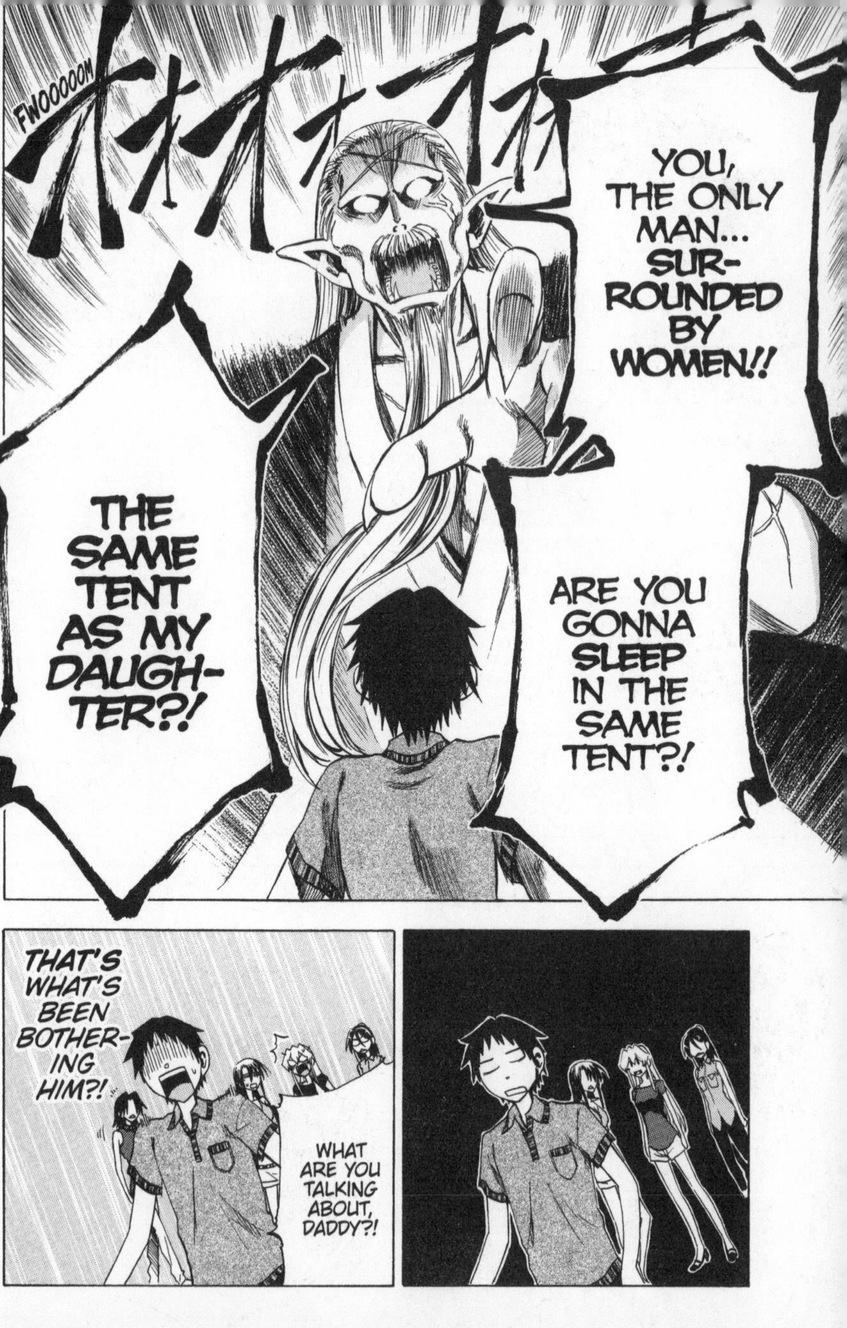
FWOOOOOM
YOU, THE ONLY MAN... SUR-ROUNDED BY WOMEN!!
ARE YOU GONNA SLEEP IN THE SAME TENT?!
THE SAME TENT AS MY DAUGH-TER?!
WHAT ARE YOU TALKING ABOUT, DADDY?!
THAT'S WHAT'S BEEN BOTHER-ING HIM?!

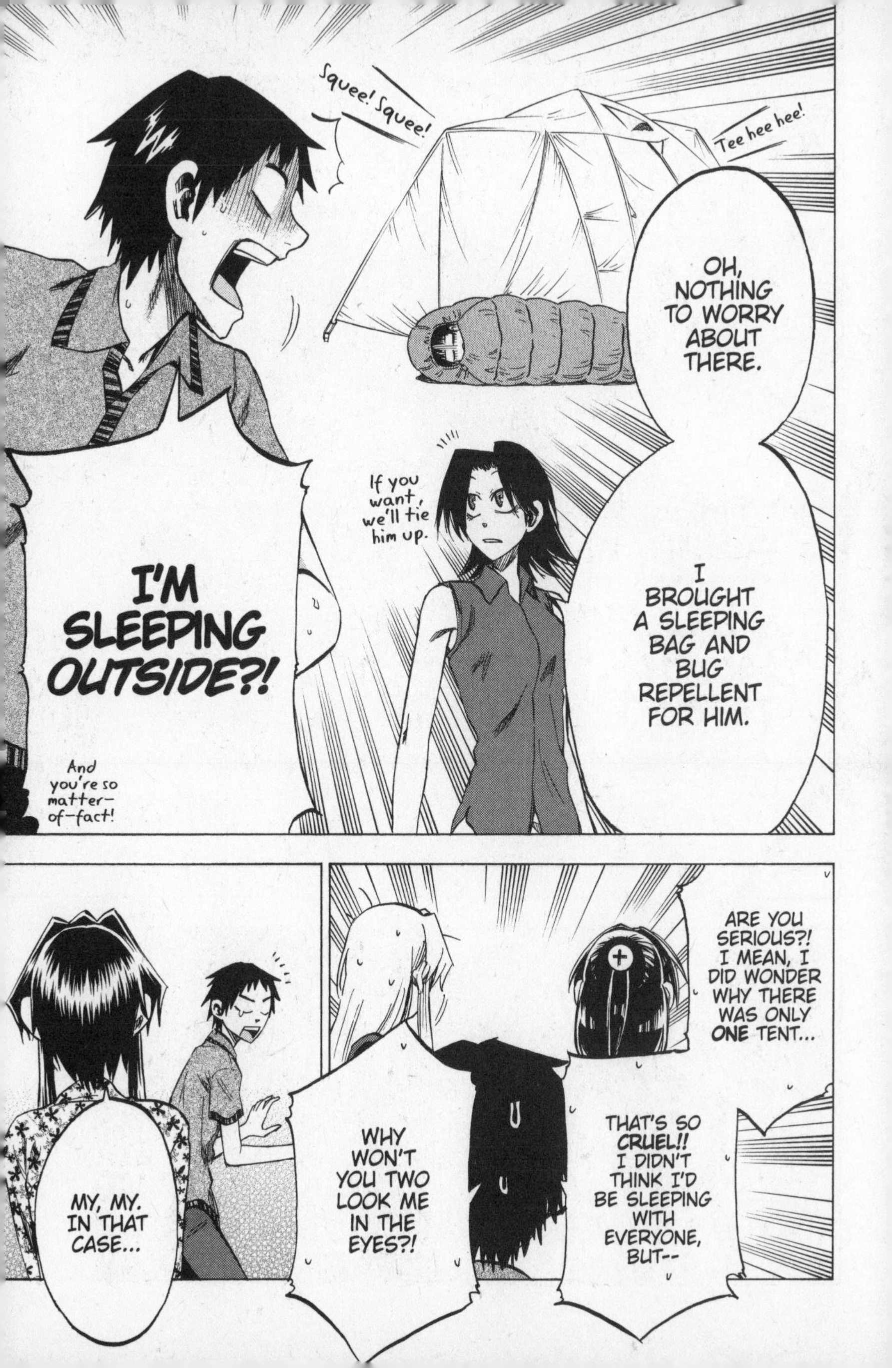
Tee hee hee!
Squee! Squee!
OH, NOTHING TO WORRY ABOUT THERE.
I BROUGHT A SLEEPING BAG AND BUG REPELLENT FOR HIM.
If you want, we'll tie him up.
I'M SLEEPING OUTSIDE?!
And you're so matter-of-fact!
ARE YOU SERIOUS?! I MEAN, I DID WONDER WHY THERE WAS ONLY ONE TENT...
THAT'S SO CRUEL!! I DIDN'T THINK I'D BE SLEEPING WITH EVERYONE, BUT--
WHY WON'T YOU TWO LOOK ME IN THE EYES?!
MY, MY. IN THAT CASE...

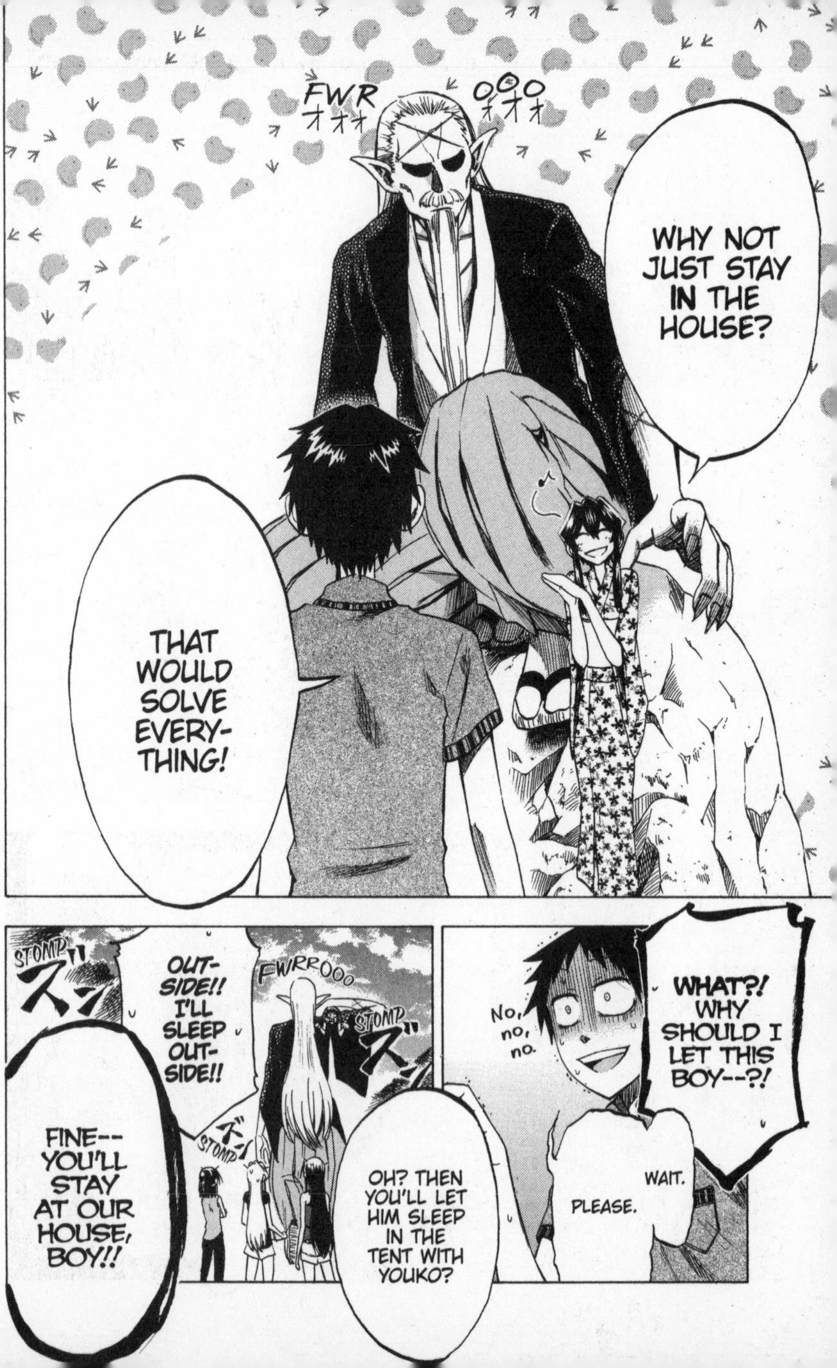
FWR オオオ
OOO オオオ
WHY NOT JUST STAY IN THE HOUSE?
THAT WOULD SOLVE EVERYTHING!
WHAT?! WHY SHOULD I LET THIS BOY--?!
No, no, no.
WAIT.
PLEASE.
OH? THEN YOU'LL LET HIM SLEEP IN THE TENT WITH YOUKO?
OUT-SIDE!! I'LL SLEEP OUT-SIDE!!
FWRROOO
STOMP ズ
STOMP ズ
STOMP スッ
FINE-- YOU'LL STAY AT OUR HOUSE, BOY!!

Chapter 31: "Let's Sleep Over at the Shirogami's!"

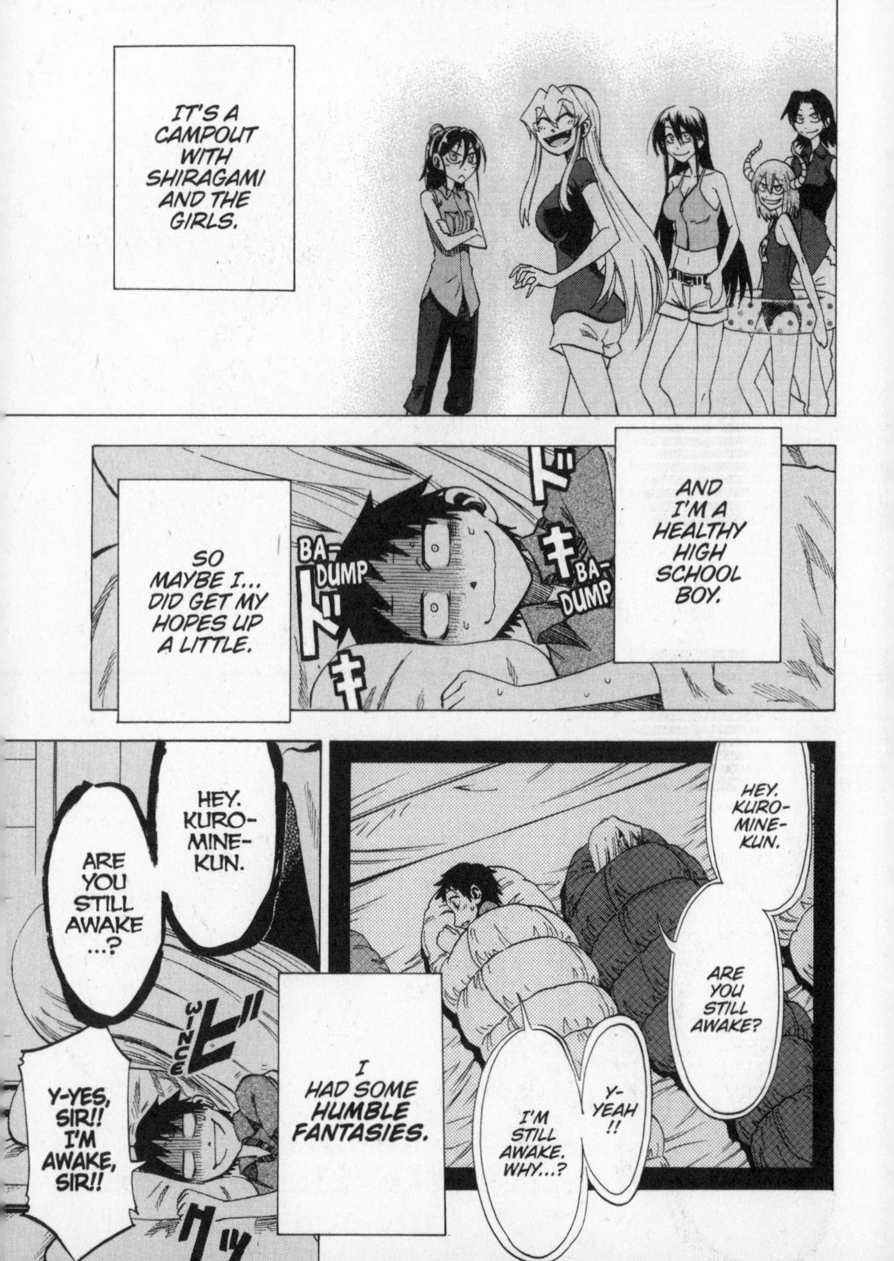
IT'S A CAMPOUT WITH SHIRAGAMI AND THE GIRLS.
AND I'M A HEALTHY HIGH SCHOOL BOY.
BA-DUMP
ドキ
BA-DUMP
ドキ
SO MAYBE I... DID GET MY HOPES UP A LITTLE.
HEY. KURO-MINE-KUN.
ARE YOU STILL AWAKE?
Y-YEAH!!
I'M STILL AWAKE. WHY...?
I HAD SOME HUMBLE FANTASIES.
HEY. KURO-MINE-KUN.
ARE YOU STILL AWAKE...?
WINCE
Y-YES, SIR!! I'M AWAKE, SIR!!

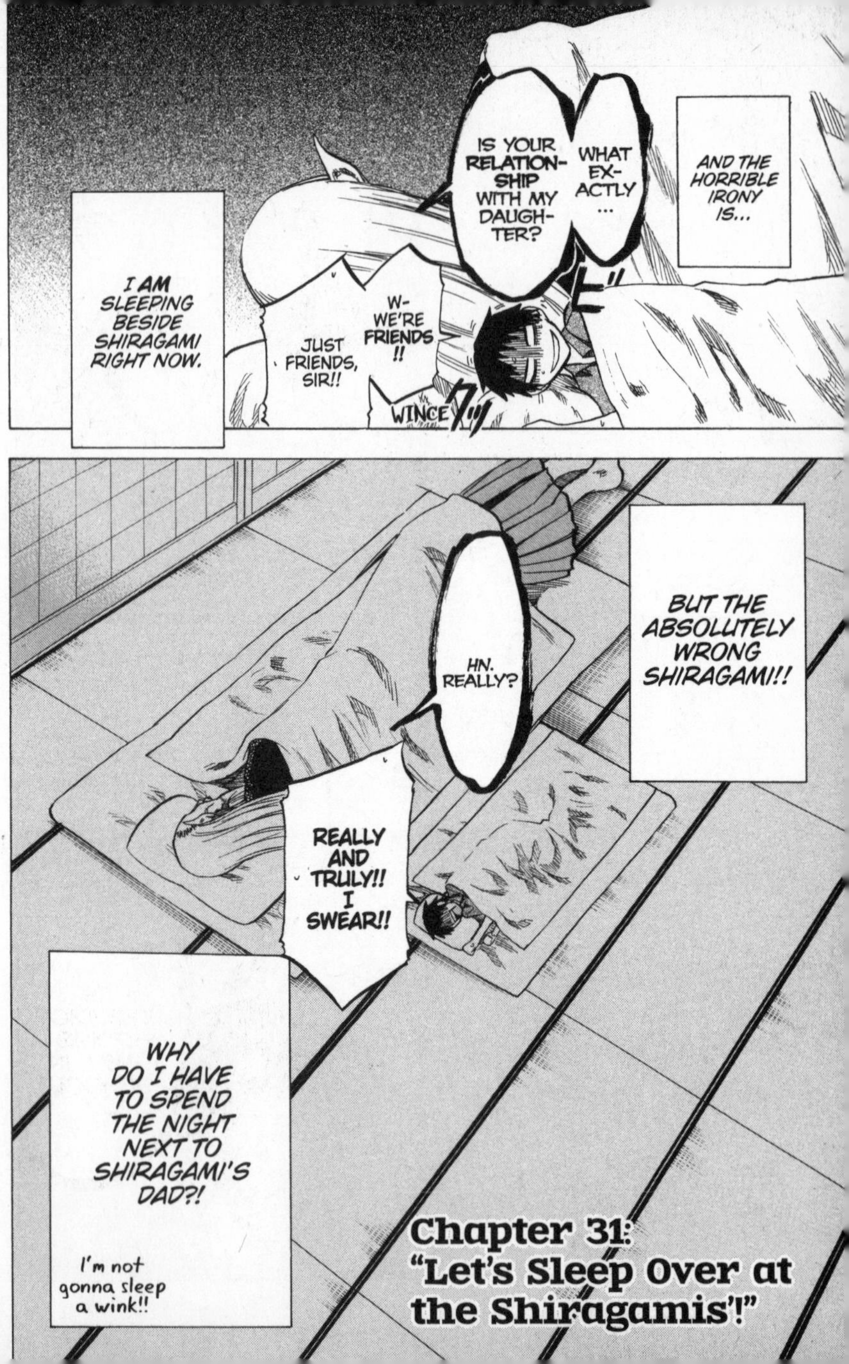
AND THE HORRIBLE IRONY IS...
WHAT EX-ACTLY...
IS YOUR RELATION-SHIP WITH MY DAUGH-TER?
W-WE'RE FRIENDS!!
JUST FRIENDS, SIR!!
WINCE
I AM SLEEPING BESIDE SHIRAGAMI RIGHT NOW.
BUT THE ABSOLUTELY WRONG SHIRAGAMI!!
HN. REALLY?
REALLY AND TRULY!! I SWEAR!!
WHY DO I HAVE TO SPEND THE NIGHT NEXT TO SHIRAGAMI'S DAD?!
I'm not gonna sleep a wink!!
Chapter 31: "Let's Sleep Over at the Shiragamis'!"

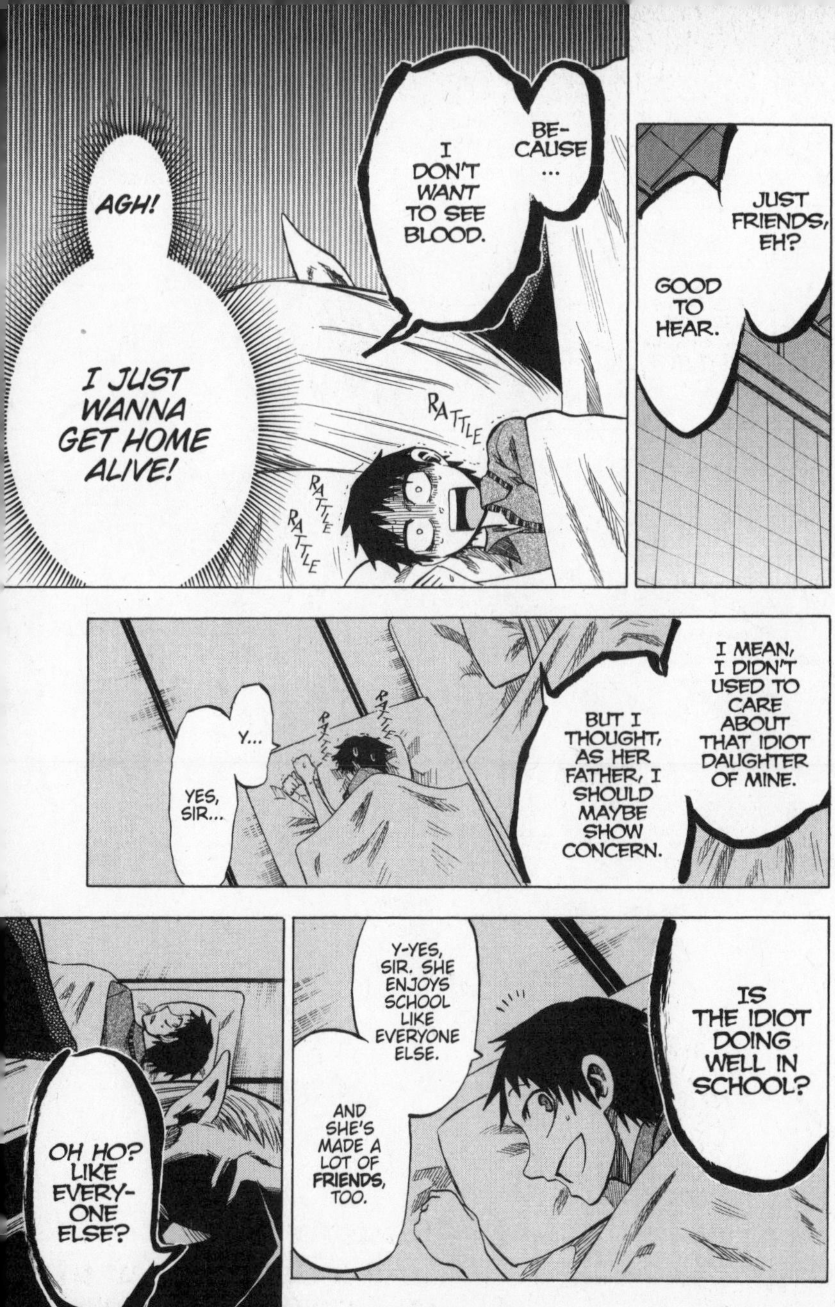
JUST FRIENDS, EH?
GOOD TO HEAR.
BE-CAUSE ...
I DON'T WANT TO SEE BLOOD.
AGH!
I JUST WANNA GET HOME ALIVE!
RATTLE
RATTLE
RATTLE
I MEAN, I DIDN'T USED TO CARE ABOUT THAT IDIOT DAUGHTER OF MINE.
BUT I THOUGHT, AS HER FATHER, I SHOULD MAYBE SHOW CONCERN.
RATTLE
RATTLE
Y...
YES, SIR...
IS THE IDIOT DOING WELL IN SCHOOL?
Y-YES, SIR. SHE ENJOYS SCHOOL LIKE EVERYONE ELSE.
AND SHE'S MADE A LOT OF **FRIENDS**, TOO.
OH HO? LIKE EVERY-ONE ELSE?

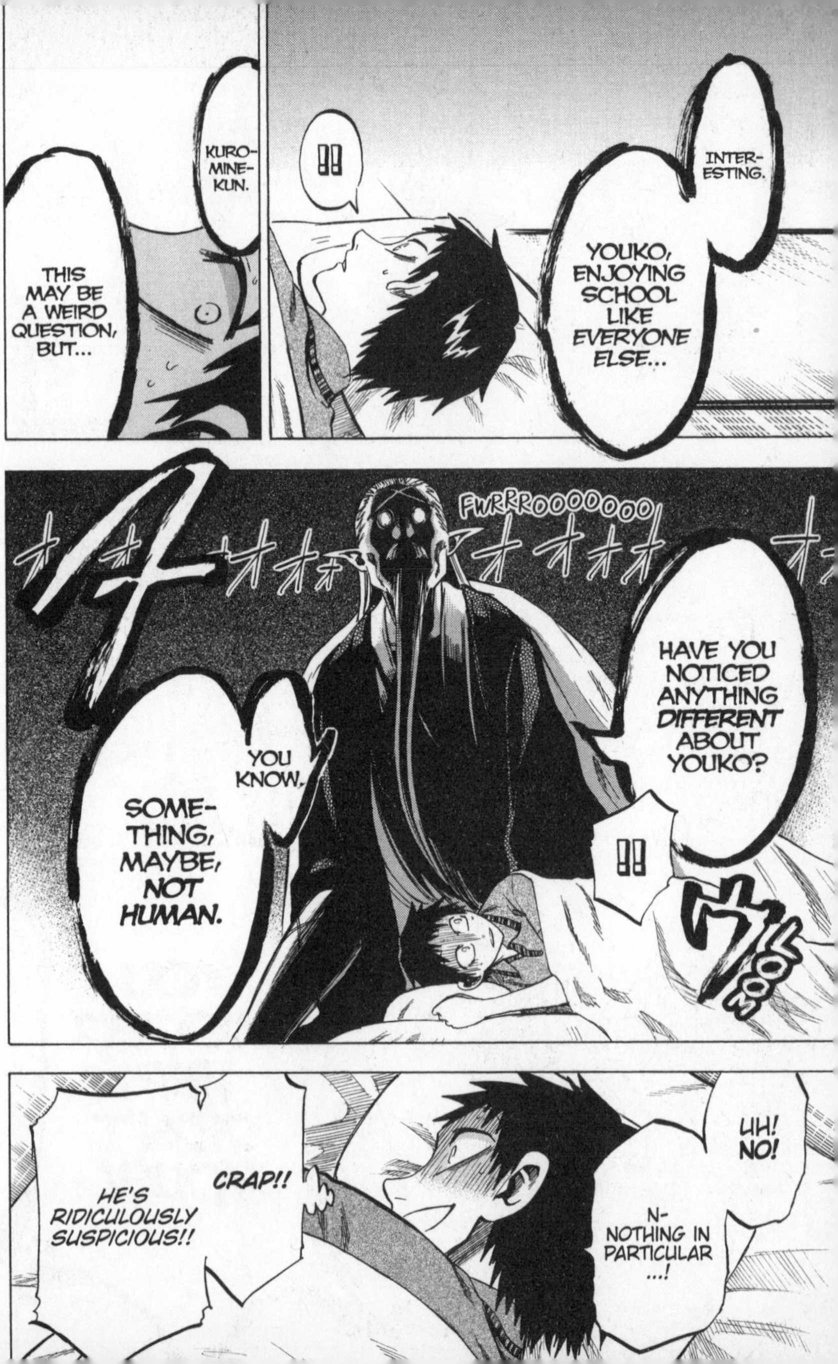
INTER-ESTING.
YOUKO, ENJOYING SCHOOL LIKE EVERYONE ELSE...
!!
KURO-MINE-KUN.
THIS MAY BE A WEIRD QUESTION, BUT...
FWRRROOOOOOOO
HAVE YOU NOTICED ANYTHING DIFFERENT ABOUT YOUKO?
YOU KNOW,
SOME-THING, MAYBE, NOT HUMAN.
!!
UH! NO!
N-NOTHING IN PARTICULAR ...!
CRAP!!
HE'S RIDICULOUSLY SUSPICIOUS!!

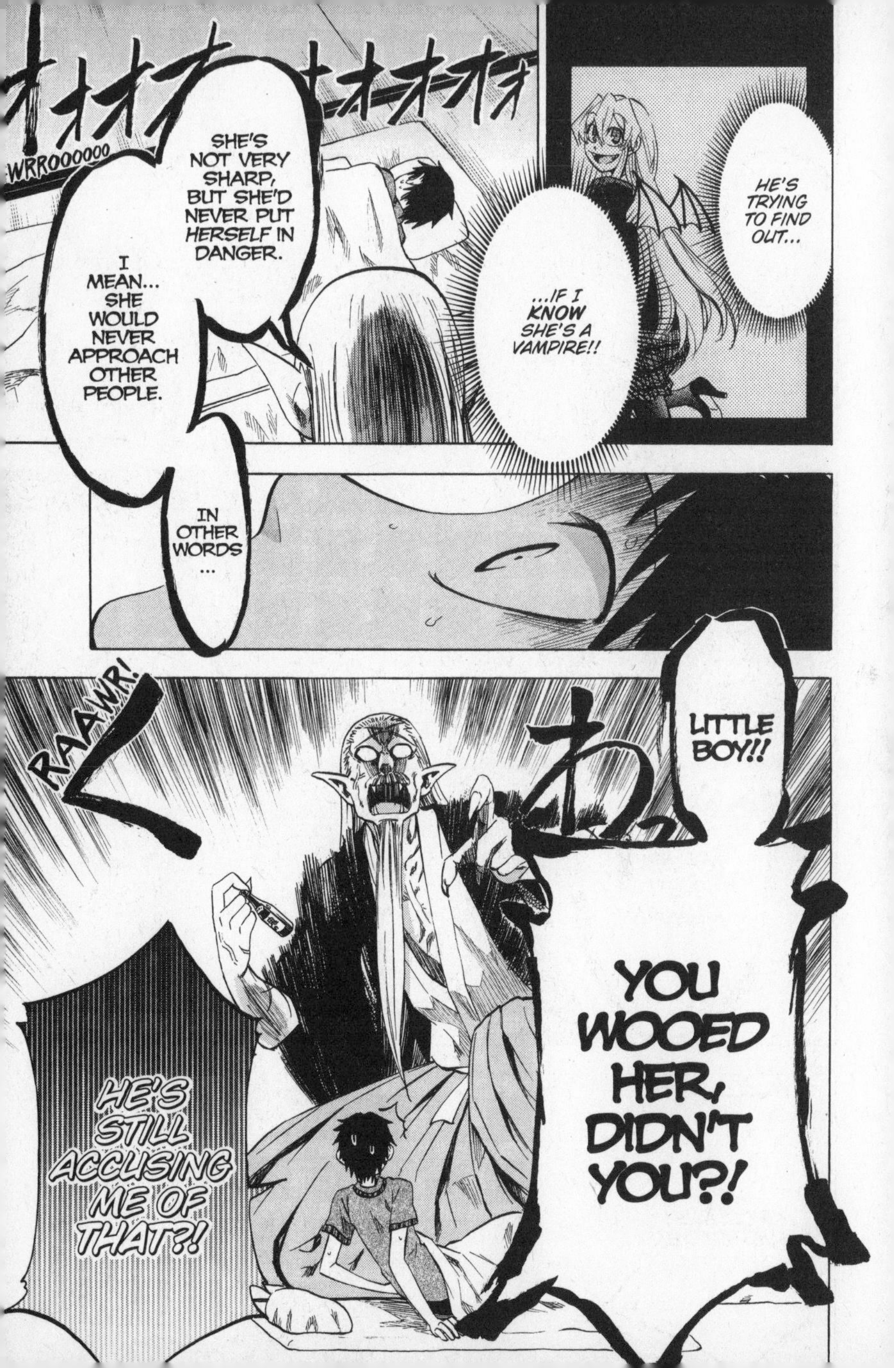
HE'S TRYING TO FIND OUT...
...IF I KNOW SHE'S A VAMPIRE!!
WRROOOOOOO
SHE'S NOT VERY SHARP, BUT SHE'D NEVER PUT HERSELF IN DANGER.
I MEAN... SHE WOULD NEVER APPROACH OTHER PEOPLE.
IN OTHER WORDS ...
LITTLE BOY!!
YOU WOOED HER, DIDN'T YOU?!
RAAAWR!
HE'S STILL ACCUSING ME OF THAT?!

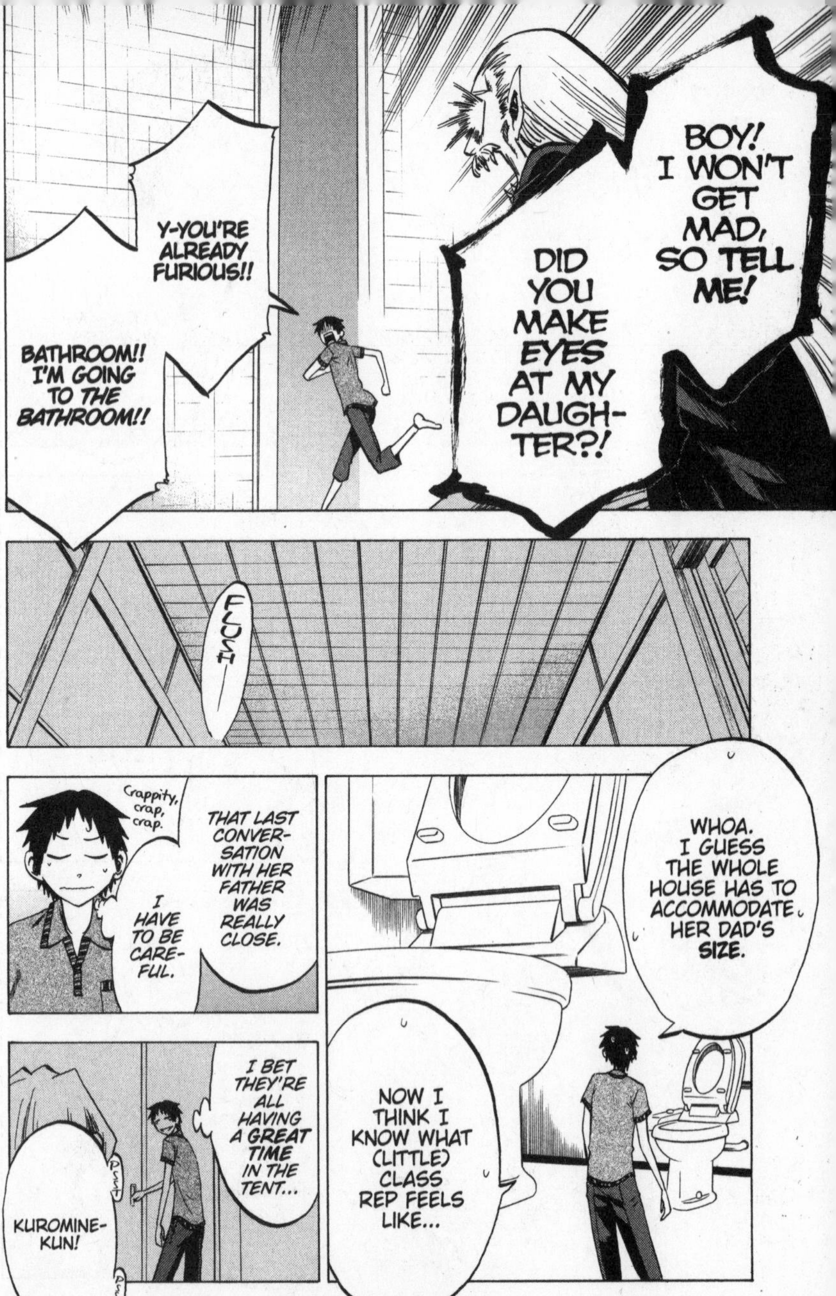
BOY! I WON'T GET MAD, SO TELL ME!
DID YOU MAKE EYES AT MY DAUGHTER?!
Y-YOU'RE ALREADY FURIOUS!!
BATHROOM!! I'M GOING TO THE BATHROOM!!
FLUSH
WHOA. I GUESS THE WHOLE HOUSE HAS TO ACCOMMODATE HER DAD'S SIZE.
NOW I THINK I KNOW WHAT (LITTLE) CLASS REP FEELS LIKE...
THAT LAST CONVERSATION WITH HER FATHER WAS REALLY CLOSE.
I HAVE TO BE CAREFUL.
Crappity, crap, crap.
I BET THEY'RE ALL HAVING A GREAT TIME IN THE TENT...
PSST
KUROMINE-KUN!
PSST

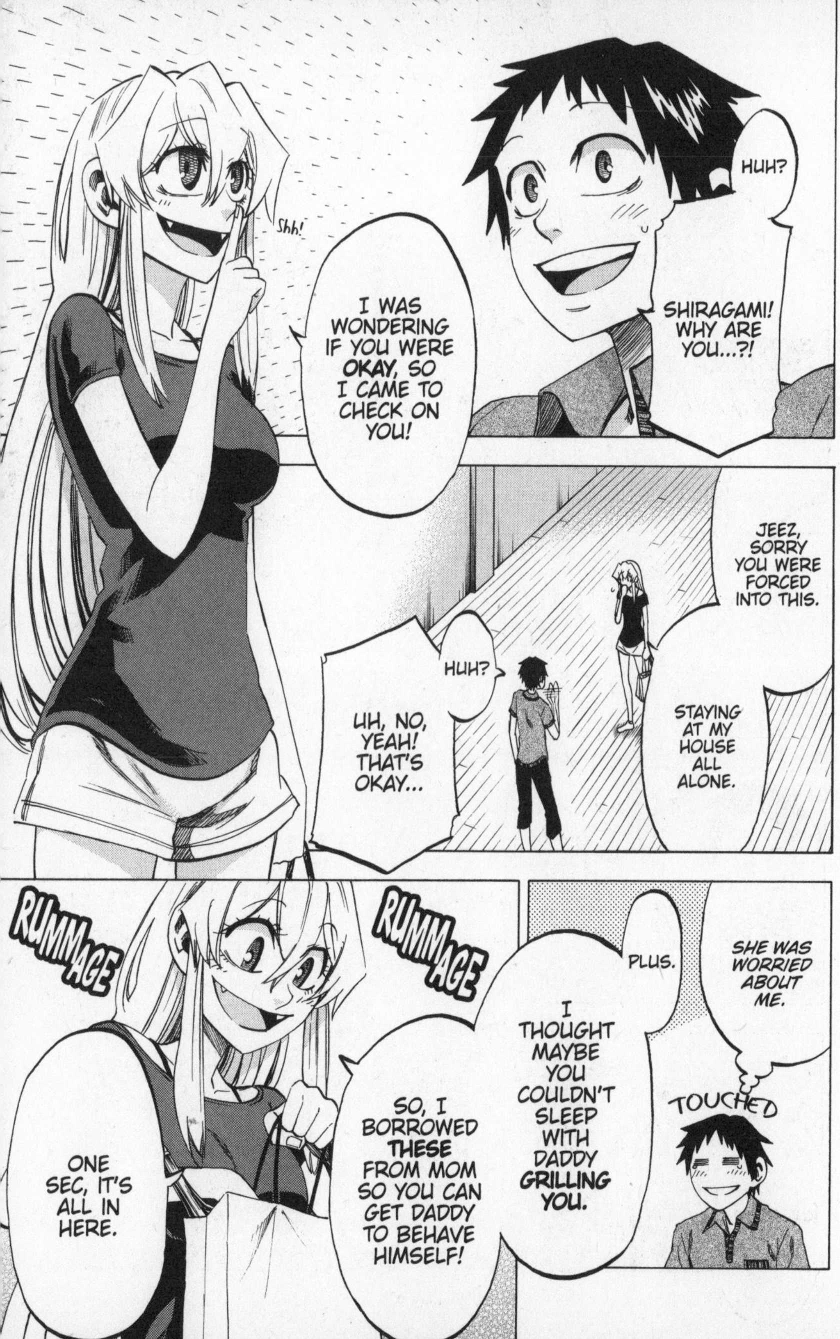
HUH?
SHIRAGAMI! WHY ARE YOU...?!
Shh!
I WAS WONDERING IF YOU WERE **OKAY**, SO I CAME TO CHECK ON YOU!
JEEZ, SORRY YOU WERE FORCED INTO THIS.
STAYING AT MY HOUSE ALL ALONE.
HUH?
UH, NO, YEAH! THAT'S OKAY...
PLUS.
I THOUGHT MAYBE YOU COULDN'T SLEEP WITH DADDY **GRILLING YOU.**
SHE WAS WORRIED ABOUT ME.
TOUCHED
RUMMAGE
RUMMAGE
SO, I BORROWED **THESE** FROM MOM SO YOU CAN GET DADDY TO BEHAVE HIMSELF!
ONE SEC, IT'S ALL IN HERE.

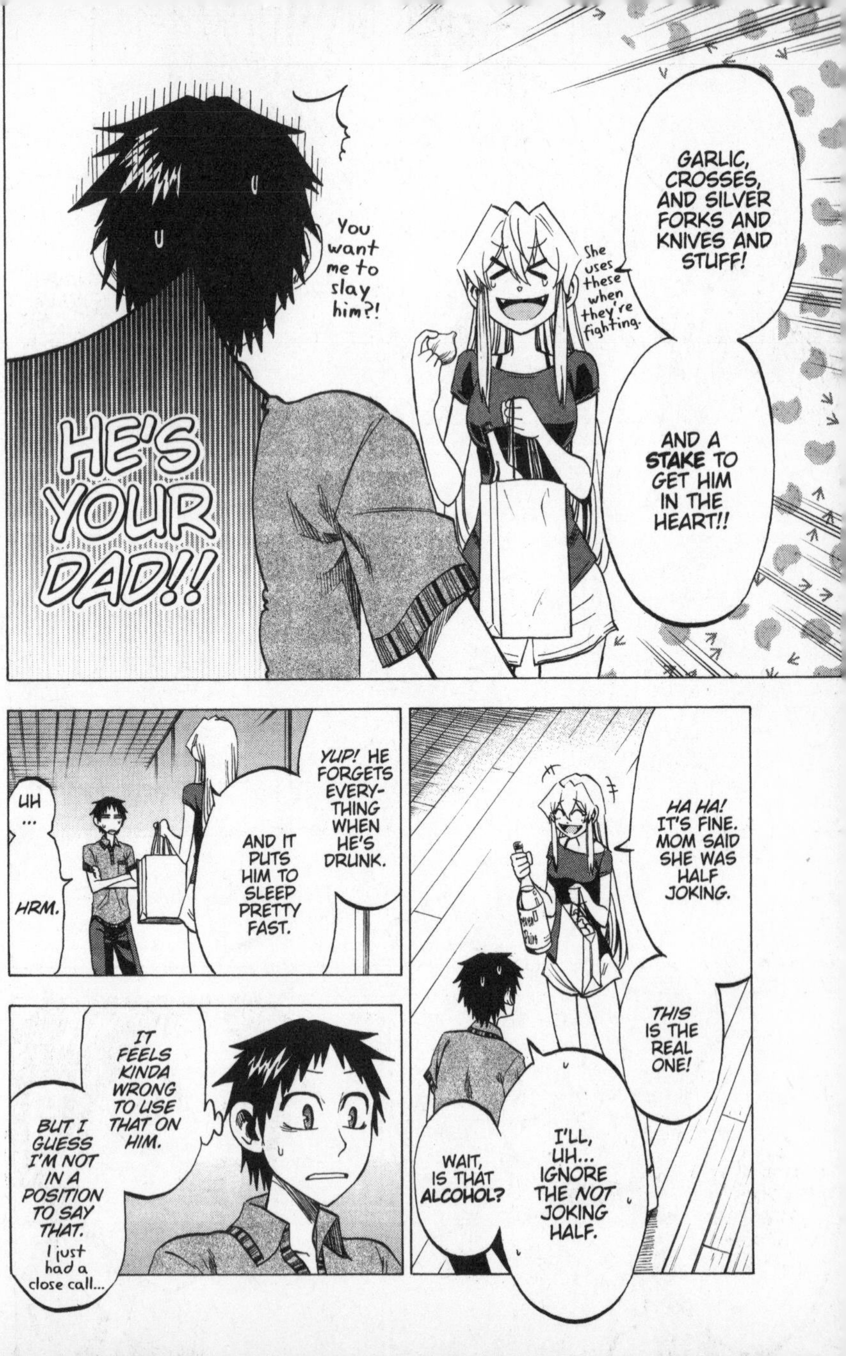
GARLIC, CROSSES, AND SILVER FORKS AND KNIVES AND STUFF!
AND A STAKE TO GET HIM IN THE HEART!!
She uses these when they're fighting.
You want me to slay him?!
HE'S YOUR DAD!!
HA HA! IT'S FINE. MOM SAID SHE WAS HALF JOKING.
THIS IS THE REAL ONE!
I'LL, UH... IGNORE THE NOT JOKING HALF.
WAIT, IS THAT ALCOHOL?
YUP! HE FORGETS EVERYTHING WHEN HE'S DRUNK.
AND IT PUTS HIM TO SLEEP PRETTY FAST.
UH ...
HRM.
IT FEELS KINDA WRONG TO USE THAT ON HIM.
BUT I GUESS I'M NOT IN A POSITION TO SAY THAT.
I just had a close call...

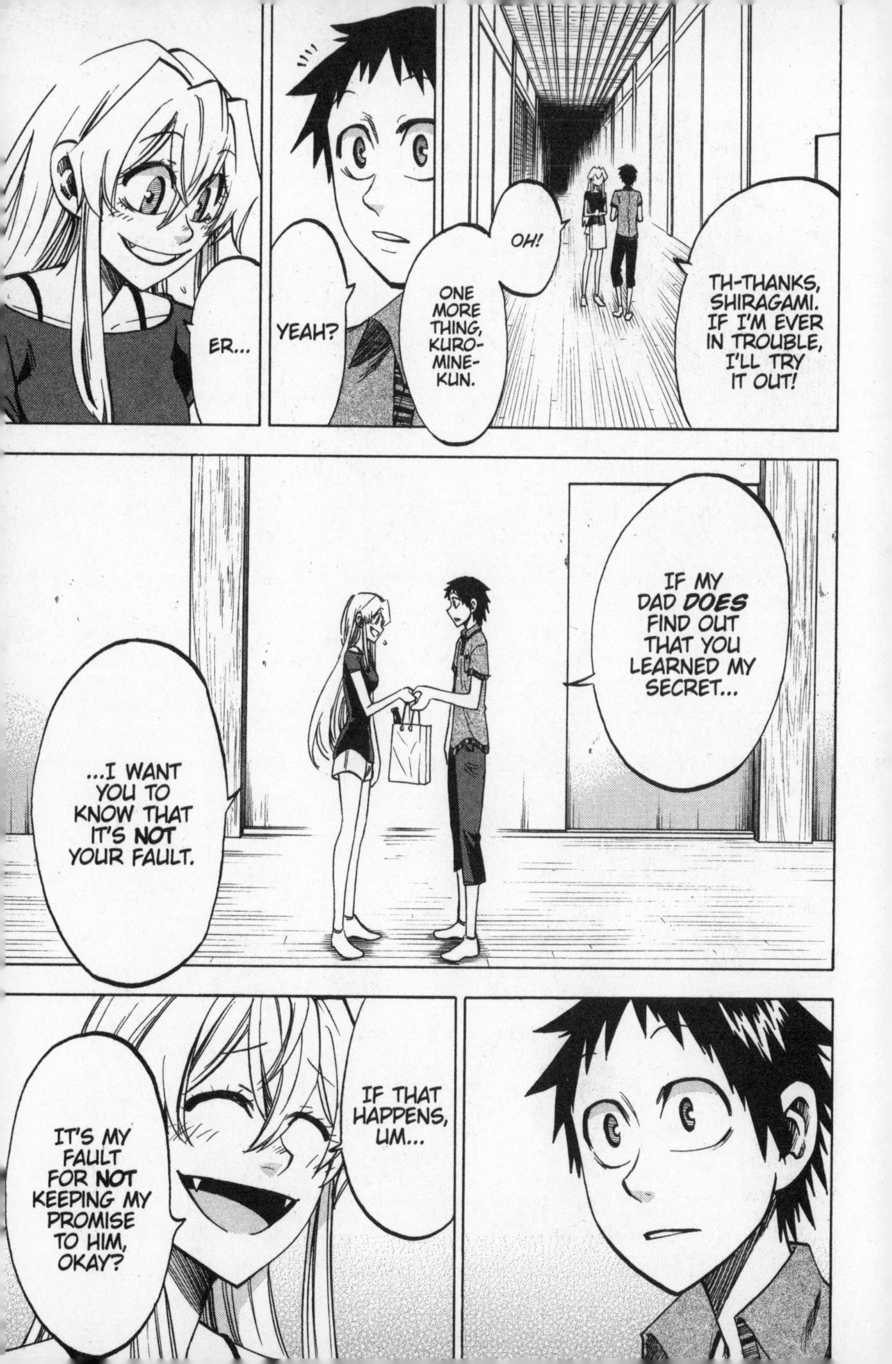
TH-THANKS, SHIRAGAMI. IF I'M EVER IN TROUBLE, I'LL TRY IT OUT!
OH!
ONE MORE THING, KURO-MINE-KUN.
YEAH?
ER...
IF MY DAD DOES FIND OUT THAT YOU LEARNED MY SECRET...
...I WANT YOU TO KNOW THAT IT'S NOT YOUR FAULT.
IF THAT HAPPENS, UM...
IT'S MY FAULT FOR NOT KEEPING MY PROMISE TO HIM, OKAY?

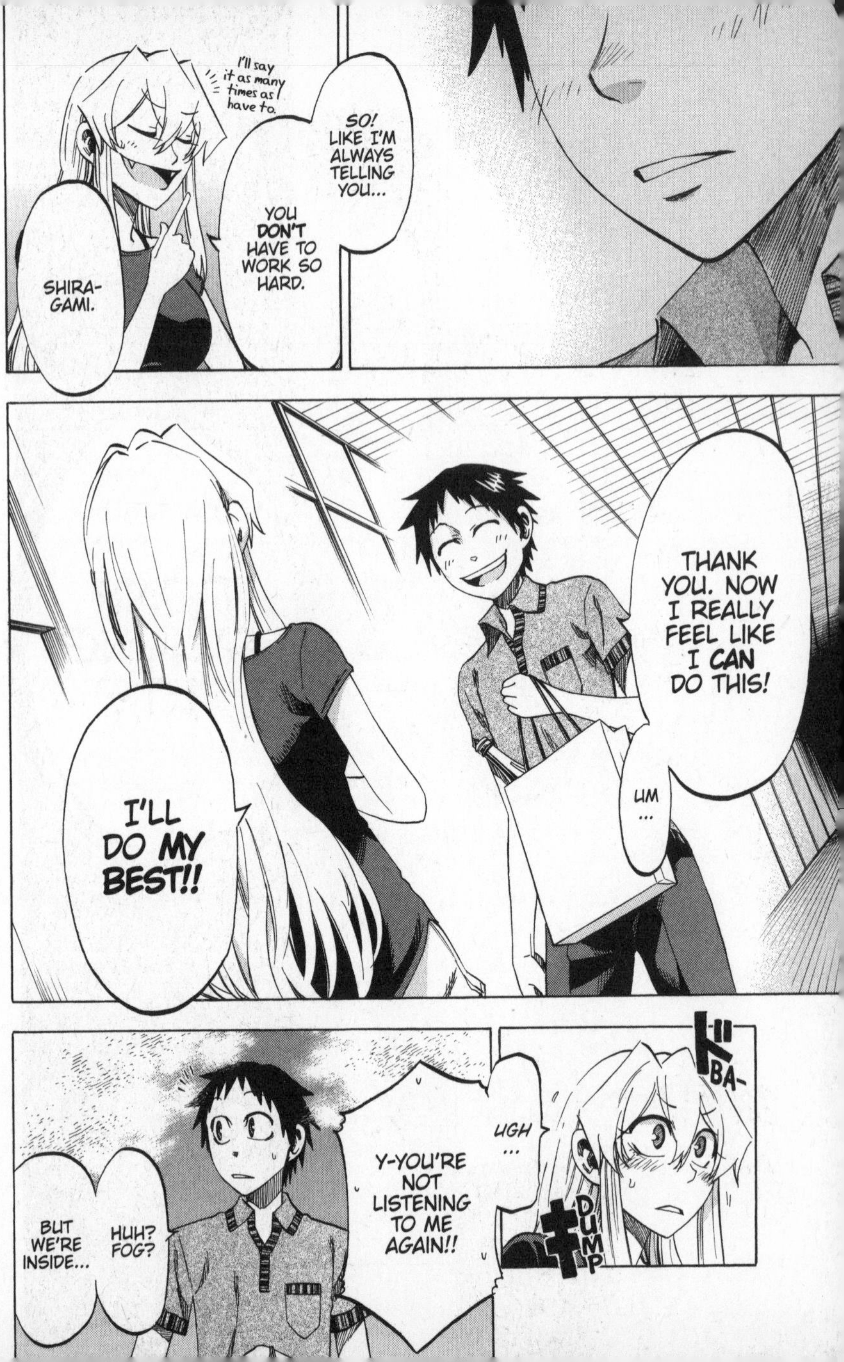
SO! LIKE I'M ALWAYS TELLING YOU...
I'll say it as many times as I have to.
YOU DON'T HAVE TO WORK SO HARD.
SHIRA-GAMI.
THANK YOU. NOW I REALLY FEEL LIKE I CAN DO THIS!
UM ...
I'LL DO MY BEST!!
BA-
UGH ...
DUMP
Y-YOU'RE NOT LISTENING TO ME AGAIN!!
HUH? FOG?
BUT WE'RE INSIDE...

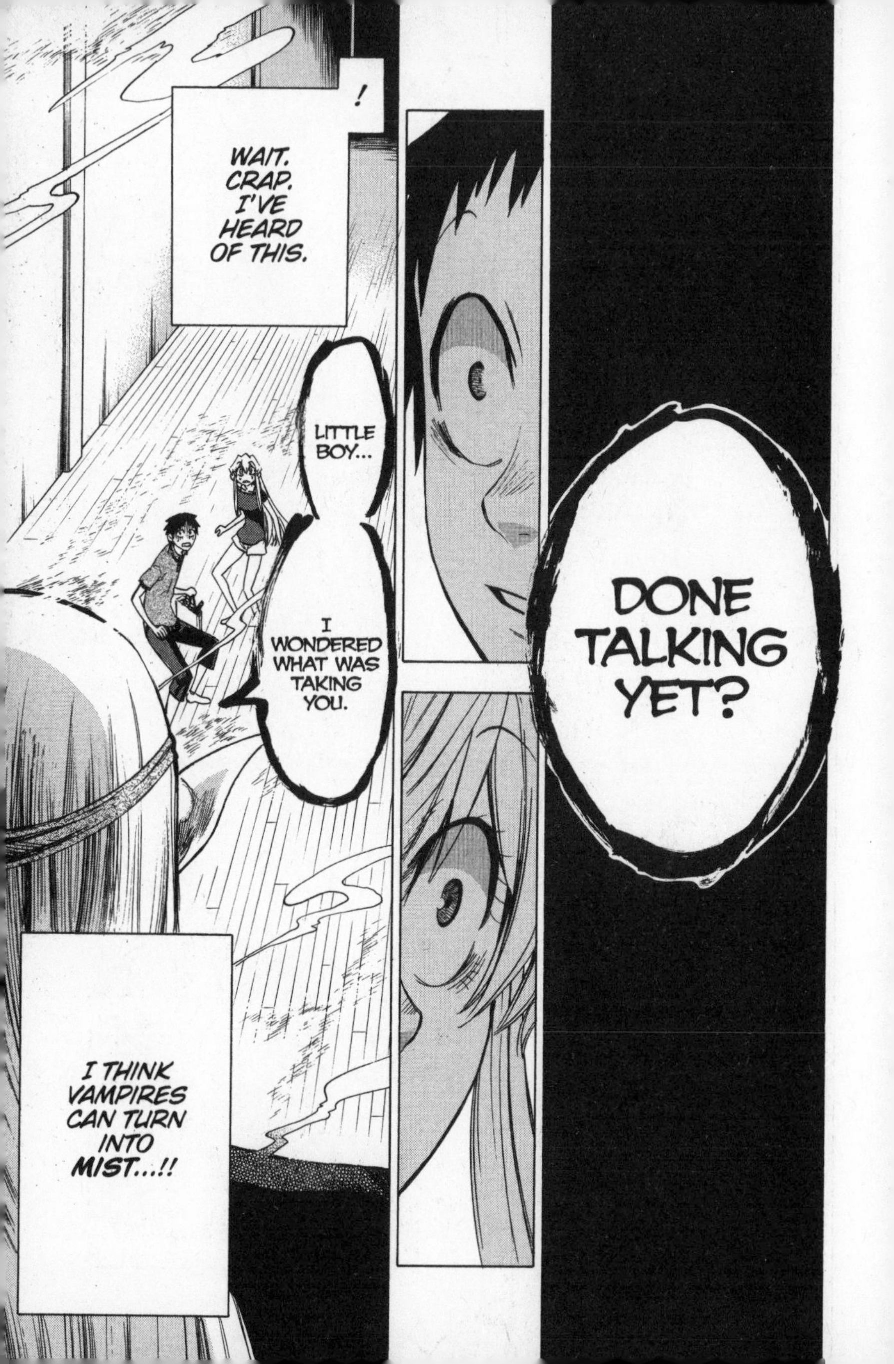
DONE TALKING YET?
!
WAIT. CRAP. I'VE HEARD OF THIS.
LITTLE BOY...
I WONDERED WHAT WAS TAKING YOU.
I THINK VAMPIRES CAN TURN INTO MIST...!!

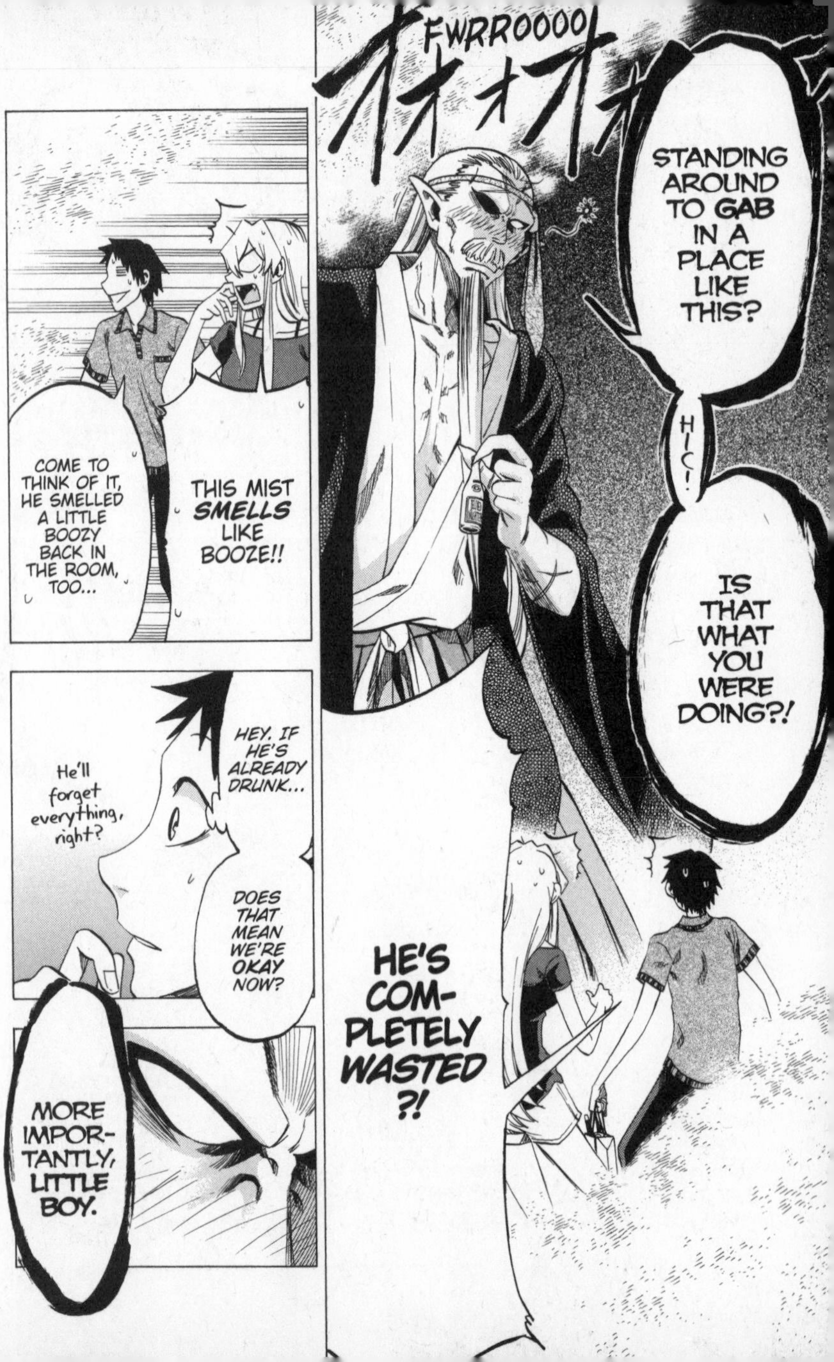
FWRROOOO
STANDING AROUND TO GAB IN A PLACE LIKE THIS?
HIC!
IS THAT WHAT YOU WERE DOING?!
HE'S COM-PLETELY WASTED?!
THIS MIST SMELLS LIKE BOOZE!!
COME TO THINK OF IT, HE SMELLED A LITTLE BOOZY BACK IN THE ROOM, TOO...
HEY. IF HE'S ALREADY DRUNK...
He'll forget everything, right?
DOES THAT MEAN WE'RE OKAY NOW?
MORE IMPOR-TANTLY, LITTLE BOY.

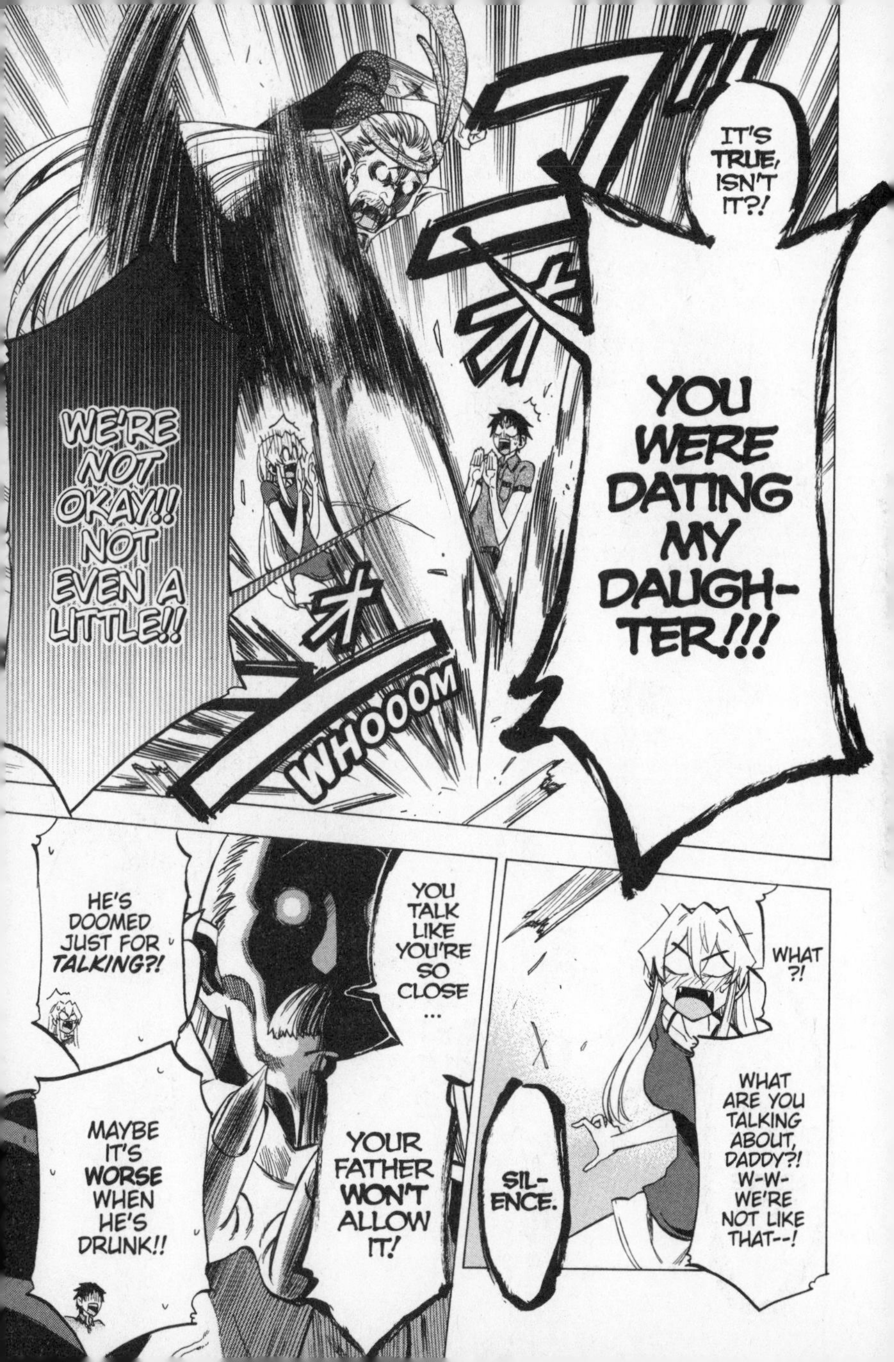
IT'S TRUE, ISN'T IT?!
YOU WERE DATING MY DAUGHTER!!!
WHOOOM
WE'RE NOT OKAY!! NOT EVEN A LITTLE!!
WHAT?!
WHAT ARE YOU TALKING ABOUT, DADDY?! W-W-WE'RE NOT LIKE THAT--!
SILENCE.
YOU TALK LIKE YOU'RE SO CLOSE ...
YOUR FATHER WON'T ALLOW IT!
HE'S DOOMED JUST FOR TALKING?!
MAYBE IT'S WORSE WHEN HE'S DRUNK!!

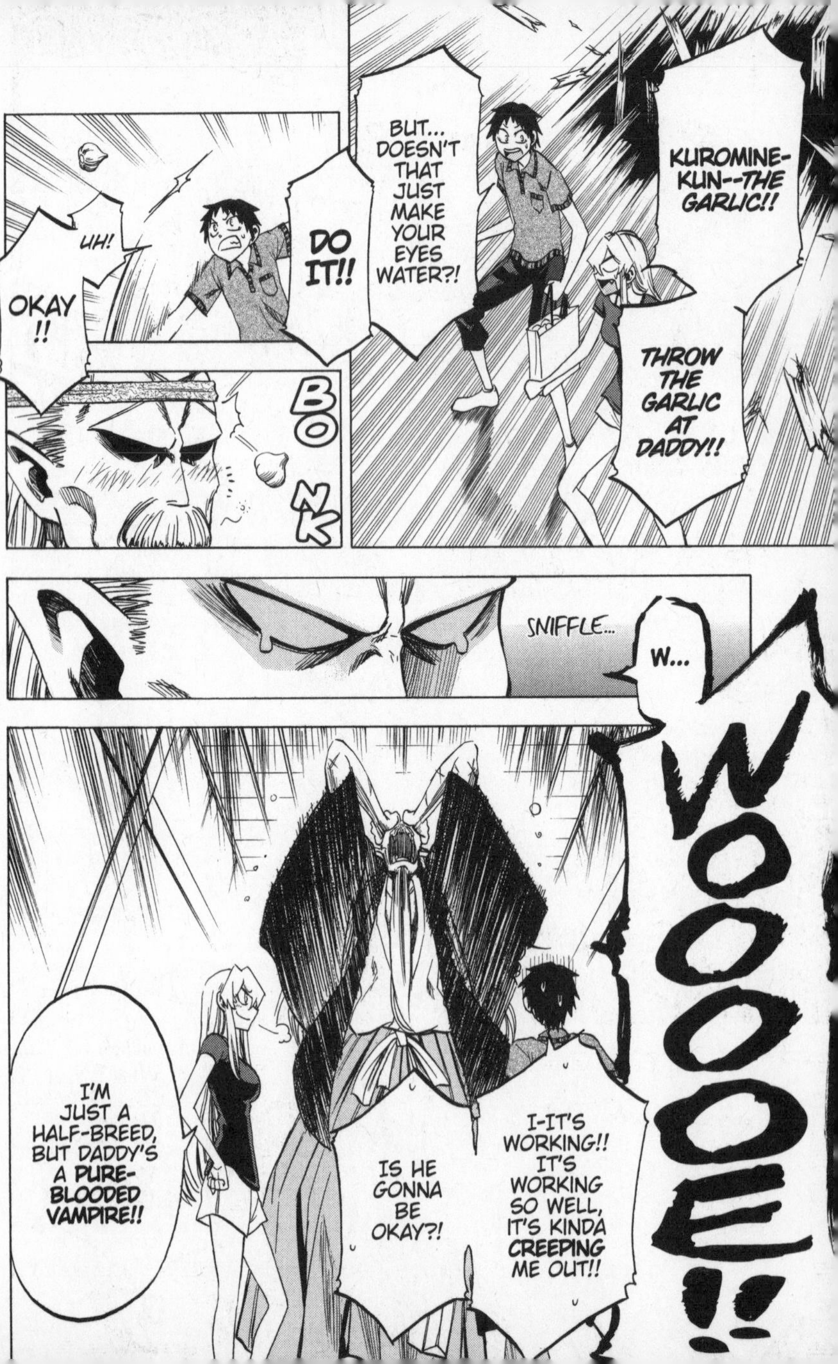
KUROMINE-KUN--THE GARLIC!!
THROW THE GARLIC AT DADDY!!
BUT... DOESN'T THAT JUST MAKE YOUR EYES WATER?!
DO IT!!
UH!
OKAY!!
BONK
SNIFFLE...
W...
WOOOOE!!
I-IT'S WORKING!! IT'S WORKING SO WELL, IT'S KINDA CREEPING ME OUT!!
IS HE GONNA BE OKAY?!
I'M JUST A HALF-BREED, BUT DADDY'S A PURE-BLOODED VAMPIRE!!

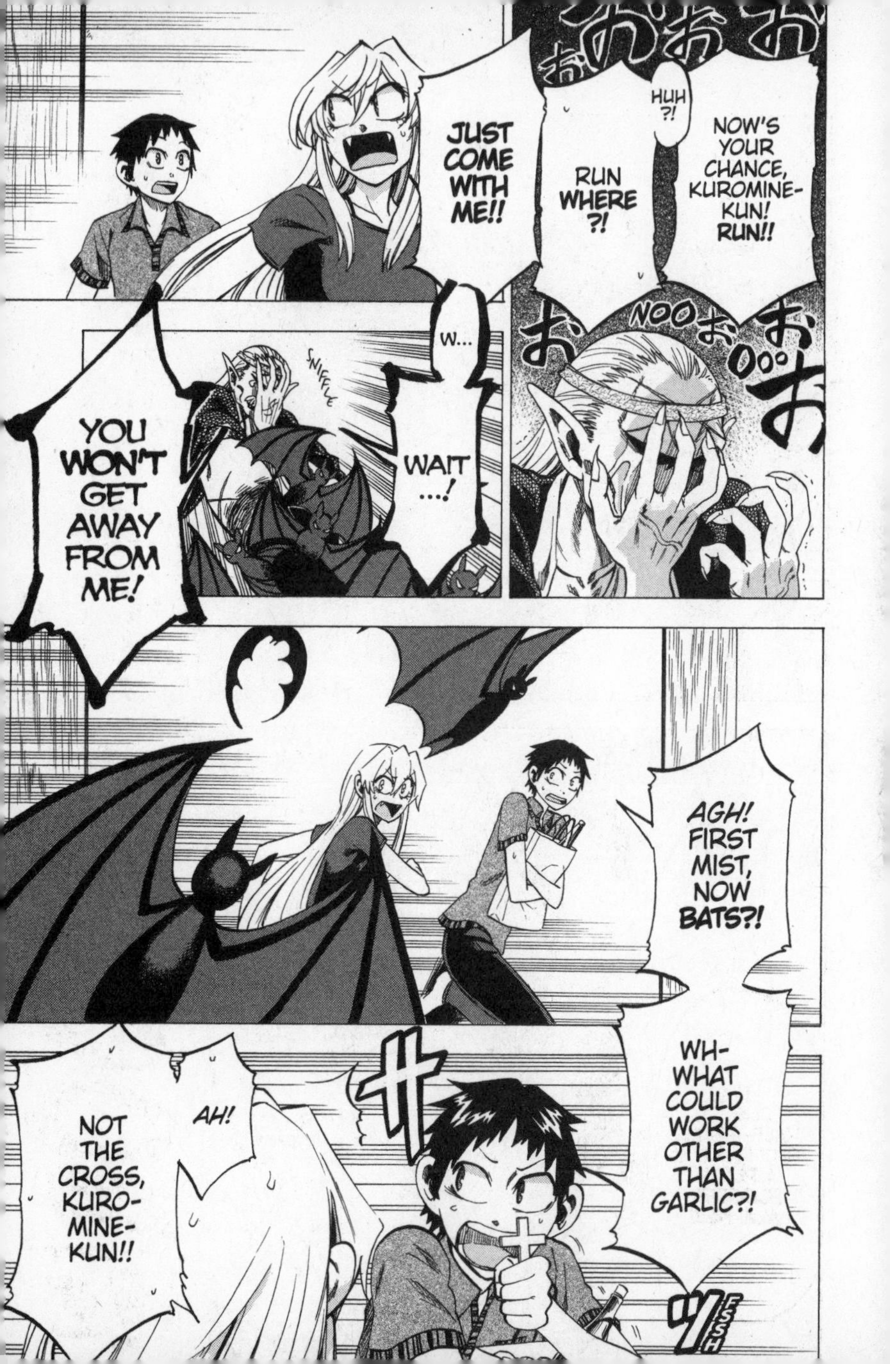

NOW'S YOUR CHANCE, KUROMINE-KUN! RUN!!
HUH?!
RUN WHERE?!
JUST COME WITH ME!!
NOOO
W...
WAIT...!
SNIFFLE
YOU WON'T GET AWAY FROM ME!
AGH! FIRST MIST, NOW BATS?!
WH-WHAT COULD WORK OTHER THAN GARLIC?!
AH!
NOT THE CROSS, KUROMINE-KUN!!
FSSH

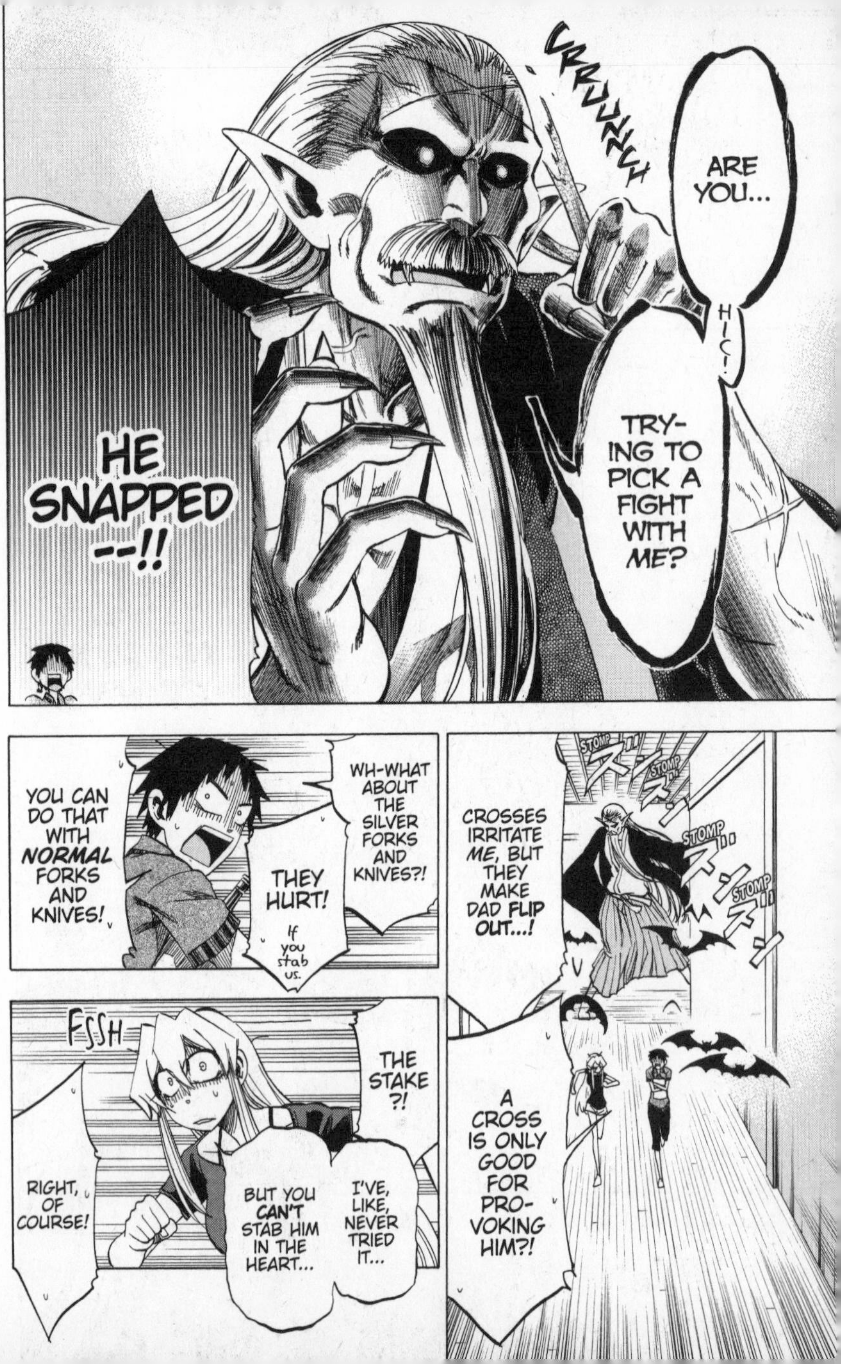
CRRUNNCH
ARE YOU...
HIC!
TRYING TO PICK A FIGHT WITH ME?
HE SNAPPED--!!
STOMP STOMP STOMP STOMP
CROSSES IRRITATE ME, BUT THEY MAKE DAD FLIP OUT...!
A CROSS IS ONLY GOOD FOR PROVOKING HIM?!
WH-WHAT ABOUT THE SILVER FORKS AND KNIVES?!
THEY HURT!
If you stab us.
YOU CAN DO THAT WITH NORMAL FORKS AND KNIVES!
THE STAKE?!
FSSH
I'VE, LIKE, NEVER TRIED IT...
BUT YOU CAN'T STAB HIM IN THE HEART...
RIGHT, OF COURSE!

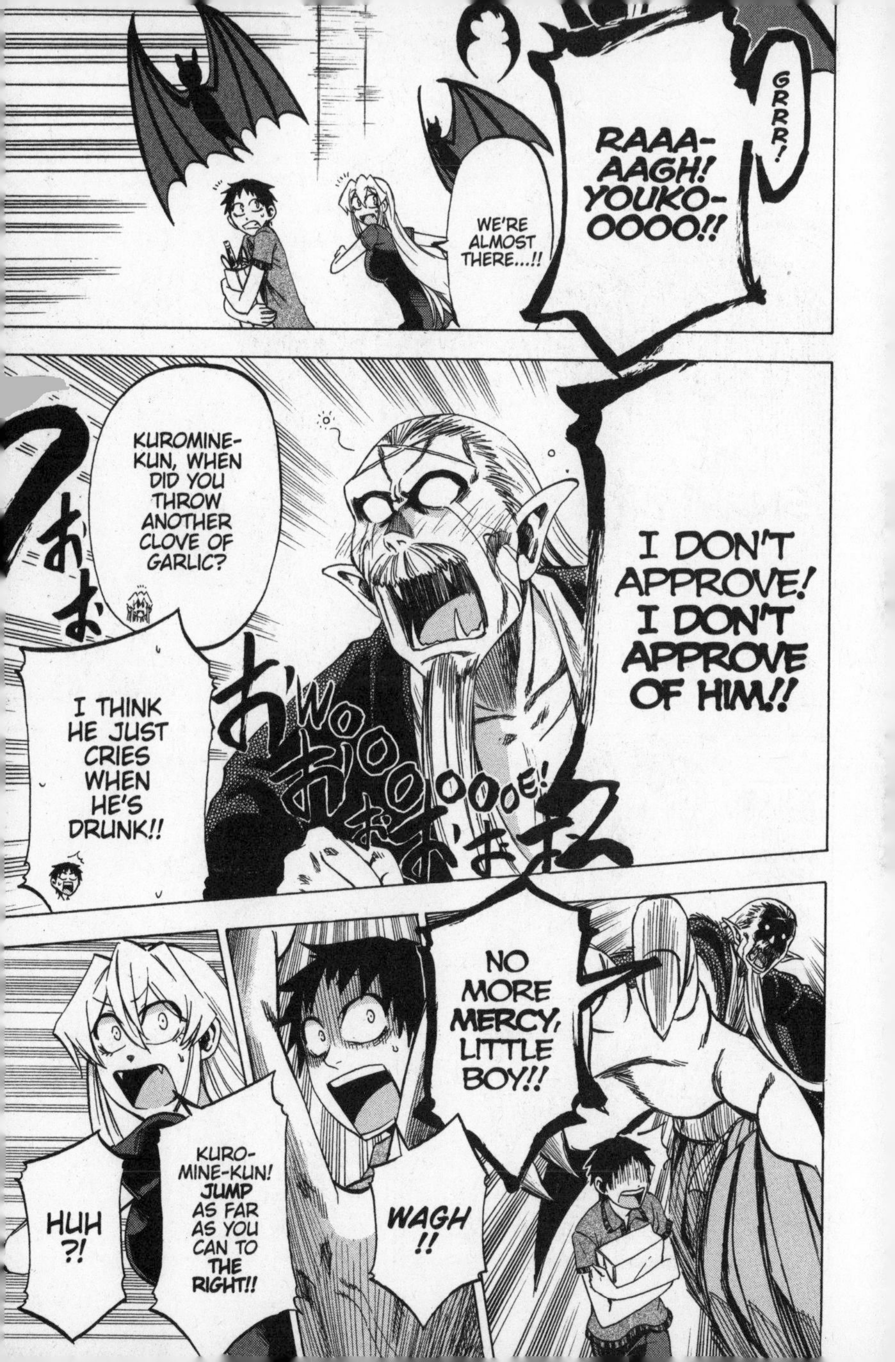
GRRR!
RAAA-AAGH! YOUKO-OOOO!!
WE'RE ALMOST THERE...!!
I DON'T APPROVE! I DON'T APPROVE OF HIM!!
WOOOOOOE!
KUROMINE-KUN, WHEN DID YOU THROW ANOTHER CLOVE OF GARLIC?
I THINK HE JUST CRIES WHEN HE'S DRUNK!!
NO MORE MERCY, LITTLE BOY!!
WAGH!!
KURO-MINE-KUN! JUMP AS FAR AS YOU CAN TO THE RIGHT!!
HUH?!

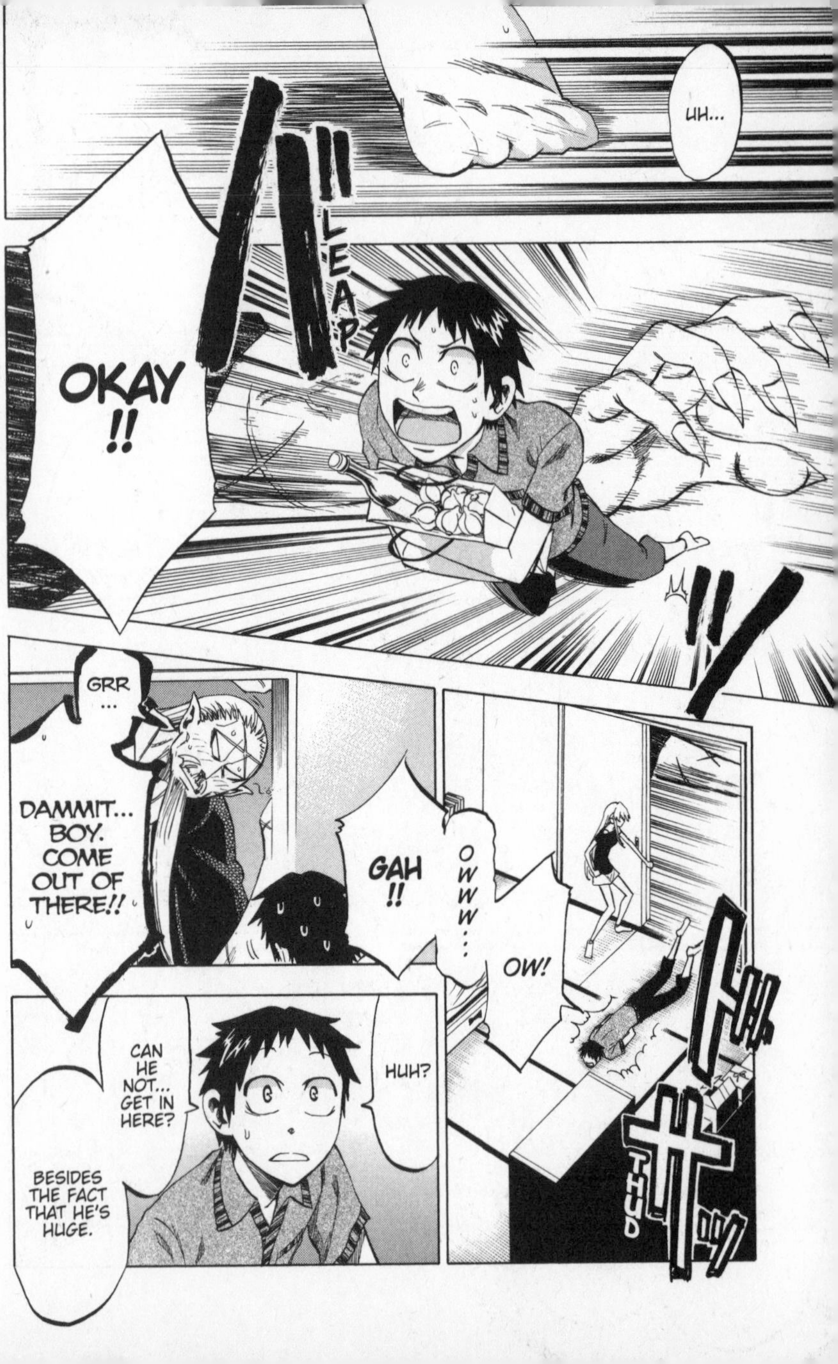
UH...
LEAP
OKAY !!
THUD
OW!
OWWW...
GAH !!
GRR ...
DAMMIT... BOY. COME OUT OF THERE!!
HUH?
CAN HE NOT... GET IN HERE?
BESIDES THE FACT THAT HE'S HUGE.

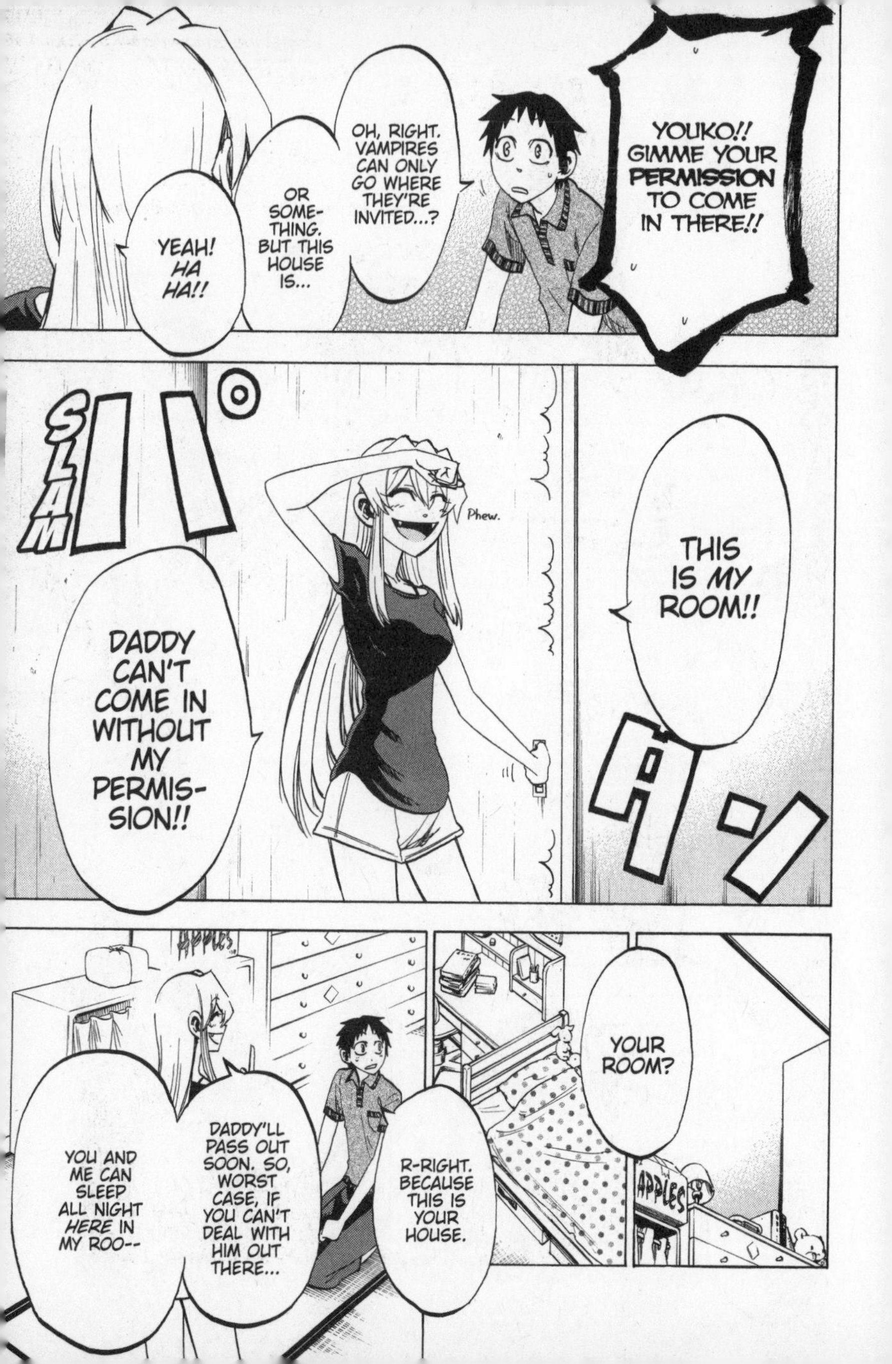
YOUKO!! GIMME YOUR PERMISSION TO COME IN THERE!!
OH, RIGHT. VAMPIRES CAN ONLY GO WHERE THEY'RE INVITED...?
OR SOMETHING. BUT THIS HOUSE IS...
YEAH! HA HA!!
THIS IS MY ROOM!!
SLAM
Phew.
DADDY CAN'T COME IN WITHOUT MY PERMISSION!!
YOUR ROOM?
APPLES
R-RIGHT. BECAUSE THIS IS YOUR HOUSE.
DADDY'LL PASS OUT SOON. SO, WORST CASE, IF YOU CAN'T DEAL WITH HIM OUT THERE...
YOU AND ME CAN SLEEP ALL NIGHT *HERE* IN MY ROO--

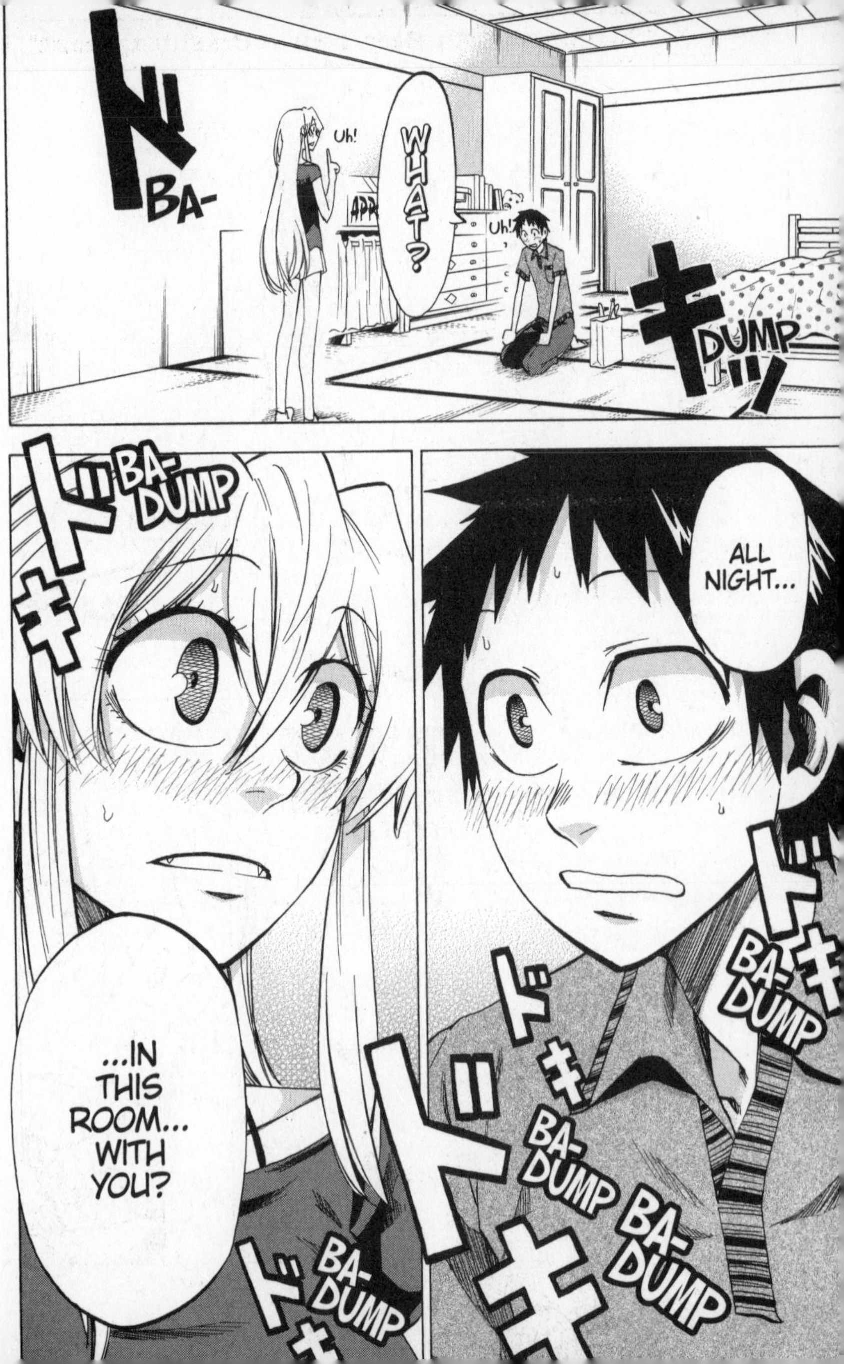
ドキ
BA-DUMP
WHAT?
Uh!
Uh!
ドキ
BA-
ALL NIGHT...
ドキ
BA-DUMP
ドキ
BA-DUMP
ドキ
BA-DUMP
...IN THIS ROOM... WITH YOU?
ドキ
BA-DUMP
ドキ
BA-DUMP

Chapter 32: "Let's Sleep Over at the Shiragamis'!!"

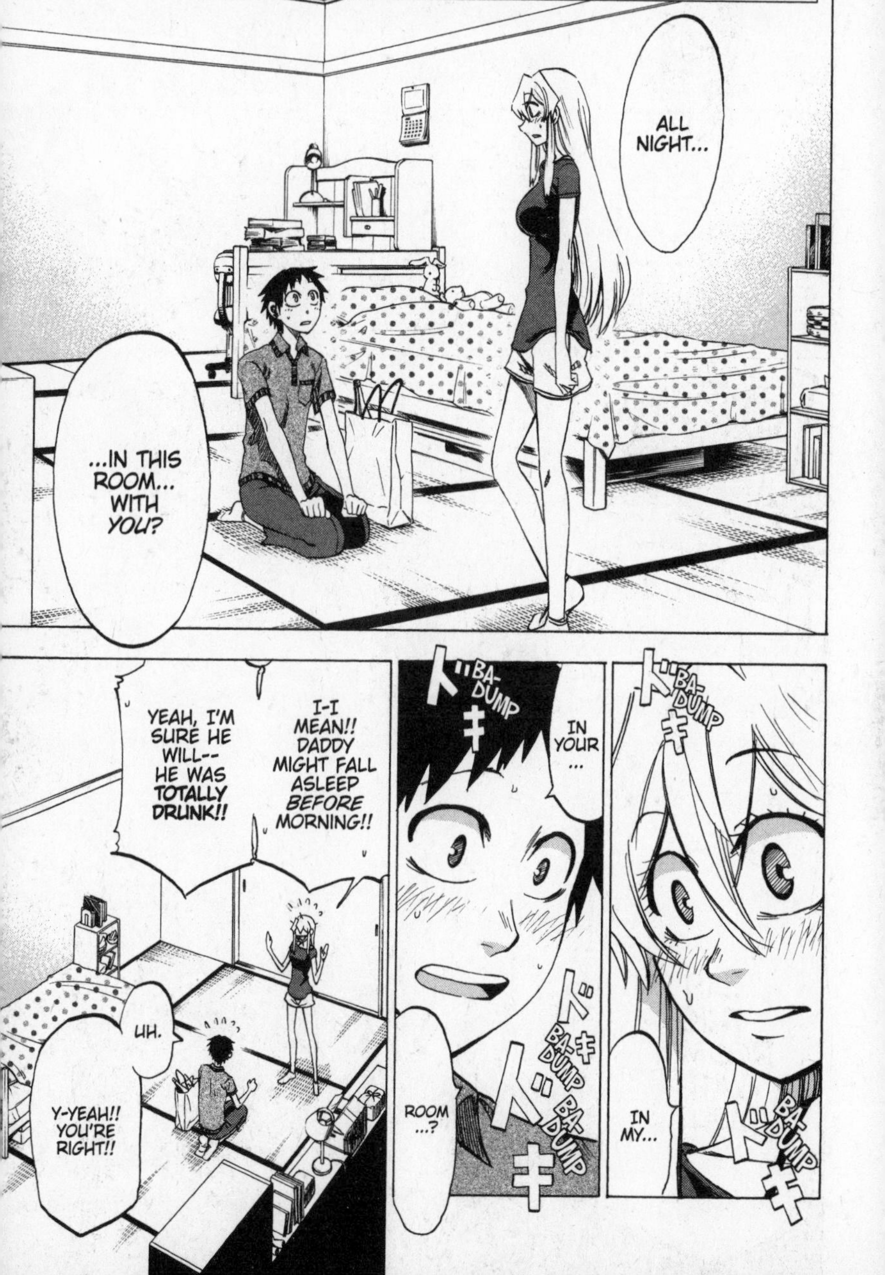

ALL NIGHT...
...IN THIS ROOM... WITH YOU?
ドキ BA-DUMP
IN MY...
ドキ BA-DUMP
ドキ BA-DUMP
IN YOUR ...
ROOM ...?
ドキ BA-DUMP
ドキ BA-DUMP
I-I MEAN!! DADDY MIGHT FALL ASLEEP BEFORE MORNING!!
YEAH, I'M SURE HE WILL-- HE WAS TOTALLY DRUNK!!
UH.
Y-YEAH!! YOU'RE RIGHT!!

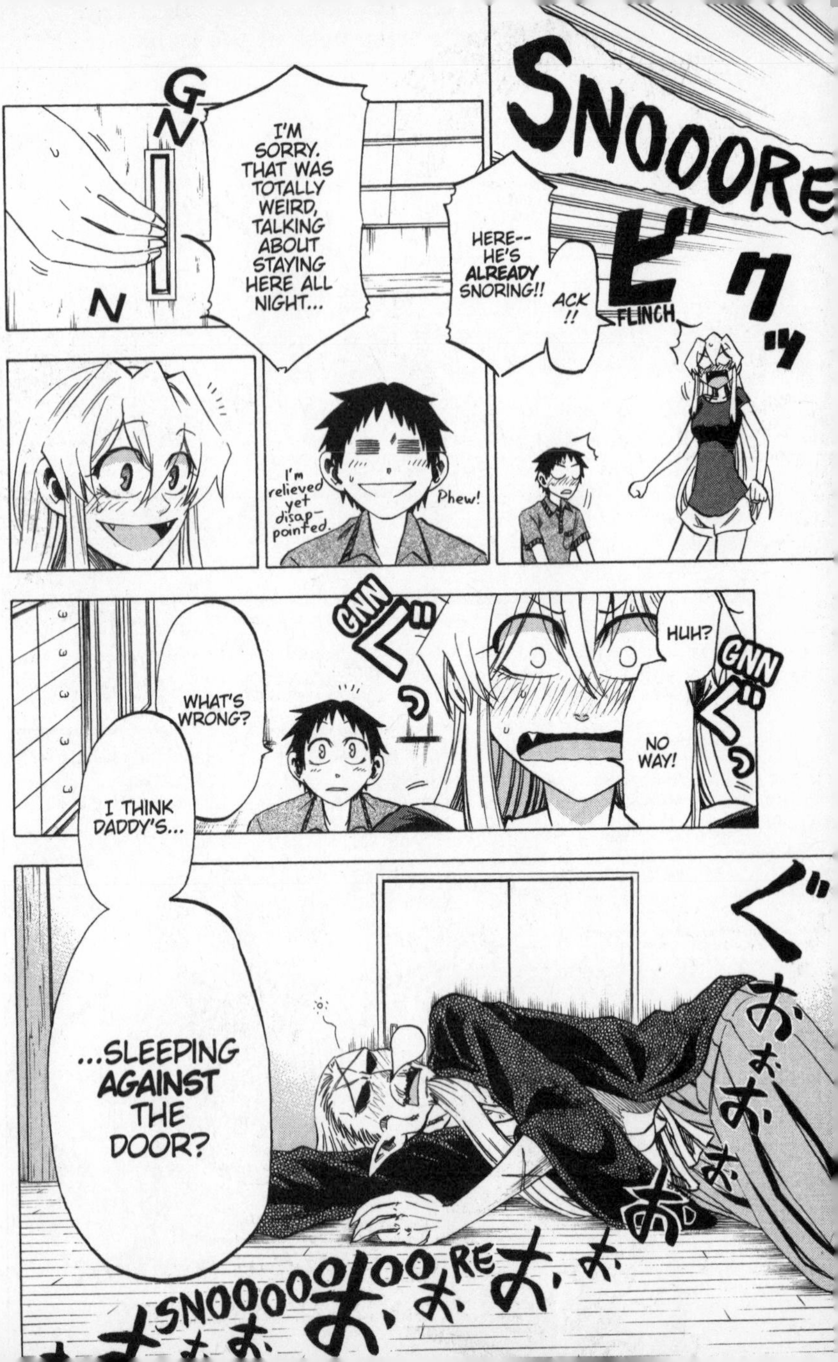
SNOOORE
ビクッ
FLINCH
ACK!!
HERE-- HE'S ALREADY SNORING!!
I'M SORRY. THAT WAS TOTALLY WEIRD, TALKING ABOUT STAYING HERE ALL NIGHT...
GN N
Phew!
I'm relieved yet disap-pointed.
HUH?
GNN
ぐっ
NO WAY!
GNN
ぐっ
WHAT'S WRONG?
I THINK DADDY'S...
...SLEEPING AGAINST THE DOOR?
SNOOOOOORE

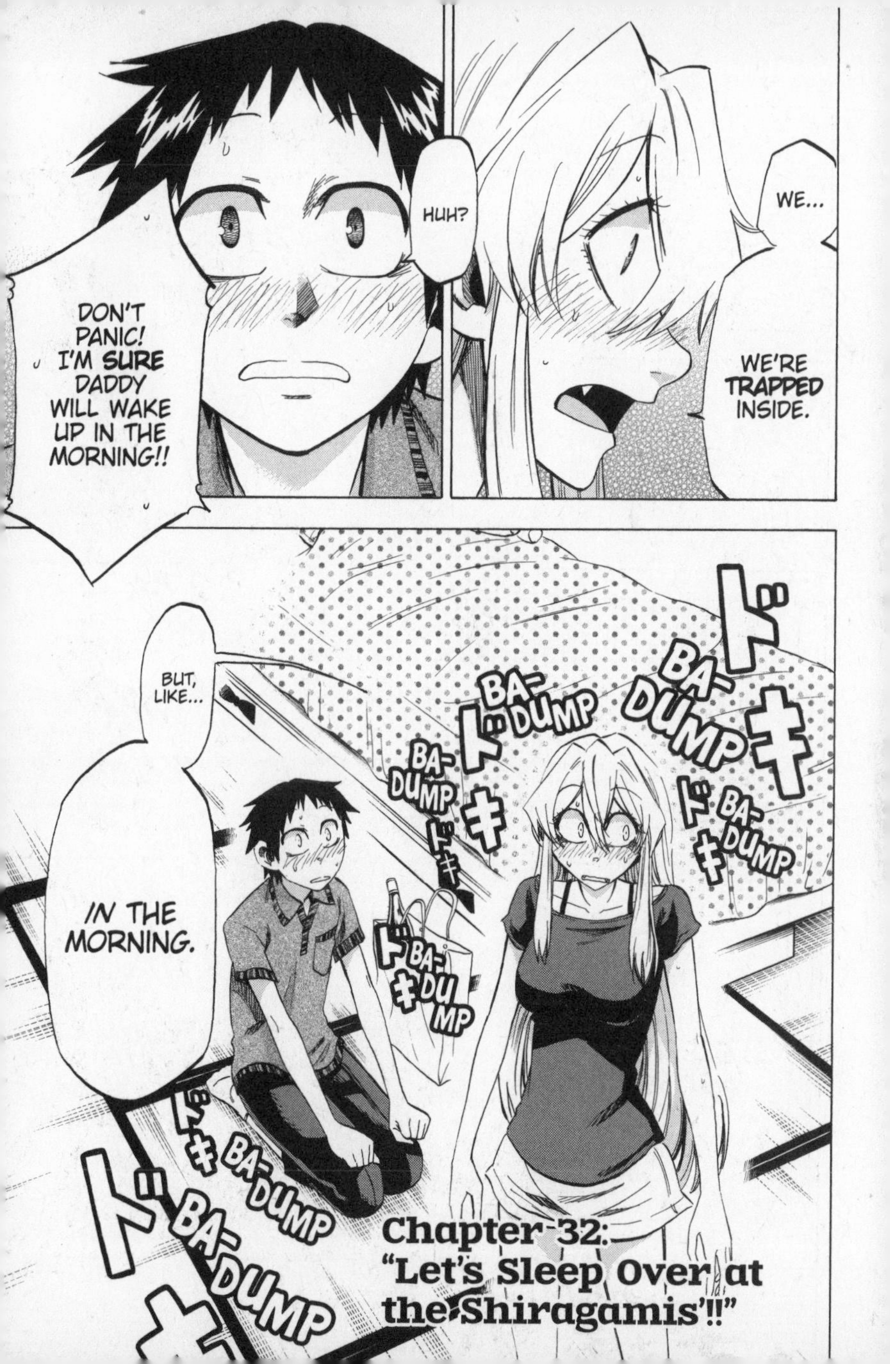
WE...
WE'RE TRAPPED INSIDE.
HUH?
DON'T PANIC! I'M SURE DADDY WILL WAKE UP IN THE MORNING!!
BUT, LIKE...
IN THE MORNING.
ド BA-DUMP キ
ドキ BA-DUMP
ド BA-DUMP
BA-DUMP キ ドキ
ド BA-DUMP キ
ドキ BA-DUMP
ド BA-DUMP キ
Chapter 32: "Let's Sleep Over at the Shiragamis'!!"

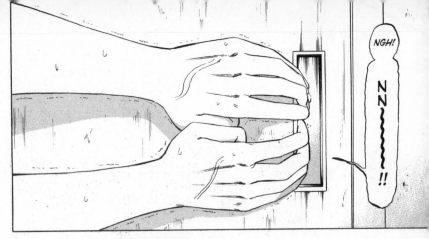

NGH!

NN~~~~~~~!!

SORRY... IT WON'T EVEN BUDGE.

UM, DOES THIS ROOM HAVE ANY WINDOWS...?

N-NO.

TO, LIKE, KEEP OUT THE SUN.

WHEEZE

WHEEZE

WHAT DO I DO?!

I MEAN, I'M NOT COMPLETELY UNHAPPY TO BE ALONE WITH SHIRAGAMI HERE...

BA-DUMP

BA-DUMP

BA-DUMP

BUT NOW THAT I'M CONFRONTED WITH IT... I DON'T KNOW WHAT TO DO.

I'M SOOO SORRY, KUROMINE-KUN.

UGH.

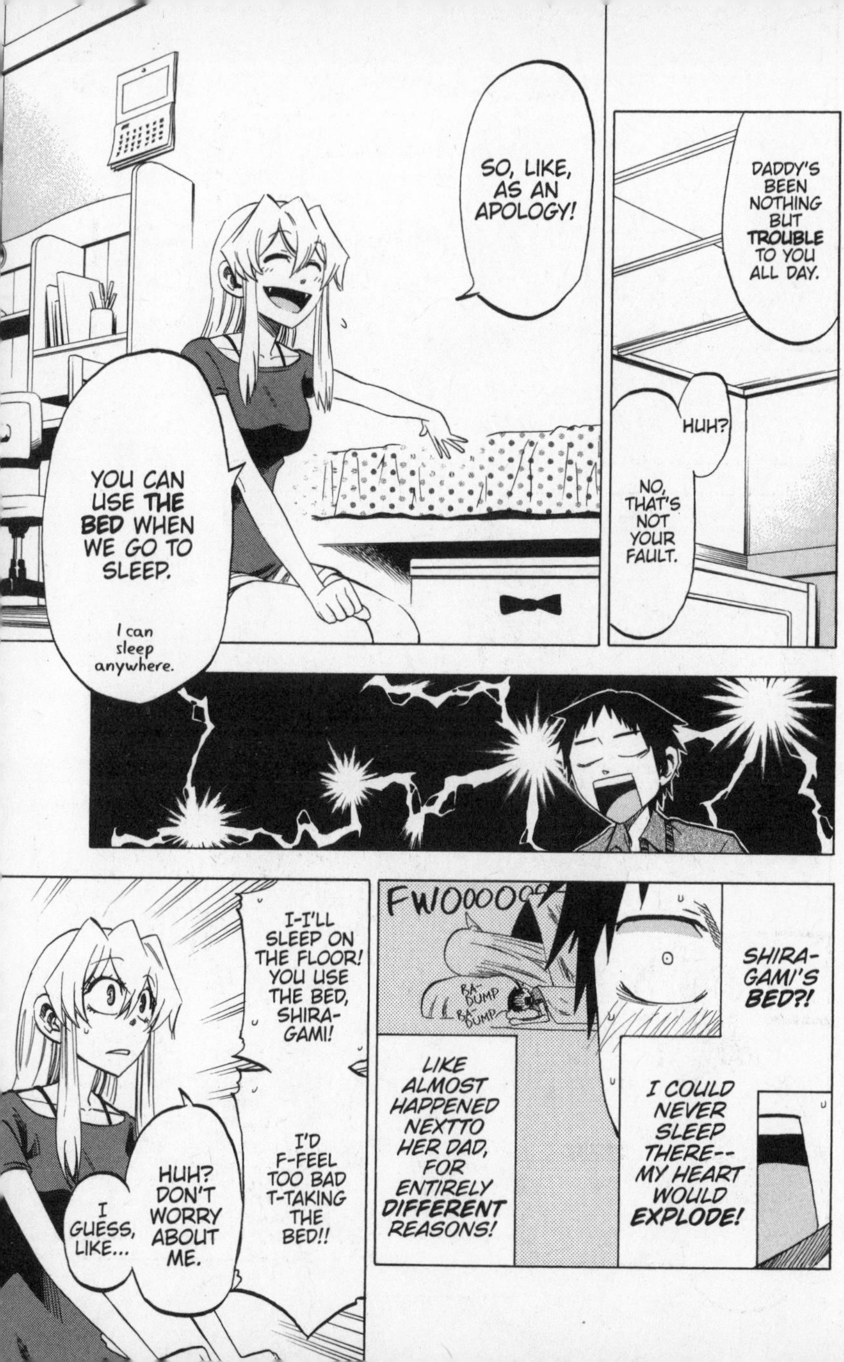
DADDY'S BEEN NOTHING BUT **TROUBLE** TO YOU ALL DAY.
HUH?
NO, THAT'S NOT YOUR FAULT.
SO, LIKE, AS AN APOLOGY!
YOU CAN USE **THE BED** WHEN WE GO TO SLEEP.
I can sleep anywhere.
FWOOOO
SHIRA-GAMI'S BED?!
BA-DUMP BA-DUMP
I COULD NEVER SLEEP THERE-- MY HEART WOULD **EXPLODE!**
LIKE ALMOST HAPPENED NEXTTO HER DAD, FOR ENTIRELY **DIFFERENT** REASONS!
I-I'LL SLEEP ON THE FLOOR! YOU USE THE BED, SHIRA-GAMI!
I'D F-FEEL TOO BAD T-TAKING THE BED!!
HUH? DON'T WORRY ABOUT ME.
I GUESS, LIKE...

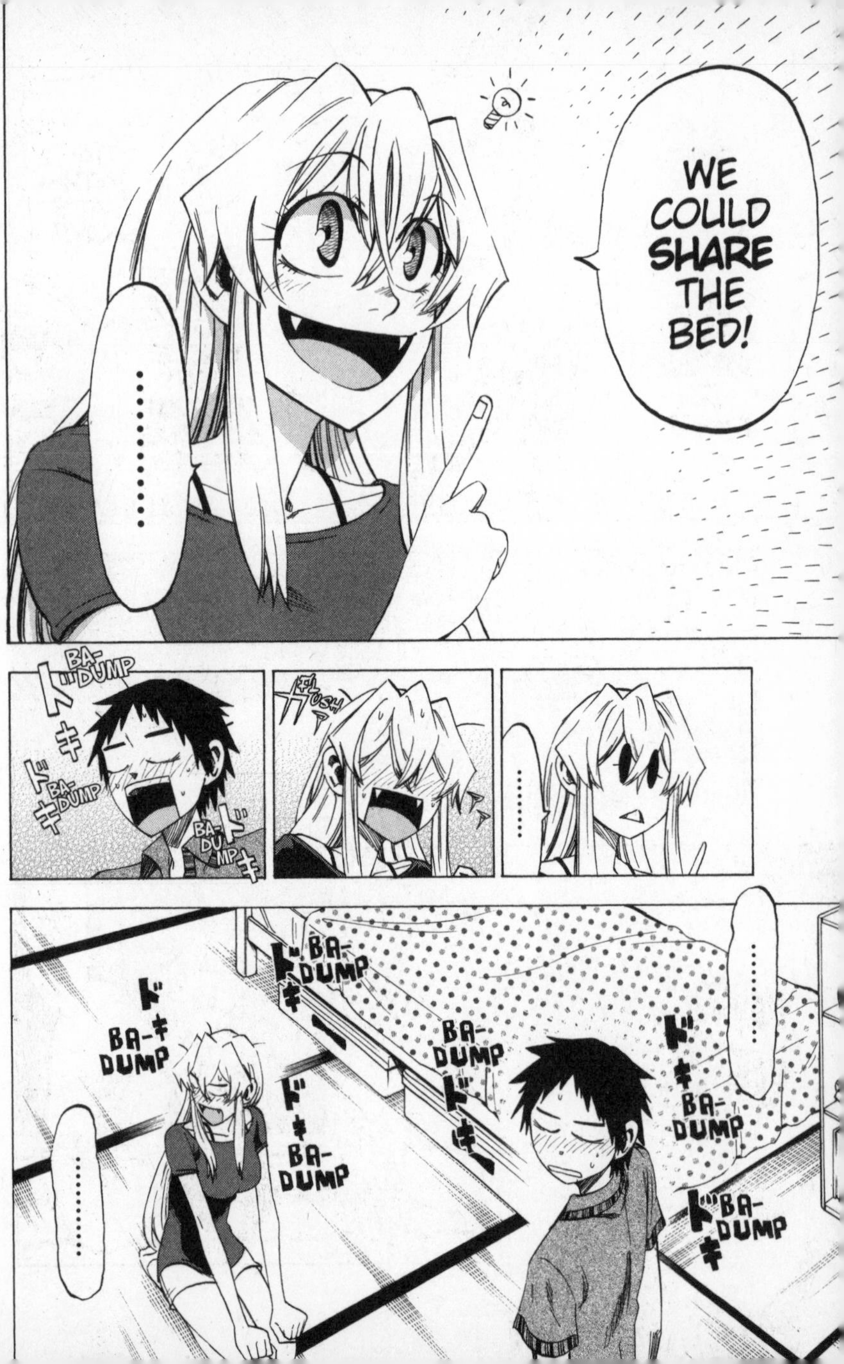
WE COULD SHARE THE BED!
....
......
FLUSH
BA-DUMP
BA-DUMP
BA-DUMP
....
BA-DUMP
BA-DUMP
BA-DUMP
BA-DUMP
BA-DUMP
BA-DUMP
....

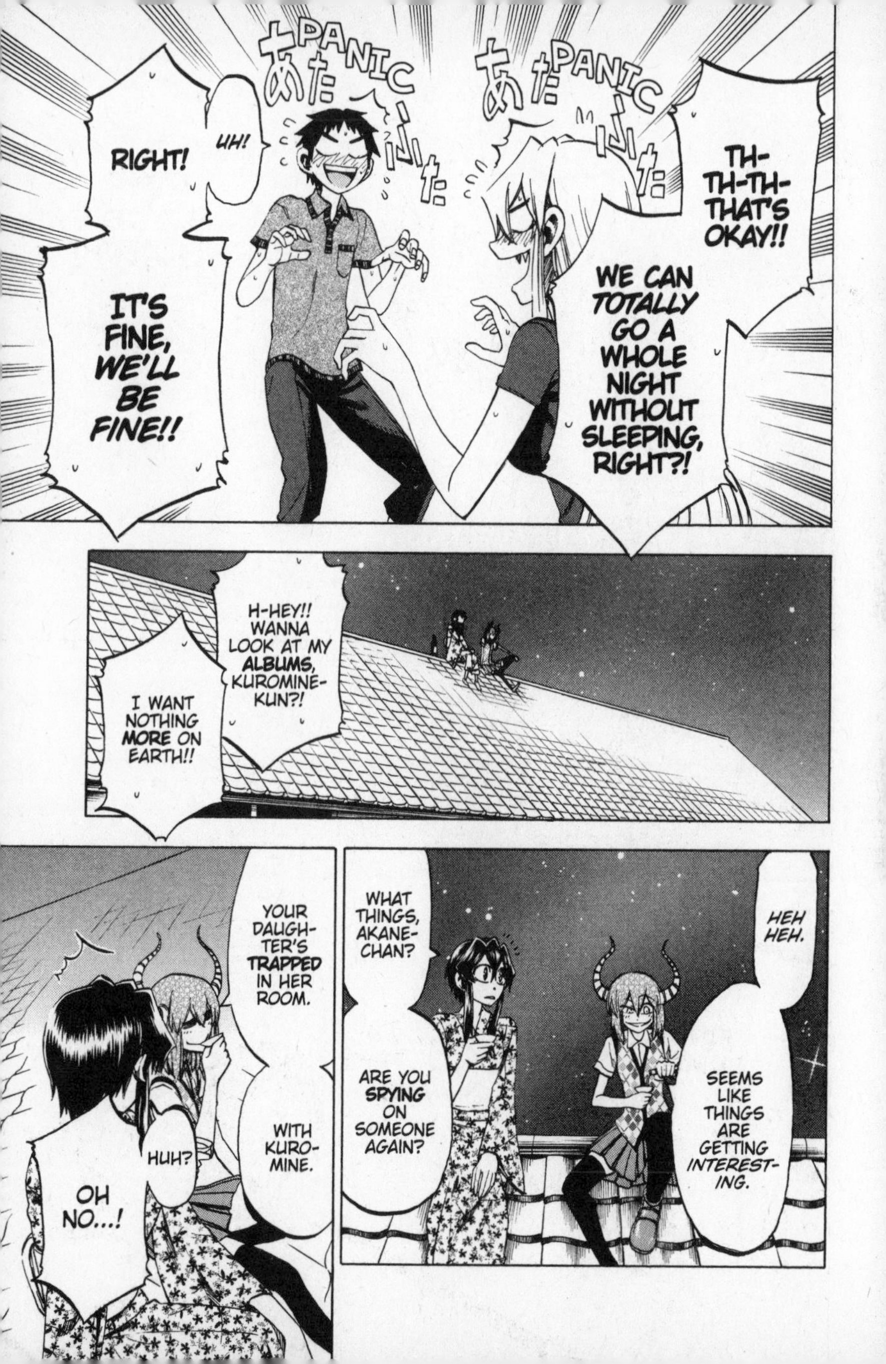
TH-TH-TH-THAT'S OKAY!!
WE CAN TOTALLY GO A WHOLE NIGHT WITHOUT SLEEPING, RIGHT?!
あたふた PANIC
UH!
RIGHT!
IT'S FINE, WE'LL BE FINE!!
あたふた PANIC
H-HEY!! WANNA LOOK AT MY ALBUMS, KUROMINE-KUN?!
I WANT NOTHING MORE ON EARTH!!
HEH HEH.
SEEMS LIKE THINGS ARE GETTING INTEREST-ING.
WHAT THINGS, AKANE-CHAN?
ARE YOU SPYING ON SOMEONE AGAIN?
YOUR DAUGH-TER'S TRAPPED IN HER ROOM.
WITH KURO-MINE.
HUH?
OH NO...!

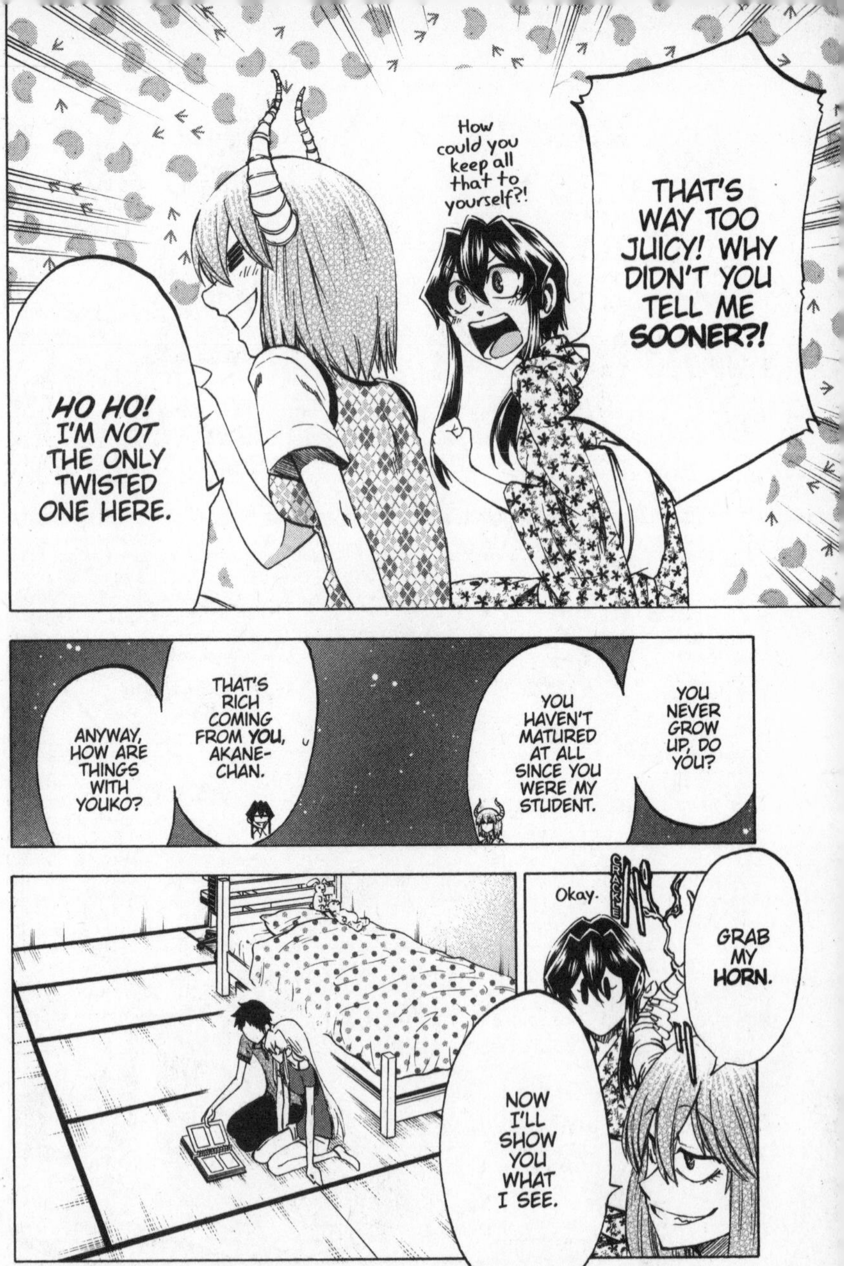
THAT'S WAY TOO JUICY! WHY DIDN'T YOU TELL ME SOONER?!
How could you keep all that to yourself?!
HO HO! I'M NOT THE ONLY TWISTED ONE HERE.
YOU NEVER GROW UP, DO YOU?
YOU HAVEN'T MATURED AT ALL SINCE YOU WERE MY STUDENT.
THAT'S RICH COMING FROM YOU, AKANE-CHAN.
ANYWAY, HOW ARE THINGS WITH YOUKO?
GRAB MY HORN.
CRACKLE
Okay.
NOW I'LL SHOW YOU WHAT I SEE.

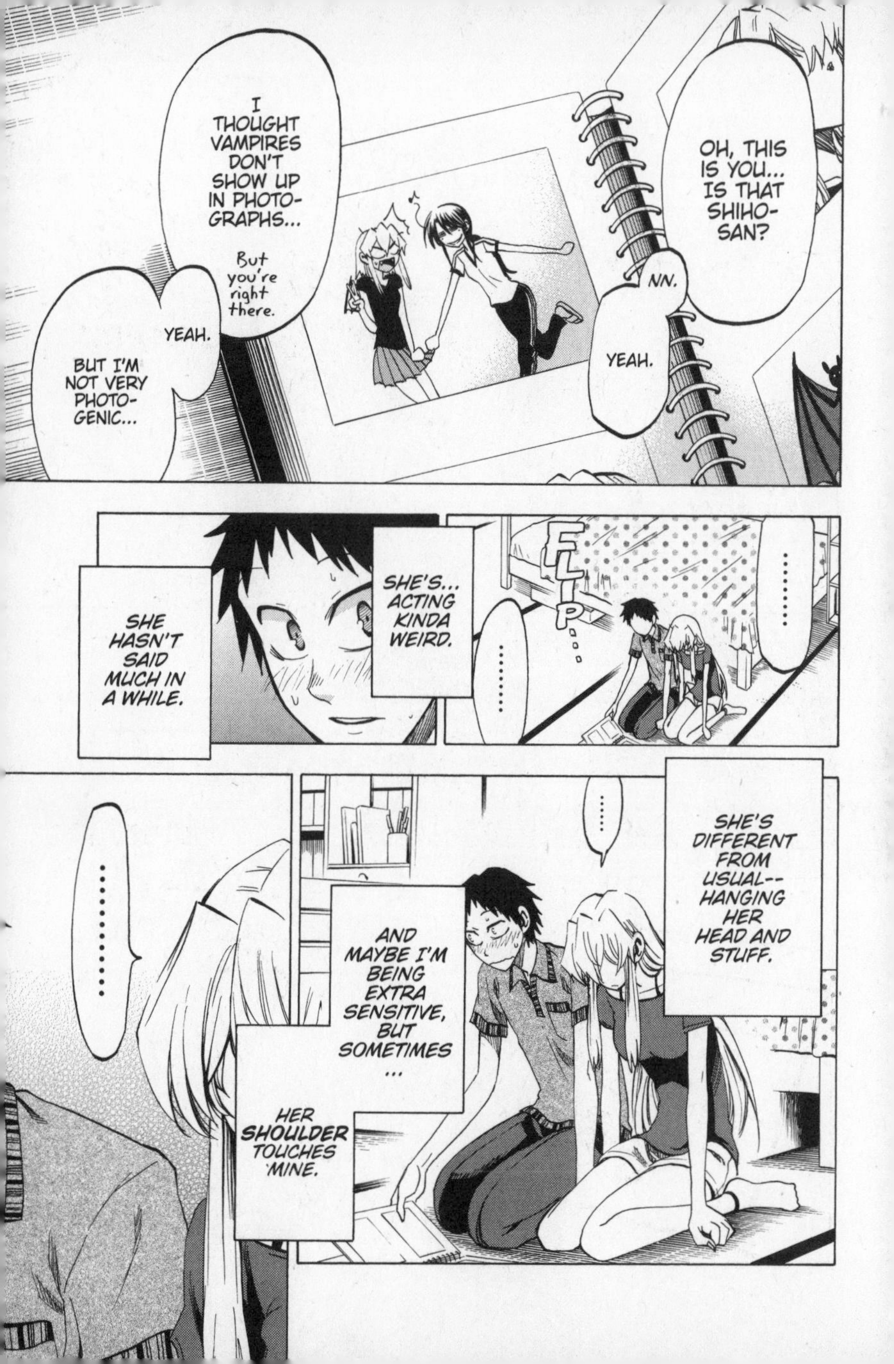
OH, THIS IS YOU... IS THAT SHIHO-SAN?
NN.
YEAH.
I THOUGHT VAMPIRES DON'T SHOW UP IN PHOTOGRAPHS...
But you're right there.
YEAH.
BUT I'M NOT VERY PHOTOGENIC...
......
FLIP...
SHE'S... ACTING KINDA WEIRD.
......
SHE HASN'T SAID MUCH IN A WHILE.
SHE'S DIFFERENT FROM USUAL--HANGING HER HEAD AND STUFF.
......
AND MAYBE I'M BEING EXTRA SENSITIVE, BUT SOMETIMES ...
HER SHOULDER TOUCHES MINE.
......

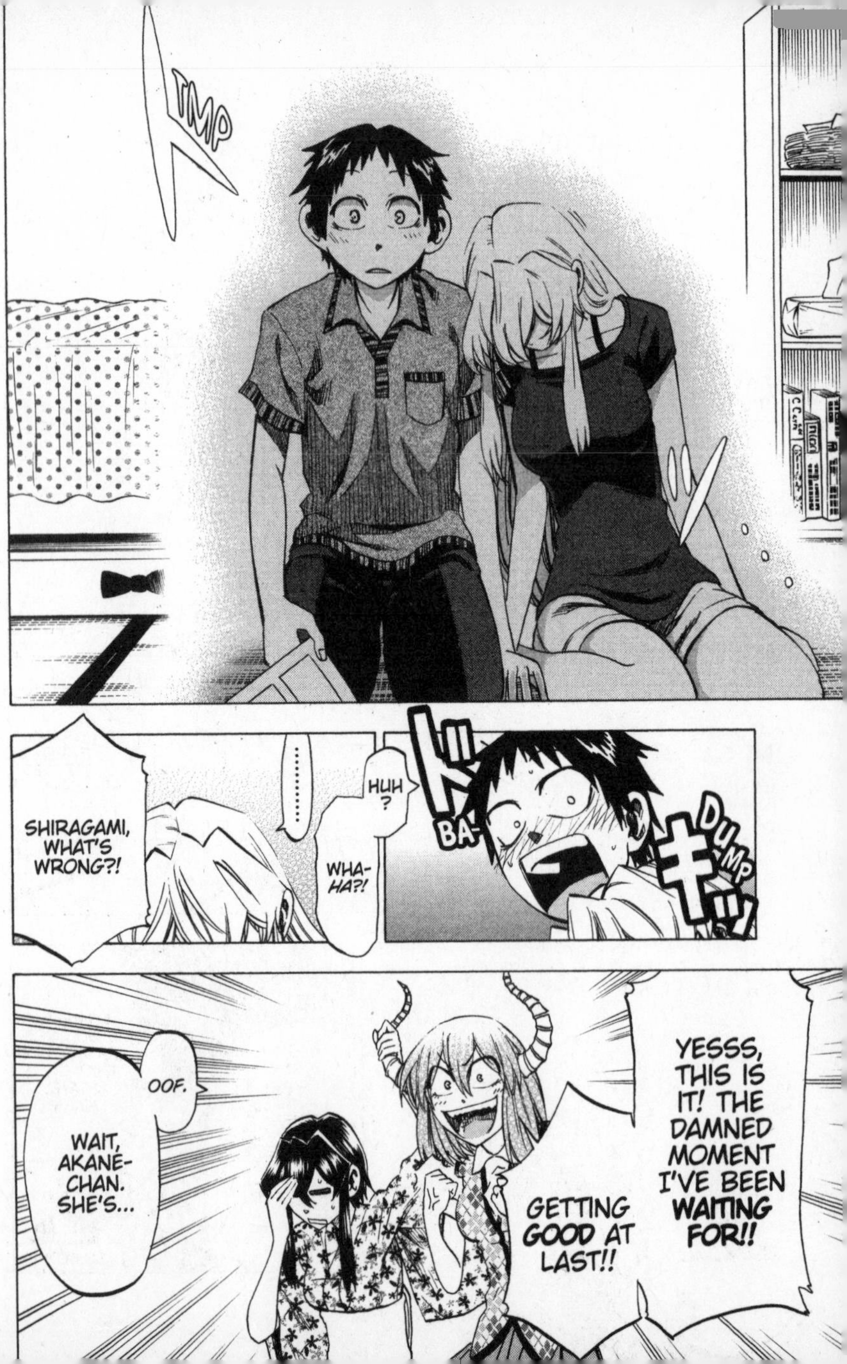
TMP
BA-
DUMP
HUH?
......
WHA-HA?!
SHIRAGAMI, WHAT'S WRONG?!
YESSS, THIS IS IT! THE DAMNED MOMENT I'VE BEEN WAITING FOR!!
GETTING GOOD AT LAST!!
OOF.
WAIT, AKANE-CHAN. SHE'S...

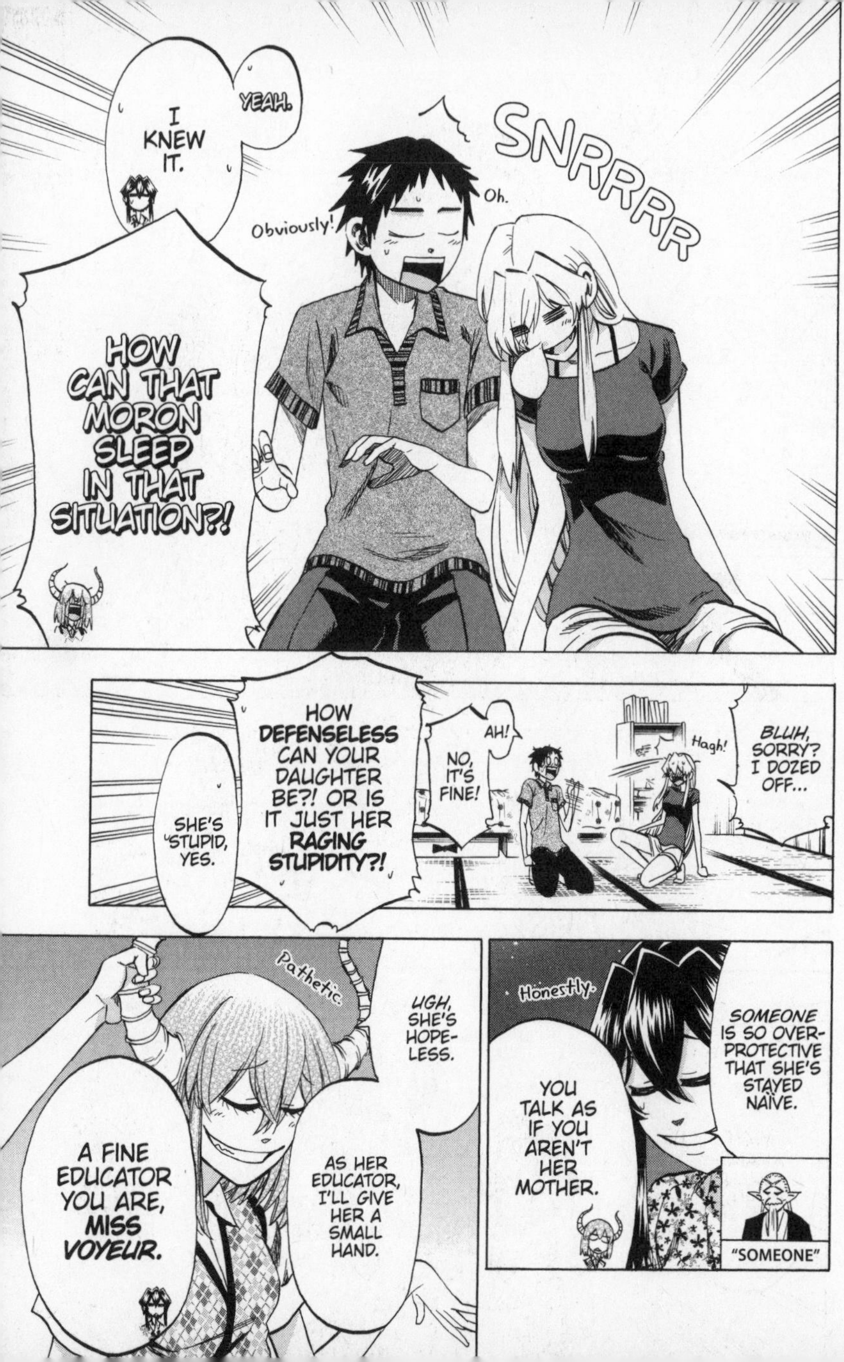
SNRRRRR
Oh.
YEAH.
I KNEW IT.
Obviously!
HOW CAN THAT MORON SLEEP IN THAT SITUATION?!
BLUH, SORRY? I DOZED OFF...
Hagh!
AH!
NO, IT'S FINE!
HOW DEFENSELESS CAN YOUR DAUGHTER BE?! OR IS IT JUST HER RAGING STUPIDITY?!
SHE'S STUPID, YES.
SOMEONE IS SO OVER-PROTECTIVE THAT SHE'S STAYED NAÏVE.
Honestly.
YOU TALK AS IF YOU AREN'T HER MOTHER.
"SOMEONE"
UGH, SHE'S HOPE-LESS.
Pathetic.
AS HER EDUCATOR, I'LL GIVE HER A SMALL HAND.
A FINE EDUCATOR YOU ARE, MISS VOYEUR.

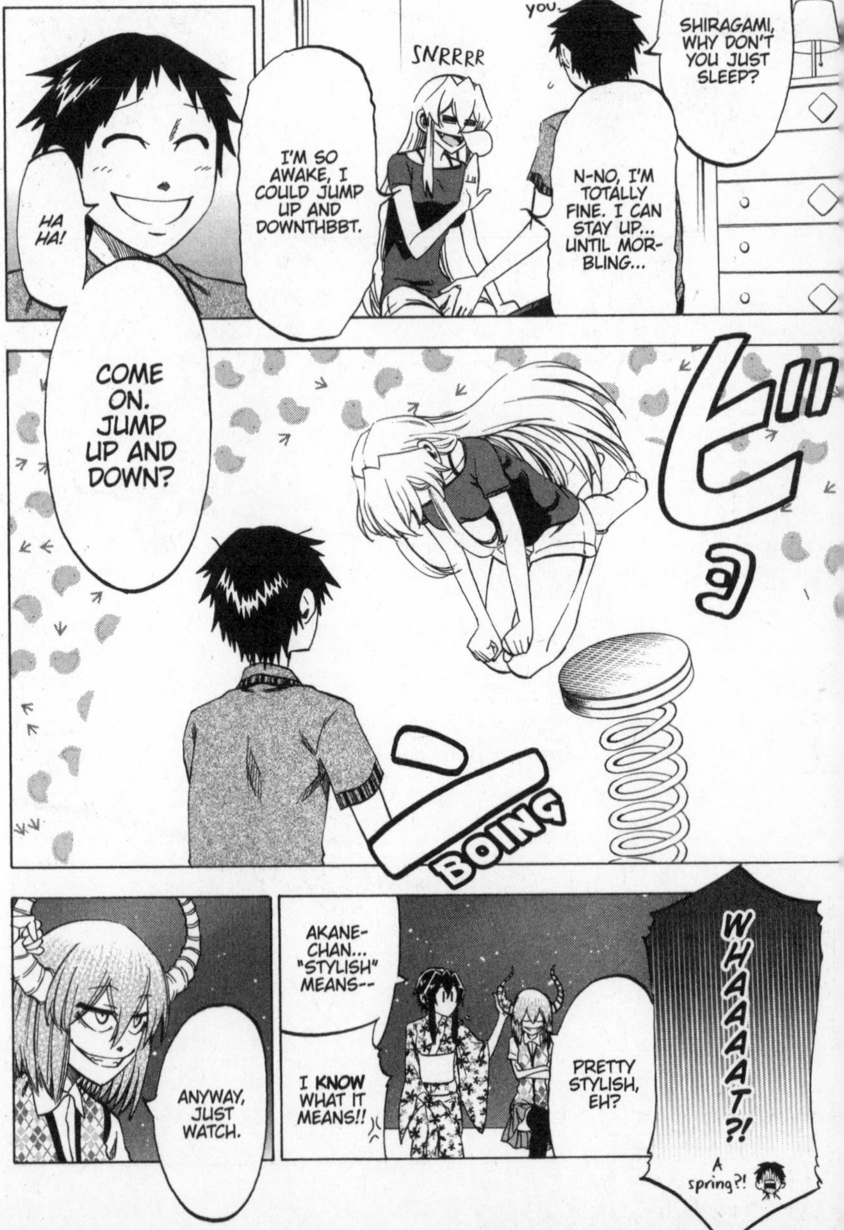
SHIRAGAMI, WHY DON'T YOU JUST SLEEP?
I'm losing you.
N-NO, I'M TOTALLY FINE. I CAN STAY UP... UNTIL MOR-BLING...
SNRRRR
I'M SO AWAKE, I COULD JUMP UP AND DOWNTHBBT.
HA HA!
COME ON. JUMP UP AND DOWN?
BOING
WHAAAAAT?!
A spring?!
PRETTY STYLISH, EH?
AKANE-CHAN... "STYLISH" MEANS--
I KNOW WHAT IT MEANS!!
ANYWAY, JUST WATCH.

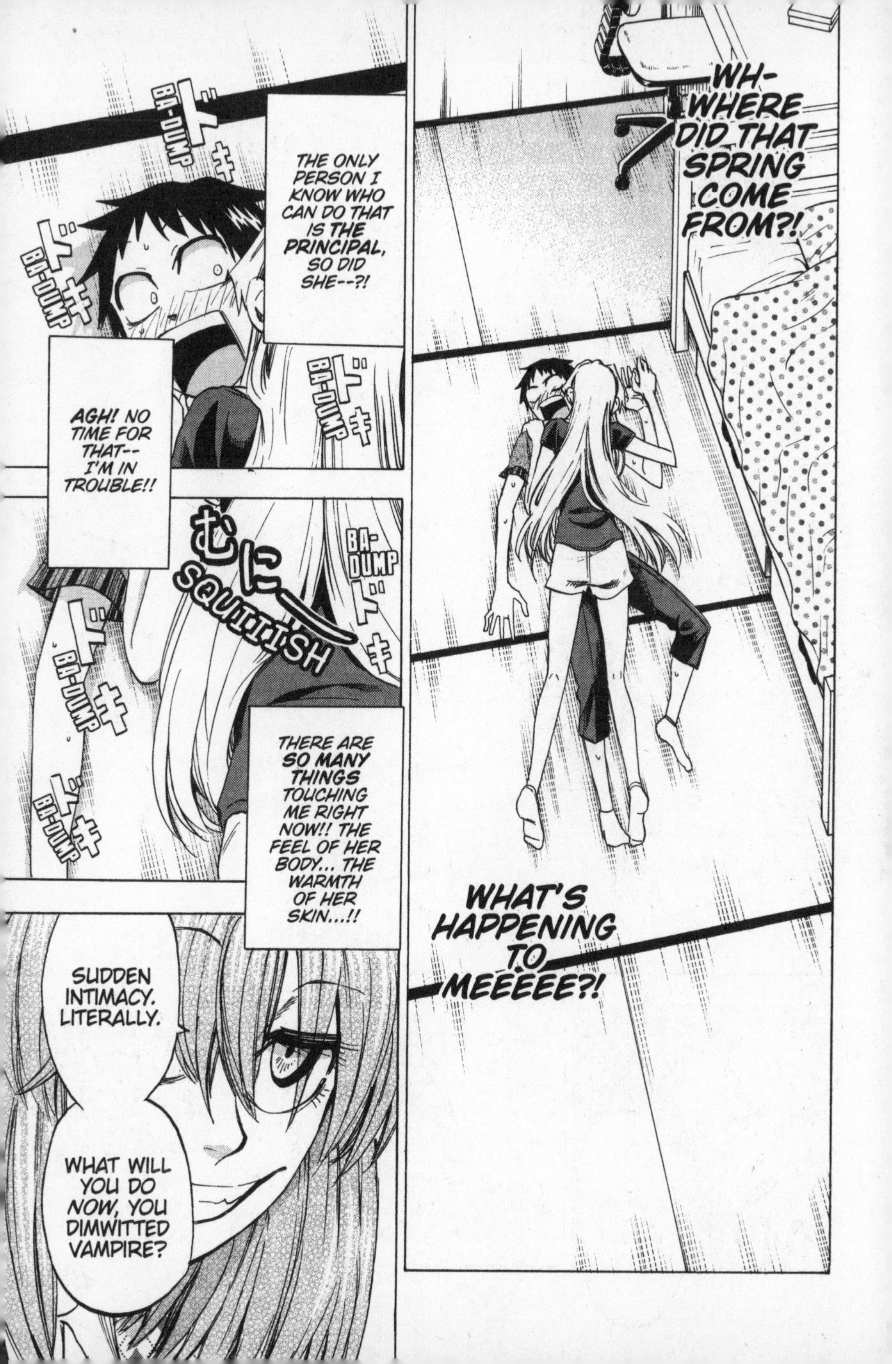
WH-WHERE DID THAT SPRING COME FROM?!
WHAT'S HAPPENING TO MEEEEE?!
ドキ BA-DUMP
THE ONLY PERSON I KNOW WHO CAN DO THAT IS THE PRINCIPAL, SO DID SHE--?!
ドキ BA-DUMP
ドキ BA-DUMP
AGH! NO TIME FOR THAT-- I'M IN TROUBLE!!
BA-DUMP ドキ
むにー SQUIIIISH
ドキ BA-DUMP
ドキ BA-DUMP
THERE ARE SO MANY THINGS TOUCHING ME RIGHT NOW!! THE FEEL OF HER BODY... THE WARMTH OF HER SKIN...!!
SUDDEN INTIMACY. LITERALLY.
WHAT WILL YOU DO NOW, YOU DIMWITTED VAMPIRE?

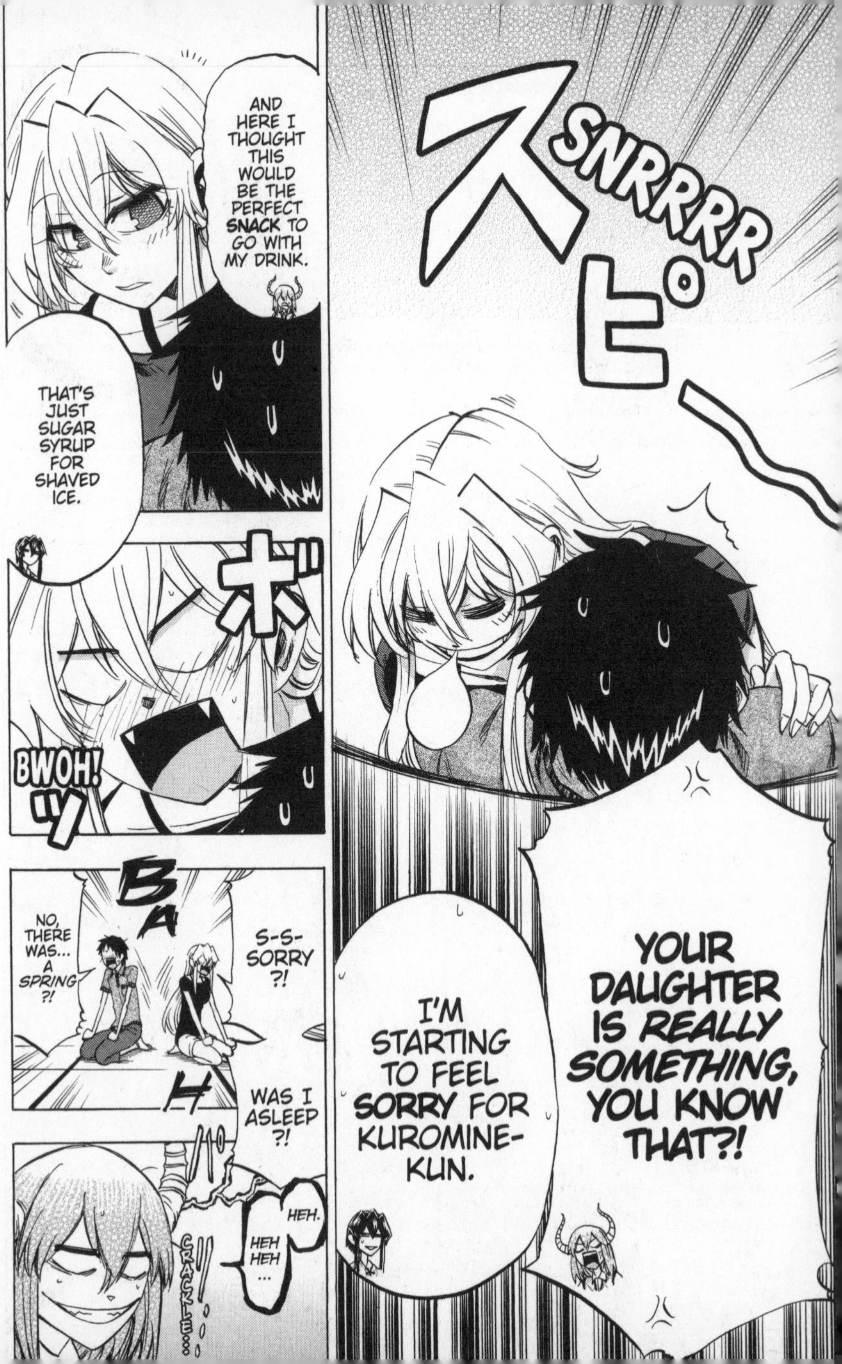
SNRRRRR
スピ〜
YOUR DAUGHTER IS *REALLY SOMETHING*, YOU KNOW THAT?!
I'M STARTING TO FEEL **SORRY** FOR KUROMINE-KUN.
AND HERE I THOUGHT THIS WOULD BE THE PERFECT **SNACK** TO GO WITH MY DRINK.
THAT'S JUST SUGAR SYRUP FOR SHAVED ICE.
ボッ
BWOH!
BAH
S-S-SORRY?!
NO, THERE WAS... A *SPRING*?!
WAS I ASLEEP?!
HEH.
HEH HEH...
CRACKLE...

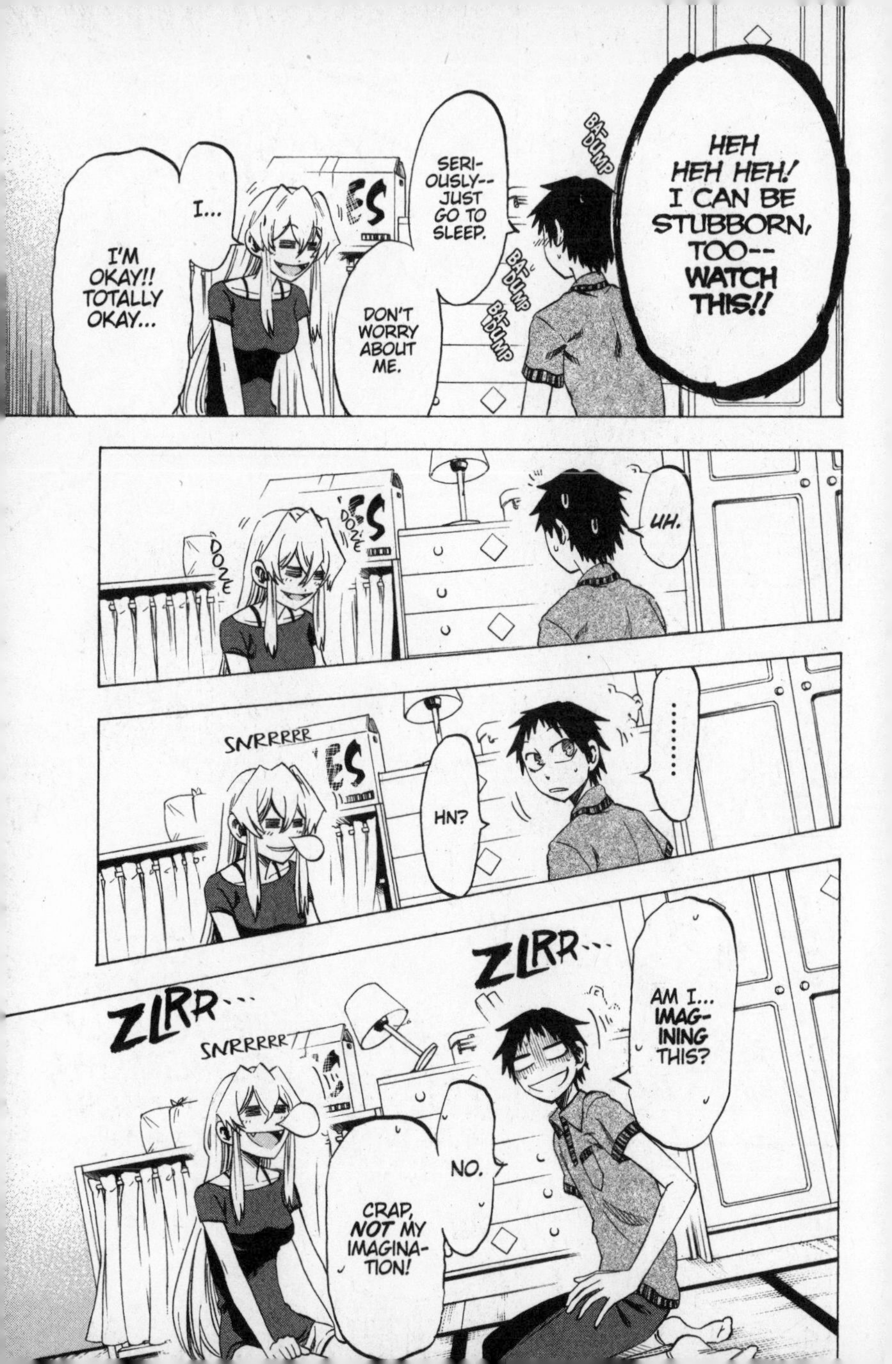
HEH HEH HEH! I CAN BE STUBBORN, TOO-- WATCH THIS!!
BA-DUMP
BA-DUMP
BA-DUMP
SERI-OUSLY-- JUST GO TO SLEEP.
DON'T WORRY ABOUT ME.
I...
I'M OKAY!! TOTALLY OKAY...
UH.
DOZE
DOZE
......
HN?
SNRRRRR
AM I... IMAG-INING THIS?
ZLRR...
ZLRR...
SNRRRRR
NO.
CRAP, *NOT* MY IMAGINA-TION!

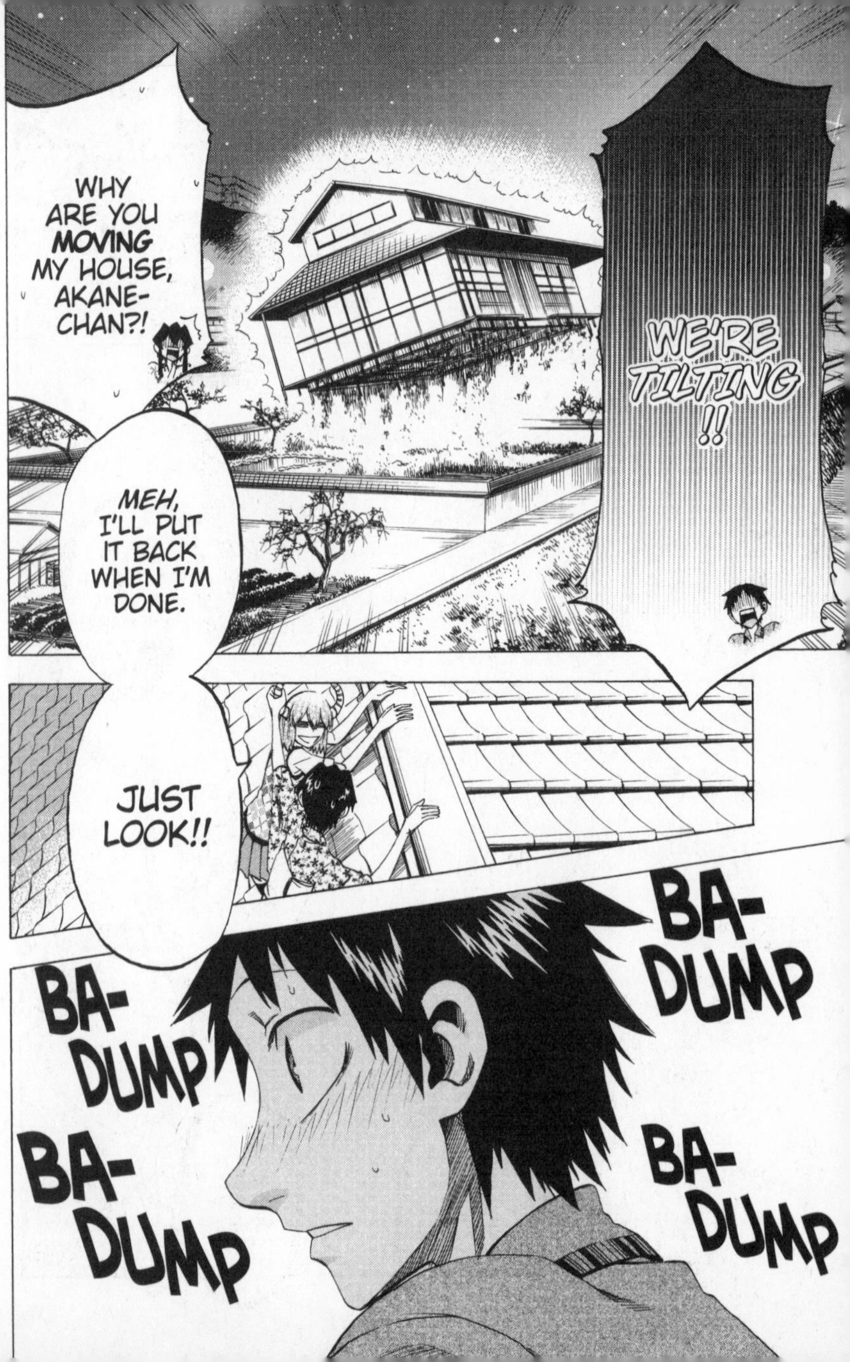
WE'RE TILTING!!
WHY ARE YOU MOVING MY HOUSE, AKANE-CHAN?!
MEH, I'LL PUT IT BACK WHEN I'M DONE.
JUST LOOK!!
BA-DUMP
BA-DUMP
BA-DUMP
BA-DUMP
BA-DUMP

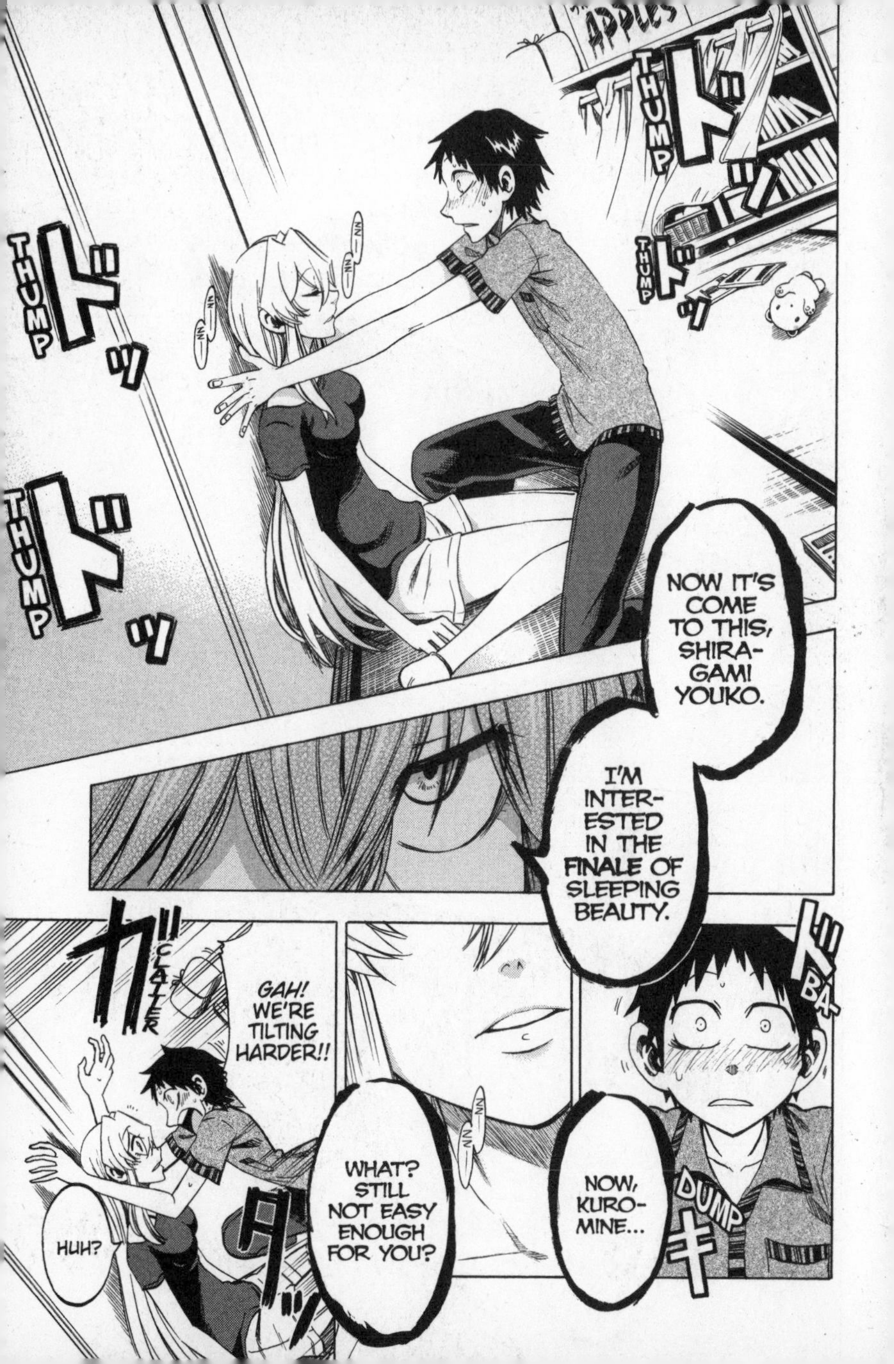
APPLES
THUMP
THUMP
NN— NN—
NN— NN—
THUMP
THUMP
NOW IT'S COME TO THIS, SHIRAGAMI YOUKO.
I'M INTERESTED IN THE FINALE OF SLEEPING BEAUTY.
BA-
NOW, KUROMINE...
DUMP
NN— NN—
WHAT? STILL NOT EASY ENOUGH FOR YOU?
CLATTER
GAH! WE'RE TILTING HARDER!!
HUH?

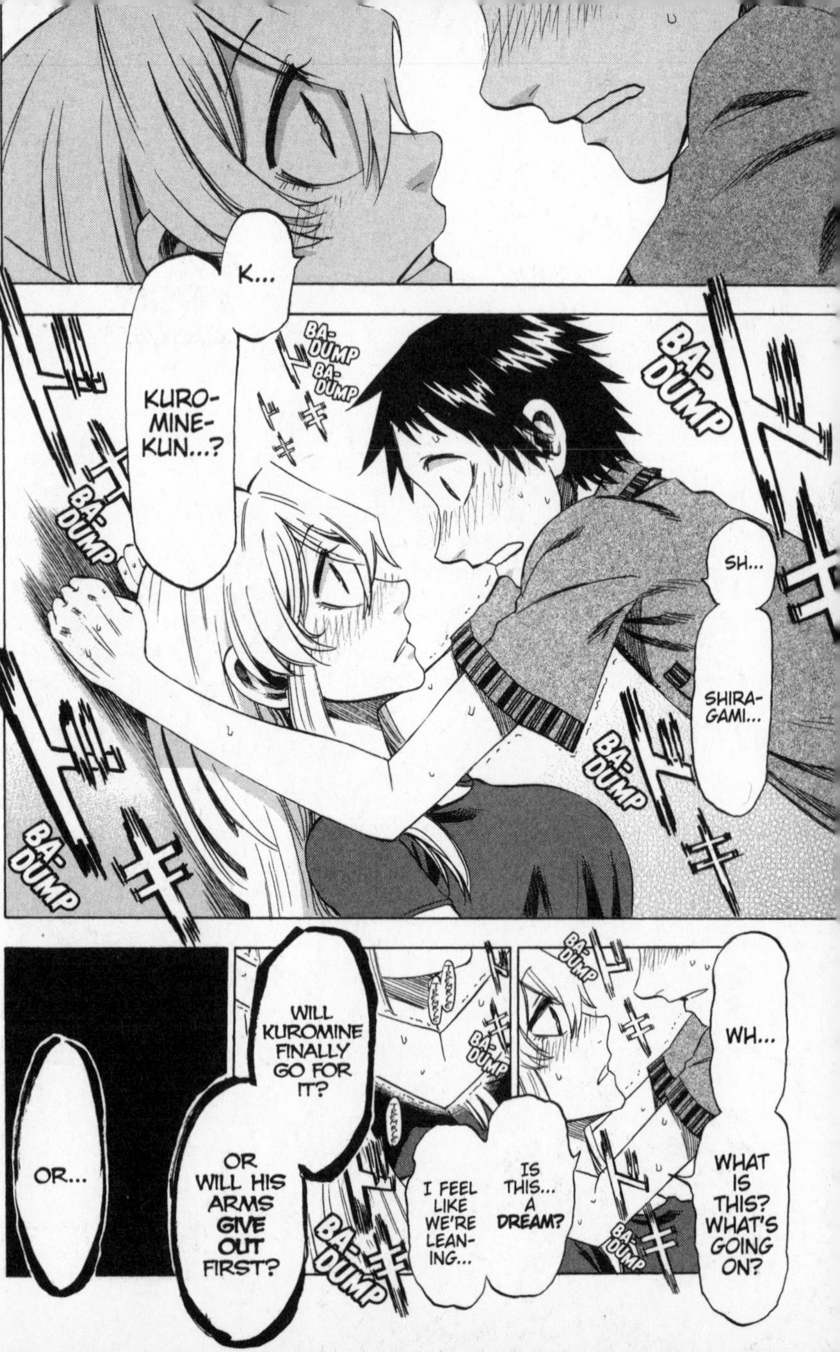
K...
BA-DUMP
SH...
SHIRAGAMI...
BA-DUMP
KURO-MINE-KUN...?
BA-DUMP BA-DUMP
BA-DUMP
BA-DUMP
WH...
BA-DUMP
WHAT IS THIS? WHAT'S GOING ON?
BA-DUMP
IS THIS... A DREAM?
I FEEL LIKE WE'RE LEANING...
BA-DUMP
WILL KUROMINE FINALLY GO FOR IT?
OR WILL HIS ARMS GIVE OUT FIRST?
BA-DUMP
OR...

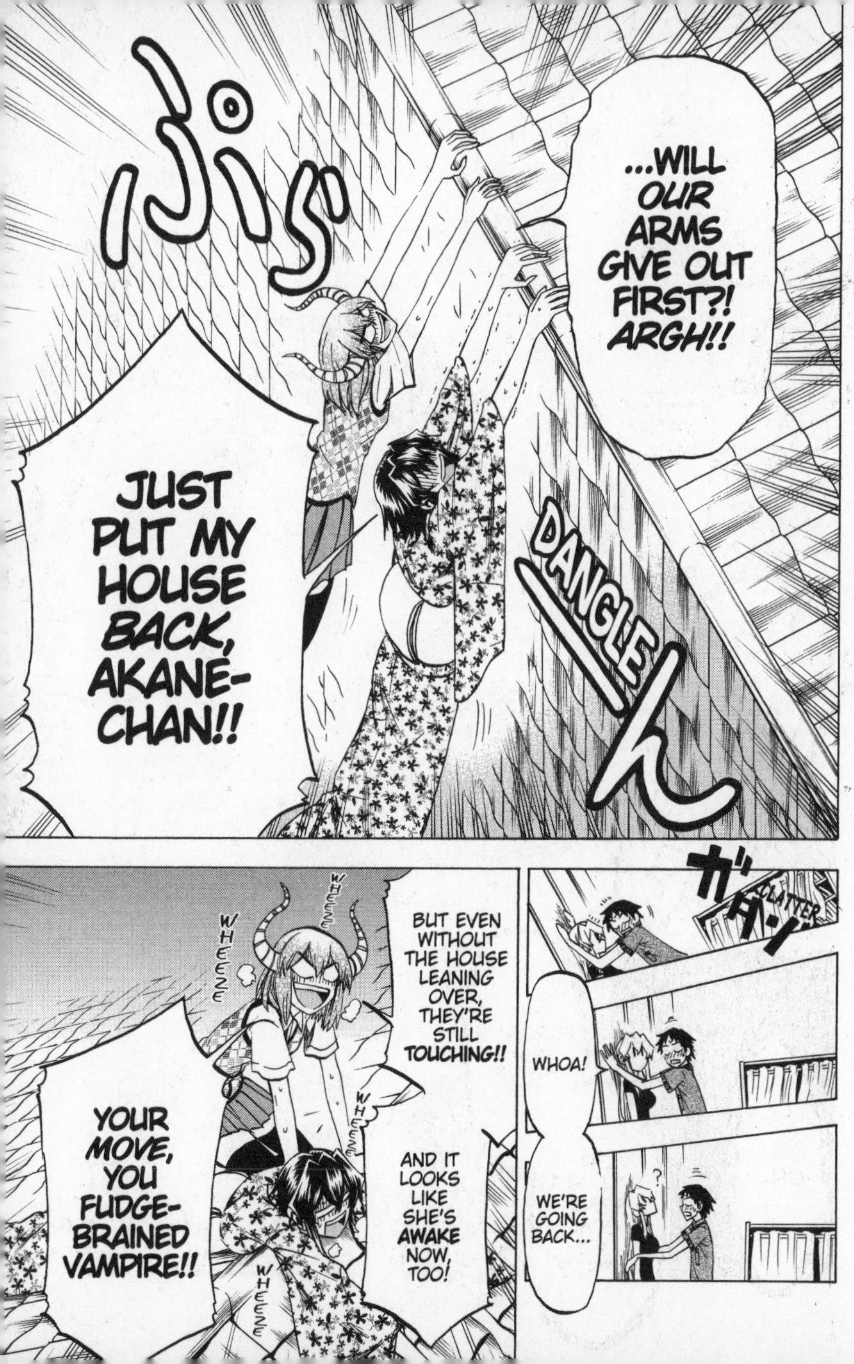
...WILL OUR ARMS GIVE OUT FIRST?! ARGH!!
ぷら
DANGLE
ん
JUST PUT MY HOUSE BACK, AKANE-CHAN!!
ガダ・!
CLATTER
WHOA!
WE'RE GOING BACK...
BUT EVEN WITHOUT THE HOUSE LEANING OVER, THEY'RE STILL TOUCHING!!
AND IT LOOKS LIKE SHE'S AWAKE NOW, TOO!
WHEEZE
WHEEZE
YOUR MOVE, YOU FUDGE-BRAINED VAMPIRE!!
WHEEZE
WHEEZE

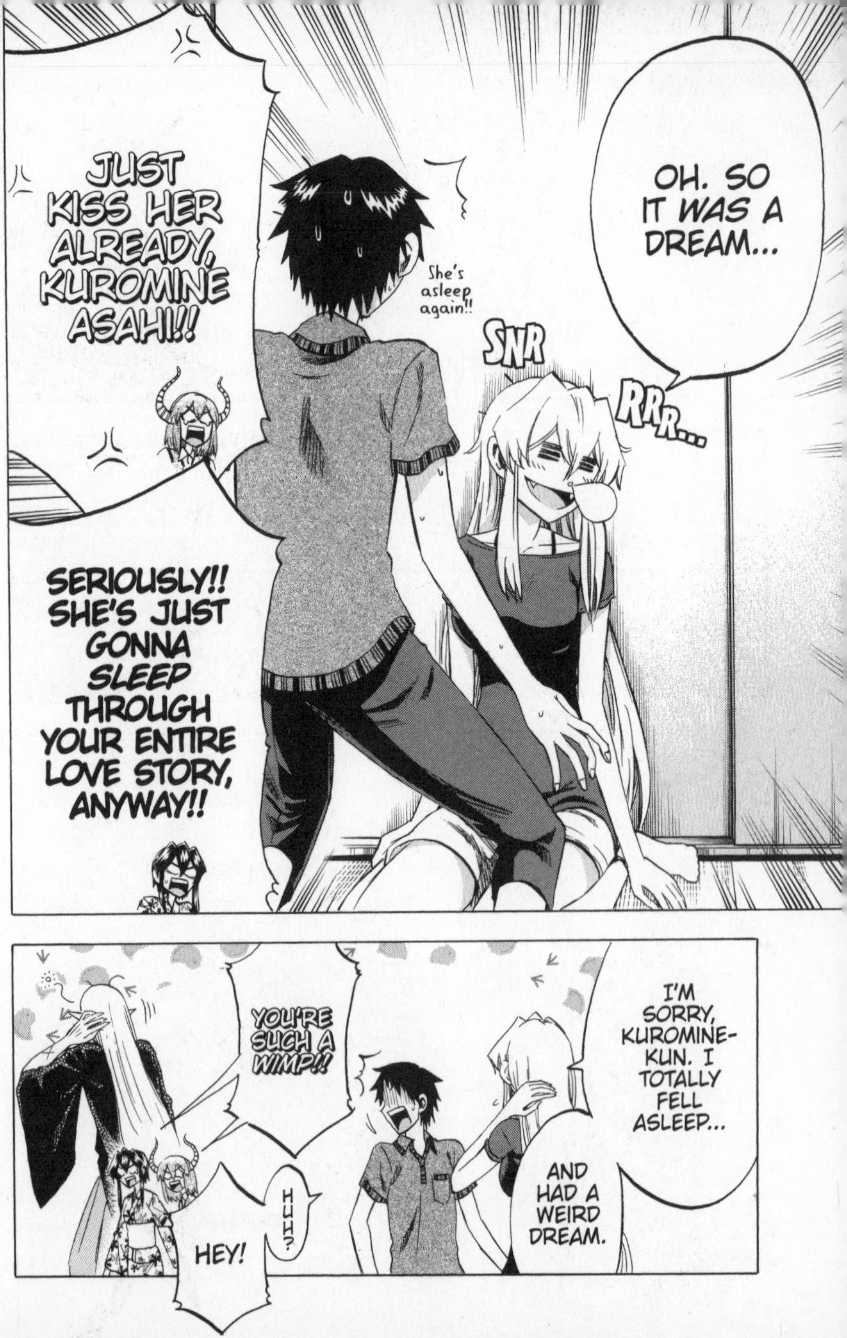
OH. SO IT WAS A DREAM...
SNR
RRR...
She's asleep again!!
JUST KISS HER ALREADY, KUROMINE ASAHI!!
SERIOUSLY!! SHE'S JUST GONNA SLEEP THROUGH YOUR ENTIRE LOVE STORY, ANYWAY!!
I'M SORRY, KUROMINE-KUN. I TOTALLY FELL ASLEEP...
AND HAD A WEIRD DREAM.
HUH?
YOU'RE SUCH A WIMP!!
HEY!

Chapter 33: "See You Later!"

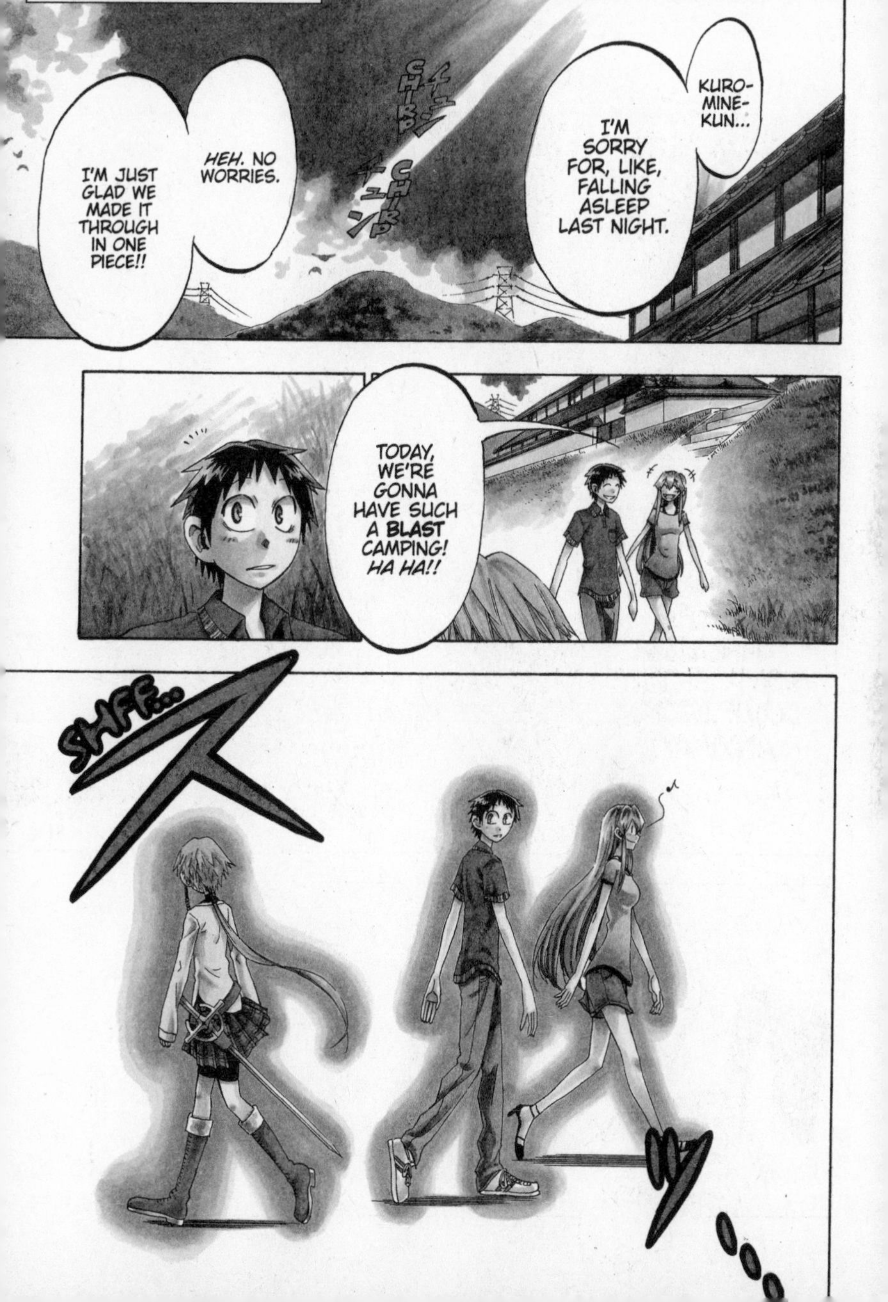
KURO-MINE-KUN...
I'M SORRY FOR, LIKE, FALLING ASLEEP LAST NIGHT.
CHIRP CHIRP
HEH. NO WORRIES.
I'M JUST GLAD WE MADE IT THROUGH IN ONE PIECE!!
TODAY, WE'RE GONNA HAVE SUCH A BLAST CAMPING! HA HA!!
SHFF...

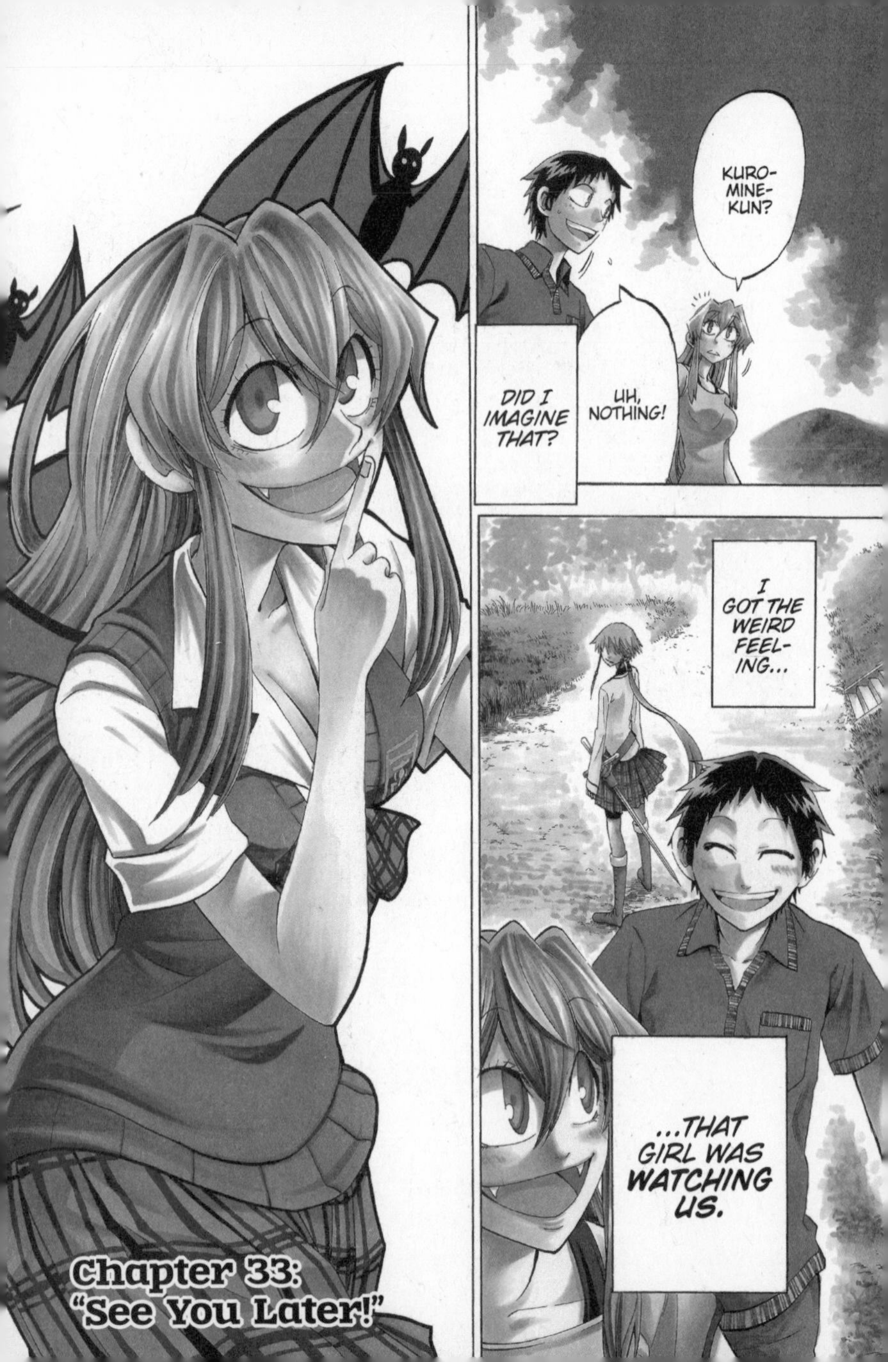
KURO-MINE-KUN?
UH, NOTHING!
DID I IMAGINE THAT?
I GOT THE WEIRD FEEL-ING...
...THAT GIRL WAS WATCHING US.
Chapter 33: "See You Later!"

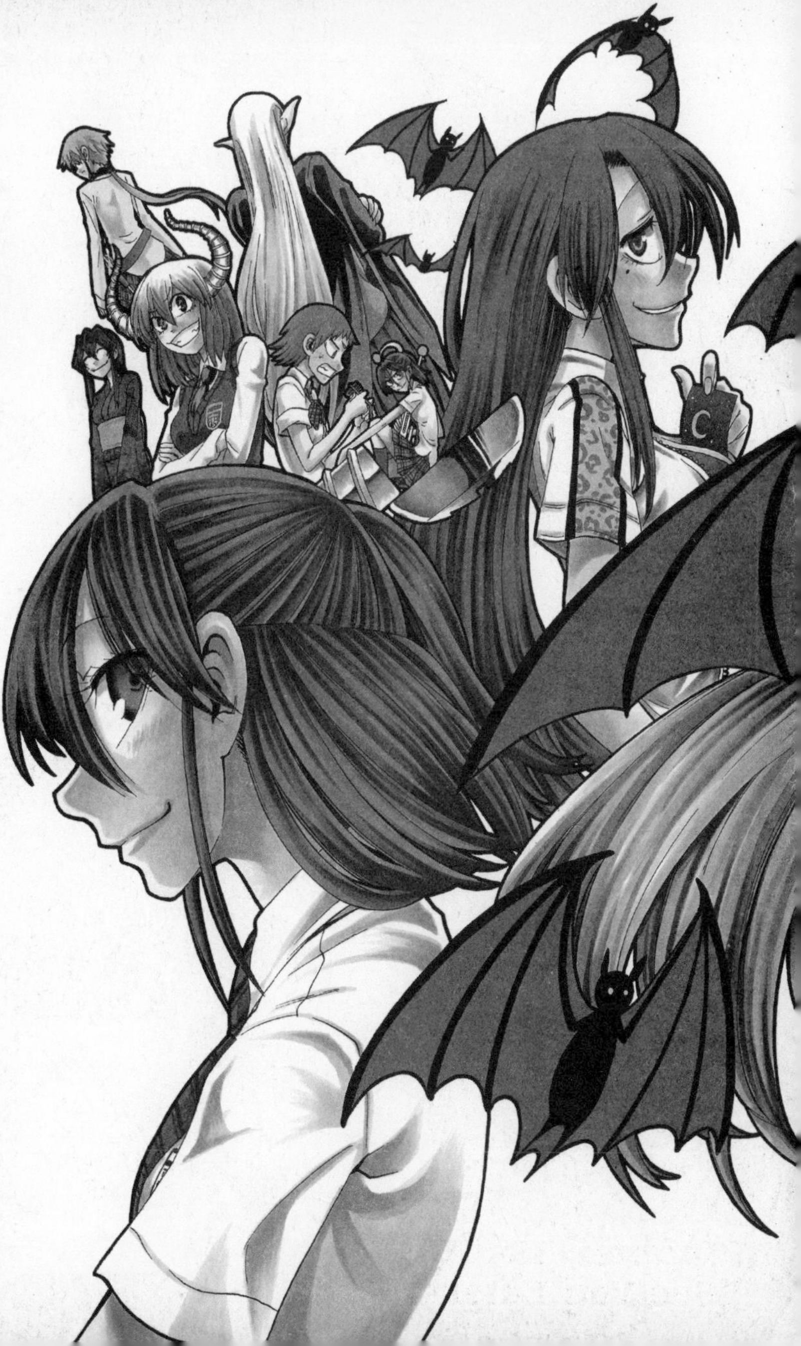

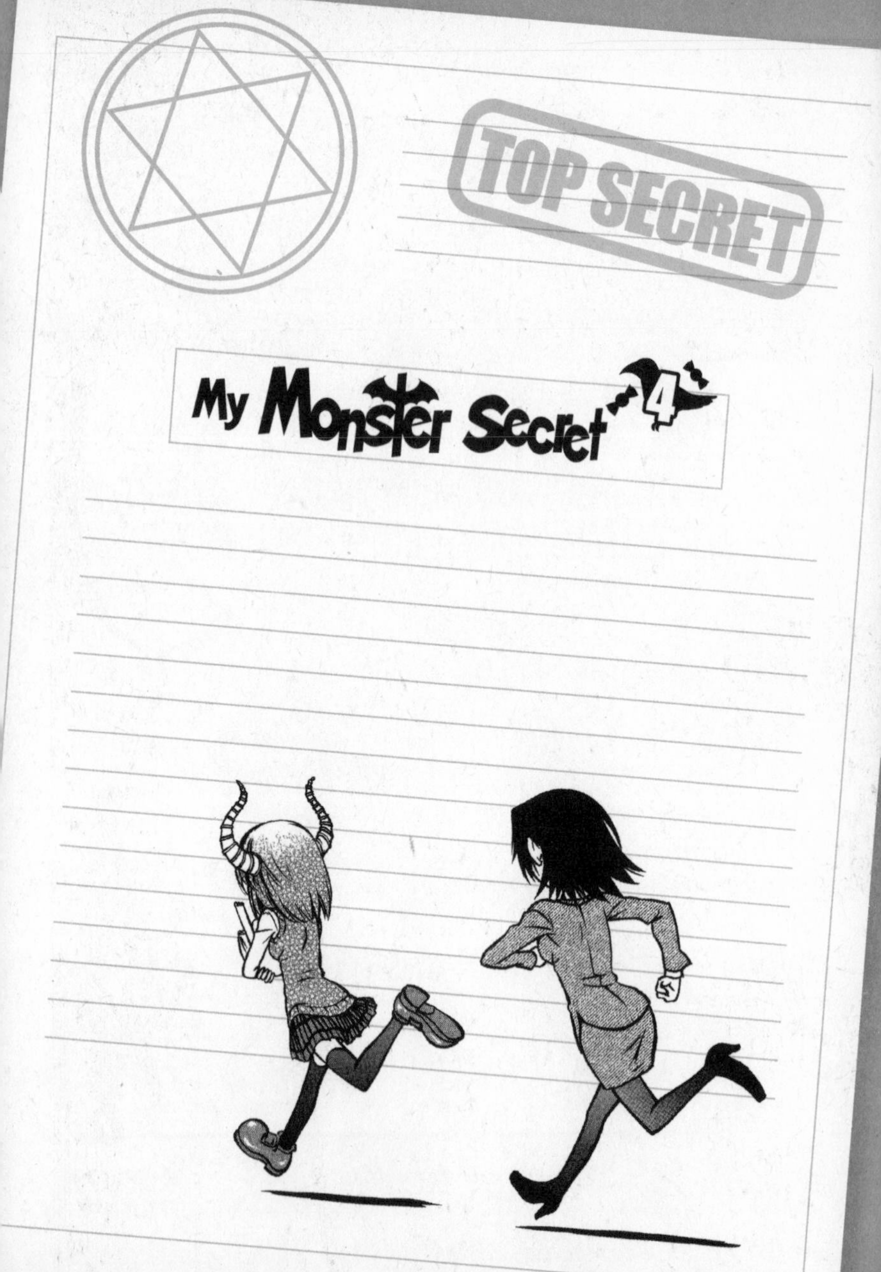
TOP SECRET
My Monster Secret 4

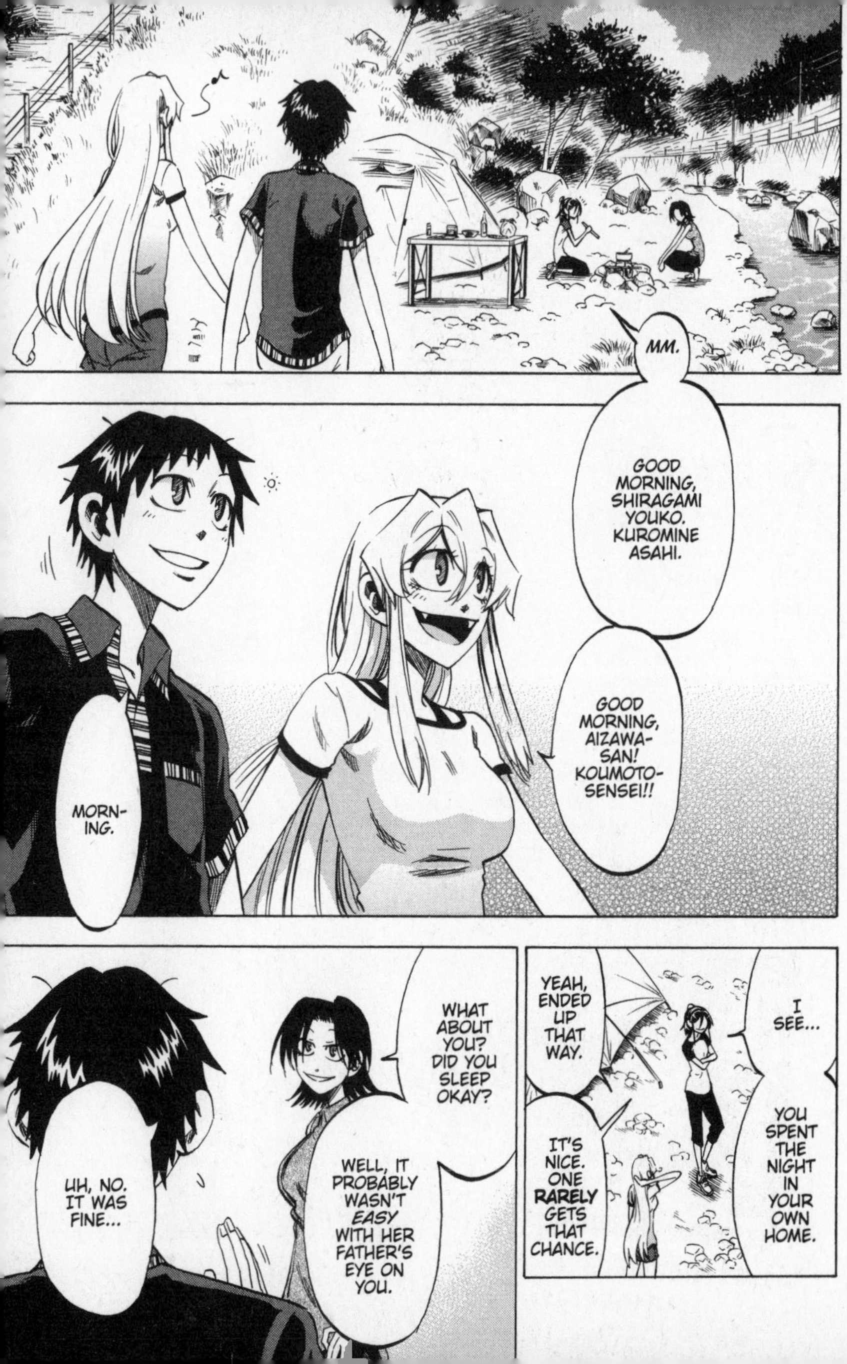
MM.
GOOD MORNING, SHIRAGAMI YOUKO. KUROMINE ASAHI.
GOOD MORNING, AIZAWA-SAN! KOUMOTO-SENSEI!!
MORN-ING.
I SEE...
YOU SPENT THE NIGHT IN YOUR OWN HOME.
YEAH, ENDED UP THAT WAY.
IT'S NICE. ONE RARELY GETS THAT CHANCE.
WHAT ABOUT YOU? DID YOU SLEEP OKAY?
WELL, IT PROBABLY WASN'T EASY WITH HER FATHER'S EYE ON YOU.
UH, NO. IT WAS FINE...

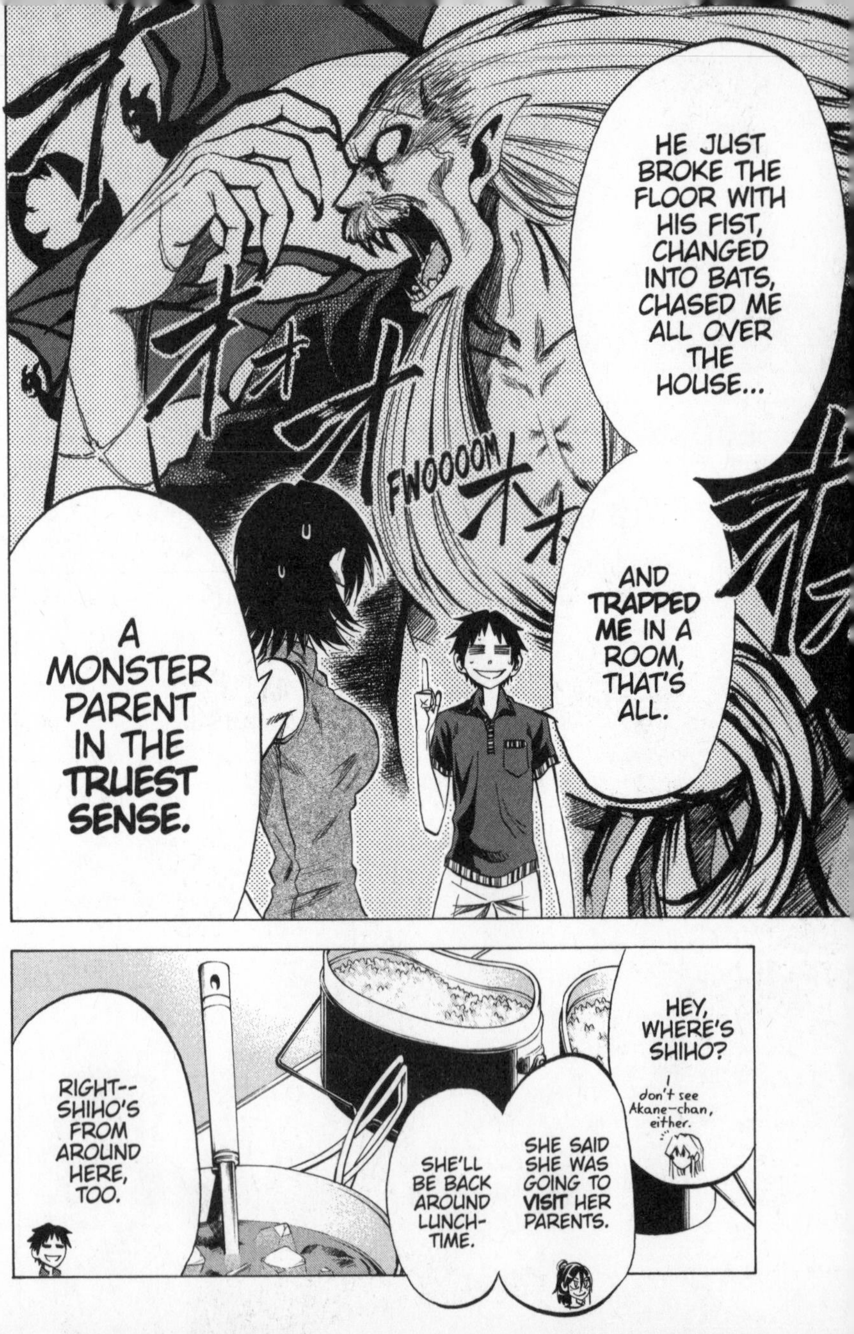
HE JUST BROKE THE FLOOR WITH HIS FIST, CHANGED INTO BATS, CHASED ME ALL OVER THE HOUSE...
FWOOOOM
AND TRAPPED ME IN A ROOM, THAT'S ALL.
A MONSTER PARENT IN THE TRUEST SENSE.
HEY, WHERE'S SHIHO?
I don't see Akane-chan, either.
SHE SAID SHE WAS GOING TO VISIT HER PARENTS.
SHE'LL BE BACK AROUND LUNCH-TIME.
RIGHT-- SHIHO'S FROM AROUND HERE, TOO.

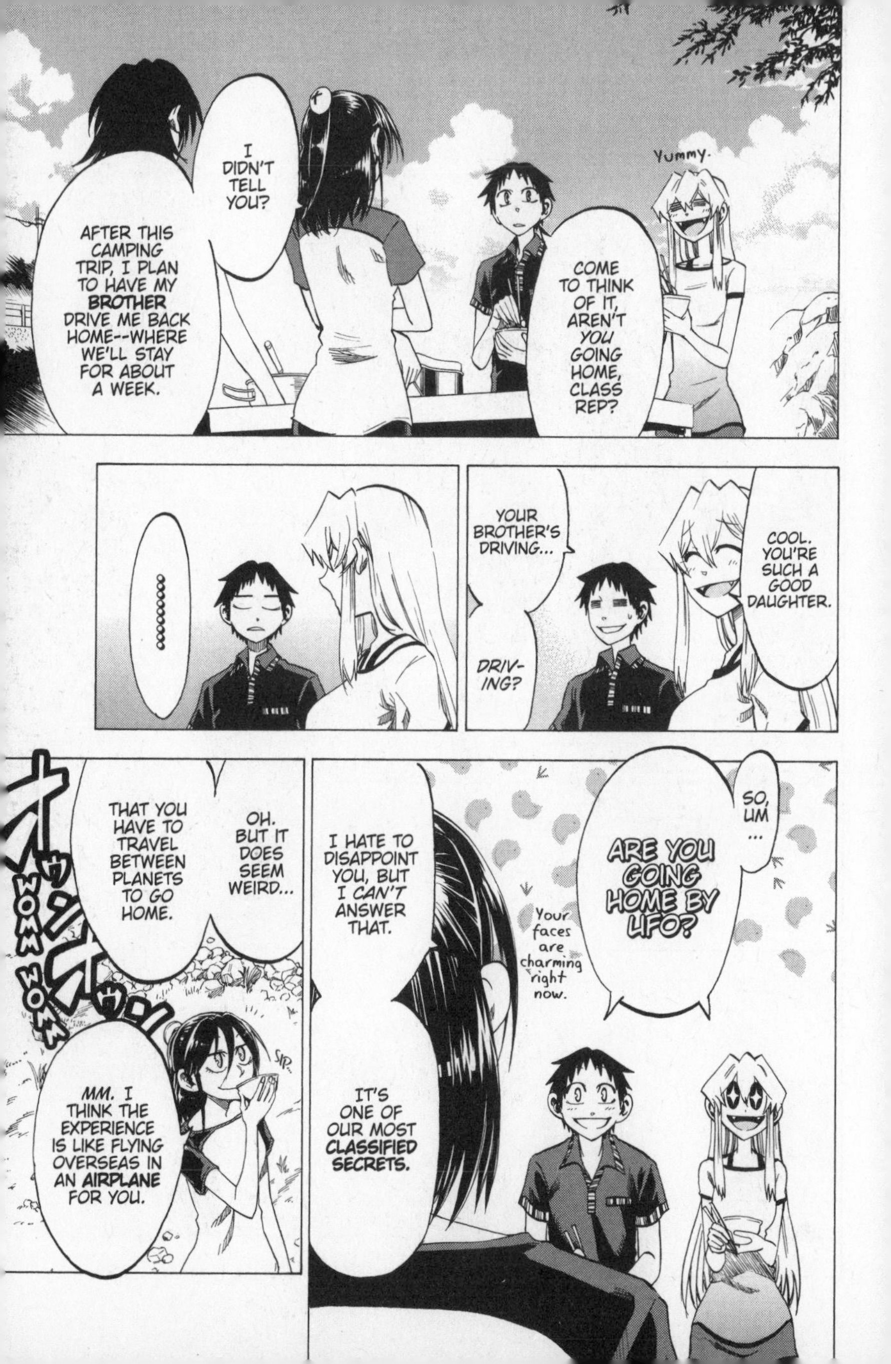
Yummy.
COME TO THINK OF IT, AREN'T YOU GOING HOME, CLASS REP?
I DIDN'T TELL YOU?
AFTER THIS CAMPING TRIP, I PLAN TO HAVE MY BROTHER DRIVE ME BACK HOME--WHERE WE'LL STAY FOR ABOUT A WEEK.
COOL. YOU'RE SUCH A GOOD DAUGHTER.
YOUR BROTHER'S DRIVING...
DRIV-ING?
....
SO, UM ...
ARE YOU GOING HOME BY UFO?
Your faces are charming right now.
I HATE TO DISAPPOINT YOU, BUT I CAN'T ANSWER THAT.
IT'S ONE OF OUR MOST CLASSIFIED SECRETS.
OH. BUT IT DOES SEEM WEIRD...
THAT YOU HAVE TO TRAVEL BETWEEN PLANETS TO GO HOME.
WOMM WOMM WOMM
SIP..
MM. I THINK THE EXPERIENCE IS LIKE FLYING OVERSEAS IN AN AIRPLANE FOR YOU.

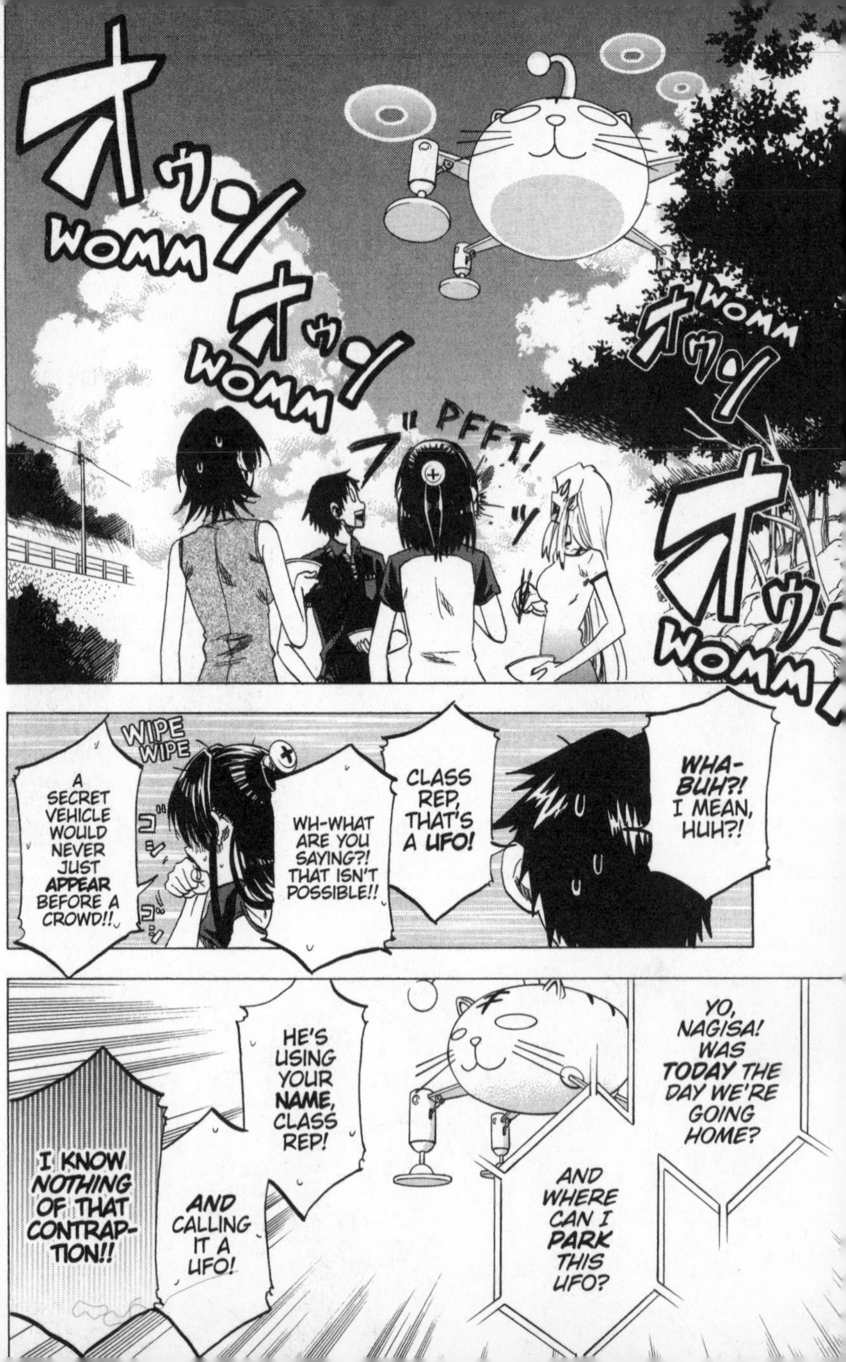
WOMM
オウン
WOMM
オウン
PFFT!
ブッ
WOMM
オウン
WOMM
オウン
WHA-BUH?! I MEAN, HUH?!
CLASS REP, THAT'S A UFO!
WH-WHAT ARE YOU SAYING?! THAT ISN'T POSSIBLE!!
WIPE WIPE
A SECRET VEHICLE WOULD NEVER JUST APPEAR BEFORE A CROWD!!
YO, NAGISA! WAS TODAY THE DAY WE'RE GOING HOME?
AND WHERE CAN I PARK THIS UFO?
HE'S USING YOUR NAME, CLASS REP!
AND CALLING IT A UFO!
I KNOW NOTHING OF THAT CONTRAPTION!!

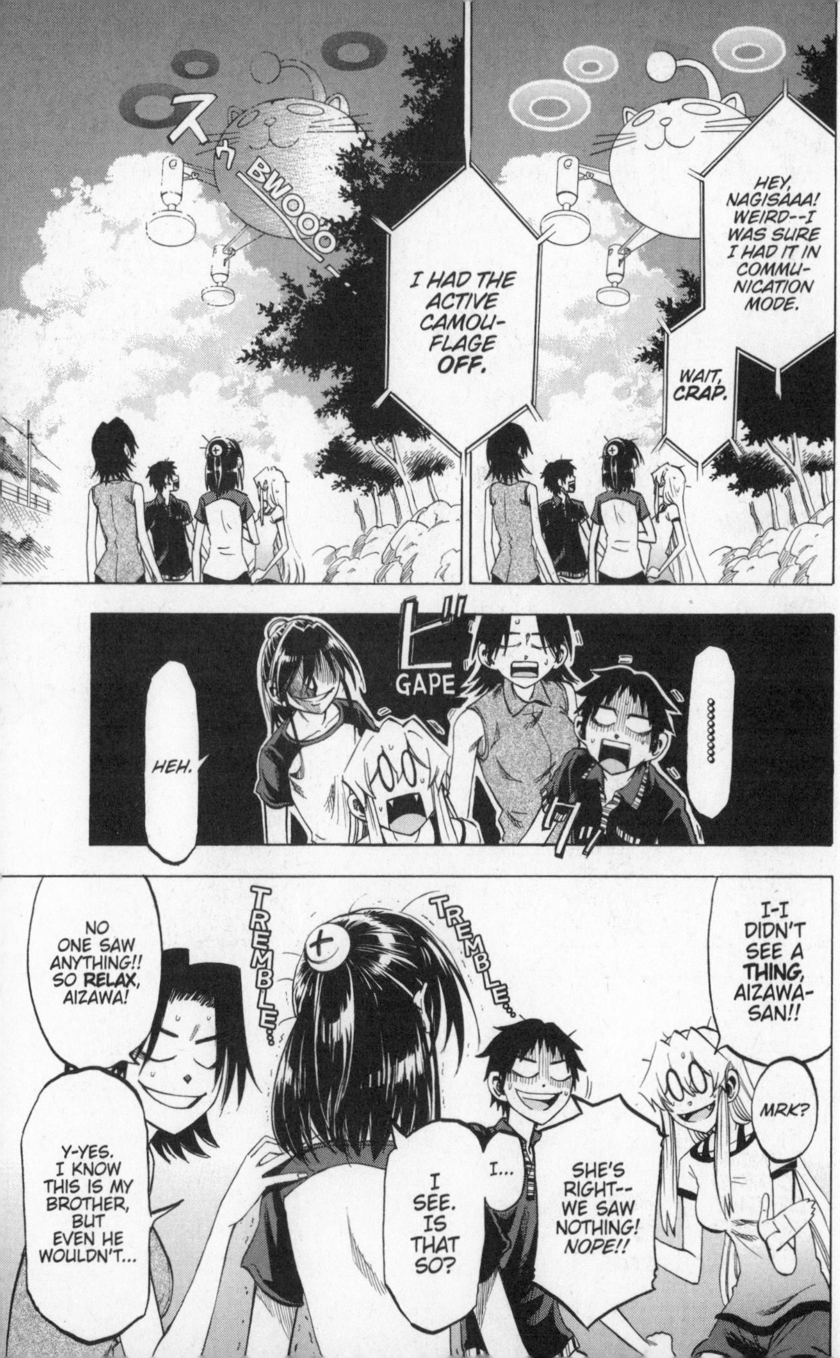
HEY, NAGISAAA! WEIRD--I WAS SURE I HAD IT IN COMMUNICATION MODE.
WAIT, CRAP.
I HAD THE ACTIVE CAMOUFLAGE OFF.
スゥ
BWOOO
......
GAPE
HEH.
I-I DIDN'T SEE A THING, AIZAWA-SAN!!
MRK?
SHE'S RIGHT-- WE SAW NOTHING! NOPE!!
I...
TREMBLE TREMBLE...
I SEE. IS THAT SO?
NO ONE SAW ANYTHING!! SO RELAX, AIZAWA!
Y-YES. I KNOW THIS IS MY BROTHER, BUT EVEN HE WOULDN'T...

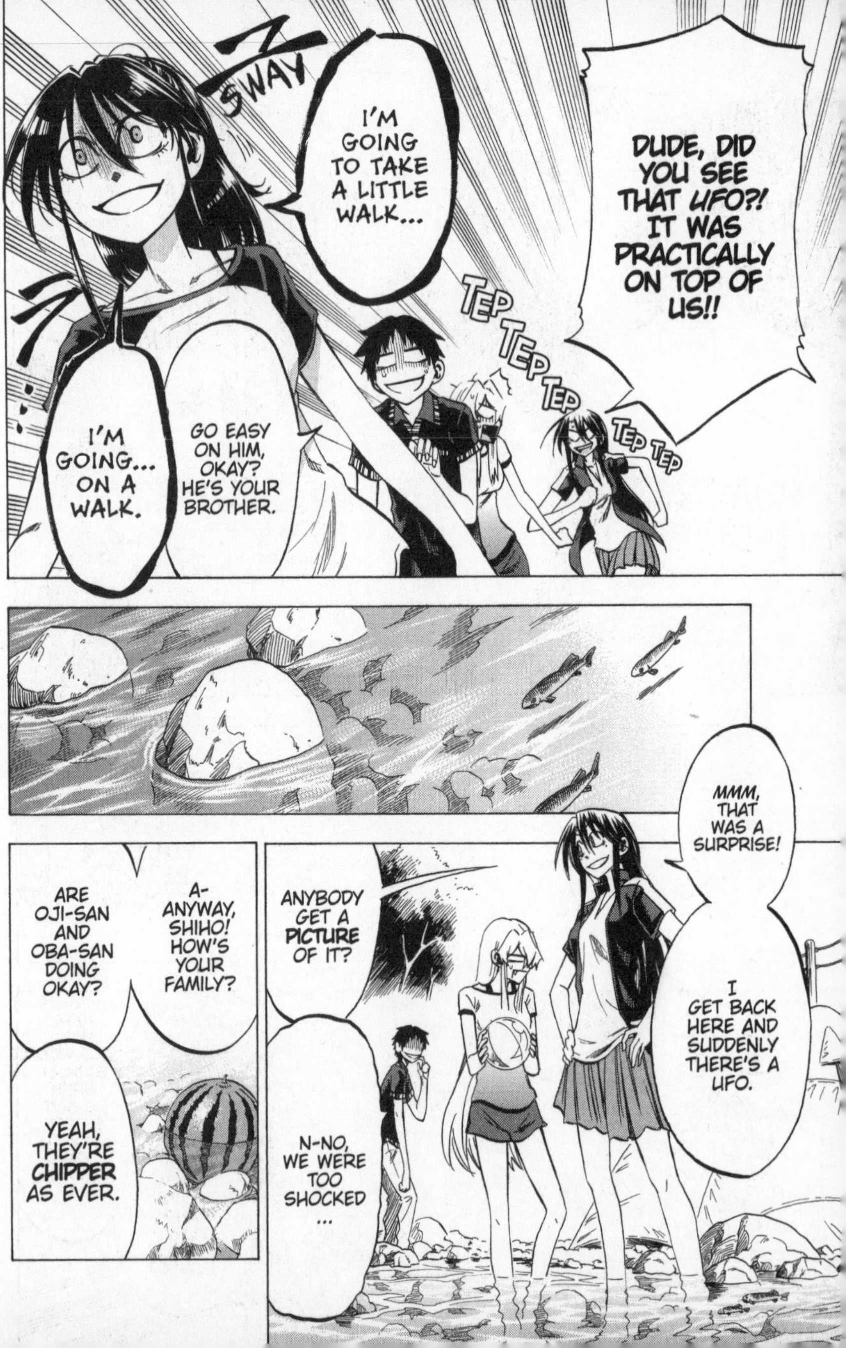
DUDE, DID YOU SEE THAT UFO?! IT WAS PRACTICALLY ON TOP OF US!!
TEP TEP TEP TEP TEP
I'M GOING TO TAKE A LITTLE WALK...
SWAY
GO EASY ON HIM, OKAY? HE'S YOUR BROTHER.
I'M GOING... ON A WALK.
MMM, THAT WAS A SURPRISE!
I GET BACK HERE AND SUDDENLY THERE'S A UFO.
ANYBODY GET A PICTURE OF IT?
N-NO, WE WERE TOO SHOCKED ...
A-ANYWAY, SHIHO! HOW'S YOUR FAMILY?
ARE OJI-SAN AND OBA-SAN DOING OKAY?
YEAH, THEY'RE CHIPPER AS EVER.

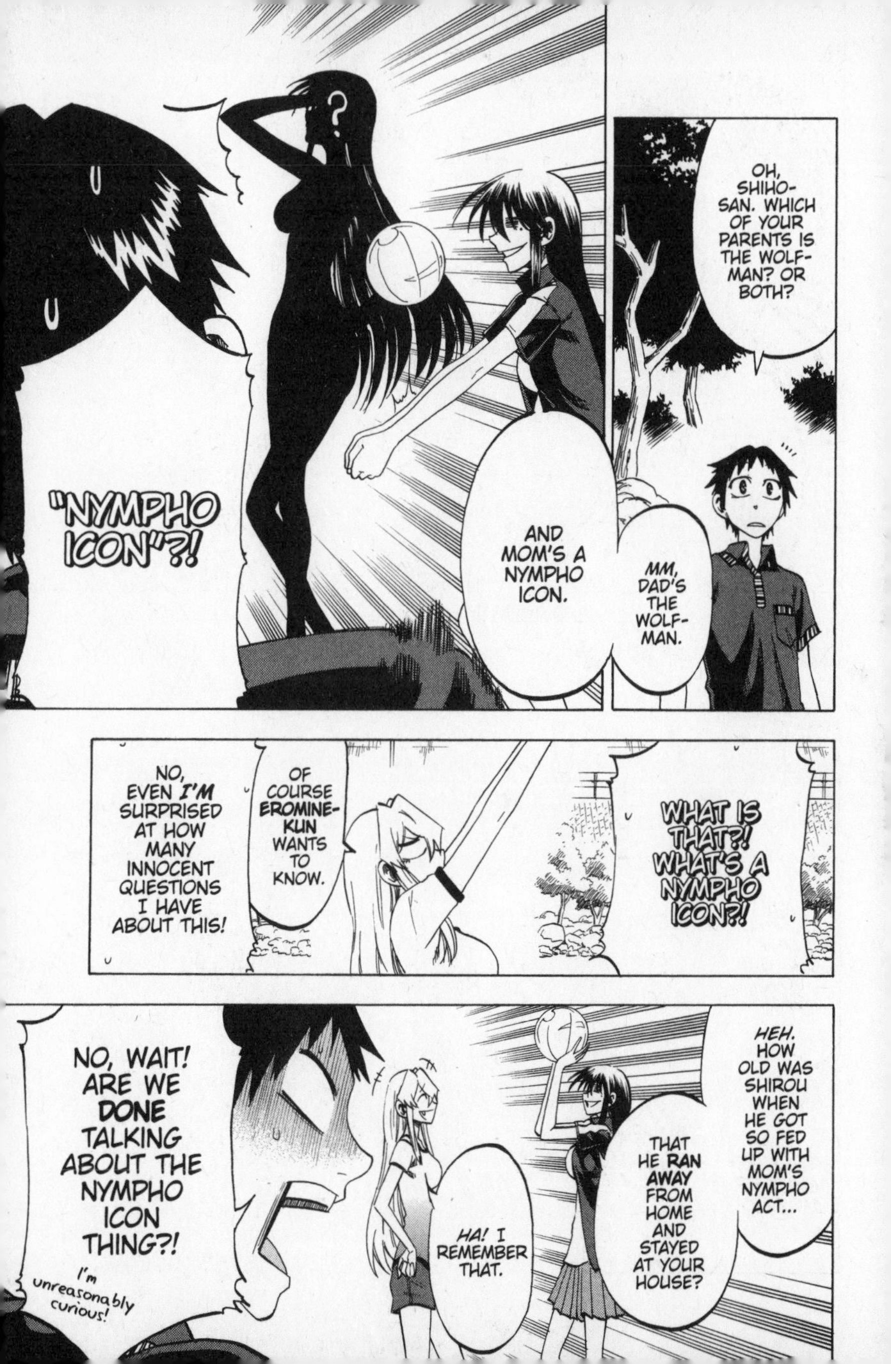
OH, SHIHO-SAN. WHICH OF YOUR PARENTS IS THE WOLF-MAN? OR BOTH?
MM, DAD'S THE WOLF-MAN.
AND MOM'S A NYMPHO ICON.
"NYMPHO ICON"?!
WHAT IS THAT?! WHAT'S A NYMPHO ICON?!
OF COURSE EROMINE-KUN WANTS TO KNOW.
NO, EVEN I'M SURPRISED AT HOW MANY INNOCENT QUESTIONS I HAVE ABOUT THIS!
HEH. HOW OLD WAS SHIROU WHEN HE GOT SO FED UP WITH MOM'S NYMPHO ACT...
THAT HE RAN AWAY FROM HOME AND STAYED AT YOUR HOUSE?
HA! I REMEMBER THAT.
NO, WAIT! ARE WE DONE TALKING ABOUT THE NYMPHO ICON THING?!
I'm unreasonably curious!

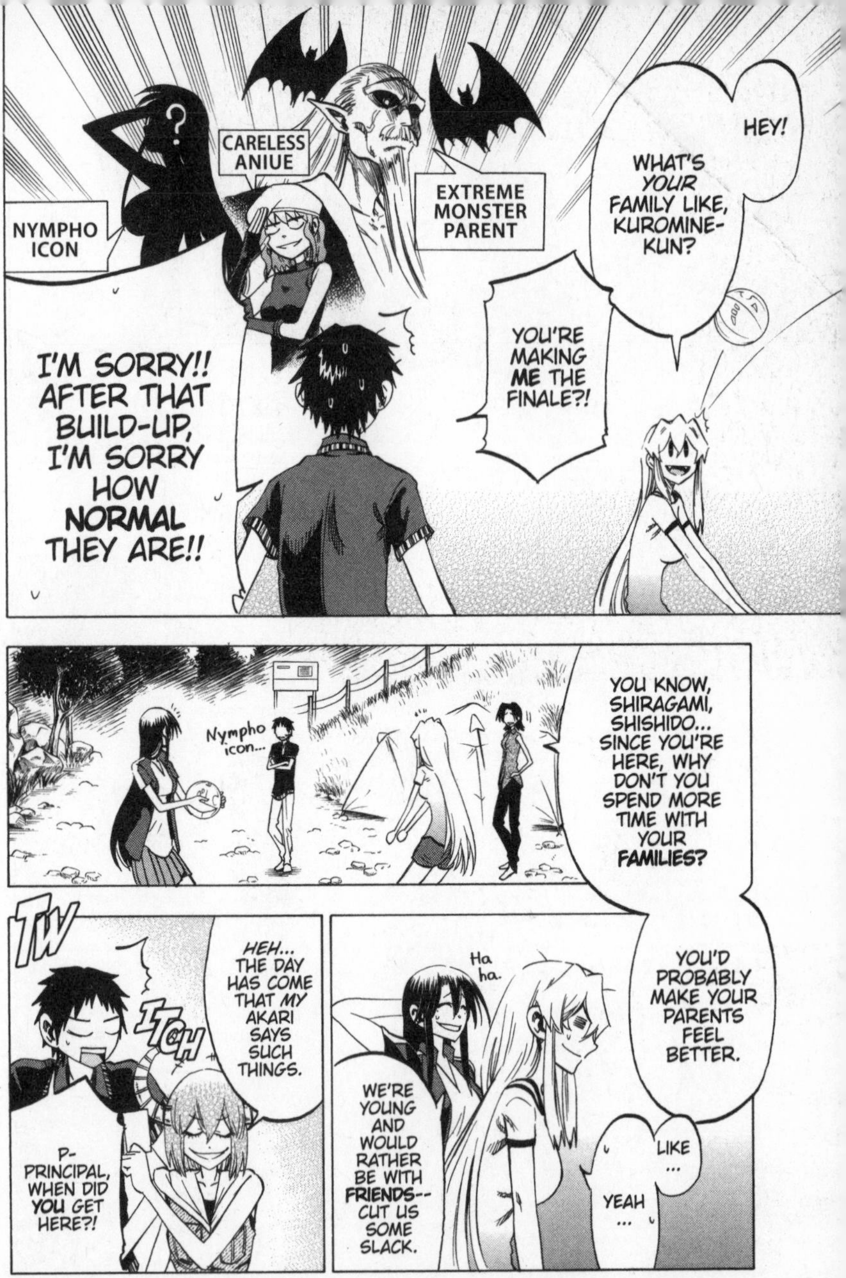
HEY!
WHAT'S YOUR FAMILY LIKE, KUROMINE-KUN?
EXTREME MONSTER PARENT
CARELESS ANIUE
NYMPHO ICON
YOU'RE MAKING ME THE FINALE?!
I'M SORRY!! AFTER THAT BUILD-UP, I'M SORRY HOW NORMAL THEY ARE!!
YOU KNOW, SHIRAGAMI, SHISHIDO... SINCE YOU'RE HERE, WHY DON'T YOU SPEND MORE TIME WITH YOUR FAMILIES?
Nympho icon...
YOU'D PROBABLY MAKE YOUR PARENTS FEEL BETTER.
LIKE...
YEAH...
Ha ha.
WE'RE YOUNG AND WOULD RATHER BE WITH FRIENDS-- CUT US SOME SLACK.
HEH... THE DAY HAS COME THAT MY AKARI SAYS SUCH THINGS.
TW
ITCH
P-PRINCIPAL, WHEN DID YOU GET HERE?!

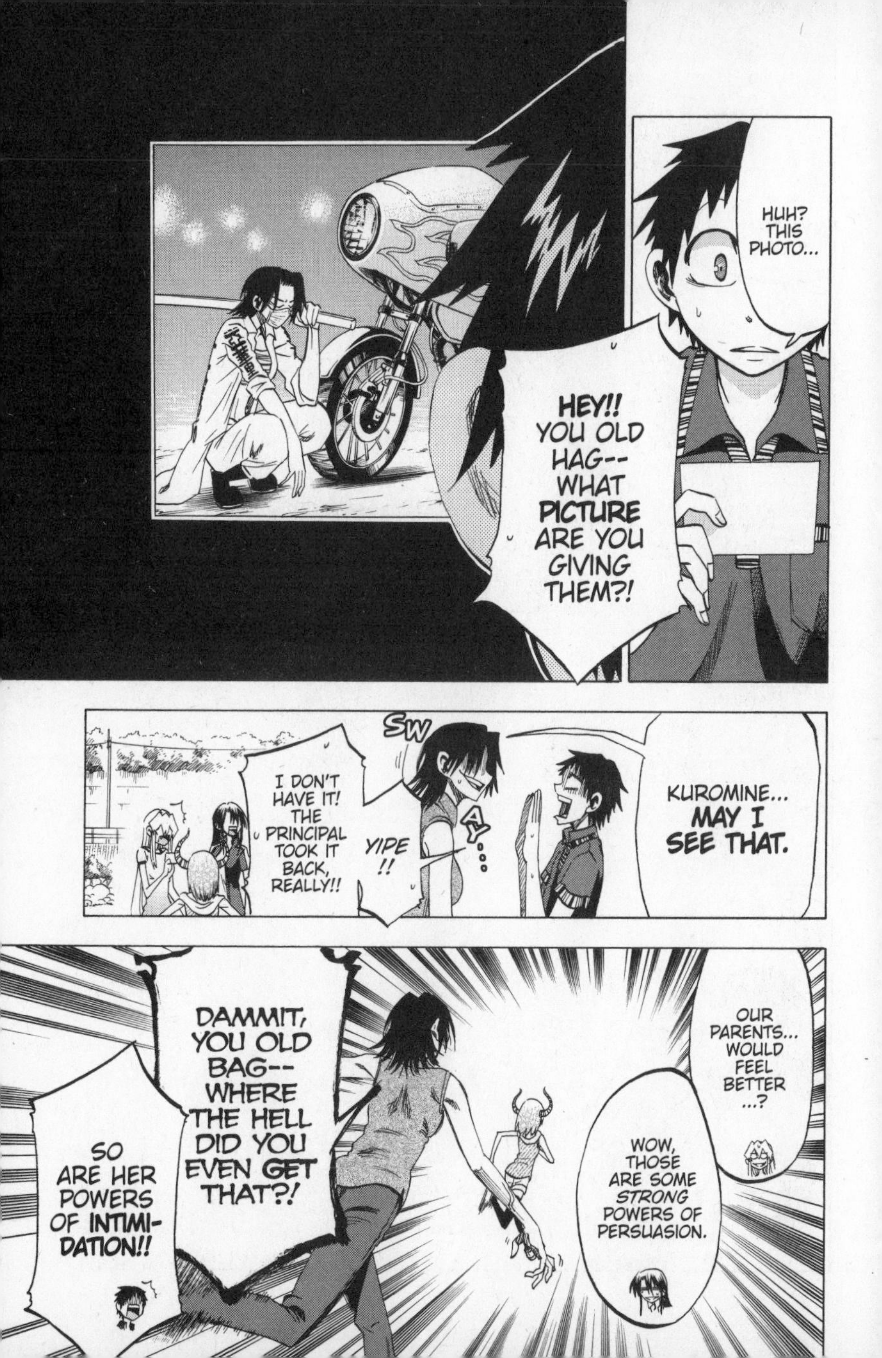
HUH? THIS PHOTO...
HEY!! YOU OLD HAG-- WHAT PICTURE ARE YOU GIVING THEM?!
KUROMINE... MAY I SEE THAT.
SW
AY...
YIPE!!
I DON'T HAVE IT! THE PRINCIPAL TOOK IT BACK, REALLY!!
OUR PARENTS... WOULD FEEL BETTER ...?
WOW, THOSE ARE SOME STRONG POWERS OF PERSUASION.
DAMMIT, YOU OLD BAG-- WHERE THE HELL DID YOU EVEN GET THAT?!
SO ARE HER POWERS OF INTIMIDATION!!

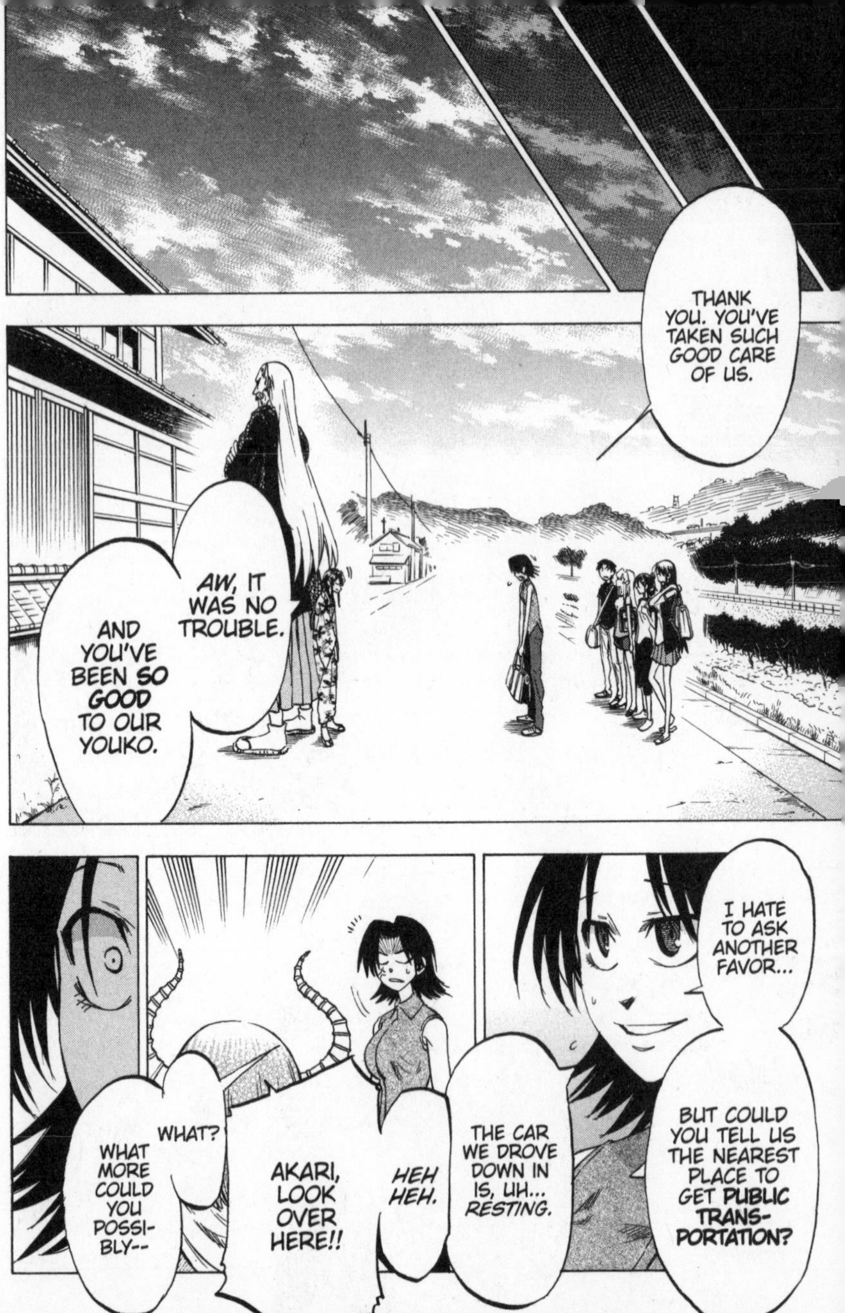
THANK YOU. YOU'VE TAKEN SUCH GOOD CARE OF US.
AW, IT WAS NO TROUBLE.
AND YOU'VE BEEN SO GOOD TO OUR YOUKO.
I HATE TO ASK ANOTHER FAVOR...
BUT COULD YOU TELL US THE NEAREST PLACE TO GET PUBLIC TRANS-PORTATION?
THE CAR WE DROVE DOWN IN IS, UH... RESTING.
HEH HEH.
AKARI, LOOK OVER HERE!!
WHAT?
WHAT MORE COULD YOU POSSI-BLY--

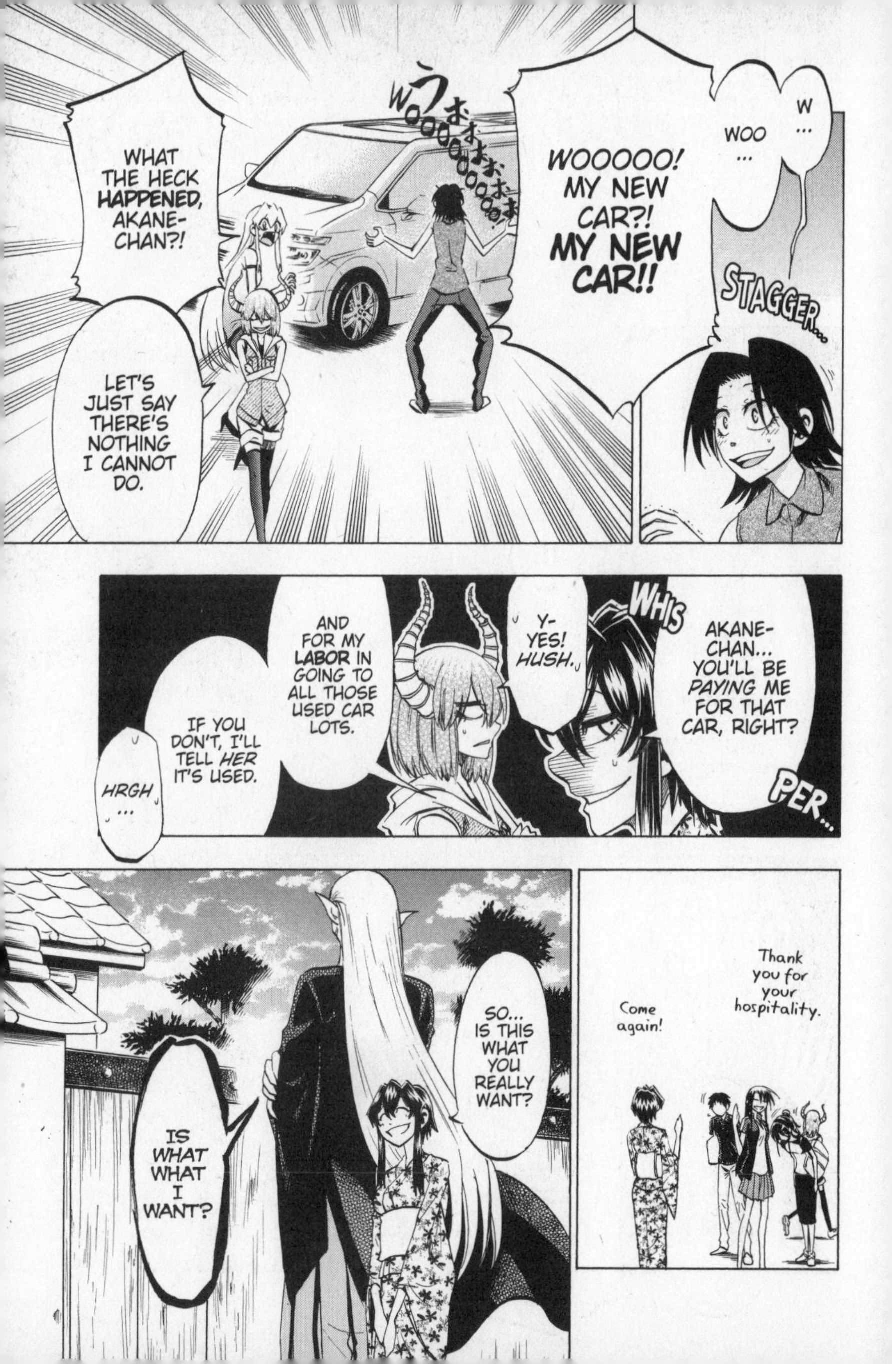
W ...
WOO ...
STAGGER...
WOOOOO! MY NEW CAR?! MY NEW CAR!!
WOOOOOOOOOO
WHAT THE HECK HAPPENED, AKANE-CHAN?!
LET'S JUST SAY THERE'S NOTHING I CANNOT DO.
WHIS
PER...
AKANE-CHAN... YOU'LL BE PAYING ME FOR THAT CAR, RIGHT?
Y-YES! HUSH.
AND FOR MY LABOR IN GOING TO ALL THOSE USED CAR LOTS.
IF YOU DON'T, I'LL TELL HER IT'S USED.
HRGH ...
Thank you for your hospitality.
Come again!
SO... IS THIS WHAT YOU REALLY WANT?
IS WHAT WHAT I WANT?

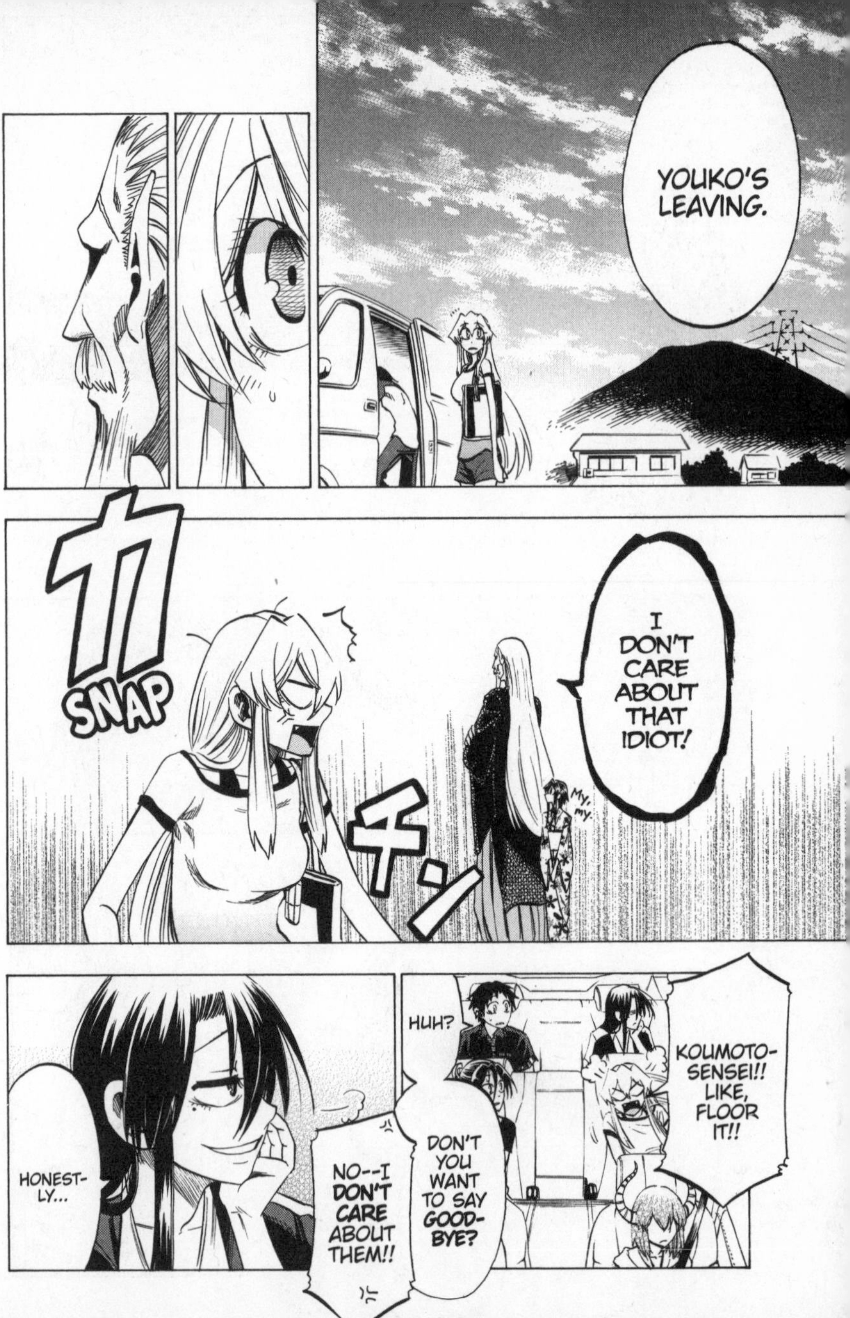
YOUKO'S LEAVING.
I DON'T CARE ABOUT THAT IDIOT!
My, my.
チッ
カ
SNAP
KOUMOTO-SENSEI!! LIKE, FLOOR IT!!
HUH?
DON'T YOU WANT TO SAY GOOD-BYE?
NO--I DON'T CARE ABOUT THEM!!
HONESTLY...

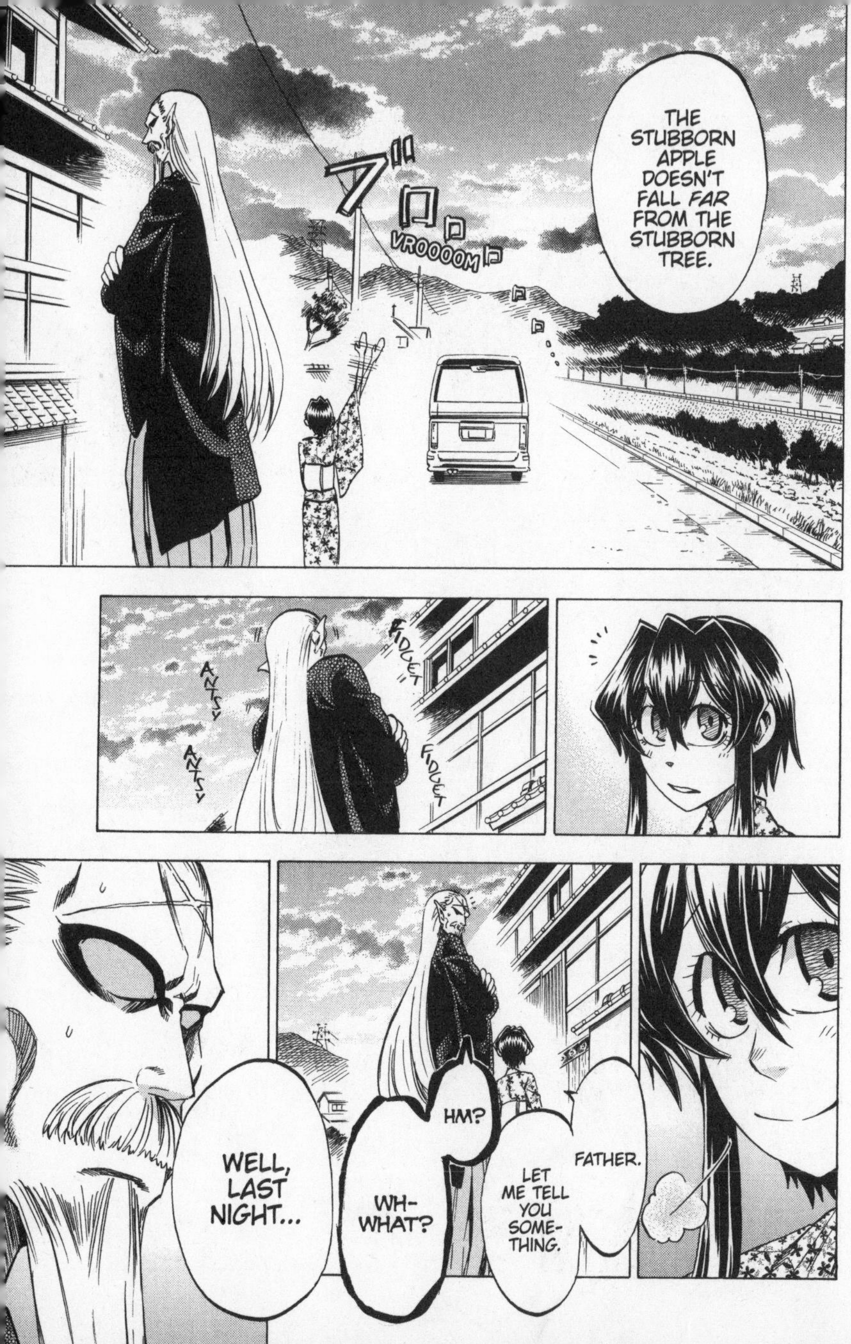
VROOOOM
THE STUBBORN APPLE DOESN'T FALL *FAR* FROM THE STUBBORN TREE.
FIDGET FIDGET
ANTSY ANTSY
FATHER.
HM?
LET ME TELL YOU SOMETHING.
WH- WHAT?
WELL, LAST NIGHT...

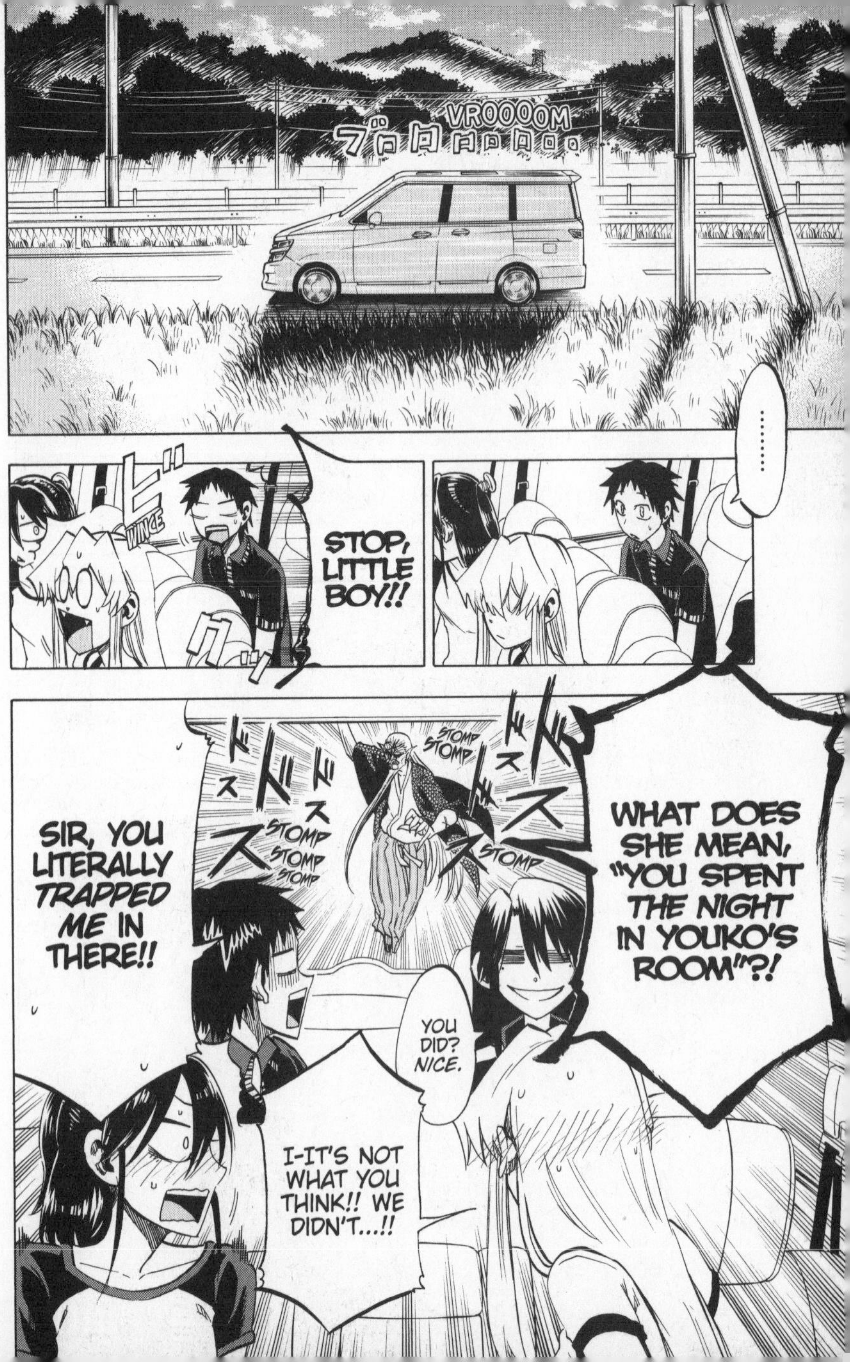
VROOOOM
ブロロロロロロロ
......
STOP, LITTLE BOY!!
ビ
WINCE
WHAT DOES SHE MEAN, "YOU SPENT THE NIGHT IN YOUKO'S ROOM"?!
ドスドス
STOMP STOMP
STOMP
STOMP STOMP STOMP
SIR, YOU LITERALLY TRAPPED ME IN THERE!!
YOU DID? NICE.
I-IT'S NOT WHAT YOU THINK!! WE DIDN'T...!!

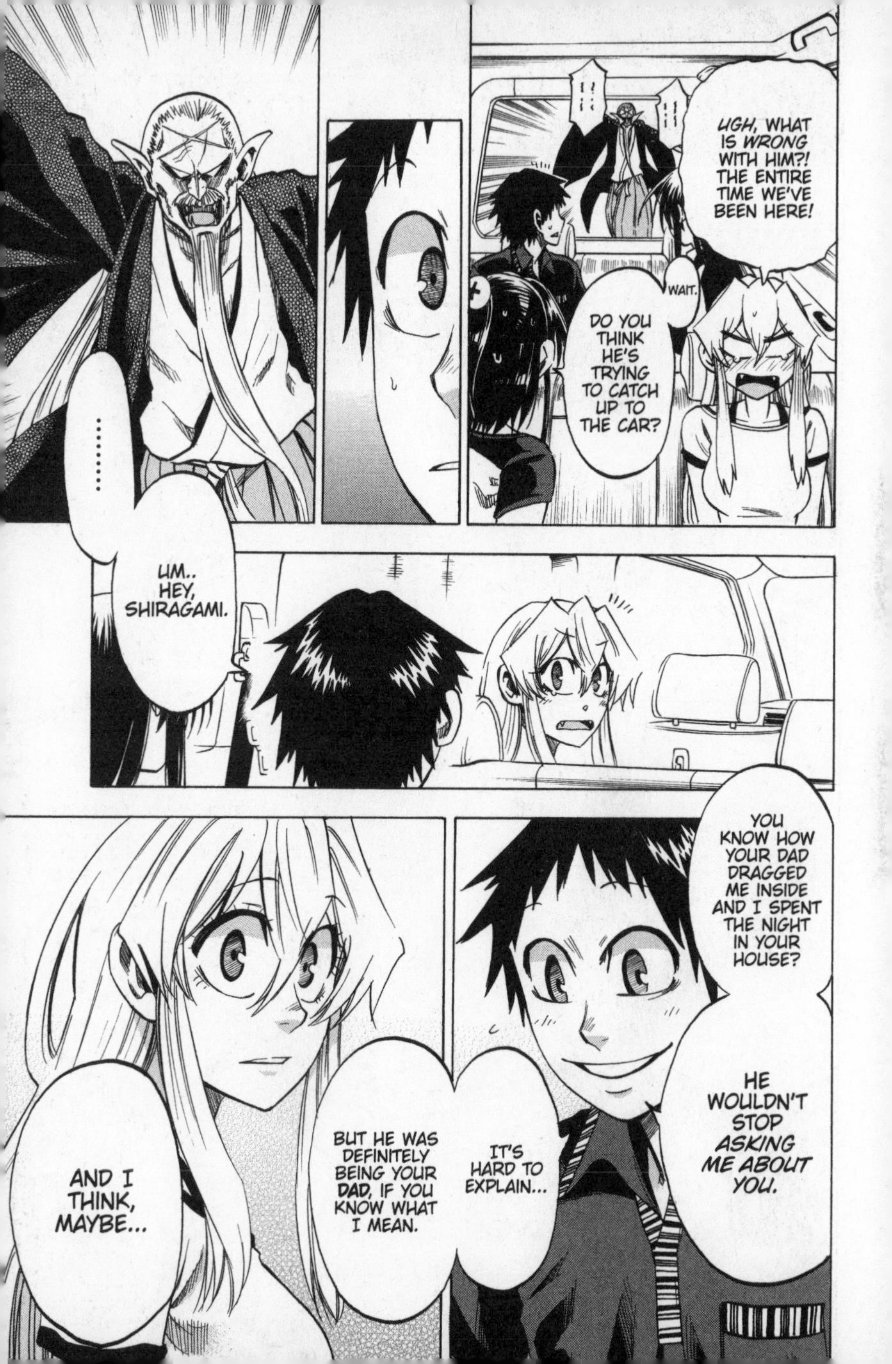
UGH, WHAT IS WRONG WITH HIM?! THE ENTIRE TIME WE'VE BEEN HERE!
WAIT.
DO YOU THINK HE'S TRYING TO CATCH UP TO THE CAR?
......
UM.. HEY, SHIRAGAMI.
YOU KNOW HOW YOUR DAD DRAGGED ME INSIDE AND I SPENT THE NIGHT IN YOUR HOUSE?
HE WOULDN'T STOP ASKING ME ABOUT YOU.
IT'S HARD TO EXPLAIN...
BUT HE WAS DEFINITELY BEING YOUR DAD, IF YOU KNOW WHAT I MEAN.
AND I THINK, MAYBE...

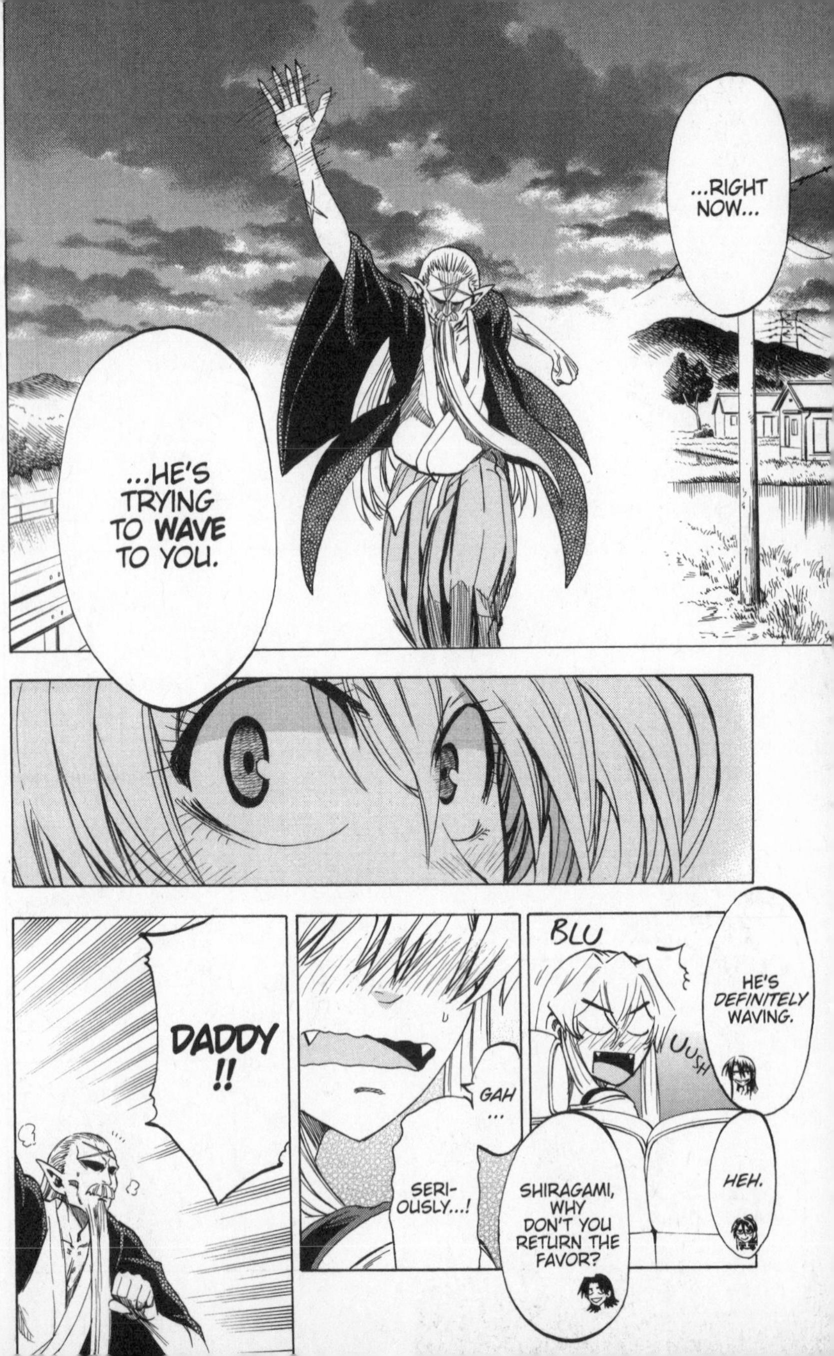
...RIGHT NOW...
...HE'S TRYING TO WAVE TO YOU.
HE'S DEFINITELY WAVING.
BLU
UUSH
HEH.
SHIRAGAMI, WHY DON'T YOU RETURN THE FAVOR?
GAH ...
SERI- OUSLY...!
DADDY !!

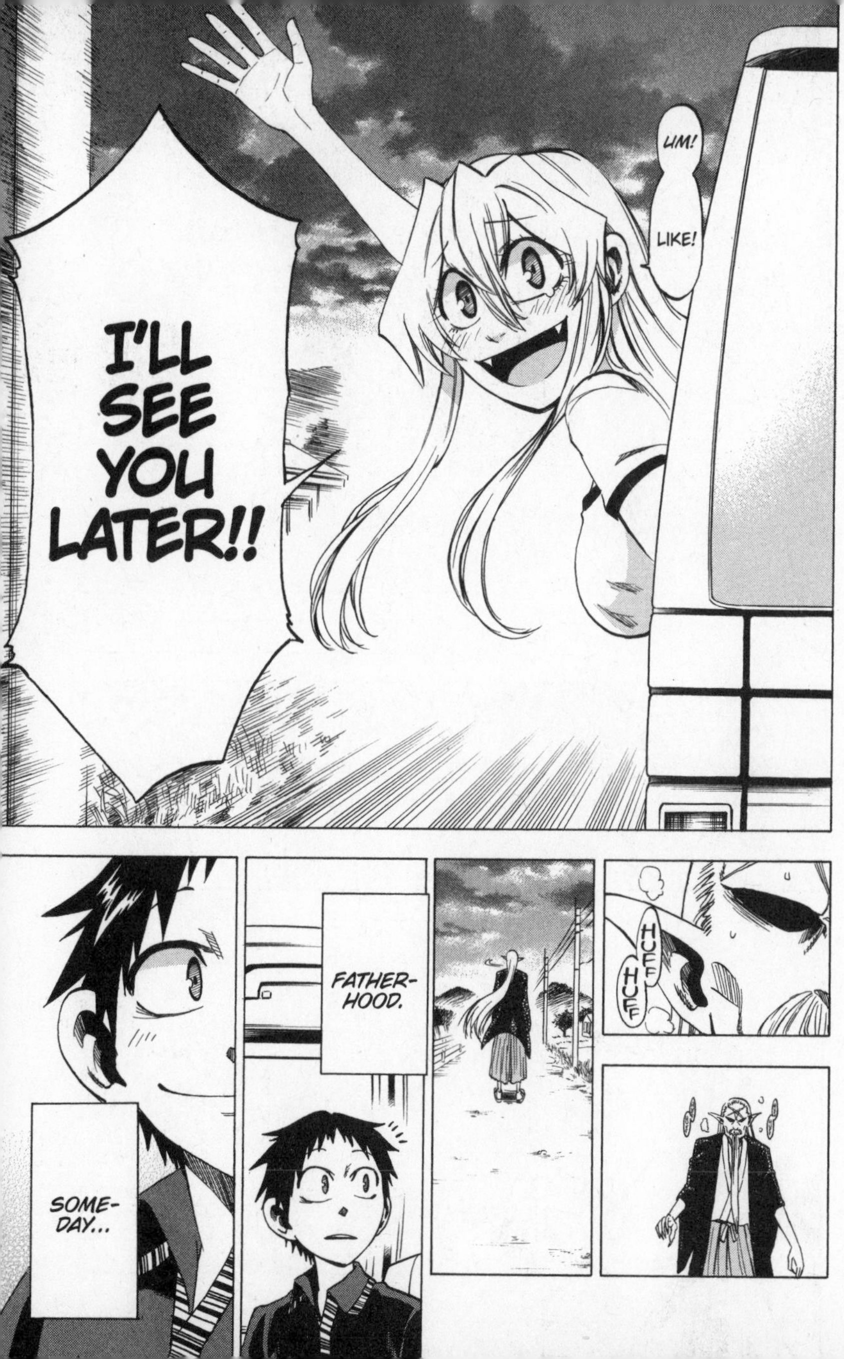
UM! LIKE!
I'LL SEE YOU LATER!!
HUFF HUFF
FATHER-HOOD.
SOME-DAY...

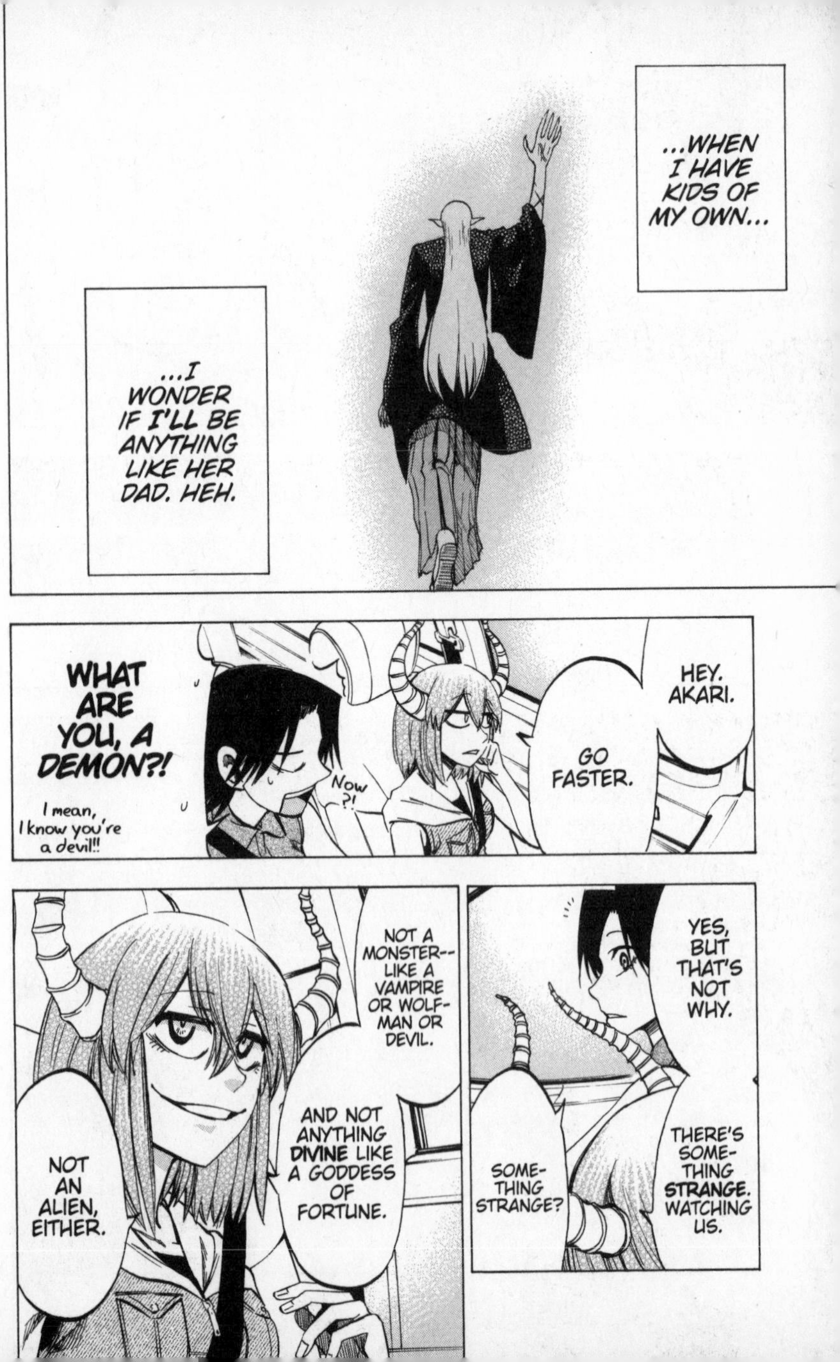
...WHEN I HAVE KIDS OF MY OWN...
...I WONDER IF I'LL BE ANYTHING LIKE HER DAD. HEH.
HEY. AKARI.
GO FASTER.
Now?!
WHAT ARE YOU, A DEMON?!
I mean, I know you're a devil!!
YES, BUT THAT'S NOT WHY.
THERE'S SOME-THING STRANGE. WATCHING US.
SOME-THING STRANGE?
NOT A MONSTER-- LIKE A VAMPIRE OR WOLF-MAN OR DEVIL.
AND NOT ANYTHING DIVINE LIKE A GODDESS OF FORTUNE.
NOT AN ALIEN, EITHER.

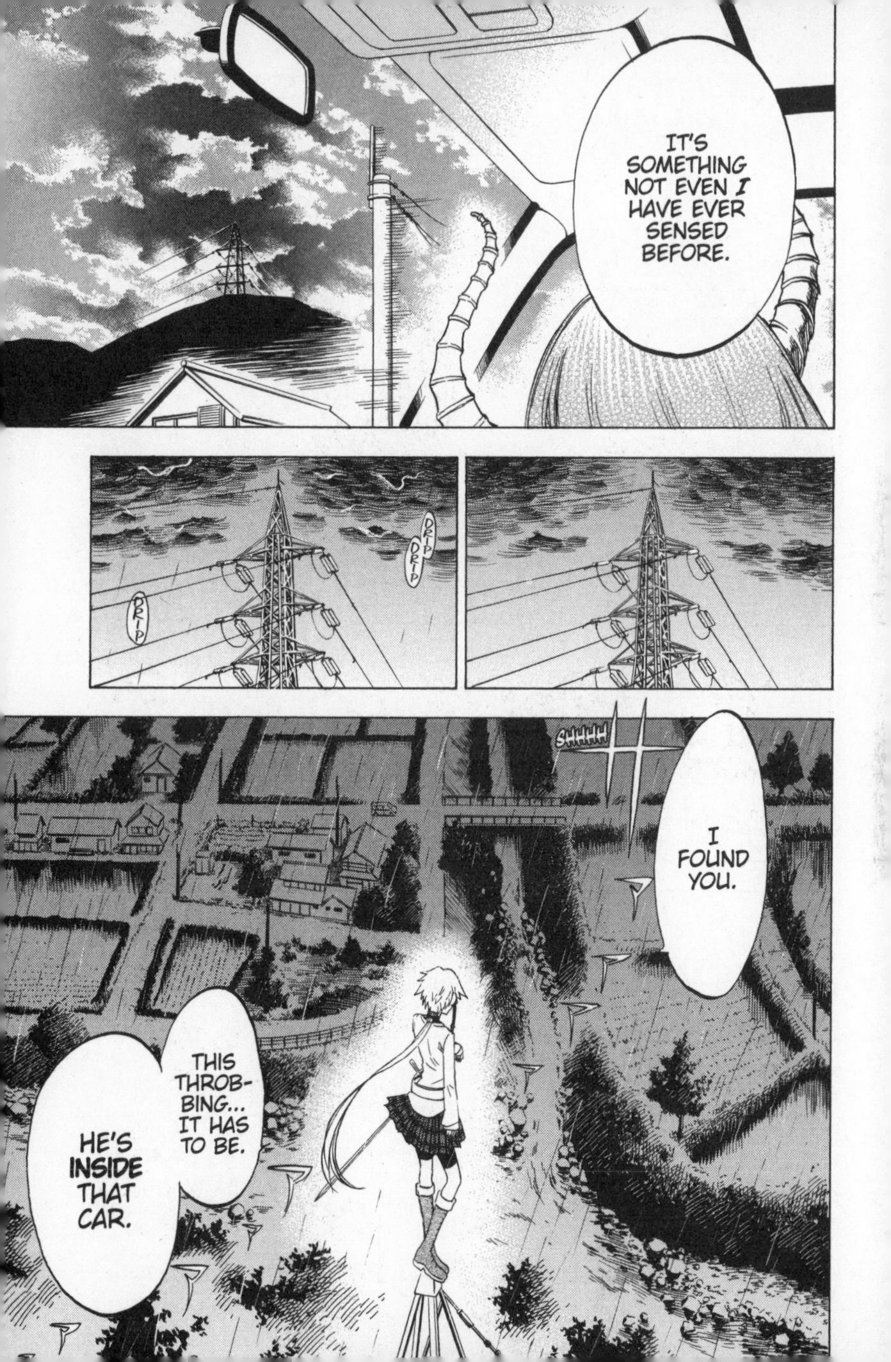
IT'S SOMETHING NOT EVEN I HAVE EVER SENSED BEFORE.
DRIP DRIP
DRIP
SHHHHH
I FOUND YOU.
THIS THROBBING... IT HAS TO BE.
HE'S INSIDE THAT CAR.

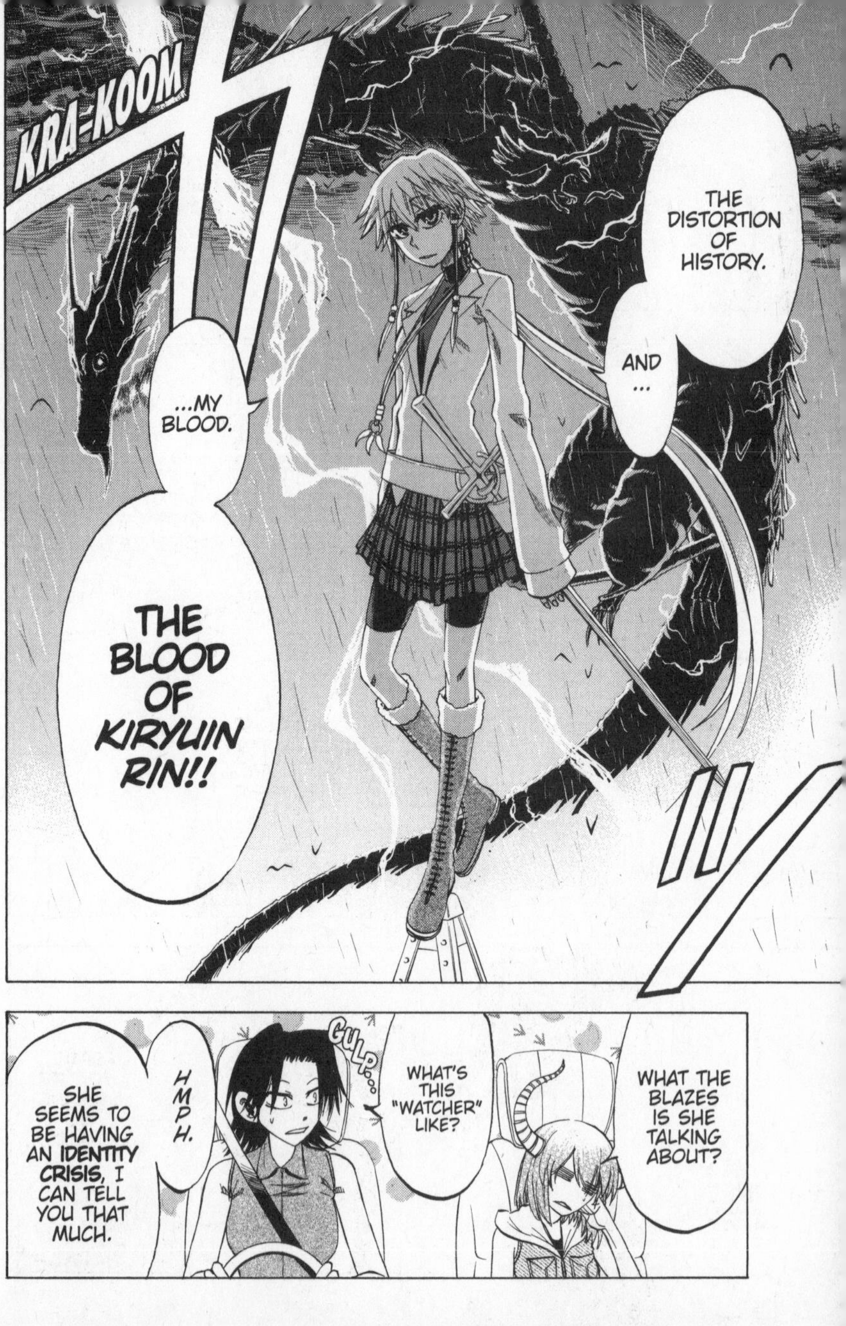
KRA-KOOM
THE DISTORTION OF HISTORY.
AND ...
...MY BLOOD.
THE BLOOD OF KIRYUIN RIN!!
WHAT THE BLAZES IS SHE TALKING ABOUT?
WHAT'S THIS "WATCHER" LIKE?
GULP...
HMPH.
SHE SEEMS TO BE HAVING AN IDENTITY CRISIS, I CAN TELL YOU THAT MUCH.

Chapter 34: "Let's Clear Up This Misunderstanding!"

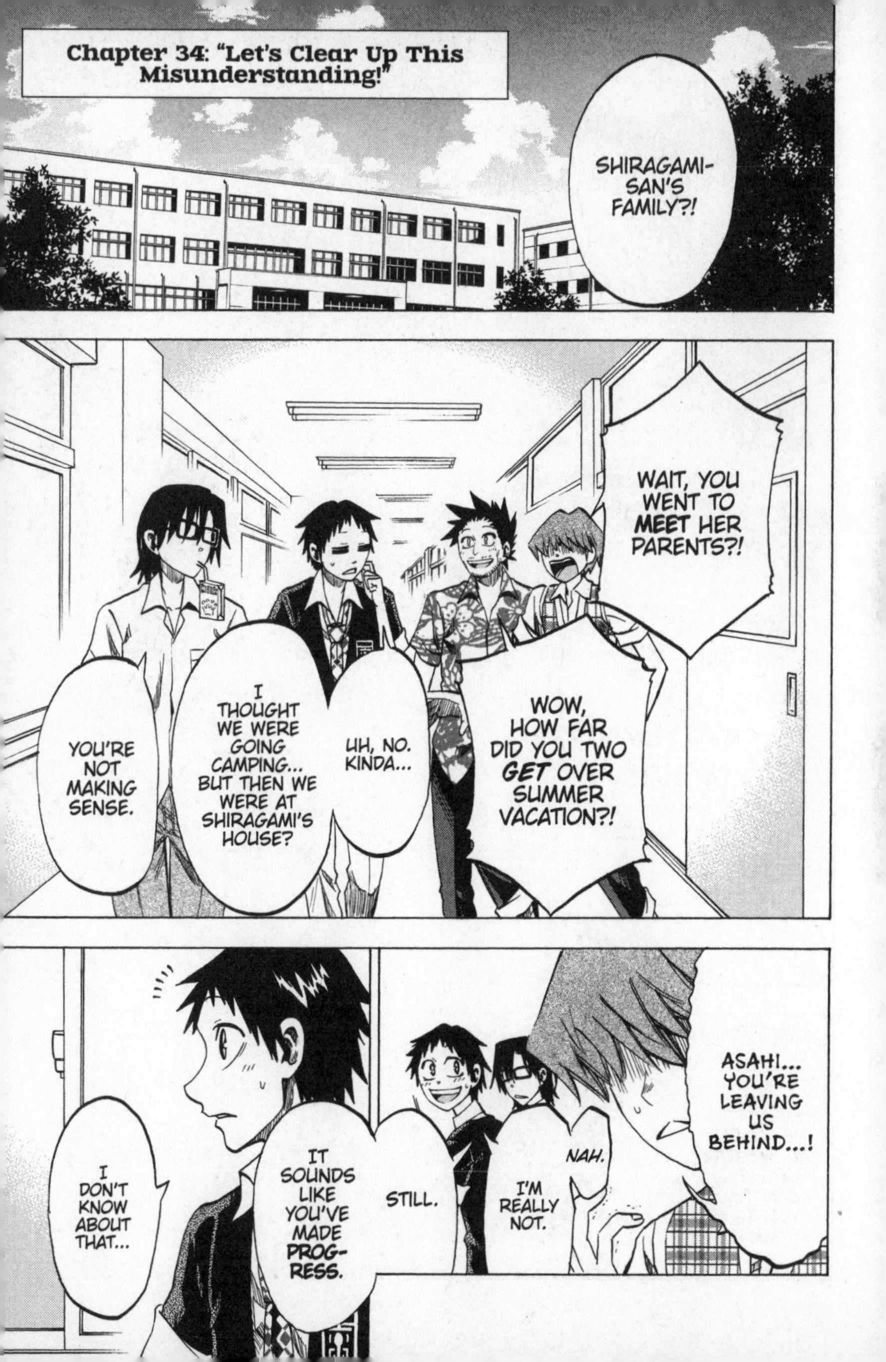
SHIRAGAMI-SAN'S FAMILY?!
WAIT, YOU WENT TO MEET HER PARENTS?!
WOW, HOW FAR DID YOU TWO GET OVER SUMMER VACATION?!
UH, NO. KINDA...
I THOUGHT WE WERE GOING CAMPING... BUT THEN WE WERE AT SHIRAGAMI'S HOUSE?
YOU'RE NOT MAKING SENSE.
ASAHI... YOU'RE LEAVING US BEHIND...!
NAH.
I'M REALLY NOT.
STILL.
IT SOUNDS LIKE YOU'VE MADE PROG-RESS.
I DON'T KNOW ABOUT THAT...

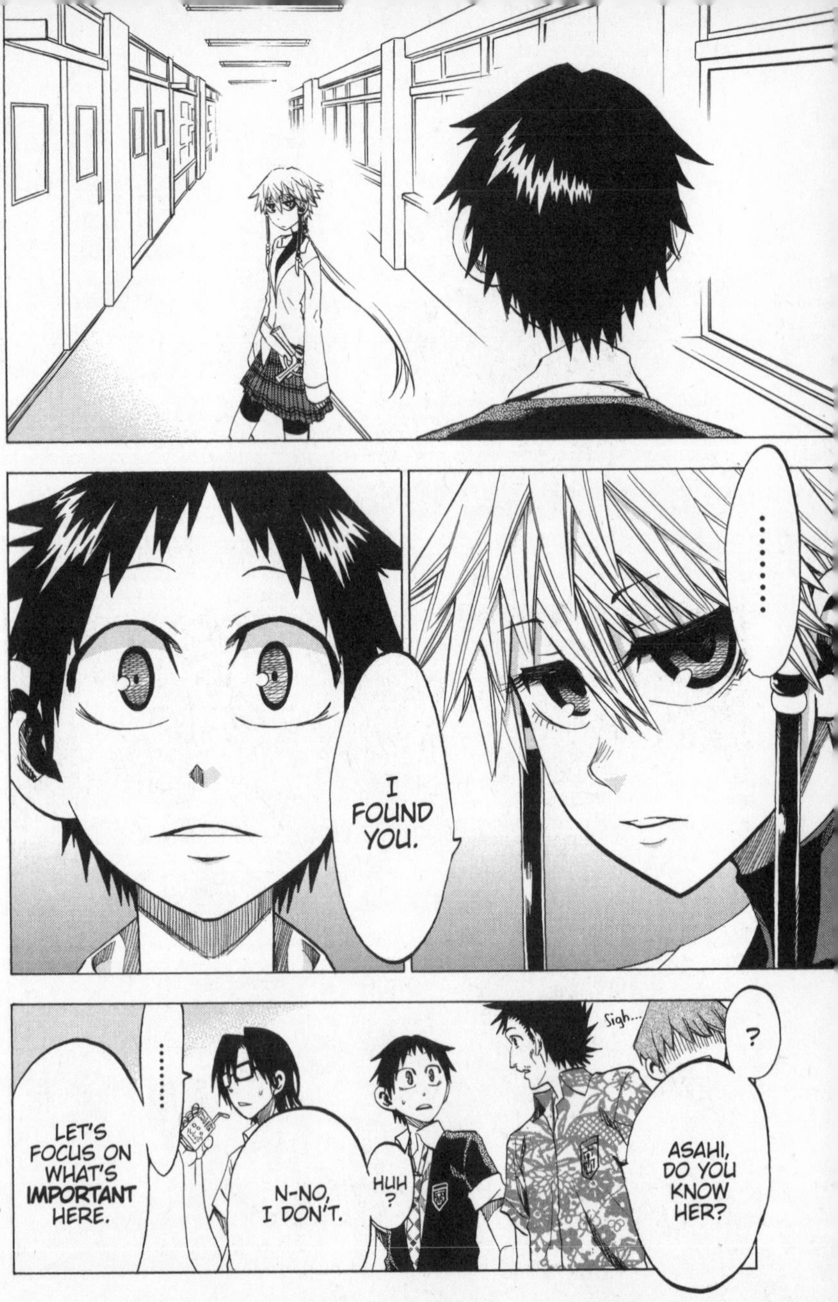
......
I FOUND YOU.
?
Sigh...
ASAHI, DO YOU KNOW HER?
HUH?
N-NO, I DON'T.
......
LET'S FOCUS ON WHAT'S IMPORTANT HERE.

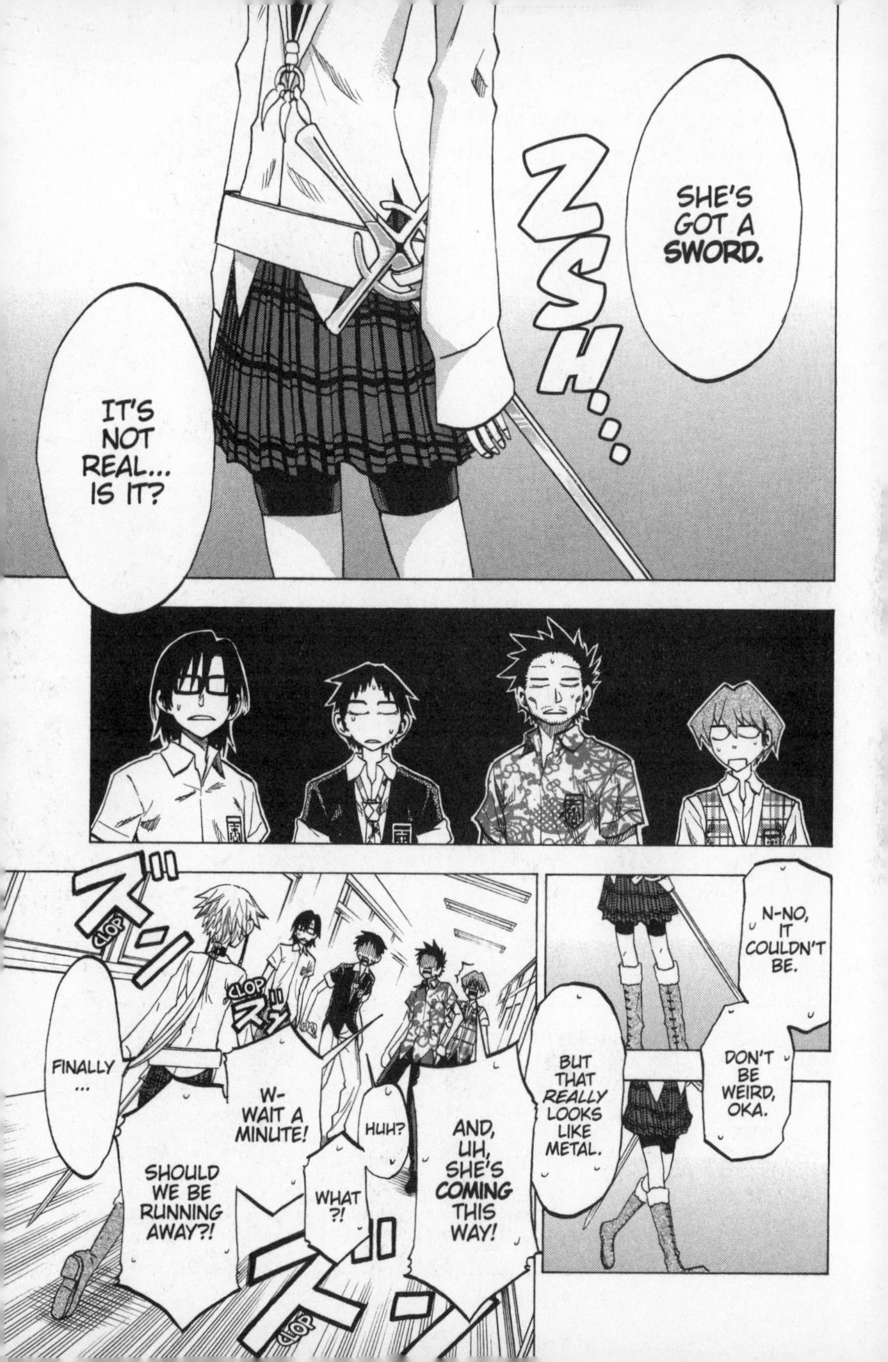

SHE'S GOT A SWORD.
ZSH...
IT'S NOT REAL... IS IT?
N-NO, IT COULDN'T BE.
DON'T BE WEIRD, OKA.
BUT THAT *REALLY* LOOKS LIKE METAL.
AND, UH, SHE'S **COMING** THIS WAY!
HUH?
WHAT?!
W-WAIT A MINUTE!
SHOULD WE BE RUNNING AWAY?!
CLOP
CLOP
CLOP
FINALLY ...

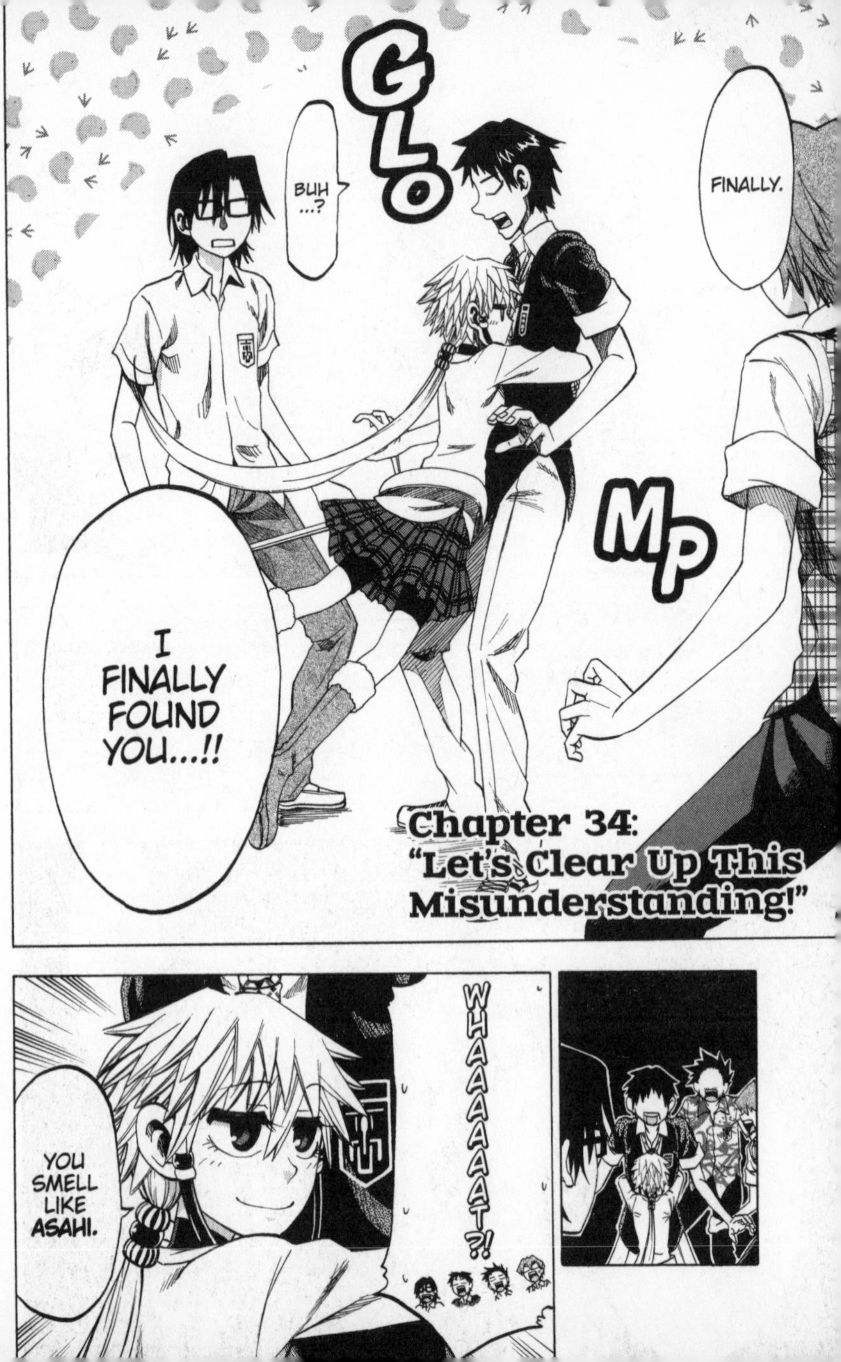
FINALLY.
GLOMP
BUH ...?
I FINALLY FOUND YOU...!!
Chapter 34: "Let's Clear Up This Misunderstanding!"
WHAAAAAAAT?!
YOU SMELL LIKE ASAHI.

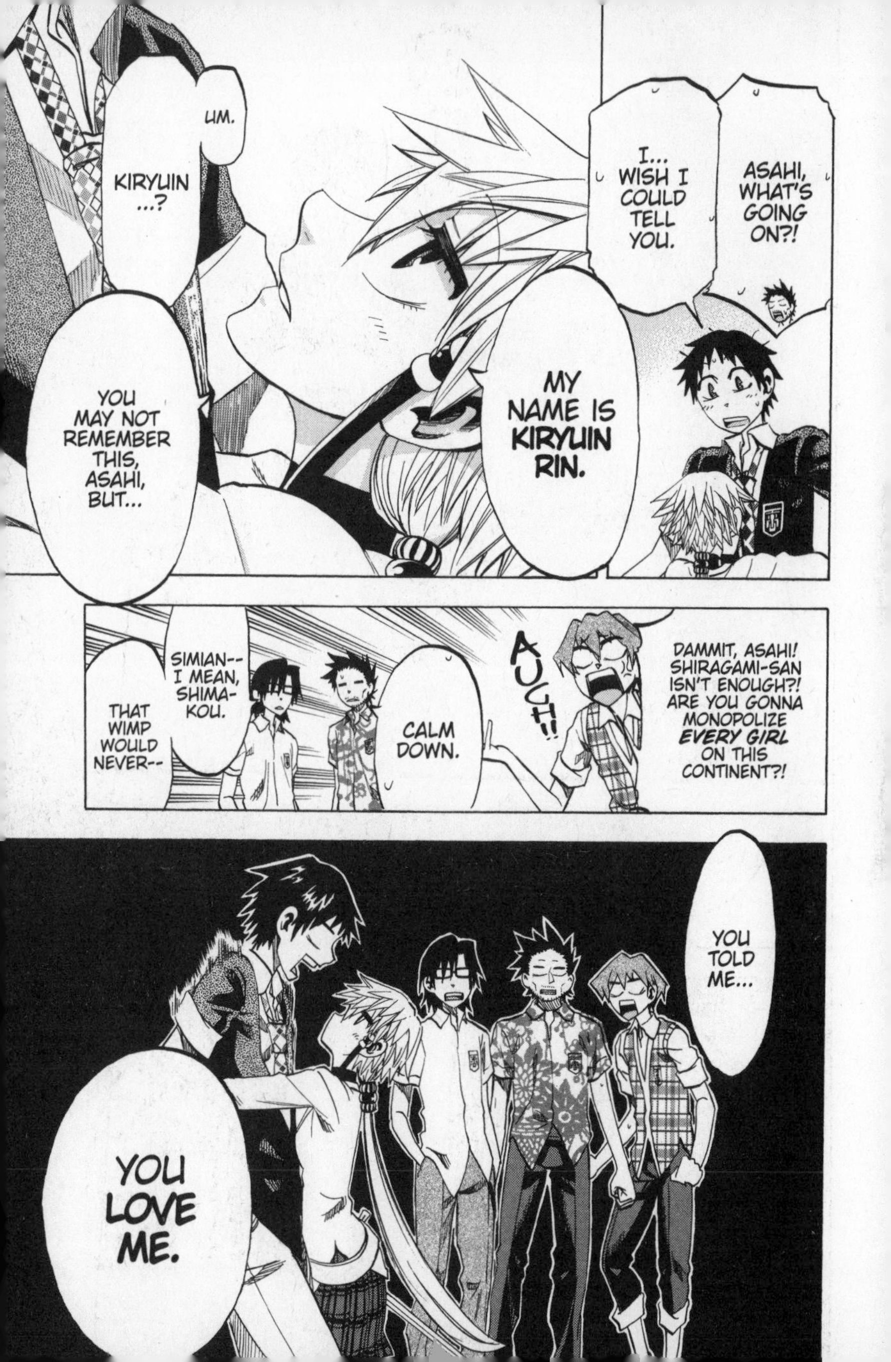
ASAHI, WHAT'S GOING ON?!
I... WISH I COULD TELL YOU.
MY NAME IS KIRYUIN RIN.
UM.
KIRYUIN ...?
YOU MAY NOT REMEMBER THIS, ASAHI, BUT...
DAMMIT, ASAHI! SHIRAGAMI-SAN ISN'T ENOUGH?! ARE YOU GONNA MONOPOLIZE EVERY GIRL ON THIS CONTINENT?!
AUCH!!
CALM DOWN.
SIMIAN-- I MEAN, SHIMAKOU.
THAT WIMP WOULD NEVER--
YOU TOLD ME...
YOU LOVE ME.

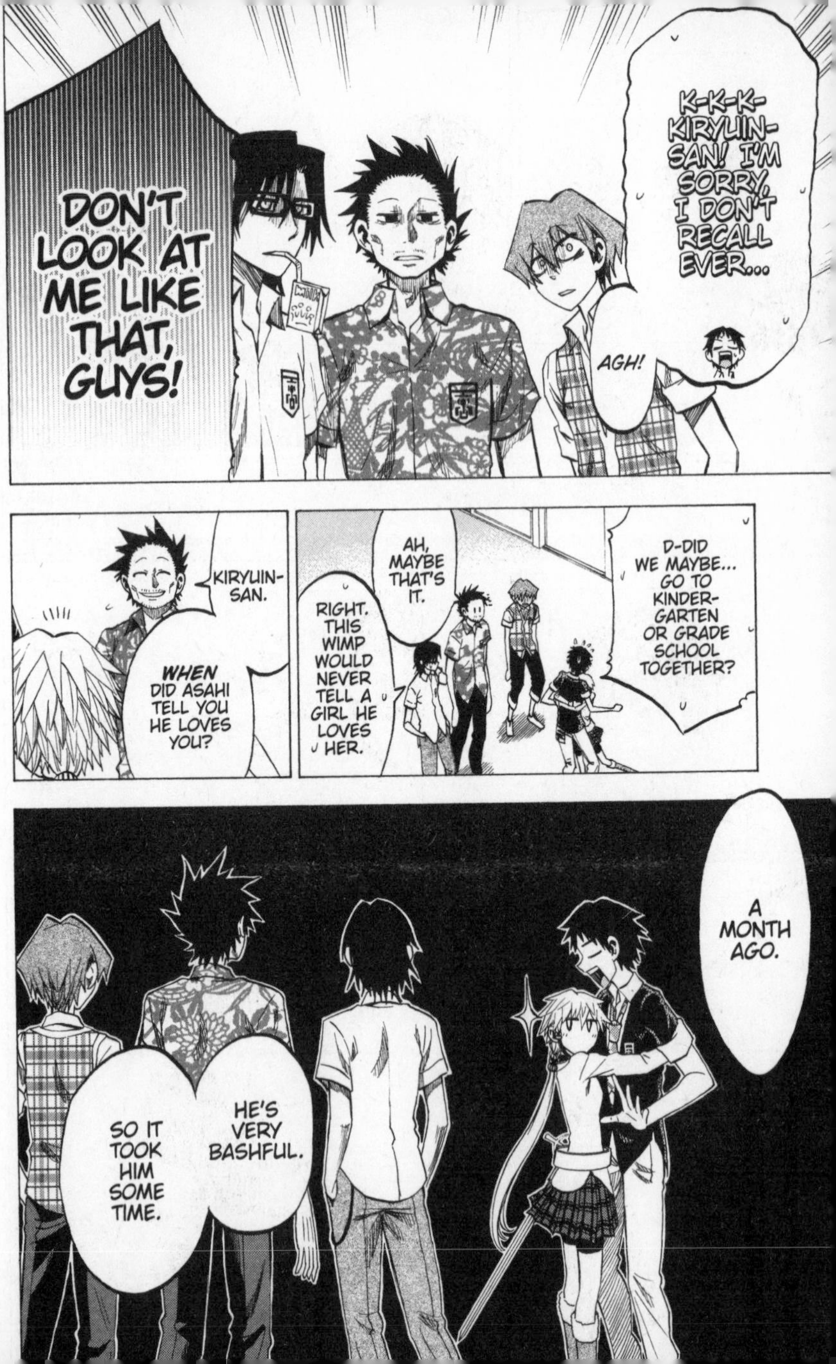
K-K-K-KIRYUIN-SAN! I'M SORRY, I DON'T RECALL EVER...
AGH!
DON'T LOOK AT ME LIKE THAT, GUYS!
D-DID WE MAYBE... GO TO KINDER-GARTEN OR GRADE SCHOOL TOGETHER?
AH, MAYBE THAT'S IT.
RIGHT. THIS WIMP WOULD NEVER TELL A GIRL HE LOVES HER.
KIRYUIN-SAN.
WHEN DID ASAHI TELL YOU HE LOVES YOU?
A MONTH AGO.
HE'S VERY BASHFUL.
SO IT TOOK HIM SOME TIME.

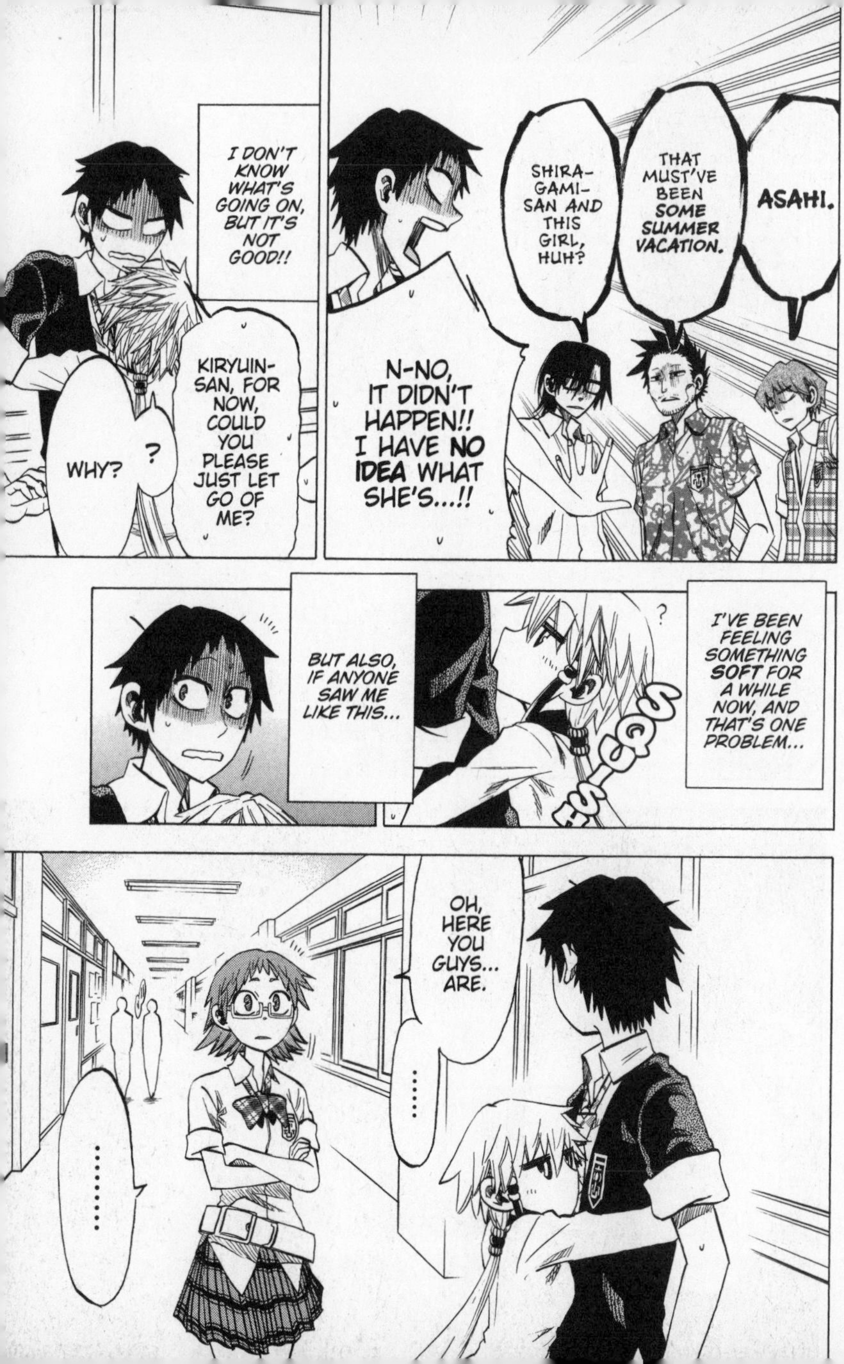
ASAHI.
THAT MUST'VE BEEN SOME SUMMER VACATION.
SHIRA-GAMI-SAN AND THIS GIRL, HUH?
N-NO, IT DIDN'T HAPPEN!! I HAVE NO IDEA WHAT SHE'S...!!
I DON'T KNOW WHAT'S GOING ON, BUT IT'S NOT GOOD!!
KIRYUIN-SAN, FOR NOW, COULD YOU PLEASE JUST LET GO OF ME?
?
WHY?
?
I'VE BEEN FEELING SOMETHING SOFT FOR A WHILE NOW, AND THAT'S ONE PROBLEM...
SQUISH
BUT ALSO, IF ANYONE SAW ME LIKE THIS...
OH, HERE YOU GUYS... ARE.
......
......

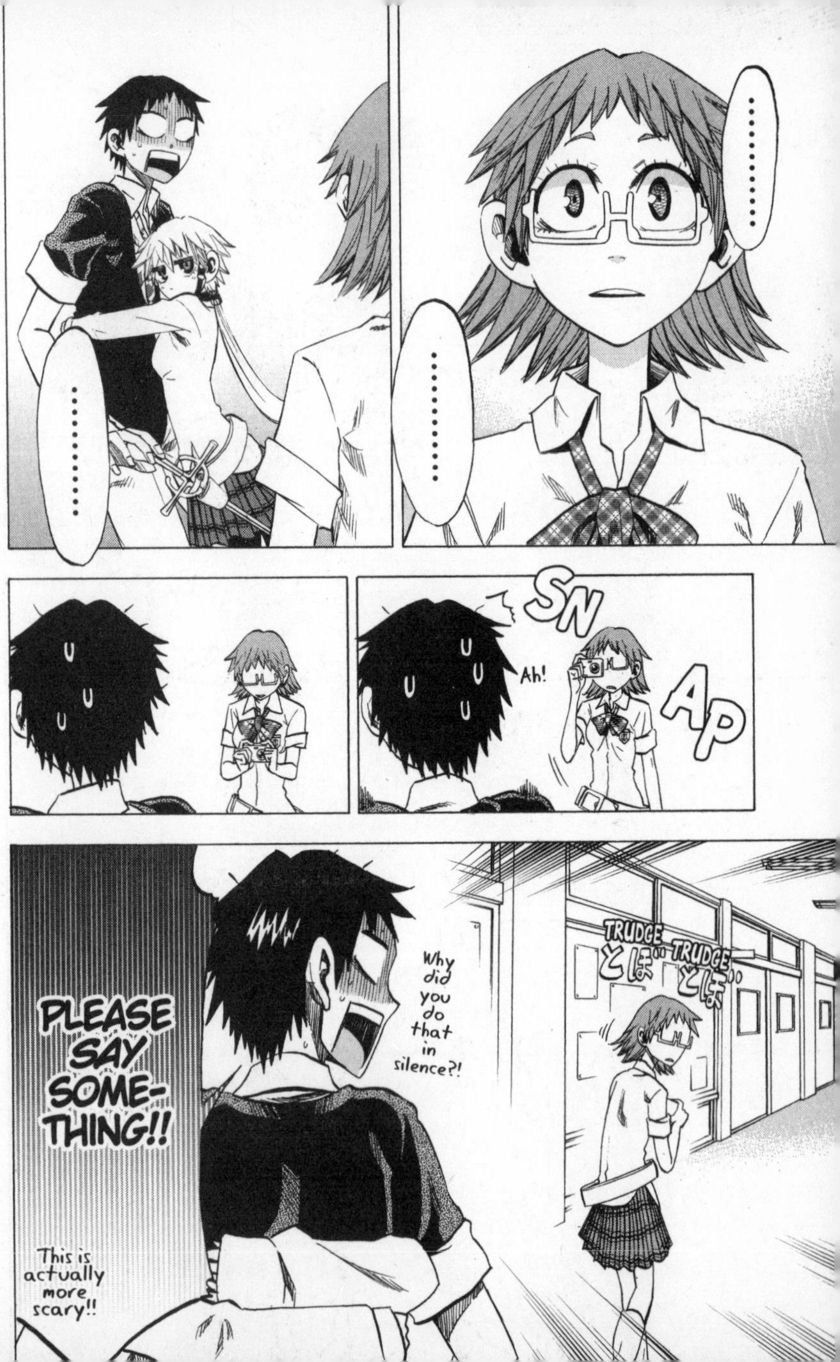
......
......
......
SN
AP
Ah!
TRUDGE とぼ TRUDGE とぼ
Why did you do that in silence?!
PLEASE SAY SOME-THING!!
This is actually more scary!!

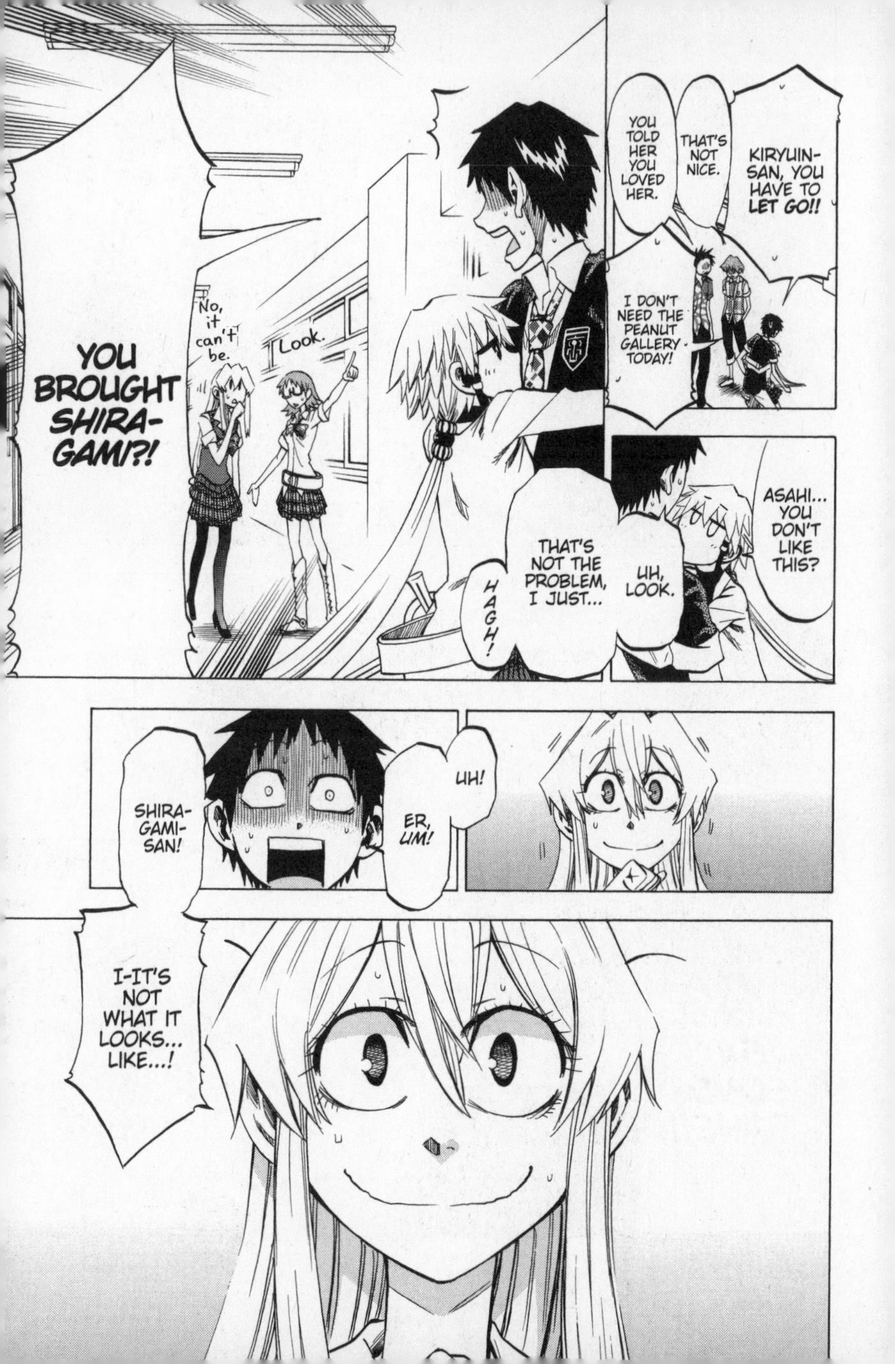
KIRYUIN-SAN, YOU HAVE TO LET GO!!
THAT'S NOT NICE.
YOU TOLD HER YOU LOVED HER.
I DON'T NEED THE PEANUT GALLERY TODAY!
ASAHI... YOU DON'T LIKE THIS?
UH, LOOK.
THAT'S NOT THE PROBLEM, I JUST...
HAGH!
Look.
No, it can't be.
YOU BROUGHT SHIRA-GAMI?!
UH!
ER, UM!
SHIRA-GAMI-SAN!
I-IT'S NOT WHAT IT LOOKS... LIKE...!

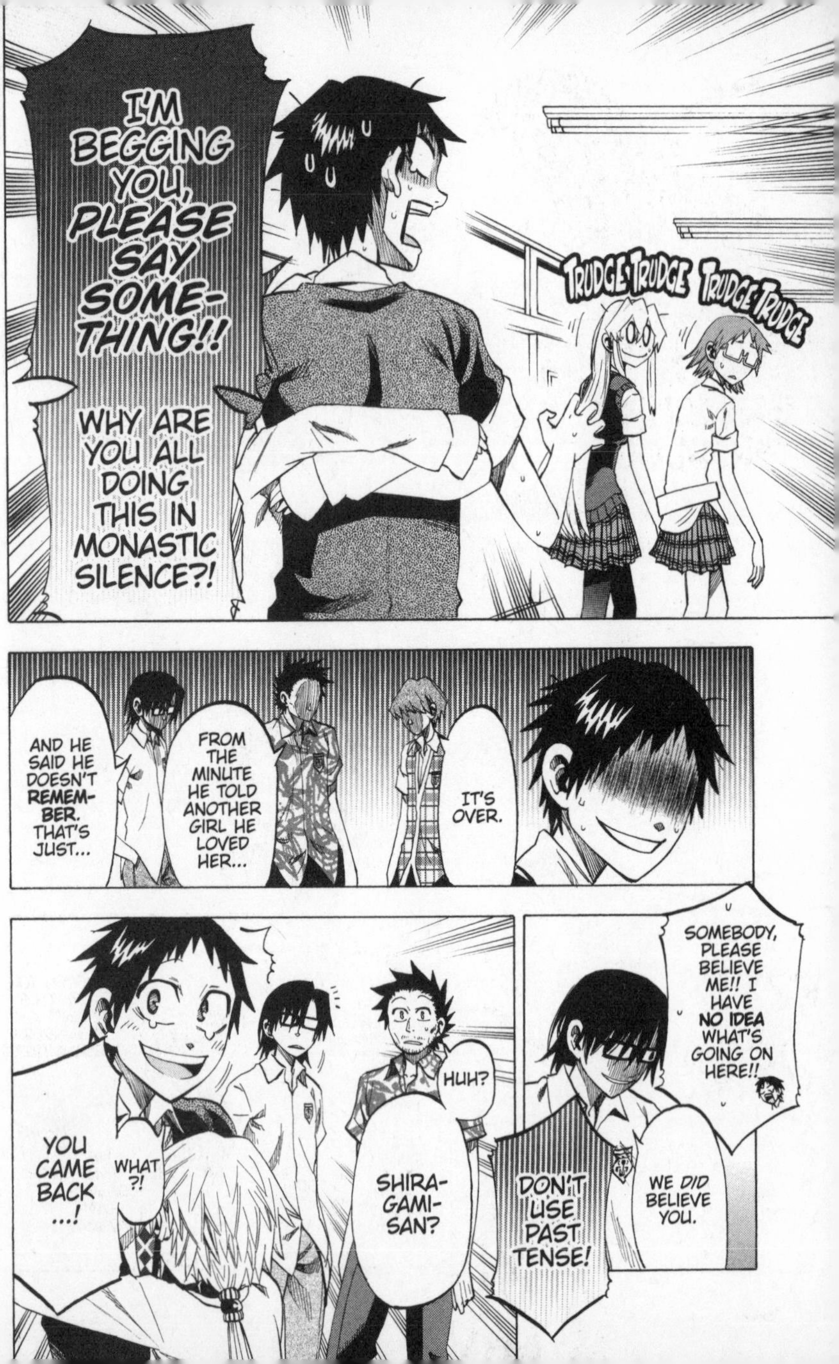
I'M BEGGING YOU, PLEASE SAY SOME-THING!!
WHY ARE YOU ALL DOING THIS IN MONASTIC SILENCE?!
TRUDGE TRUDGE TRUDGE TRUDGE
IT'S OVER.
FROM THE MINUTE HE TOLD ANOTHER GIRL HE LOVED HER...
AND HE SAID HE DOESN'T REMEMBER. THAT'S JUST...
SOMEBODY, PLEASE BELIEVE ME!! I HAVE NO IDEA WHAT'S GOING ON HERE!!
WE DID BELIEVE YOU.
DON'T USE PAST TENSE!
HUH?
SHIRA-GAMI-SAN?
WHAT?!
YOU CAME BACK...!

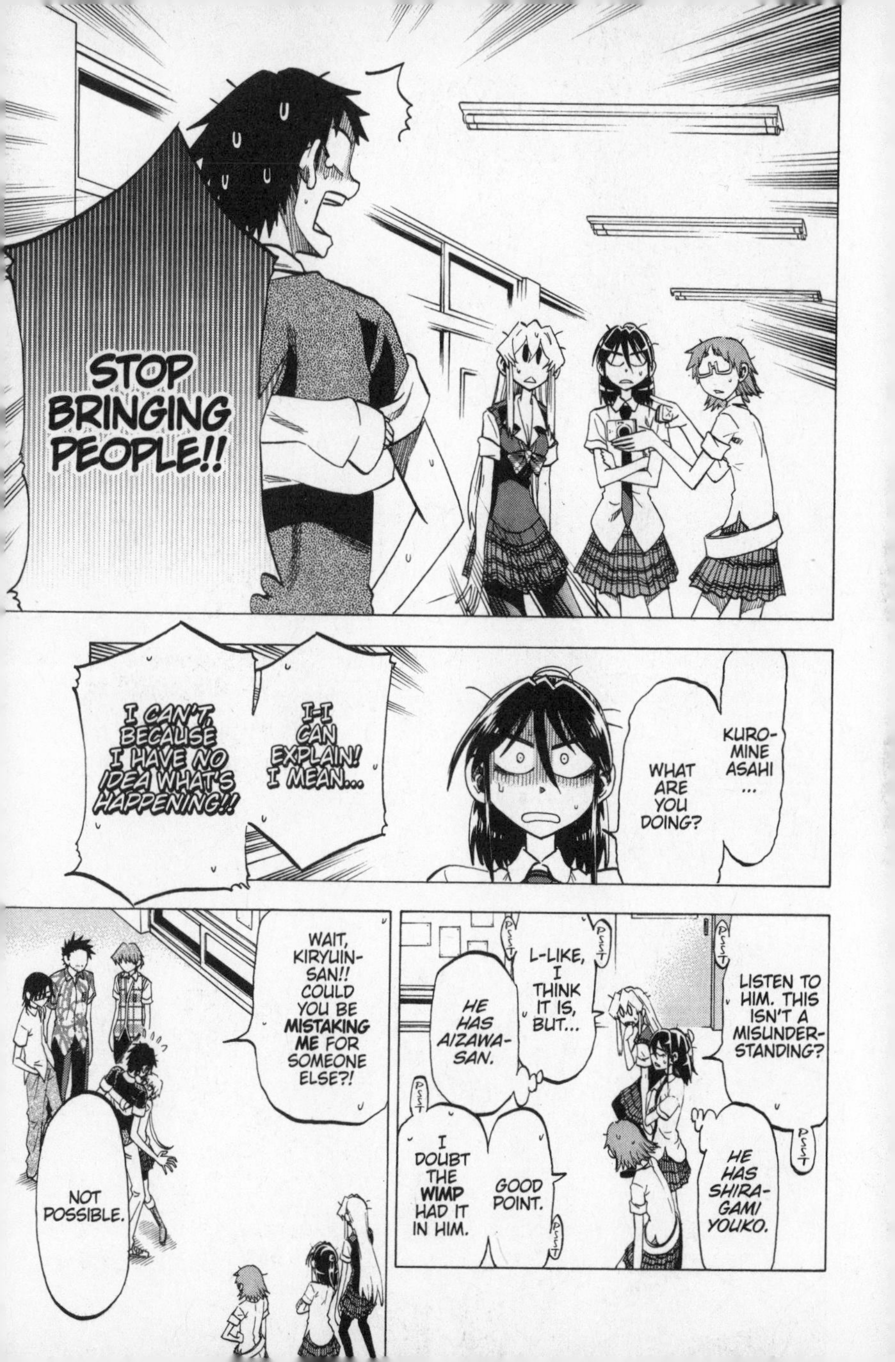
STOP BRINGING PEOPLE!!
KURO-MINE ASAHI ...
WHAT ARE YOU DOING?
I-I CAN EXPLAIN! I MEAN...
I CAN'T, BECAUSE I HAVE NO IDEA WHAT'S HAPPENING!!
PSST
LISTEN TO HIM. THIS ISN'T A MISUNDER-STANDING?
PSST
L-LIKE, I THINK IT IS, BUT...
PSST
HE HAS AIZAWA-SAN.
PSST
HE HAS SHIRAGAMI YOUKO.
PSST
GOOD POINT.
PSST
I DOUBT THE WIMP HAD IT IN HIM.
WAIT, KIRYUIN-SAN!! COULD YOU BE MISTAKING ME FOR SOMEONE ELSE?!
NOT POSSIBLE.

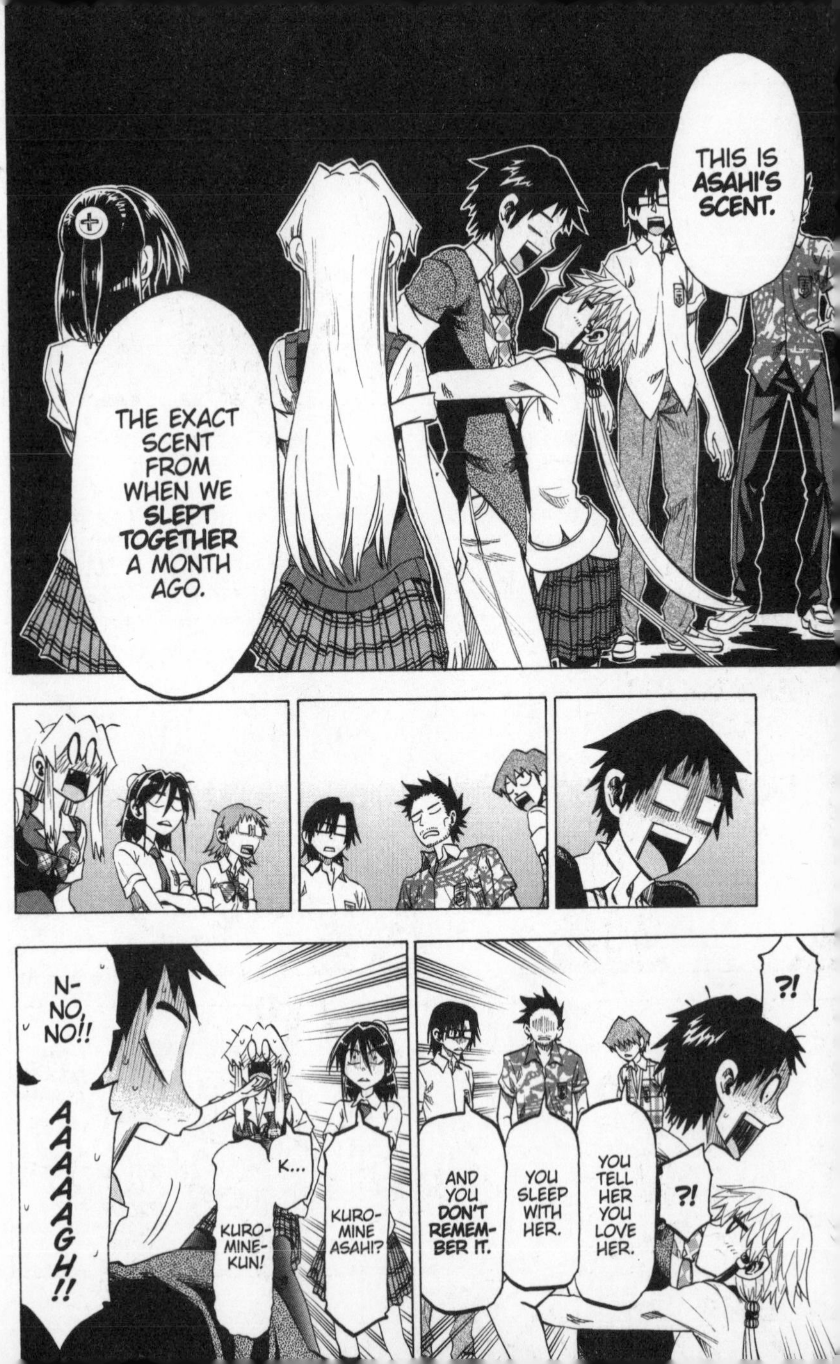
THIS IS ASAHI'S SCENT.
THE EXACT SCENT FROM WHEN WE SLEPT TOGETHER A MONTH AGO.
?!
YOU TELL HER YOU LOVE HER.
YOU SLEEP WITH HER.
AND YOU DON'T REMEMBER IT.
?!
KURO-MINE ASAHI?
K...
KURO-MINE-KUN!
N-NO, NO!!
AAAAAGH!!

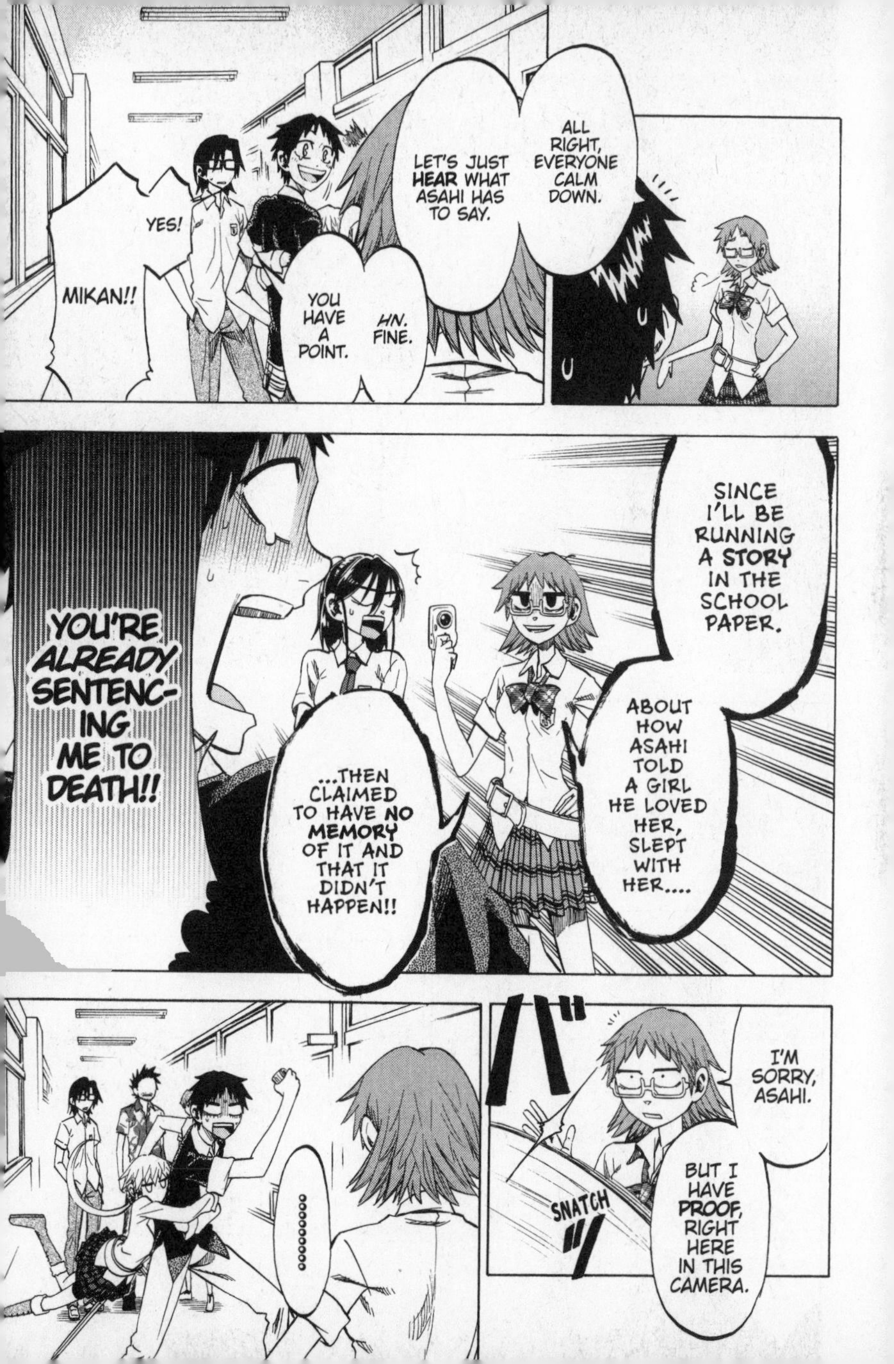
ALL RIGHT, EVERYONE CALM DOWN.
LET'S JUST HEAR WHAT ASAHI HAS TO SAY.
HN. FINE.
YOU HAVE A POINT.
YES!
MIKAN!!
SINCE I'LL BE RUNNING A STORY IN THE SCHOOL PAPER.
ABOUT HOW ASAHI TOLD A GIRL HE LOVED HER, SLEPT WITH HER....
...THEN CLAIMED TO HAVE NO MEMORY OF IT AND THAT IT DIDN'T HAPPEN!!
YOU'RE ALREADY SENTENCING ME TO DEATH!!
I'M SORRY, ASAHI.
BUT I HAVE PROOF, RIGHT HERE IN THIS CAMERA.
SNATCH
....

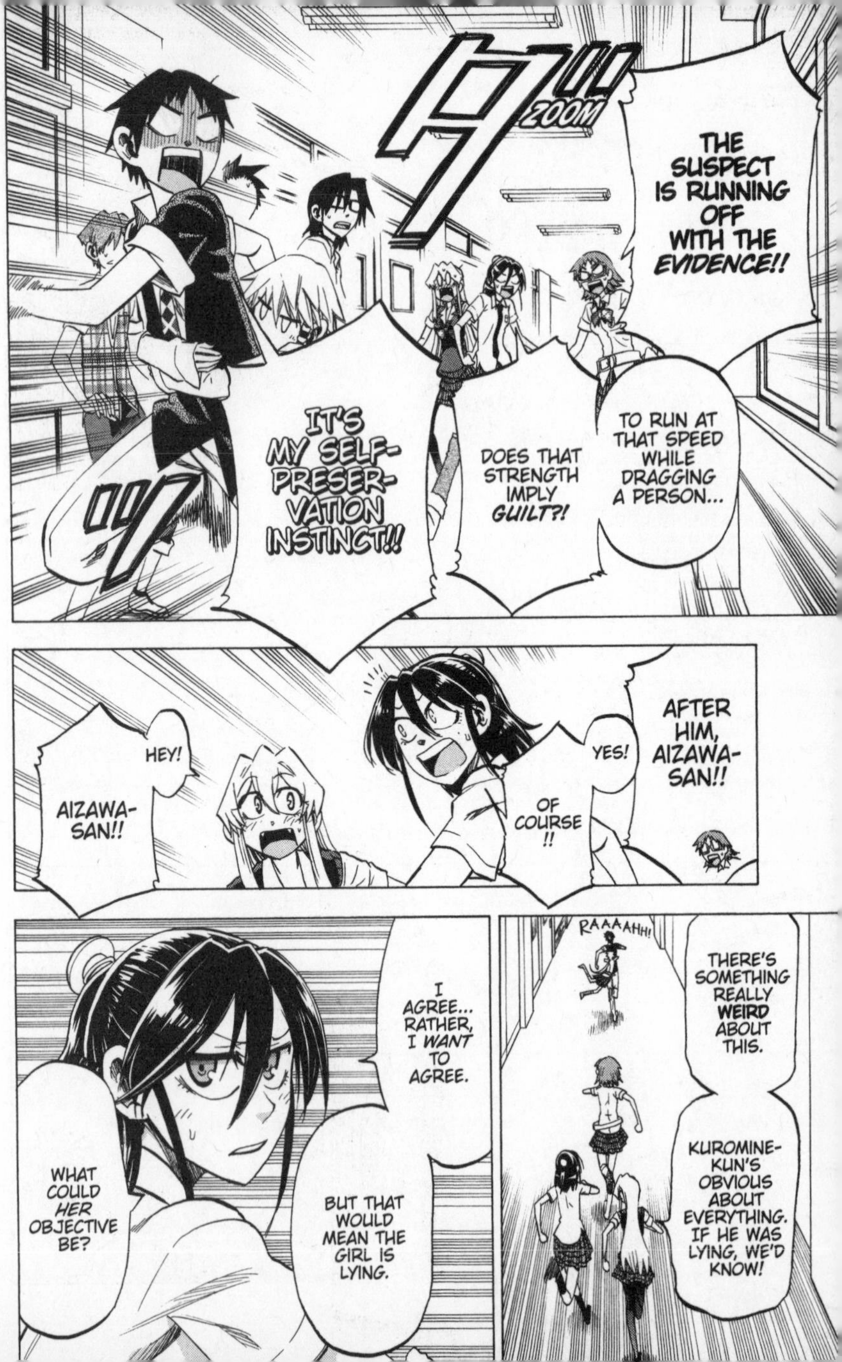
ZOOM
THE SUSPECT IS RUNNING OFF WITH THE EVIDENCE!!
TO RUN AT THAT SPEED WHILE DRAGGING A PERSON...
DOES THAT STRENGTH IMPLY GUILT?!
IT'S MY SELF-PRESERVATION INSTINCT!!
AFTER HIM, AIZAWA-SAN!!
YES!
OF COURSE!!
HEY!
AIZAWA-SAN!!
RAAAAHH!
THERE'S SOMETHING REALLY WEIRD ABOUT THIS.
KUROMINE-KUN'S OBVIOUS ABOUT EVERYTHING. IF HE WAS LYING, WE'D KNOW!
I AGREE... RATHER, I WANT TO AGREE.
BUT THAT WOULD MEAN THE GIRL IS LYING.
WHAT COULD HER OBJECTIVE BE?

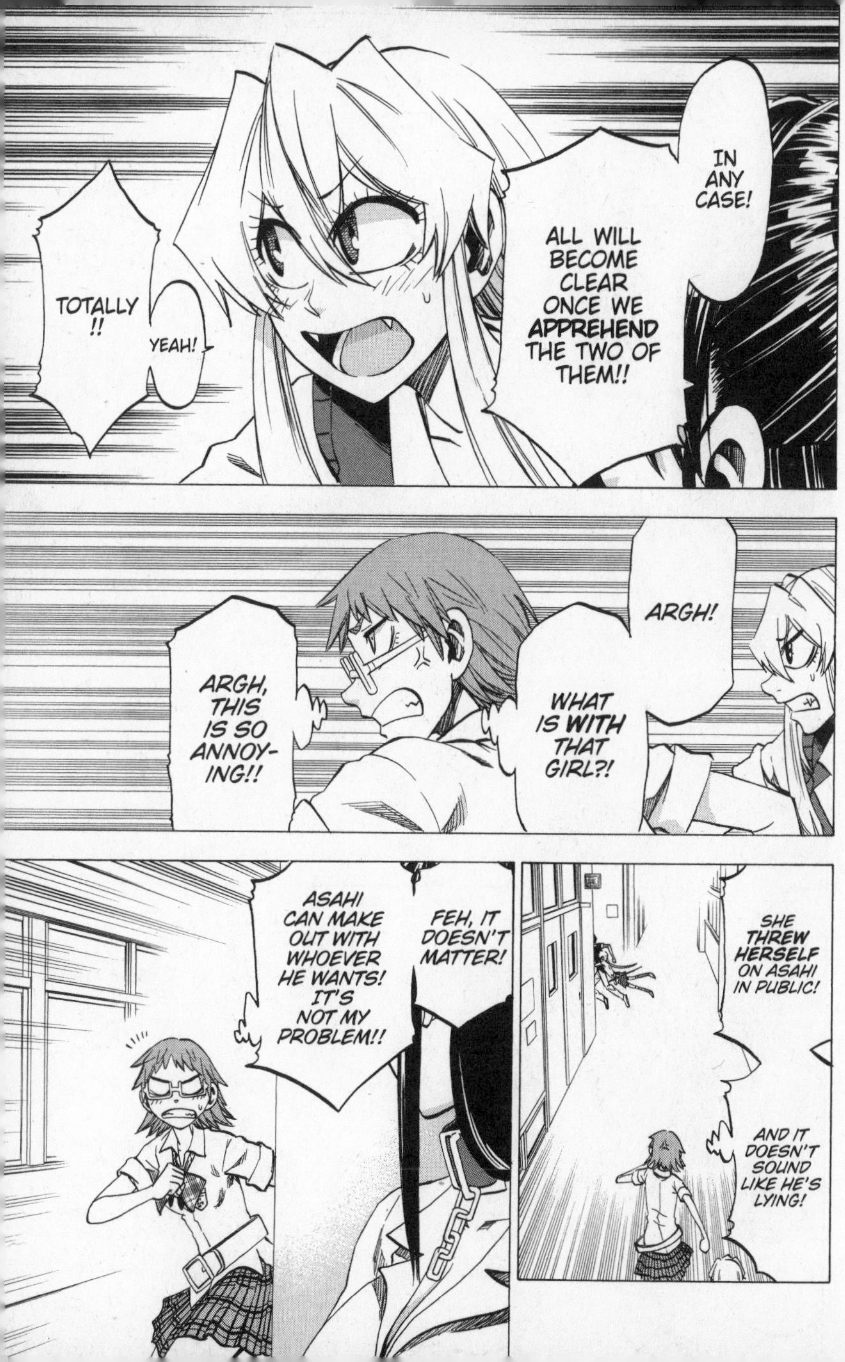
IN ANY CASE!
ALL WILL BECOME CLEAR ONCE WE APPREHEND THE TWO OF THEM!!
YEAH!
TOTALLY!!
ARGH!
WHAT IS WITH THAT GIRL?!
ARGH, THIS IS SO ANNOYING!!
SHE THREW HERSELF ON ASAHI IN PUBLIC!
AND IT DOESN'T SOUND LIKE HE'S LYING!
FEH, IT DOESN'T MATTER!
ASAHI CAN MAKE OUT WITH WHOEVER HE WANTS! IT'S NOT MY PROBLEM!!

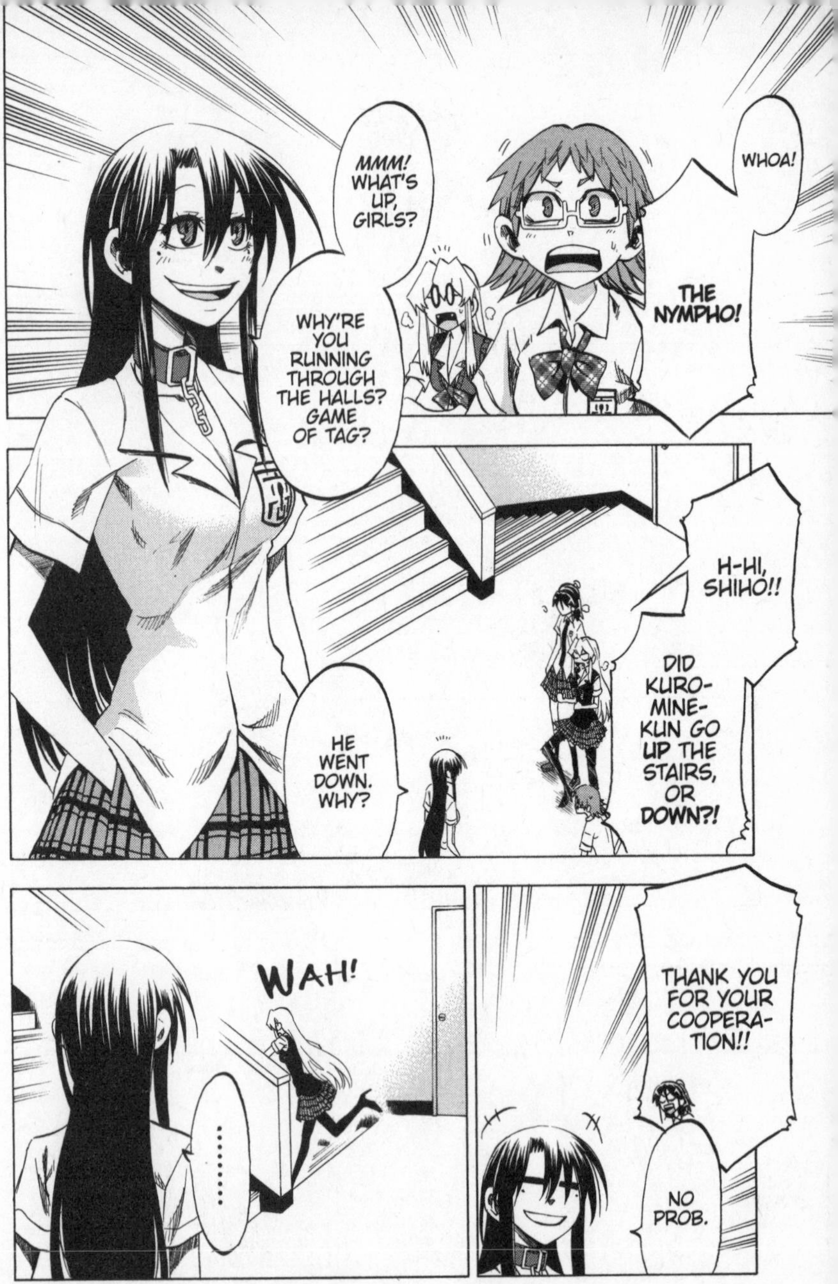
WHOA!
THE NYMPHO!
MMM! WHAT'S UP, GIRLS?
WHY'RE YOU RUNNING THROUGH THE HALLS? GAME OF TAG?
H-HI, SHIHO!!
DID KURO-MINE-KUN GO UP THE STAIRS, OR DOWN?!
HE WENT DOWN. WHY?
THANK YOU FOR YOUR COOPERA-TION!!
NO PROB.
WAH!
......

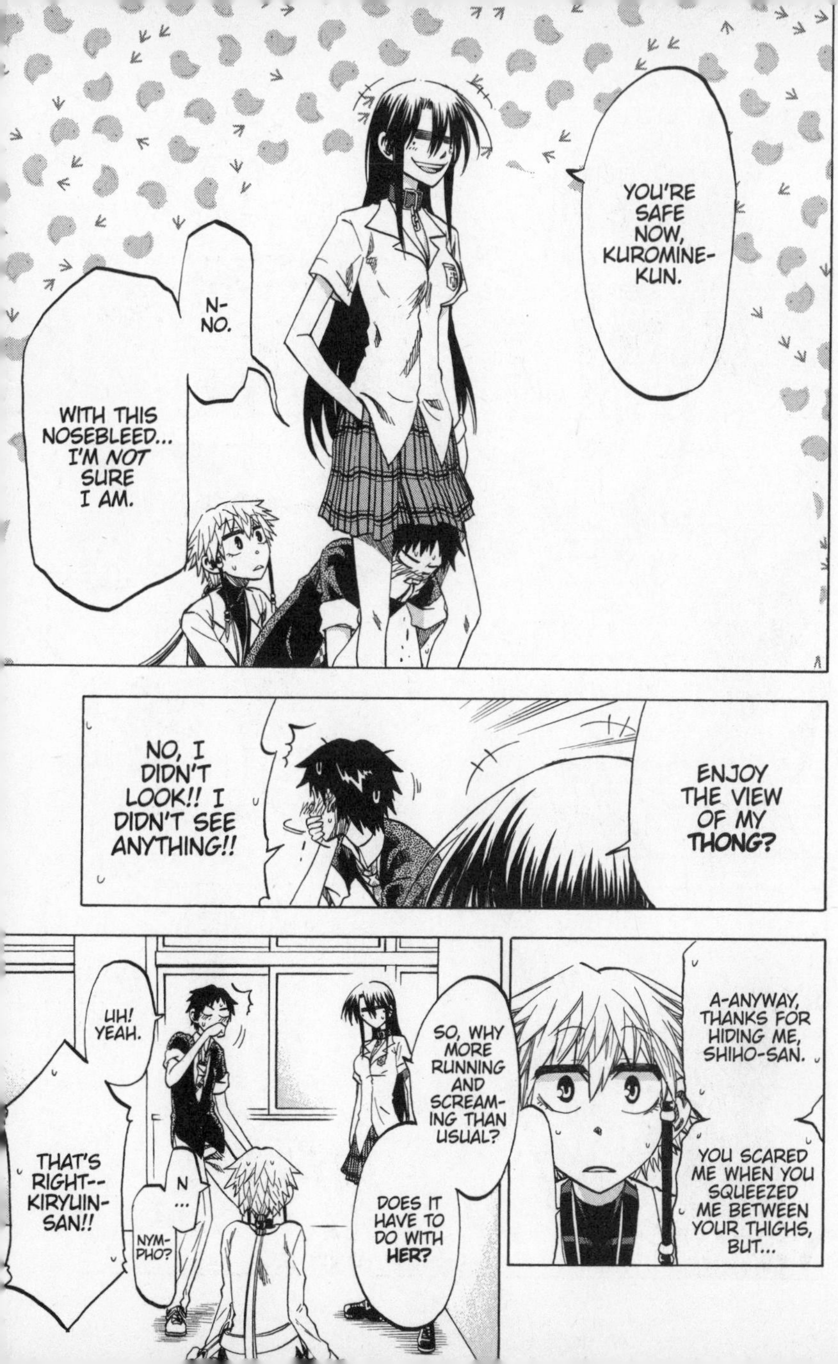
YOU'RE SAFE NOW, KUROMINE-KUN.
N-NO.
WITH THIS NOSEBLEED... I'M *NOT* SURE I AM.
ENJOY THE VIEW OF MY **THONG?**
NO, I DIDN'T LOOK!! I DIDN'T SEE ANYTHING!!
A-ANYWAY, THANKS FOR HIDING ME, SHIHO-SAN.
YOU SCARED ME WHEN YOU SQUEEZED ME BETWEEN YOUR THIGHS, BUT...
SO, WHY MORE RUNNING AND SCREAMING THAN USUAL?
DOES IT HAVE TO DO WITH **HER?**
UH! YEAH.
N ...
NYMPHO?
THAT'S RIGHT-- KIRYUIN-SAN!!

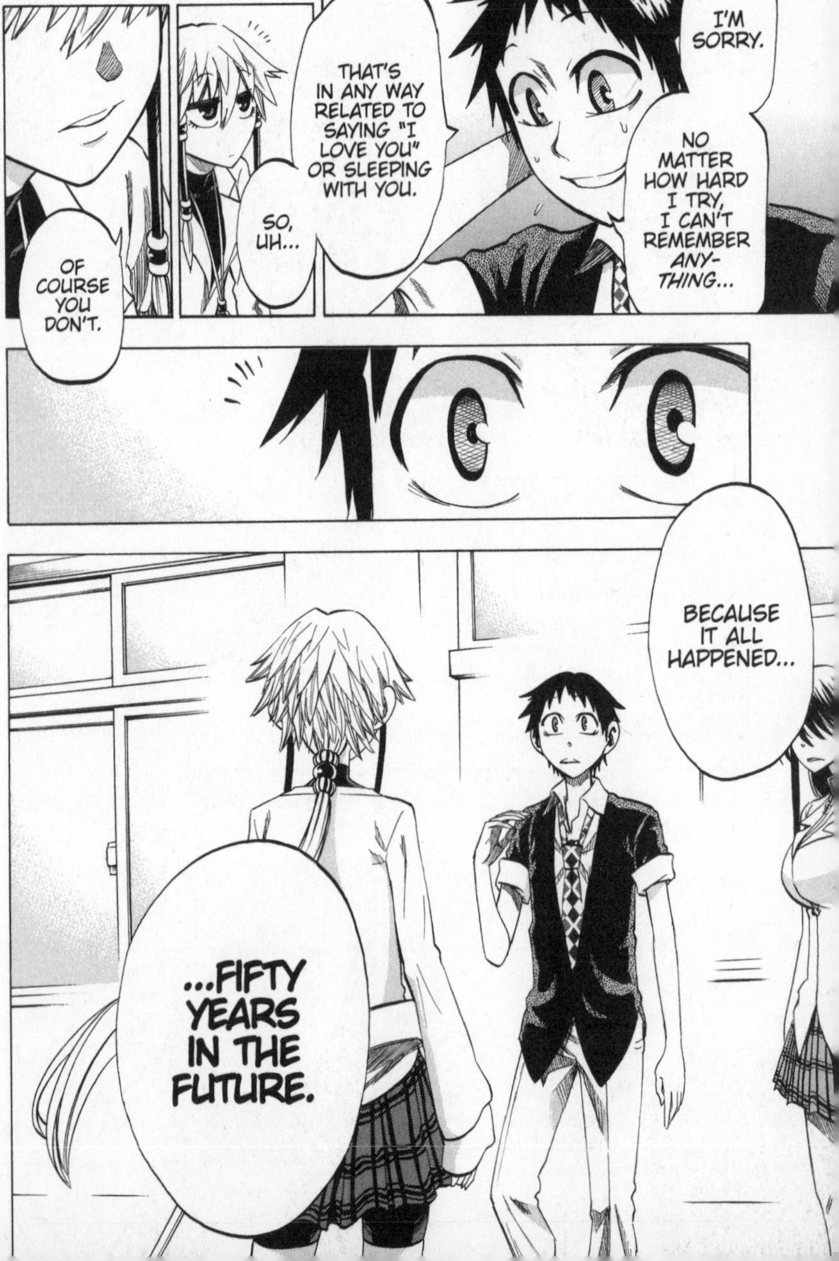
I'M SORRY.
NO MATTER HOW HARD I TRY, I CAN'T REMEMBER ANYTHING...
THAT'S IN ANY WAY RELATED TO SAYING "I LOVE YOU" OR SLEEPING WITH YOU.
SO, UH...
OF COURSE YOU DON'T.
BECAUSE IT ALL HAPPENED...
...FIFTY YEARS IN THE FUTURE.

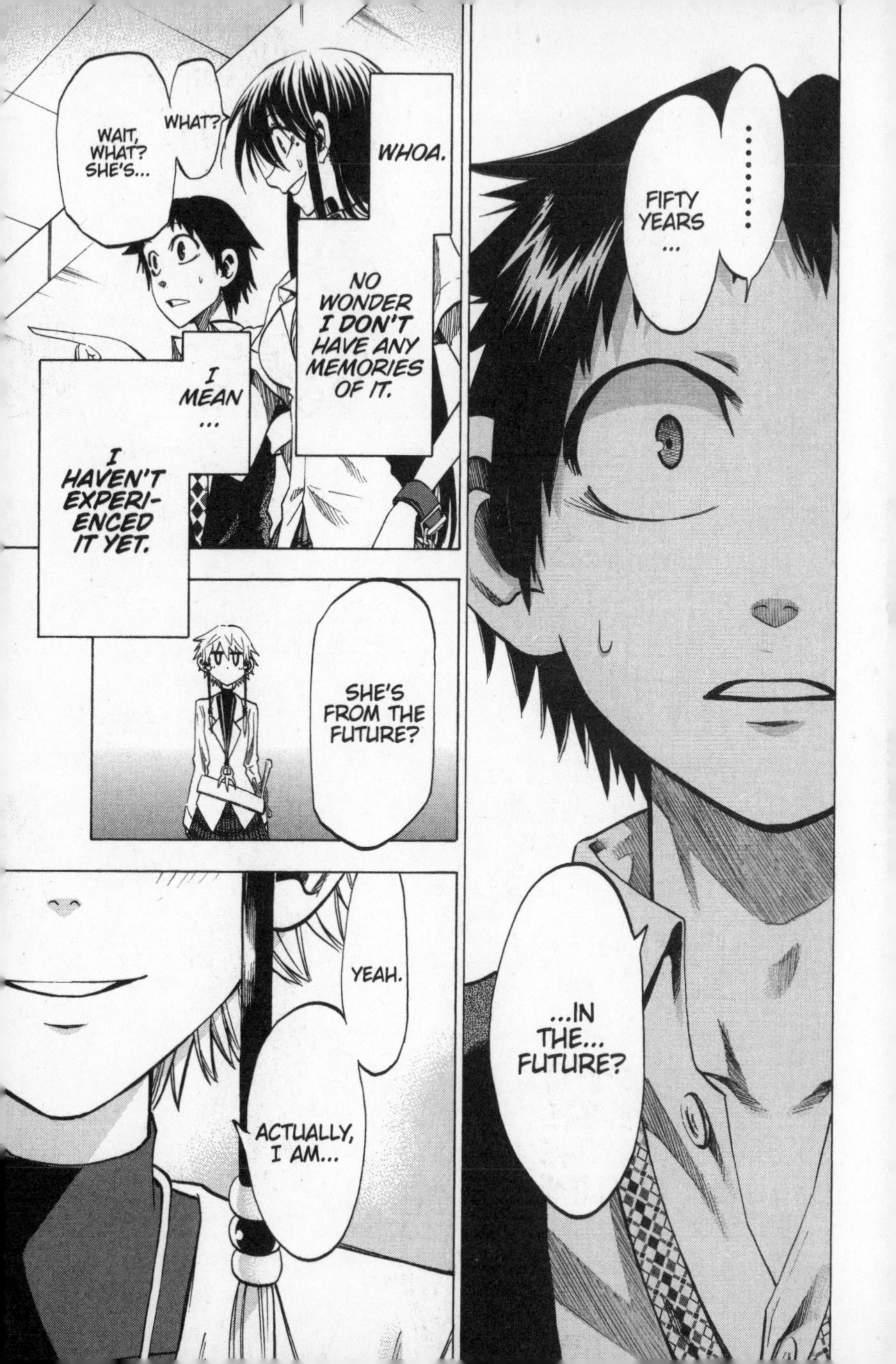
......
FIFTY YEARS ...
...IN THE... FUTURE?
WHOA.
NO WONDER I DON'T HAVE ANY MEMORIES OF IT.
I MEAN ...
I HAVEN'T EXPERIENCED IT YET.
WHAT?
WAIT, WHAT? SHE'S...
SHE'S FROM THE FUTURE?
YEAH.
ACTUALLY, I AM...

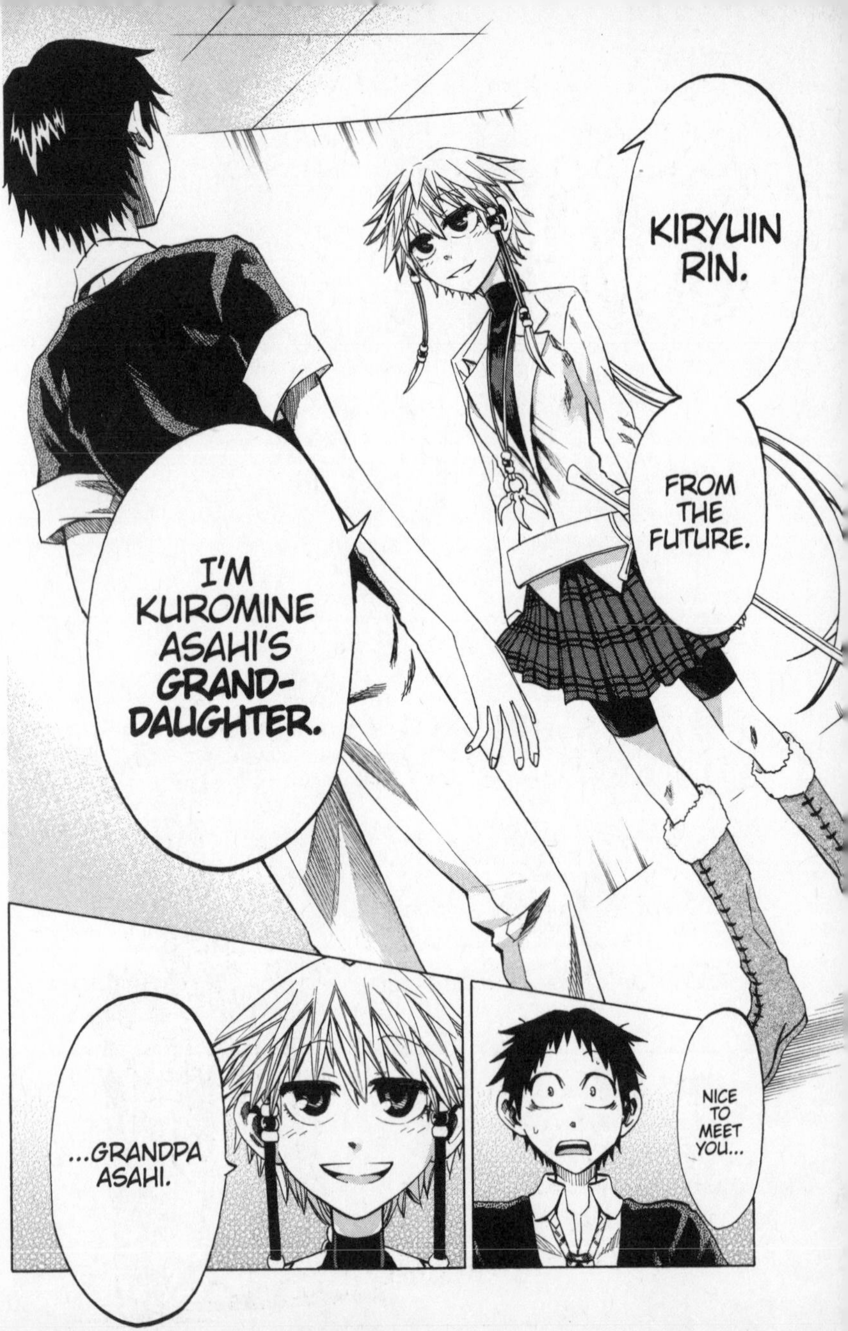
KIRYUIN RIN.
FROM THE FUTURE.
I'M KUROMINE ASAHI'S GRAND-DAUGHTER.
NICE TO MEET YOU...
...GRANDPA ASAHI.

STAFF.

- Akutsu-san
- Shuumeigiku-san
- Seijun Suzuki-san
- Hiroki Minemura-san

SPECIAL THANKS

- Ayako Matsuda-san
- Junko Yamada-san

Editor: Mukawa-san,
Otsuka-san

I give my thanks to those of you holding this book right now and everyone who let me and this work be a part of their lives.

Eiji Masuda

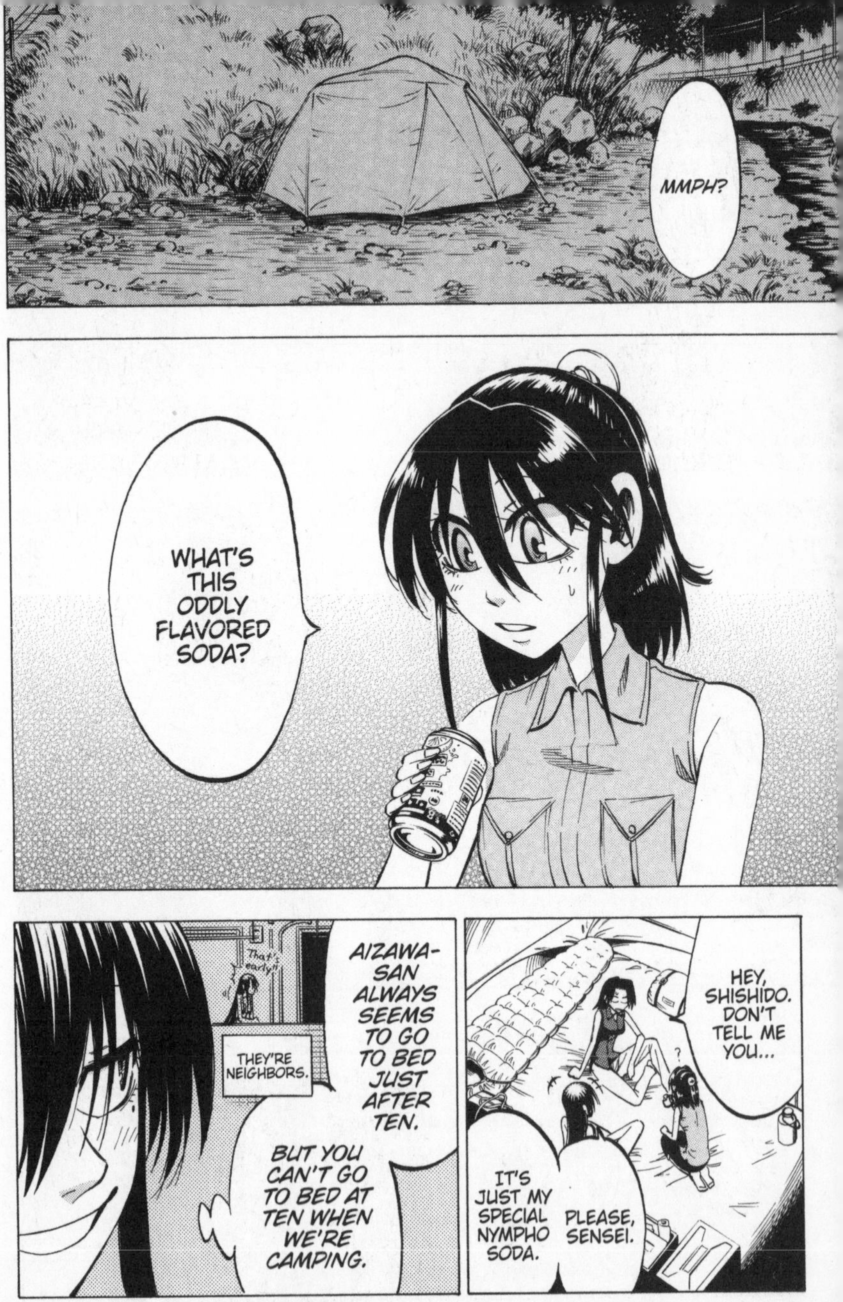
MMPH?
WHAT'S THIS ODDLY FLAVORED SODA?
HEY, SHISHIDO. DON'T TELL ME YOU...
IT'S JUST MY SPECIAL NYMPHO SODA.
PLEASE, SENSEI.
AIZAWA-SAN ALWAYS SEEMS TO GO TO BED JUST AFTER TEN.
BUT YOU CAN'T GO TO BED AT TEN WHEN WE'RE CAMPING.
That's early!!
THEY'RE NEIGHBORS.

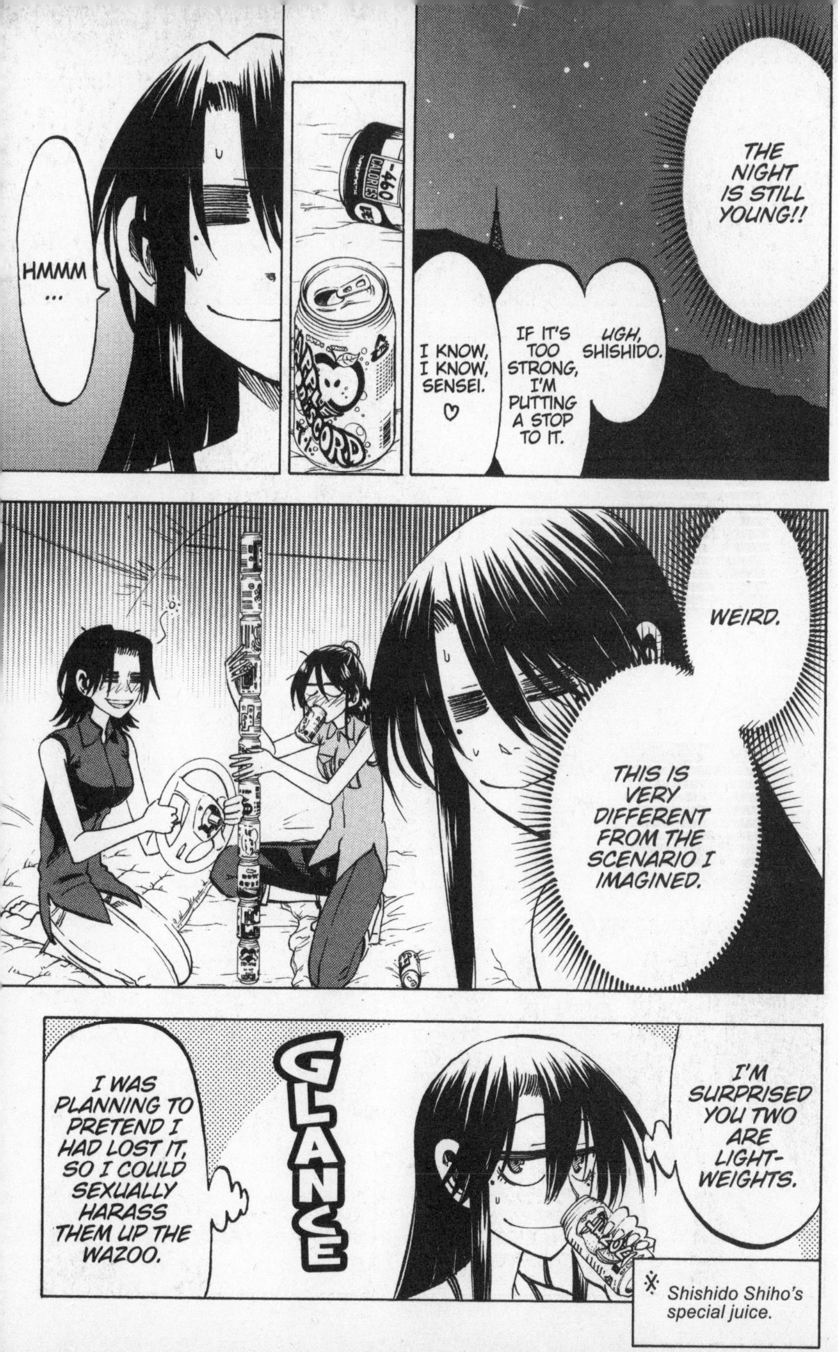
THE NIGHT IS STILL YOUNG!!
UGH, SHISHIDO.
IF IT'S TOO STRONG, I'M PUTTING A STOP TO IT.
I KNOW, I KNOW, SENSEI. ♡
-460 CALORIES
HMMM ...
WEIRD.
THIS IS VERY DIFFERENT FROM THE SCENARIO I IMAGINED.
I'M SURPRISED YOU TWO ARE LIGHT-WEIGHTS.
GLANCE
I WAS PLANNING TO PRETEND I HAD LOST IT, SO I COULD SEXUALLY HARASS THEM UP THE WAZOO.
※ Shishido Shiho's special juice.

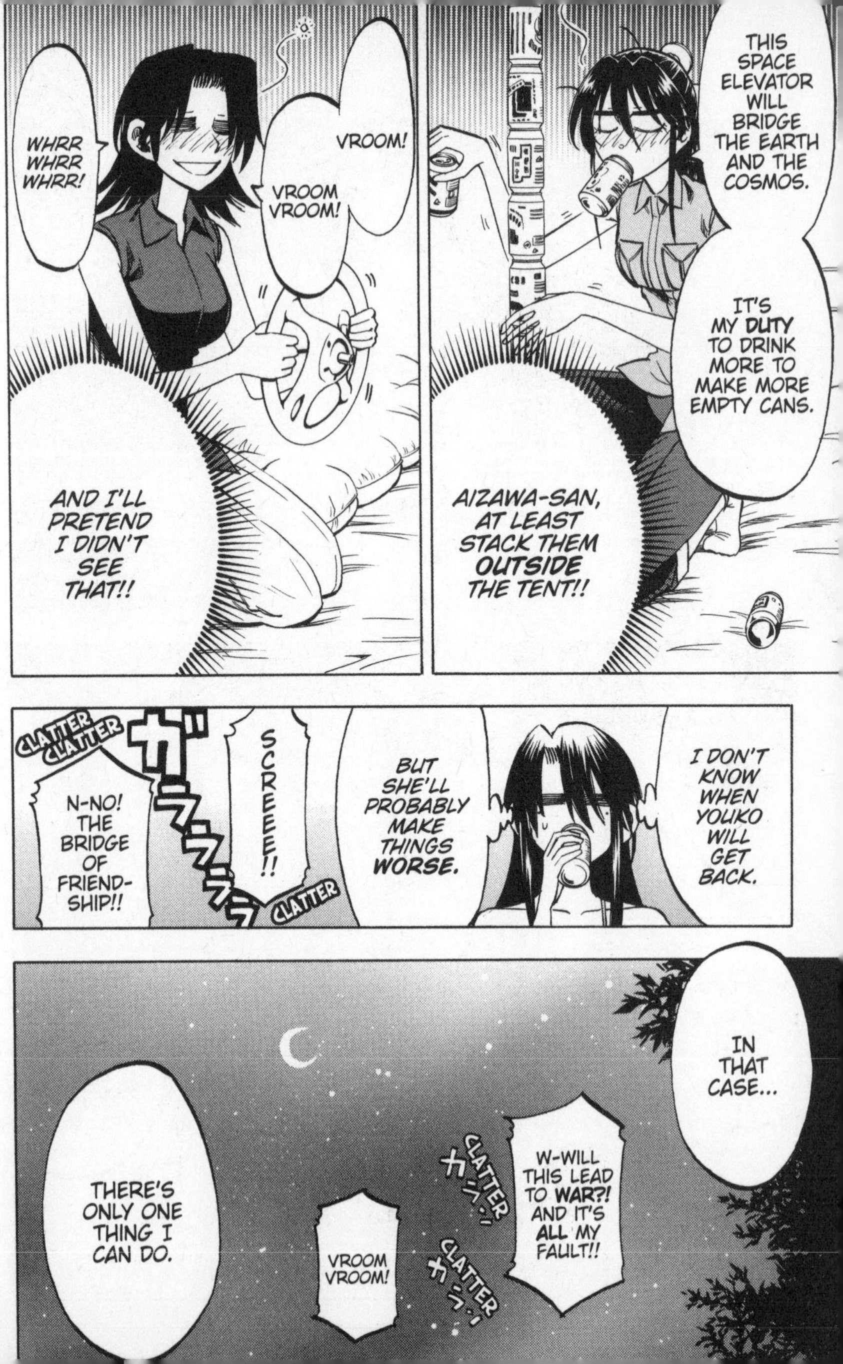
THIS SPACE ELEVATOR WILL BRIDGE THE EARTH AND THE COSMOS.
IT'S MY DUTY TO DRINK MORE TO MAKE MORE EMPTY CANS.
AIZAWA-SAN, AT LEAST STACK THEM OUTSIDE THE TENT!!
VROOM!
VROOM VROOM!
WHRR WHRR WHRR!
AND I'LL PRETEND I DIDN'T SEE THAT!!
I DON'T KNOW WHEN YOUKO WILL GET BACK.
BUT SHE'LL PROBABLY MAKE THINGS WORSE.
SCREEEE!!
CLATTER
CLATTER CLATTER
N-NO! THE BRIDGE OF FRIEND-SHIP!!
IN THAT CASE...
W-WILL THIS LEAD TO WAR?! AND IT'S ALL MY FAULT!!
CLATTER
CLATTER
VROOM VROOM!
THERE'S ONLY ONE THING I CAN DO.

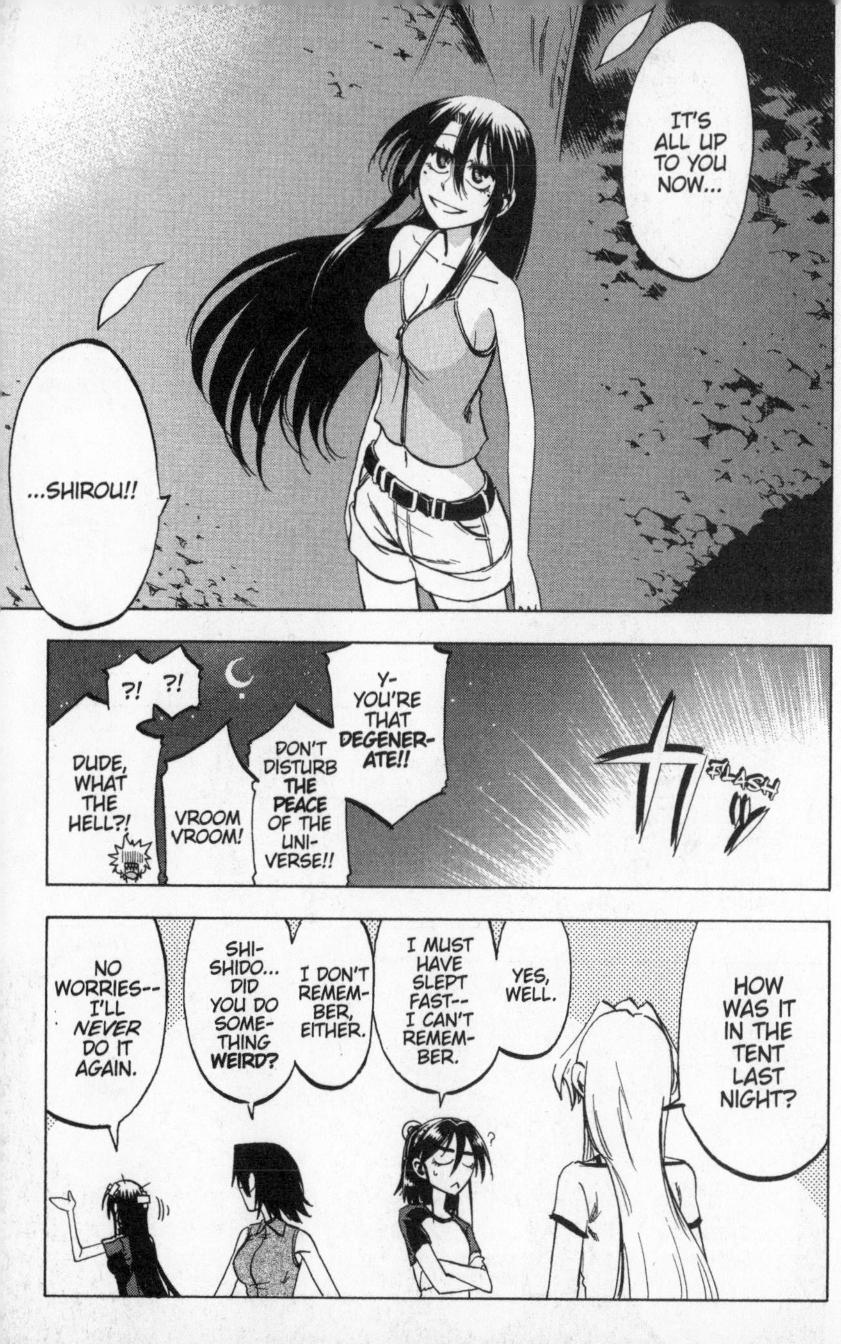
IT'S ALL UP TO YOU NOW...
...SHIROU!!
FLASH
Y-YOU'RE THAT DEGENERATE!!
DON'T DISTURB THE PEACE OF THE UNIVERSE!!
VROOM VROOM!
?! ?!
DUDE, WHAT THE HELL?!
HOW WAS IT IN THE TENT LAST NIGHT?
YES, WELL.
I MUST HAVE SLEPT FAST-- I CAN'T REMEMBER.
I DON'T REMEMBER, EITHER.
SHISHIDO... DID YOU DO SOMETHING WEIRD?
NO WORRIES-- I'LL NEVER DO IT AGAIN.

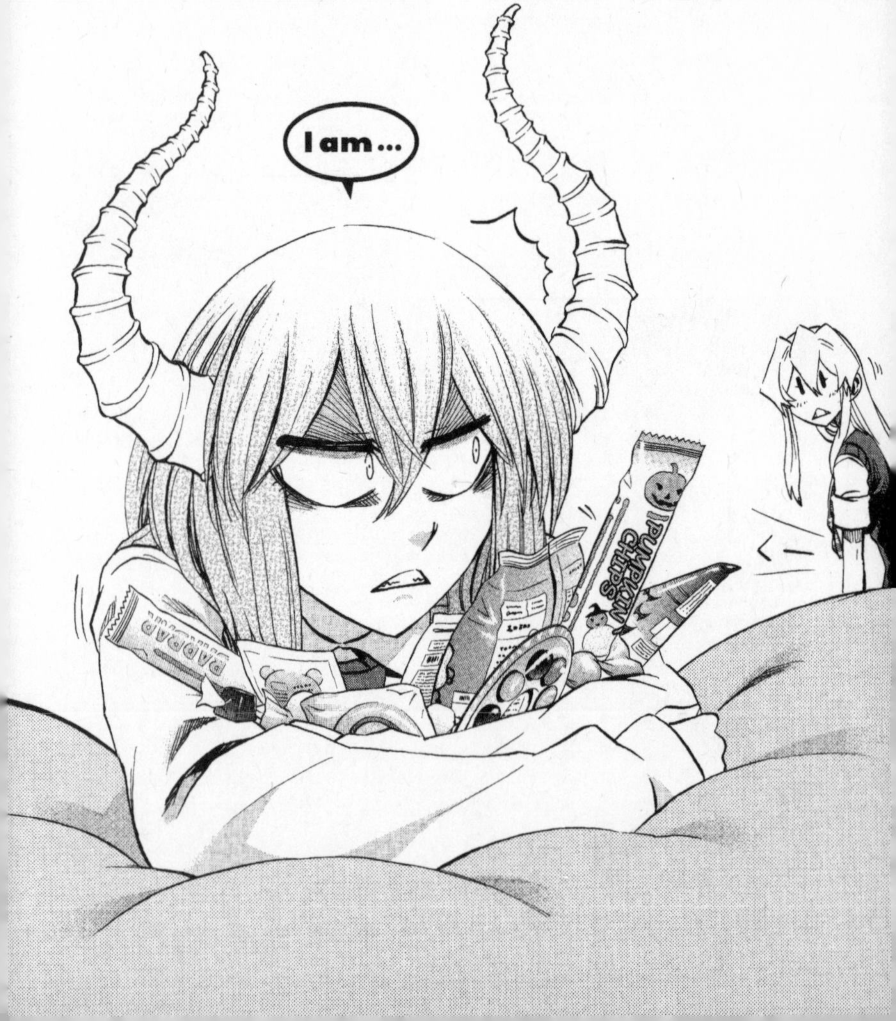
I am...
PUMPKIN CHIPS
BABBAB